CW01080247

1

JACK THE RIPPER THE SUSPECTS

C J MORLEY

INTRODUCTION

Within the pages of this book are 365 individuals who have at one time or another come under suspicion of being Jack the Ripper. Many of the names in this book are only suspects in the very loosest of terms. Their involvement coming about by them having committed or attempting to commit a Ripper-style murder. Some by confessing to being Jack the Ripper while suffering from mental illness or while under the influence of alcohol. Others have been linked to Jack the Ripper by the press, police and by contemporary and recent theorists. Some have come under suspicion as a consequence of unusual behaviour towards family, friends and neighbours. Only a select few of these individuals can realistically be considered genuine and credible suspects. Many of the suspects have since been exonerated by history, but at one time or another proof or no proof they were suspected of being Jack the Ripper. All have been included in this book for the purpose of completion, however, improbable the suggestion. Making this the most comprehensive Jack the Ripper suspect book available.

Jack the Ripper, eluded apprehension despite the best efforts of the police, who in an era before modern day fingerprinting, DNA forensics, surveillance cameras and criminal profiling, were simply out of their depth in hunting what was then a new phenomenon, but which today has become all too commonplace. "The serial killer." The investigation was hampered by a barrage of false confessions and the police faced a hostile press and an angry public clamouring for swift justice. Taunting letters using the moniker "Jack the Ripper" were reportedly sent by the killer. Hope of a successful conviction relied almost entirely upon catching the perpetrator in the act. The only clue the killer left behind was a piece of dirty bloodied apron found in Goulston Street. Cut from the apron of Catherine Eddowes. The item having been discarded near a chalk written message which read: The Juwes [sic] are the men that will not be blamed for nothing.' Top police officials of the time dropped hints in their memoirs and newspaper interviews that the identity of the killer was known. And that the perpetrator was safely locked away in an asylum. Or at the bottom of the Thames. The killer's identity remains to this day unknown.

At least five women met their fate at the hands of Jack the Ripper in the autumn of 1888. The first generally accepted Ripper victim was 43-year old Mary Ann Nichols known as "Polly" to her friends. Polly was murdered in Buck's Row, in the early hours of Friday 31 August 1888. The second murder occurred in Hanbury Street, on Saturday 8 September. Annie Chapman, was 47 years of age. The third and fourth murders were committed on the same night 30 September in what has become known as the double event. The first of these was 44-year old Elizabeth Stride murdered in Dutfield's Yard, Berner Street. The second victim that night was 46-year old Catherine "Kate" Eddowes, murdered in Mitre Square, Aldgate. The last murder occurred over a month later on Friday 9 November 1888. Mary Jane Kelly, also known as "Marie Jeanette Kelly" was the youngest, 25-years old, and the only victim to be murdered indoors. Other murders were attributed to the Ripper. Emma Elizabeth Smith on 3 April 1888, Alice McKenzie, on 17 July 1889, and Martha Tabram on 7, August 1888. The last Ripper scare occurred on 13 February 1891 when 31 year old Frances Coles nicknamed "Carroty Nell" was murdered in Swallow Gardens.

Eyewitness descriptions were varied and unreliable.

Joseph Lawende: Described a suspect seen with Catherine Eddowes: Aged 30, 5'7", fair complexion, brown moustache, salt-

and-pepper coat, red neckerchief, grey peaked cloth cap. Sailor-like.

George Hutchinson: Described a suspect seen with Mary Kelly: Aged 34-35, 5'6", pale complexion, dark hair, slight moustached curled at each end, long dark coat, collar cuffs of Astrakhan, dark jacket underneath. Light waistcoat, thick gold chain with a red stone seal, dark trousers and button boots, gaiters, white buttons. White shirt, black tie fastened with a horseshoe pin. Dark hat turned down in middle. Red neckerchief. Jewish and respectable in appearance.

Mary Ann Cox: Described a suspect seen with Mary Kelly: Short, stout man, shabbily dressed. Billy-cock hat, blotchy face, carroty moustache, holding quart can of beer.

Israel Schwartz: Described two suspects seen with Elizabeth Stride: First man: Aged 30, 5'5", brown haired, fair complexion, small brown moustache, full face, broad shoulders, dark jacket and trousers, black cap with peak. Second man: Aged 35, 5'11", fresh complexion, light brown hair, dark overcoat, and an old black hard felt hat with a wide brim, clay pipe.

Elizabeth Long: Described a suspect seen with Annie Chapman: Dark complexion, brown deerstalker hat, possibly a dark overcoat. Aged over 40, a little taller than Chapman (who was 5 feet tall). A foreigner of shabby genteel appearance.

Please note the text in this book was written using English spelling. Where possible the letters and original newspaper articles were copied in their entirety from the original source complete with grammatical and factual errors.

FREDERICK GEORGE ABBERLINE

Frederick George Abberline was born 8 January 1843 in Blandford Forum, Dorset. His parents, Edward Abberline a saddle-maker and minor local government official, and his wife Hannah (née Chinn) were married at Holyrood Church Southampton Hampshire on the 13 September 1832. In the 1841 census, they were living in Salisbury Street, Blandford Forum. Edward Abberline died in 1849. In the 1851 census Hannah now a widow is living in East Street, Blandford Forum. Upon the death of her husband, she opened a small shop and brought her children up alone. Frederick had three older siblings, Emily, Miriam Harriet, and Edward. In the 1861 census Edward is a cabinet maker, he later joined the Royal Engineers. Frederick at the age of sixteen took up work as an apprentice clockmaker and worked at the shop for four years until he left home for London. On 5 January 1863, he joined the Metropolitan Police as a constable and was appointed to N Division (Islington) with the warrant number 43519. He was told by his sergeant, "Just make yourself visible on the streets". He was 20 years of age, 5 ft. 9 ½ inches tall, with hazel eyes, dark brown hair, and a fresh complexion. His record of making more arrests than any other PC at his station earned him a promotion to sergeant in November 1865, whereupon he moved to Y Division (Highgate). In 1867 he was assigned to plain clothes to investigate Fenian activities. On 18 March 1868, in Islington, he married 25-year old Martha Mackness, the daughter of a labourer, Tobias Mackness. Martha died two months after the marriage from tuberculosis. Promoted to Inspector on 10 March 1873, and transferred to H Division (Whitechapel) where he remained for the next 14 years. He married a second time in December 1876, 32-year old Emma Beament, the daughter of a merchant Henry Beament, from Hoxton New Town, Shoreditch. The marriage lasted over 50 years. Appointed Local Inspector in charge of H Division's CID in April 1878. Transferred to A Division (Whitehall) in February 1887. Moved to CO Division (Central Office) at Scotland Yard in November 1887. Promoted to Inspector First Class in February 1888, and to Chief Inspector in December 1890. In July 1889, Abberline was involved in the investigation of the Cleveland Street scandal. A police raid on Number 19, exposed a male brothel run by Charles Hammond, offering telegraph boys to elite men for sexual services. The existence of his establishment had remained unknown to the authorities for a number of years. On 4 July 1889, 15 year old telegraph boy Charles Swinscow was searched as part of an ongoing investigation into money theft at his employers, the General Post Office. Eighteen shillings were found in his pockets, his weekly wage would have been about eleven shillings. Swinscow was taken in for questioning as part of the police operation. When asked how he came to have such a large sum of money in his possession, Swinscow panicked and confessed he'd been recruited by Charles Hammond to work at a house in Cleveland Street. A major cover-up ensured to protect, its prominent clientele among others, allegedly the Duke of Clarence. The young male prostitutes received sentences from four to nine months imprisonment with hard labour, no clients were prosecuted. Male homosexuality was illegal and punishable, if convicted of buggery, to penal servitude for life or for any term of not less than ten years. The death penalty for buggery had only recently been abolished in 1861. Abberline retired from the police on full pension on 8 February 1892 at the age of 49, having received 84 commendations and awards. He later worked as a private enquiry agent, before taking over the European Agency of the Pinkerton National Detective Agency of America, for whom he worked for 12 years. Abberline retired again in 1904 at the age of 61, to the seaside resort of Bournemouth, and died at his home

"Estcourt" 195 Holdenhurst Road, 10 December 1929, from bronchitis and heart disease at the age of 86. A blue plaque was unveiled in his honour in 2001, which incorrectly states his year of birth as 1813. He was buried in Wimborne Road cemetery in an unmarked grave. His wife, Emma, died 15 March 1930 at the age of 86. In his memoirs, former Detective Chief Inspector Walter Dew had this to say about his old boss:

Inspector Abberline was portly and gentle speaking. The type of police officer – and there have been many – who might easily have been mistaken for the manager of a bank or a solicitor. He also was a man who had proved himself in many previous big cases. His strong suit was his knowledge of crime and criminals in the East End, for he had been for many years the detective-inspector of the Whitechapel Division, or as it was called then the 'Local Inspector.' Inspector Abberline was my chief when I first went to Whitechapel. He left only on promotion to the Yard, to the great regret of myself and others who had served under him. No question at all of Inspector Abberline's abilities as a criminal hunter.

Abberline's preferred suspect in the Ripper case was Severin Antoniovich Klosowski, aka George Chapman, a Polish immigrant who was hanged in 1903 for murdering three of his mistresses, with poison. In interviews with the Pall Mall Gazette in 1903, Abberline put forward the idea that George Chapman may have been the Ripper saying: "I cannot help feeling that this is the man we struggled so hard to capture fifteen years ago. However, he also said that Scotland Yard is really no wiser on the subject than it was fifteen years ago." The claim that Abberline was Jack the Ripper was made by 84-year old Spanish handwriting expert Jose Luis Abad. In the (2011) book: Jack the Ripper The Most Intelligent Murderer in History. Mr Abad studied the handwriting of

Abberline and compared it to the writing in the Ripper diary which surfaced in Liverpool in 1992, and purported to have been written by Liverpool cotton dealer James Maybrick. Despite many experts believing the diary was a hoax; Abad believes it is genuine and was written not by Maybrick, but by Inspector Abberline. Mr Abad, says: "I have no doubt Abberline was the Ripper. Handwriting does not lie."

CHARLES AKEHURST

Charles Akehurst, a young man of 27 Canterbury Road, Ball's Pond Road, North, Islington, London, was arrested in a tenement house of doubtful repute in Flower and Dean Street, Spitalfields, on 18 November 1888, after he accompanied a woman to her room. There he made use of expressions and acted in a manner which caused her to jump to the conclusion that she was in the hands of the man responsible for the recent crimes. She ran trembling to a nearby policeman, who promptly arrested the man. He was taken to the Commercial Street Police Station. After a short detention, he satisfied the police of his innocence and was subsequently released.

ALASKA

An American sailor named George M. Dodge, (erroneously referred to as George M. Hodge in some newspaper accounts) told the story of how on 13 August 1888, after arriving in London from China aboard the English steamship Glenorley, (the ship he arrived on was also referred to as the Glenorchy, Glenartney, or Glenrolie in various newspaper accounts) he met a Malay cook named Alaska, at the luxuriously appointed Queens Music Hall Poplar. The Malay told him a tale of how a few days before he had received (2 years owed pay amounting to more than $500, in other newspaper reports, the amount is $100). He had purchased clothing and a fine gold watch, but had been robbed by a woman of the town, and said that unless he found the woman in question he would kill and mutilate every woman in Whitechapel that he met until he had recovered his property. To further substantiate his boast, he showed Dodge a fearsome looking knife some fifteen inches long and sharpened on both edges, which it is claimed he always carried about his person. The Malay was described as having a very coppery complexion, about 5 ft. 7 inches tall. 35 years of age, very dark in appearance, with straight black hair, black eyes, high cheekbones, black moustache, good looking with fine features and weighed about 10-11 stone. It is claimed he spoke fair English, broken, but could easily be understood. Dodge stated that the Malay lived in a street near the East India Dock Road, though, would not reveal exactly where until he had checked if there was a reward offered. Detectives were sent to make inquiries at the Glen Line Steamship Company, though could find no trace of the man. Mr Wood, the manager of the Queen's Music Hall, where Dodge claimed to have met Alaska, said that he had heard nothing of the alleged robbery of the Malay neither had his two assistants Alexander Nowlan and Henry Pierce who looked after the boxes in which sailors disport themselves of their valuables. Both men declared that no robbery could have taken place on the premises without their hearing of it. Axel Welin, the long-time warden of the Scandinavian Sailor's Temperance Home, West India Docks, which was extremely popular with foreign sailors, scanned the books but could find no trace of Dodge, nor the Malay. Mr Freeman, the manager and superintendent of the East End Home for Asiatics, said that he had been at the home for thirty years and had never heard of a Malay named Alaska. Malays, he said: "Are Mohammedans and do not use European names, but the word 'Lascar' is the Mohammedan name for seamen, and Dodge might

13

have been misled." Messrs. James McGregor, Son & Company, owners of the Glen Line of steamers trading from Singapore and China stated that the Glenorley sailed in April from London to China, and returned on 14 August 1888, after taking in cargo at Antwerp. She sailed again for China on 8 September 1888 and was last reported 23 September 1888 at Suez. They had no one on board named Alaska. The chief cook on the Glenorley, a thoroughly respectable Chinaman who had been in the employ of the firm for many years, said they had been no Malays on board. The newspapers appeared to be of the opinion that the story was nothing more than a sailor's yarn.

FREDERICO ALBERRICI

Alberrici an Italian-American, is identified as a footman called Frederick, employed by the eminent surgeon and Ripper suspect Sir William Gull, at 78 Brook Street, by Melvyn Fairclough in the (1991) book: The Ripper And The Royals. Alberrici is included, not because he was suspected of being Jack the Ripper himself, but because he was said to be part of the Masonic conspiracy theory, and was alleged to have aided Gull in his search for the prostitutes who knew of the alleged secret marriage between Prince Albert Victor and commoner Annie Crook. According to Fairclough, Alberrici, along with coachman John Netley, first questioned and then murdered 45-year old Emma Elizabeth Smith, in April 1888 because she was friends with Ripper victims Mary Ann Nichols and Annie Chapman, and presented a danger. Smith was threatened, then beaten up. The beating was particularly brutal and a stick or blunt object was pushed forcibly into her vagina, tearing her perineum; she died in hospital the following day from her Injuries. Smith, shortly before she slipped into a coma and died, claimed she was assaulted by three or possibly four men, one a youth of about 19 years. Fairclough in his book makes the claim that Alberrici and Netley, acting on the orders of Lord Randolph Churchill, travelled to Scotland on the pretext of safeguarding some furniture which had been delivered, and attempted to push Eddy over a cliff; he survived the murder attempt though was confined at Balmoral for the rest of his days. Fairclough also states that Albericci subsequently murdered John Netley. The claims are based on the Abberline diaries. The diaries, three leather-bound volumes; authenticity, however, is extremely dubious. The diaries author, allegedly Inspector Frederick George Abberline misspells his own name and claims to be G F. Abberline. Alberrici was known in the East End as Freddy Fingers, or American Freddy, due to his criminal history.

ALBERT EDWARD THE PRINCE OF WALES

Those who allege that Albert Edward, the Prince of Wales was a Ripper suspect, appear to be confusing him with his son Prince Albert Victor, who was a Ripper suspect. John Wilding in the (1993) book: Jack the Ripper Revealed. Claims that the Prince was involved; by getting Ripper victim Mary Kelly pregnant. It was rumoured that the Prince had a flat above a butcher's shop in Watling Street, where he and his companions could change into more inconspicuous clothing before going out fire-watching. It was also claimed to be a venue for wild orgies involving prostitutes. It is probably from these rumours that the Mary Kelly pregnancy story arises. Bertie, as he was affectionately known, was the eldest son of Queen Victoria and Prince Albert. He was born at 10:48 am on 9 November 1841 at Buckingham Palace, and it was said had a strict and unhappy childhood. Described as a rebel with a reluctance to study, he tried, but would always fall below the high standards of perfection expected from him by his mother. In a typical letter to him, she wrote:

None of you could ever be proud enough of being the child of such a father who has not his equal in this world, so great, so good, so faultless, I delight in the fact that I possess such a perfect husband.

Bertie in 1861 at the age of 20, spent 10 weeks at Curragh Camp in Ireland with the Grenadier Guards; his sexual inexperience caused merriment amongst his colleagues who decided one evening to play a joke on him. Nellie Clifden, a young Irish actress, (some reports say prostitute), was smuggled in to share his bed. News reached the palace and was soon the talk of London. It caused his father, Prince Albert great consternation and he wrote to his son:

You have caused me the greatest pain I have yet felt in this life, you must not, you dare not be lost.

His father, travelled to Cambridge despite the bad weather to see his son and castigate him. During the trip home, Albert became feverish after contracting a virulent bout of typhoid fever and died at the age of 42, on 14 December 1861. Some have theorised that he may not have died from typhoid fever, but from untreated renal failure or possibly cancer. Historian Helen Rappaport, in the (2011) book: Magnificent Obsession, suggest Albert may have in fact had an underlying medical condition, Crohn's disease, a totally unknown condition at the time, the anxiety and stress over his son may have caused a major flare-up claims, Rappaport, and contributed to his early death. The Queen always held Bertie to blame for her beloved husband's death, and once said of him to one of her daughters: "Much as I pity, I never can or shall look at him without a shudder." For the duration of his life, he struggled with the burden of knowing that she blamed him. Her refusal to allow him any role in state affairs would leave him with too much energy and free time on his hands, she also considered him frivolous, incompetent, indiscreet and feared him competing with her for the affection of her subjects. A popular joke from this period, perhaps best summed up the situation:

Why is the Queen like the weather? Because she reigns (rains) and reigns and reigns and never gives the poor son (sun) a chance.

On 10 March 1863, he married Princess Alexandra, daughter of the heir to the Danish throne, Prince Christian of Glucksburg, and they had five children. Queen Victoria, still in mourning 15 months after the death of her husband, attended the wedding dressed entirely in black, complete with a widow's cap. Throughout the service, she frequently burst into tears whenever she glanced at the spot where her husband's coffin had previously laid. After the wedding, she wrote: "What a dismal affair, it was." Edward treated his marriage with indifference, and he continued to lead a scandalous playboy lifestyle, full of mistresses and parties. His lists of conquests seemed endless; actress Lilly Langtry was replaced by the socialite Daisy Brooke, who in turn was replaced by the actress Sarah Bernhardt, followed by society matron Alice Keppel. A court appearance in a notorious divorce case (he was named as one of the many lovers of Lady Mordant; he denied the affair and her Lady-ship was certified insane and institutionalised), brought him bad press, and his lifestyle made him unpopular with the public. During a tour of Cork in 1885, the crowd hissed, booed and threw onions at him. On the death of Queen Victoria, he was crowned King. Now portly, balding, bearded and nearly 60 years of age, his reign lasted from 1901 until 1910. In March and April 1910 while in France, he was reported as suffering from severe bronchitis. Despite suffering several heart attacks, throughout the day he continued to work. His last words were, "I am very glad," after being told that his horse, 'Witch of the Air,' had won at Kempton Park that Afternoon. He sank into a coma and passed away at 11:45 pm on the 6 May 1910 at Buckingham Palace. He was succeeded by his only son George V. He had the distinction of being the heir apparent to the throne longer than anyone in English history and his reign is often seen as the beginning of the monarchy's modern incarnation. As King, his main interests lay in foreign affairs and military matters. He carefully fostered relationships with other countries and was largely responsible for the Entente Cordial with France, which provided Britain with an ally in Europe. Fluent in French and German, he became the first British monarch to visit Russia. An active Freemason throughout his life he was installed as Grand Master in 1874 and regularly appeared in public as such, both at home and abroad. Apart from womanising, cigars, horse racing and the love of food, the Prince had another passion in life; he loved fires and firefighting and never missed attending a big London fire. The head of the London fire brigade was under strict orders, to notify the Prince immediately should any significant fires break out. He volunteered his services in assisting the London fire service and would enthusiastically muck in and socialise with the other firemen. His generosity amongst his colleagues, particularly with his cigars, afforded him great respect and he would work unnoticed and unrecognised by the public.

ALBERT EDWARD VICTOR DUKE OF CLARENCE

Bertie's son, Albert Victor Christian Edward, known to his family as Eddy, was born 8 January 1864 at Frogmore House Windsor, Berkshire. At the time of his birth, he was second in the line of succession to the throne after his father Albert Edward, the Prince of Wales. Queen Victoria decided that the boy should be named Albert, after her beloved late husband; much to the dismay of his parents. Eddy was no stranger to scandal and gossip throughout his life and was reputed, while at Cambridge, to have conducted relationships with both sexes. Michael Harrison in the (1972) book: Clarence Was He Jack the Ripper? Wonders if there might have been a homosexual relationship between Eddy and fellow Ripper suspect James Kenneth Stephen. While there is no direct evidence to support this claim, it does remain a possibility. A poem was written by Stephen under the euphemism 'Sucking Peppermints,' does hint at such a relationship, though is rather vague:

See where the K in sturdy self-reliance, thoughtful and placid as a brooding dove, stands firmly sucking in the cause of science, just such a peppermint as schoolboys love. Suck placid K the world will they debtor, though their eyes water and thine heart grow faint. Suck and the less thou likest it the better. Suck for our sake and utter no complaint.

Eddy, by all accounts, was a slow child, considered educationally subnormal, it was reported that he could not concentrate for more than a few minutes at a time. Tutored by the Reverend John Neale Dalton, the young prince was given a strict programme of study, which included games and military drills. Dalton complained that Albert Victor's mind was "abnormally dormant." Without any proper education, he grew up to be described as a rather dull adult. In 1877, at the age of 13, he sailed with his younger brother George on the naval training ship HMS Bacchante; it was hoped travel might stimulate his desire for education. While George developed a natural passion for the sea and decided on a naval career, Eddy displayed no such aptitude and continued his education on land. He was tutored at Trinity College, Cambridge 1883-85 by James Kenneth Stephen. Eddy's dandy-ism earned him the nickname "collars and cuffs" on account of the high starched collars he wore to cover an unusually long thin swan-like neck. He was also, due to a hereditary condition from his mother's side of the family, partially deaf. In an attempt to mask these insecurities and to portray his public image as being more masculine, he took up hunting and joined the Tenth Hussars Cavalry Regiment, where he gained the rank of Major. Pictures from this period often depicted him in the uniform of the Tenth Hussars. It is claimed he chose this regiment because he liked the look of the uniform. It was rumoured that he was known at several homosexual establishments, and was also a regular visitor at 19 Cleveland Street, which was a homosexual brothel run by Charles Hammond. The raid made headlines as a number of men in British high society were implicated in the scandal. Though none of the male prostitutes in the brothel ever named Eddy as a client, there was a great deal of talk that seemed to suggest his frequent presence there The release in 1975 of Public Record Office police papers, and more importantly the publication of the letters of Lord Arthur Somerset, one of the principal players in the Cleveland Street affair, clearly show a cover-up had taken place and that the prince was involved beyond a reasonable doubt in the 1889 Scandal. Two recently discovered confidential letters written by the Prince to his surgeon, in 1885 and 1886, reveal he was suffering from gonorrhoea, in the first letter He describes suffering from "glete," a term used to describe the discharge caused by gonorrhoea, writing:

I have taken those capsules regularly, four a day. There is still a slight sign of glete, but so slight, that it is hardly percep[tive] and only when I get up of a morning.

In the second letter, he asked his surgeon named only as Roche to send him more pills. He wrote:

I think I had better go on taking them for a bit. I still continue to have this tiresome glete which comes on at times, although at present it has stopped, it is very anoying (sic) as I really thought it had stopped for good. I am perfectly well in every other respect, and really do not see why this should go on as it does.

Eddy was made the Duke of Clarence and Avondale and Earl of Athlone in 1891, and in December of that year became engaged to Princess Mary of Teck (known as Princess May), later to become Queen Mary, after marrying his younger brother George. She was, in Queen Victoria's words, "charming, sensible and pretty". He died of pneumonia at Sandringham House on 14 January 1892, during the flu epidemic which swept the country. He was 28-years old. The suggestion that Eddy was Jack the Ripper was first made by Phillipe Jullien in the (1962) book: Edouard VII (Edward and the Edwardians). Jullien makes a reference to rumours that Eddy and the Duke of Bedford were responsible for the murders, though, did not say which Duke of Bedford was actually involved. The ninth Duke was 69 years of age in 1888, his son and heir, the Marquis of Tavistock, was 36 years of age. It was an article by Dr Thomas Edmund Alexander Stowell, writing in the Criminologist in November 1970 which caused a sensation. Stowell apparently used the private papers of eminent surgeon Sir William Gull as his source material and pointed the finger of suspicion at Eddy without actually naming him, instead using the letter "S" when referring to his suspect. Stowell claims; "S" was nicknamed "collar and cuffs" and was heir to power and wealth, the article went on to say:

The killer was a gentleman who had contracted syphilis in his youth, and now in the final stages of the illness suffered delusions. He became sadistically aroused when watching deer being dressed, and when his warped sexual passion exploded

21

committed the murders. He was assisted by the authorities who helped to conceal it from the public.

Stowell, who died shortly after writing the article, allegedly left a folder labelled "Jack the Ripper," which, according to his son Dr T Eldon Stowell, was destroyed unread. Stowell further claims that the royal family knew that Eddy was Jack the Ripper for definite after the second murder, but made no attempt to restrain him until after the double event. He was taken to a private mental hospital in Sandringham. He soon escaped and headed for London, and killed Mary Kelly. He was recaptured and returned to the asylum where he died, not from the flu as claimed, but of softening of the brain due to syphilis. A variation of this story appeared in the (1978) book: Prince Jack by Frank Spiering. The author suggests that Lord Salisbury, along with Albert Edward, had Eddy killed by a morphine overdose. The extreme agony which, Eddy exhibited at death, Spiering speculates, was due to him having been poisoned, and cites his overall unsuitability for the throne as the reasoning behind this suspicion. It is here the story becomes convoluted. According to a tale told by Joseph Gorman, an obscure London artist who took the name Joseph Sickert, and claimed to be the illegitimate son of the artist Walter Sickert, suggests Eddy, on one of his visits to a homosexual brothel in Cleveland Street, met and fell in love with a young woman named Elizabeth Crook, who worked in a nearby tobacconist's shop at 22 Cleveland Street. A secret marriage took place, despite the fact that she was a Roman Catholic. The marriage bore a daughter Alice Margaret. One of the witnesses to the marriage was Mary Kelly. Eddy had his wife and daughter settled in an apartment at 6 Cleveland Street though, when news of an illegitimate great-grandchild came to Queen Victoria's attention, she informed the Prime Minister Lord Salisbury, who afraid that knowledge of the existence of Alice as a Catholic heir to the throne would result in a revolution, ordered a raid on the apartment. Annie was placed in Guy's Hospital under the custodianship of Sir William Gull, who allegedly conducted experiments on her, which drove her insane. She died on 23 February 1920 at the age of 55, after spending more than thirty years in various hospitals, workhouses and institutions. Alice survived and was cared for by Mary Kelly, and was later said to have become Walter Sickert's mistress; they allegedly had a son Joseph. Mary Kelly then began to blackmail the government and was murdered, along with all the friends that she had confided her secret to, by a group of high-ranking Freemasons, led by the Prime Minister, Robert Cecil, Sir William Gull, Lord Randolph Churchill, Sir Robert Anderson; and whichever variation of the story is told, Montague John Druitt and James Kenneth Stephens. Other theories have the Prince, not dying in 1892 but living on until 1930, locked away in Glamis Castle, hopelessly insane. Stowell's theory is without foundation. Annie Crooks death certificate clearly shows that she belonged to the Church of England, and was not a Roman Catholic as claimed. Number six Cleveland Street, was demolished in 1886, and so could not have been raided in 1888. There is no record to prove such a marriage ever took place. There is also no evidence that any of the Ripper victims knew each other, it is merely speculation. Lastly, Robert Cecil was not a Freemason. Court circulars show that when Mary Ann Nichols was murdered, Eddy was staying with Viscount Downe at Dandy Lodge Grossmont in Yorkshire from the 29 August to the 7 September 1888. When Annie Chapman was murdered, he was in York, at the Cavalry Barracks 7-10 September. On the night Elizabeth Stride and Catherine Eddowes were murdered, he was with his Grandmother the Queen, along with several newspaper reporters at Abergeldie Scotland from the

2-30 of September and finally, when Mary Kelly was killed he was at Sandringham from the 2-12 November

JOHN ANDERSON

Anderson was a sailor, who in October 1894, according to shipmate James Everard Brame, a cook on board the clipper the Annie Speer, sailing from Shields in England to Iquique, in Chile, under Captain Carruthers, confessed on his death-bed to having committed the Whitechapel murders. This account was published in Lloyd's weekly newspaper 18 October 1896. According to Brame, Anderson had been robbed and almost ruined by a prostitute while in London. He would brood on this day and night and swore revenge on the whole prostitute class. "They did me," he said, "And I did them." Having little money, he took lodgings at a quiet little farmhouse near Bromley, a distance of 9 miles to Whitechapel. He would venture out on an evening to commit the terrible deed, the knife he used was similar to that used by a slaughterman. He had an unnamed accomplice in this tale that would keep a look out for him and wait at an appointed location with a large, clean butcher's smock, which he would draw over his bloodstained garments, thus easily avoiding any suspicion. Two days before his death, at Iquique in northern Chile, Anderson, delirious with fever, would scream out, "There's another one, how she bleeds." Anderson told Brame, who was in the hospital bunk next to Anderson, his father was a surgeon at Lowestoft, and he knew how to handle a knife pretty well, himself. Anderson wrote his confession signed it and gave it to Brame, who lost it after he was shipwrecked. Anderson was described as 38-years old, of fair complexion, red hair and moustache and his face was much pitted with smallpox scars, and was believed to have had some medical knowledge (US Navy hospital assistant). Anderson was described as; of superior appearance and spoke in an educated voice. Though there is little evidence to substantiate if this story has any truth to it, or if Anderson even existed. Some theorists have noted that Anderson resembles the description of the suspect, known as Blotchy Face, seen by Mary Ann Cox entering Miller's Court with Ripper victim Mary Kelly, shortly before she was murdered. At about 11.45pm on 8 November 1888, Cox walked into Dorset Street from Commercial Street and saw Kelly walking in front of her with a man. They turned into Miller's Court and went inside No.13, at which point Mary Ann bid Kelly goodnight. Mary Kelly was apparently very drunk and could barely answer, but managed to say goodnight in return. Shortly afterwards, she was heard singing in her room. Cox went out shortly after midnight and returned about 1.00am by which time Kelly was still singing. Cox went out again just after 1.00am and returned at 3.00am and by this time all was quiet in the court and there was no light on in No.13. She stated that after that, she heard no noise for the rest of the night. Cox described the man as "aged between 35-36 with a thick carroty moustache, small side-whiskers, a fair complexion and blotches on his face, holding a quart can of beer." Cox described as a widow and "unfortunate" living at 5 Miller's Court, claimed she had known Kelly for eight months.

ROBERT ANDERSON

Proposed as a suspect in the (1976) book: Jack the Ripper the Final Solution, by Stephen Knight, and as a co-conspirator by Melvyn Fairclough in the (1991) book: The Ripper and the Royals.

Dr. (later Sir) Robert Anderson was born in Mountjoy Square, Dublin, Ireland 29 May 1841. The son of Crown Solicitor, Matthew Anderson. Brought up in a devout Christian home. Educated privately in Dublin, Boulogne and Paris. On leaving school,

Anderson began an apprenticeship in a large brewery, but decided not to go into business, and left after 18 months. He studied in Boulogne-Sur-Mer and Paris and entered Trinity College, Dublin, where he graduated Bachelor of Arts in 1862. The following year he was called to the Irish Bar. In April 1868 Anderson was attached to the Home Office as an adviser on political crime. In 1873 he married Lady Agnes Alexandrina Moore. They had four children; three sons, Arthur, Alan, Graham, and a daughter, Augusta. Appointed assistant commissioner C.I.D. 1 September 1888, upon the resignation of James Monro. In his memoirs The Lighter Side of My Official Life Anderson wrote of his appointment:

Mr. Monro was not an easy man to follow, and my difficulties in succeeding to the post were increased by the foolish ways of the Home Office, as well as by the circumstances of the times.

Within a week of his appointment, he was prescribed sick- leave due to overwork. Anderson had not taken an adequate holiday for several years and came to his post suffering from exhaustion. Dr Gilbert Smith instructed that he takes a recuperative break of at least two months. Anderson left for Switzerland on 8 September 1888, the day of the second Ripper murder, that of Annie Chapman, and assigned the supervision of the Whitechapel murders over to Detective Chief Inspector Donald Swanson. His absence was soon noted by the press and, according to his memoirs:

Letters from Whitehall decided me to spend the last week of my holiday in Paris that I might be in touch with my office. On the night of my arrival in the French capital two more victims fell to the knife of the murder-fiend; and next day's post brought me an urgent appeal from Mr. Matthews to return to London; and of course I complied.

He was recalled after the double murder of Elizabeth Stride and Catherine Eddowes. He therefore set himself to reinvestigating the whole case' and next day he met with the Home Secretary and Sir Charles Warren.

In The Lighter Side of My Official Life, he recalled their conversation:

..."We hold you responsible to find the murderer,' was Mr. Matthews' greeting to me. My answer was to decline the responsibility. 'I hold myself responsible,' I said, 'to take all legitimate means to find him..."

He retired from the Metropolitan Police in 1901 and was knighted. Anderson died in bed on 15th November 1918 at the age of seventy-seven, from sudden heart failure following Spanish Influenza. Anderson stated on a number of occasions the identity of the Ripper was known. In his (1907) book, 'Criminals and Crimes' Anderson wrote:

That the Ripper had been safely caged in an asylum.

In 1910 Anderson published his memoirs, The Lighter Side of My Official Life. In his memoirs, he wrote:

One did not need to be a Sherlock Holmes to discover that the criminal was a sexual maniac of a virulent type; that he was living in the immediate vicinity of the scenes of the murders; and that, if he was not living absolutely alone, his people knew of his guilt and refused to give him up to justice. During my absence abroad the Police had made a house-to-house search for him, investigating the case of every man in the district whose circumstances were such that he could go and come and get rid of his blood-stains in secret. And the conclusion we came to was that he and his people were certain low-class Polish Jews; for it is a remarkable fact that people of that class in the East End will not give up one of their number to Gentile justice. And the result proved that our diagnosis was right on every point. For I may say at once that "undiscovered murders" are rare in London, and the "Jack-the-Ripper" crimes are not within that category. And if the Police here had powers such as the French Police possess, the murderer would have been brought to justice. Scotland Yard can boast that not even the subordinate officers of the department will tell tales out of school, and it would ill become me to violate the unwritten rule of the service. So I will only add here that the "Jack the Ripper" letter which is preserved in the Police Museum at New Scotland Yard is the creation of an enterprising London journalist.

Having regard to the interest attaching to this case, I am almost tempted to disclose the identity of the murderer and of the pressman who wrote the letter above referred to. But no public benefit would result from such a course and the traditions of my old department would suffer. I will merely add that the only person who had ever had a good view of the murderer unhesitatingly identified the suspect the instant he was confronted with him, but he refused to give evidence against him. In saying that he was a Polish Jew, I am merely stating a definitely ascertained fact. And my words are meant to specify race, not religion. For it would outrage all religious sentiment to talk about the religion of a loathsome creature whose utterly unmentionable vices reduced him to a lower level than that of the brute.

ANDREWS

A Man known by the name of Parnell was arrested on suspicion of connection with the Whitechapel murders. He had long been a regular lodger at the Beehive Chambers, situated on the corner of Brick Lane and Prince Street. He was absent from his lodgings on the night of the double murder and had been very irregular in his attendance there since that time, this caused the deputy at the lodging house to become suspicious, and he took these suspicions to the police. At the Commercial Street police station, the man told officers his correct name was actually Andrews, and that he was a book hawker. He explained that he slept at another lodging house on the nights in question. He gave police a satisfactory account of himself and the police believed him innocent. Andrews was described as very boyish in appearance and about 22 years of age.

APE

A woman named Mrs L. Painter from Burlington Lodge, Strand, Ryde, the Isle of Wight, considered in all seriousness that the Ripper was in fact not a man or woman, but a large ape which had escaped from a wild beast show. She wrote to the City Police 3 October 1888 and explained her theory of how this powerful and agile creature escaped at night to reclaim a knife which it had hidden previously, high up in a nearby tree; or another safe place. The ape then dispatched its victims silently, before returning the knife to its hiding place, and itself dutifully to its cage. Mrs Painter opted for her ape suspect because she believed this beast was swift, cunning, silent and strong. As amusing as this story appears, it is evidently influenced by Edgar Allan Poe's 1841 short story Murders in the Rue Morgue.

STEPHEN HERBERT APPLEFORD

Uruguayan investigator and mathematician Professor Eduardo Cuitino a probability expert at the ORT University in Montevideo, has identified surgeon Dr Stephen Herbert Appleford as Jack the Ripper. He spent 2 years painstakingly researching the case and in a paper entitled Travelling through Time to Trap Jack the

Ripper, said university rower and swimmer Appleford was strong and left handed as the Ripper was reputed to be. He claims he was around 36-years-old, what he deemed "the appropriate age of a psychopath," and had an IQ well above average, another trait common in that type of criminal. Prof Cuitino, believes Appleford began his killing spree in 1881 after the death of his mother and suggests the Ripper killings stopped because Appleford got married, and moved out of town. He also speculates Appleford may have committed suicide. Appleford died at the age of 88 on 31 August, 1940. On the same date as the first Ripper murder occurred in 1888. Cuitiño added: "He probably committed suicide, laughing at England and the English until his last sign of life." Cuitiño, also believes the physician's signature on the 1891 census form and the first known letter attributed to Jack the Ripper: were almost identical. He further claims Appleford was found nearby when a woman was stabbed in East London in 1882. John Bishop, aged 45 years, was charged with feloniously wounding his wife Ann Bishop, with intent to do her grievous bodily harm. Dr Appleford's statement to the court of the attack on the woman is reproduced here:

I am house-surgeon at the London Hospital; Ann Bishop was brought there on the morning of July 25, suffering from a clean cut incised wound on the left side of the neck, at the lower part, about two inches in length; it was superficial in most of its extent, but went to a depth of half an inch in its deepest part; she left the hospital on 1 August; it is nothing serious, and she is not being attended to now—this knife (produced) might have caused the wound; it might have been self-inflicted—I cannot say it is more likely to have been inflicted by anybody else than by herself; it is just possible, but hardly probable, that the wound was self-inflicted; it is so low down.

Stephen Herbert Appleford was born 1852, in Little Coggeshall, Essex. The son of William Appleford, and Bithiah (Née Bridge). He was awarded the freedom of the City of London on 2 May 1887. He married Mary Annie (née Sergeant) in January 1892. He left in his will effects to the value of £5020 4s.

SIR GEORGE COMPTON ARCHIBALD ARTHUR

Sir George Compton Archibald Arthur was born 30 April 1860 and was the son of Colonel Sir Frederick Leopold Arthur and Lady Elizabeth Hay-Drummond. He succeeded to the title of 3rd Baronet Arthur of Upper Canada on 1 June 1878 and married Kate Harriet Brandon on 11 August 1898. He gained the rank of Lieutenant in the service of the 2nd Life Guards and later fought in both the Boer War 1900-01 and the First World War 1914-18. Between the years 1914-16 he held the office of Personal Private Secretary to the Secretary of State for War, he also wrote a number of military biographies on Kitchener Wolseley and Haig and died at the age of 85 on 14 January 1946. At the time of the Whitechapel murders, he was a 28-year old captain in the Royal Horse Guard, and also an amateur actor, appearing as the corpse when Bancroft produced Fedora. He liked to engage in what was then a favourite and fashionable pastime of the wealthy Victorian; he liked to slum it in the poor areas. Arthur, unfortunately, chose Whitechapel at the time of the Ripper murders and thus became a suspect. Dressed in an old shooting coat, with an Astrakhan, collar and slouch hat he was spotted by two alert Constables approaching a well-known prostitute. Fitting the popular description of Jack the Ripper, he was arrested; much to the amusement of the newspapers and his friends. He protested, expostulated, and threatened them with the vengeance of Royal wrath, but in vain. He was able to satisfactorily prove his innocence.

ELIZABETH ASHWORTH

On the 26 December 1888, Elizabeth Ashworth, described as a married woman, was charged at the Peterborough Police Court with stabbing George Taylor. She was in a public house in Peterborough when she drew a knife, said, "I'm Jack the Ripper" and stabbed him four times in the head. He was a stranger to her. She was sentenced to nine months hard labour.

DICK AUSTIN

Austin was suspected of being the Ripper by fellow soldier James Oliver, who had served with him in R Troop the Fifth Lancers. Oliver, of 3 Westfield View, Rotherham, went to the local police station with his suspicions about Austin and claimed he was a real woman hater. He had overheard him say that he would kill every whore and cut her inside out, and always had revenge against women brooding in his mind. Whenever the men in the regiment would talk about women, Austin could be heard grinding his teeth. Oliver said: "Austin was a man who is most abstemious and will live on dry bread, he used many a day to save his money and live on what was knocking about in the barrack room." Oliver, when shown copies of the alleged letters by the Ripper, believed the 'Dear Boss' letter (written with a steel pen), similar to Austin's handwriting, while the 'Saucy Jack' postcard (written with a quill), less so. Efforts to find a regimental photograph of Austin were unsuccessful. He described Austin as about 40-years old, 5 ft. 8 inches tall, with light hair and eyes, a very long fair moustache and long tapering hands. He described his face as fresh, hard and healthy looking, with a small piece missing from the end of his nose, where it had been bitten off. He said, "Austin was a very powerful and active man, though not heavy or stout, and although not mad, was not right in his mind." Before joining the army, he had been a sailor, and though always respectably dressed still had the appearance of a sailor more than a soldier. It was believed he had drawn his deferred pay; about £24.00 and claimed that he was going to make London his home. Oliver was cautioned to say nothing about his suspicions. On 5 October 1888, the Rotherham Police contacted Scotland Yard, though efforts to find Austin by Inspector Abberline were without success.

JOHN AVERY

John Avery was one of a number of people who wasted valuable police time by confessing that he was Jack the Ripper while under the influence of alcohol. On the 12 November 1888, John Carvell, a private E Troop, 11th Hussars, was standing on the corner of York Road, Islington, when an intoxicated Avery came up to him and announced, "I'm Jack the Ripper, I'll show you how I do all the lot." Carvell told him to go away and not talk such nonsense. Avery, however, refused and followed him. A scuffle ensued, during which Avery's nose become scratched. Avery then said, "Come and have a glass of beer and I will tell you a secret and you can make some money." They proceeded to the Duke of York public-house, Caledonian Street, where at the bar Avery repeated his claim once more that he was the Whitechapel murderer, and claimed: "he would have committed, even more had he not lost the black bag in which he kept his knives." Carvell, clearly frustrated with the man, dragged Avery outside into the charge of PC 208A Seymour, who was on duty nearby. After questioning at the Kings Cross Road Station, he was cleared of any involvement in the Whitechapel murders and was sentenced to 14 days hard labour for being drunk and disorderly. Avery apologised for what had occurred, and to no avail begged not to be sent to prison as it would ruin him. Avery, a ticket writer, lived at Southwick House, Vicarage Road, Willesden, and was described as respectable in appearance, 43 years of age, 5 ft. 9 inches tall, with dark hair and whiskers, dressed in dark clothing.

ALBERT BACHERT

In the (2016) book: One Autumn in Whitechapel, author Mick Priestly proposes Albert Bachert as the Ripper.

Albert Bachert, was born c. 1860 in London, to German Immigrants, John and Georgina Bachert. John was a tailor. In the 1881 census they are living at 13 Newnham Street, London. Albert, in the 1881 census, was an engraver. He had three sisters Augusta, Emily, and Flora. Frequently referred to as Backert, in the newspapers. Was Chairman of the Whitechapel Vigilance Committee, having taken over from Mr George Lusk. Frequent self-publicist, he appeared in thirteen newspaper articles spread between 1887 and 1893.

This newspaper report from 30 June, 1891:-

At the Thames Police-court, Alfred Backert, the chairman the Whitechapel Murder Vigilance Committee, who described himself as an engraver and "reporter" of 13, Newnham Street Whitechapel, was charged with disorderly conduct in High Street, Whitechapel. Constable 325 H said that he saw the defendant fighting.

He had been ejected four times from a butcher's shop, and as he refused to go away he was taken into custody.

The defendant said that he knew the law better than the witness did, and would stay there as long as he liked.

Thomas Oates, a butcher, said the defendant often came to his shop after he had been drinking. He would not go away, and he shoved the witness, who then struck him.

Mr Montagu Williams: "Does he often get drunk?"

Witness: "Very often. Mostly Mondays and Tuesdays as a rule."

Mr. Montagu Williams fined the defendant five shillings, or in default, five days' imprisonment."

In February of 1891, Frances Coles was found murdered in Swallow Gardens. On 16 February, the inquest into Coles murder reconvened after an adjournment Coroner Wynne Baxter found himself short of jurymen to hear the case. Bachert offered himself as a substitute, but Baxter, seemingly all too familiar with Bachert's reputation, refused him. Bachert was furious and demanded an explanation:

Mr. Backert.-Why?
The CORONER. Because I decline.
Mr. Backert. - You decline simply because I happen to be chairman of the Vigilance Committee, and you think I shall fully investigate this matter. I have a right to be on the jury.
The CORONER. - I have decided you are not to serve on this jury.
Mr. Backert. - Yes; because you know I shall inquire into the case.
The CORONER. - You have already been told I shall decline to accept you. Mr. Backert (walking to the back of the court). - You will hear more of this. The jury, having been sworn, proceeded to view the body. On their return Mr. Backert, addressing the Coroner, said: - "It was only after you heard who I was that you would not allow me to serve on the jury." The CORONER. - If you do not keep quiet I will have you ejected from the room.

On 8 March Bachert, was sentenced to three months imprisonment for fraud. This was the last appearance of Bachert in the newspapers.

JOHN EVELYN BARLAS

Theorist David A Green, suggests John Evelyn Barlas as a Jack the Ripper suspect due to his penchant for long midnight walks, and his association with prostitutes.

John Evelyn Barlas was a decadent English poet and political activist. Born in Rangoon, Burma 13 July 1860, to John Barlas and Elizabeth Annie, a Scottish family of merchants. After the death of his father, he was brought to Glasgow, by his mother, when he was 1-years-old. He was educated at St John's Wood School then the Merchant Taylor's School. After the death of his mother in 1878, he moved into lodgings in Great Russell Street. Here he began to study Marxism, and other left wing literature. He studied at New College, Oxford, where he befriended the playwright Oscar Wilde, who became an intimate companion. Married Eveline Honoria Nelson Davies, a relation of Lord Nelson. Their daughter Evelyn Adelaide Isabella was born in May 1882, she died in June 1885. Barlas was briefly associated with the Rhymers Club, (a group of London-based poets who met regularly at Ye Olde Cheshire Cheese, a tavern off Fleet Street to discuss their work) having been sponsored by Ernest Dowson, himself also a Ripper suspect. From 1884-1893 Barlas published eight volumes of Swinburne influenced verse under the pseudonym "Evelyn Douglas." Including 1885's the Bloody Heart, 1887's Phantasmagoria: Dream-Fugues and 1889's Love Sonnets. A revolutionary anarchist, socialist in politics, Writers have claimed he demonstrated in Trafalgar Square on Bloody Sunday, November 1886, where he was heroically clubbed, falling bleeding at the feet of Eleanor Marx. This assault, it is speculated may have led to lifelong medical problems; delirium and depression. Barlas himself makes no reference in any of his letters of this incident, neither does it appear in any contemporary press accounts. So it is no longer plausible to believe, as commentators have claimed, that Barlas subsequent insanity dated from what happened to him at Trafalgar Square because there is no evidence Barlas ever attended that demonstration. A friend of Barlas wrote to him:

There has been some 'serious fighting' today as you predicted. I am glad you were not there

Possessing both fragile mental health and intense emotions, he was arrested on New Year's Eve 1891, after walking to Westminster Bridge and firing a revolver three times in the House of Commons, apparently to show his contempt for the Parliamentary procedure. He was bailed out by his friend Oscar Wilde. In the 1890s, the mere expression of socialist views was sometimes construed as evidence of insanity. In September 1892 Barlas was arrested for unprovoked assault in Crieff, Perthshire, Scotland. Certified as a lunatic he was admitted first to James Murray's Royal Asylum in Perth and later to Gartnavel Asylum, Glasgow, where he was never to be free again. Life in an asylum for a paying patient like Barlas could be highly tolerable. Amenities included a reading room with periodicals and newspapers, library, lounge with billiards and card tables, cricket grounds, a bowling green, and a croquet lawn. Gartnavel even had its own golf course. It has been suggested syphilis may have contributed to his madness after a sore was discovered when he was admitted to the asylum. He may have contracted the disease from a prostitute, he allegedly lived with after leaving his wife. Known by his friends as a brilliant conversationalist and a man of compelling personality and good looks. He died in Gartnavel 15 August 1914 at the age of 54 of a valvular disease of the heart. During his time in the asylum, he wrote 23 dramas, 20 volumes of lyrics, and many novels. Unfortunately, none of this work has survived.

DR. BARNARDO

Suggested as a possible Ripper suspect, first by Donald McCormick in 1962, and more recently by Gary Rowland's in the (1999) book: The Mammoth Book of Jack the Ripper, and by Vanessa A Hayes in the (2006) book: Revelations of the True Ripper.

Rowland's puts forward the notion that Barnardo's lonely childhood and religious zeal led him to slaughter prostitutes to clear them from the streets, and that he only stopped killing because of an accident in a swimming pool shortly after murdering Mary Kelly, left him totally deaf. He was thus unable to listen out for sounds, such as the approaching footsteps of a patrolling policeman, which in turn forced Jack the Ripper into early retirement. Hayes in her book put forward the following points. That Barnardo had medical training. That he was familiar enough with the East End to make good his escape. And that he spent time in America, which made him familiar with Americanisms such as "Boss." At the height of the Ripper murders, Barnardo was a recognisable figure in the East End of London, known for his charity work and preaching. He would visit doss houses and urge prostitutes to place their children into his care, rather than run the risk of them being suddenly orphaned. It was during one of these visits to 32 Flower and Dean Street, that Barnardo, in a letter to the Times newspaper 6 October he wrote:

Sir, Stimulated by the recently revealed Whitechapel horrors many voices are daily heard suggesting as many different schemes to remedy degraded social conditions, all of which doubtless contain some practical elements. I trust you will allow one other voice to be raised on behalf of the children. For the saddest feature of the common lodging-houses in Whitechapel and other parts of London is that so many of their inmates are children. Indeed, it is impossible to describe the state in which myriads of young people live who were brought up in these abodes of poverty and of crime. I and others are at work almost day and night rescuing boys and girls from the foul contamination of these human sewers; but while the law permits children to herd in these places, there is little that can be done except to snatch a few here and there from ruin and waiting patiently those slower changes which many have advocated. Meanwhile, a new generation is actually growing up in them. We want to make it illegal for the keepers of licensed lodging-houses to which adults resort to admitting young children upon any pretext whatever. It is also desirable that the existing laws relating to the custody and companionship of the children should be more rigidly enforced. At the same time some provision is urgently required for the shelter of young children of the casual or tramp class, something between the casual wards of the workhouse and the lodging-house itself, places where only young people under 16 would be admitted, where they would be free to enter and as free to depart, and which could be made self-supporting, or nearly so. A few enterprising efforts to open lodging-houses of this class for the young only would do immense good. Only four days before the recent murders I visited No. 32, Flower and Dean-street, the house in which the unhappy woman Stride occasionally lodged. I had been examining many of the common lodging-houses in Bethnal-Green that night, endeavouring to elicit from the inmates their opinions upon a certain aspect of the subject. In the kitchen of No. 32, there were many persons, some of them being girls and women of the same unhappy class as that to which poor Elizabeth Stride belonged. The company soon recognised me, and the conversation turned upon the previous murders. The female inmates of the kitchen seemed thoroughly frightened at the dangers to which they were presumably exposed. In an explanatory fashion, I put before them the scheme which had suggested itself to my mind, by which children at all events could be saved from the contamination of the common lodging-houses and the streets, and so to some extent the supply cut off which feeds the vast ocean of misery in this great city. The pathetic part of my story is that my remarks were manifestly followed with deep interest by all the women. Not a single scoffing voice was raised in ridicule or opposition. One poor creature, who had evidently been drinking, exclaimed somewhat bitterly to the following effect: - "We're all up to no good, and no one cares what becomes of us. Perhaps some of us will be killed next!" And then she added, if anybody had helped the likes of us long ago we would never have come to this!" Impressed by the unusual manner of the people, I could not help noticing their appearance somewhat closely, and I saw how evidently some of them were moved. I have since visited the mortuary in which was lying the remains of the poor woman Stride, and I at once recognised her as one of those who stood around me in the kitchen of the common lodging-house on the occasion of my visit last Wednesday week. In all the wretched dens where such unhappy creatures live are to be found hundreds, if not thousands, of poor children who breathe from their very birth an atmosphere fatal to all goodness. They are so heavily handicapped at the start in the race of life that the future is for most of them absolutely hopeless. They are continually surrounded by influences so vile that decency is outraged and virtue becomes impossible. Surely the awful revelations consequent upon the recent tragedies should stir the whole community up to action and to the resolve to deliver the children of to-day who will be the men and women of tomorrow from so evil an environment.

He later viewed the body of Elizabeth Stride at the mortuary and recognised her as one of the women who had stood around him in the kitchen.

Thomas John Barnardo was born in Dame Street, Dublin, on 4 July 1845, the fourth of six children. His father, John Michaelis Barnardo, a furrier, was a Jewish immigrant from Havelberg, Germany. His mother, Abigail, was John's second wife. He had lost his first wife Elizabeth, who was Abigail's older sister, during childbirth. Thomas was described as "a short, rather unattractive child with wiry hair and plain features," unlike his younger fair haired brother Henry Lionel, who was attractive and an absolute cherub, and was said to be the apple of his mother's eye. Henry was frequently summoned by his parents and shown off to family and friends, whom he would entertain with his fine singing voice, while Thomas was kept hidden away in the nursery. He attended St. Ann's Sunday school, St John's Parochial School and St. Patrick's Cathedral Grammar School. After leaving school, Barnardo found employment in a clerical capacity at a local wine merchant. As a young man, he joined various Christian Organisations and became a Sunday school teacher, spending most of his free time spreading the word of God. He took the Bible through the back streets, into the pubs and doss houses, he was mobbed, pelted with refuse, laughed at but still he hung on, with great faith and courage. In the summer of 1863, he began to hold his own prayer meetings from a room on Augier Street, which was not altogether successful. In April 1866 Barnardo left Dublin for London to train as a missionary. Upon arriving in London, he lodged at 30, Coburn Street in the East End, and in November of 1867 registered as a student at the London

Hospital, where it was said he took a keen interest in anatomy. Although he was nicknamed "The Doctor" Barnardo never actually qualified as a doctor. He returned to religion and after attempts to start a mission in the East End failed, suffered the first of several nervous breakdowns, which occurred during stressful periods in his life. On 2 March 1868, he founded his East End juvenile mission, in two small cottages in Limehouse. In 1870, at 18 Stepney Causeway, he opened his first home for underprivileged boys. The words 'No destitute child ever refused admission.' were written above the door of the first Barnardo's home in Stepney the boys were trained in carpentry, metalwork and shoemaking in the hope, these skills would lead to apprenticeships and employment. He would regularly go out at night into the slum districts to find destitute boys. By night, lantern in hand, he would catch his children, retrieving them from the gutters, roofs and doorsteps where they slept. A home for girls soon followed. In 1874 he opened a photographic department in his Stepney boy's home and over the next thirty years every child that entered one of Barnardo's homes had their photograph taken. Children were photographed when they first arrived, and again several months later, after they had recovered from their experiences of life on the streets. Critics claimed that he staged the photographs to make the children look ragged and ill to enable him to gain more sympathy, support and funds from the general public, it was a claim Barnardo strenuously denied. During his lifetime, he was said to have helped and rescued no fewer than sixty thousand children. The charitable work of Barnardo's continues to this day, and helps more than 100,000 children, young people and their families every year. He married Syrie Louise Elmslie on the 17 June 1873, and they had seven children. In 1888 Barnardo was 43 years of age, 5 ft. 3 inches tall, with a heavy moustache. In November 1889, Thomas

Barnardo became a Freemason, being initiated into Shadwell Clerke Lodge No. 1910. He ignored doctor's orders to take a period of absolute rest, worn out he died of angina at the age of 60 on 19 September 1905.

DANIEL BARNETT

Daniel Barnett was the older brother of Ripper suspect, Joseph Barnett. He was born in Whitechapel in 1853, to John and Catherine Barnett, who like many of their fellow countrymen had fled Ireland to seek a better life for themselves in London. John Barnett worked as a fish porter at Billingsgate Market; it was a trade Daniel would later follow him into. In July 1864 John Barnett died at the age of 47 after contracting pleurisy. By 1871, Daniel, like his father before him, was working as a fish porter at Billingsgate Market. On 1 July 1874, he received his porter's license and was still working there as late as 1891. When his elder brother Dennis left home to get married, the responsibility of being head of the family now fell to Daniel. Life was a struggle, and the family was forced to move to Great Pearl Street, which was considered one of the worst streets in the East End, with severe overcrowding and most homes classed as unfit for human habitation. Daniel, however, did his best in difficult circumstances and ensured that the children attended school. In the 1881 census, he is aged 28, a lodger at 9 Aldred Street. His occupation Fish Porter. Daniel's life was seemingly uneventful after this and the next we hear of him is the night that Mary Kelly was murdered. Joseph Barnett told The Star newspaper 10 November 1888 that his brother had met Kelly the night before, though does not offer us an explanation why, or at what time the alleged meeting took place. It is speculated that Joseph had turned to his older brother for advice and support in an attempt to win Mary back after their relationship had ended. Maurice Lewis, a tailor and Dorset Street resident, had claimed that he had seen Mary Kelly in the Horn Of Plenty public house, Dorset Street, between 10:00 and 11:00 pm in the company of some women, one of them named Julia (this was possibly Julia Van Turney), and a man named Dan, or Danny, who sold oranges in Billingsgate Market, and with whom she had lived with until recently. Lewis claimed to have known Kelly for five years, a claim which cannot be correct, as it pre-dates her arrival in London. The newspapers probably incorrectly quoted the time Lewis had known Kelly, from five months to five years. Lewis, regardless of the length of time he had known Kelly, would presumably also have known, and being able to recognise Joseph Barnett, the man she had, until recently, been living with. Though the man Dan – Danny is often credited as Joseph Barnett was it, in fact, Daniel Barnett. The story Joseph Barnett gave to the Star newspaper about his brother visiting Kelly appears to support this claim. Daniel Barnett, it is said bore a facial similarity to his younger brother. The man she was with in the Horn Of Plenty at around 10:00 or 11:00 pm could not have been Joseph Barnett unless the alibi he gave to the police in which claims he left Kelly at around 8:00 pm and did not see her again after returning to his lodgings, was untrue. It is entirely possible Lewis simply mistook Kelly for someone else, or simply got his days confused. Lewis is a controversial witness; he also claims he saw Kelly twice the following morning, first briefly at 8:00 am then later at around 10:00 am drinking in the Britannia public-house, (known as Ringer's) only forty-five minutes before her horrifically mutilated body was discovered, and several hours, according to the medical evidence after she was supposedly killed. Daniel Barnett, in 1888 was 36 years of age, 5 ft. 4 ½ inches tall, with a fair complexion. He lived at the Victoria Home For Working Men, co – incidentally, also living there at that time was another Ripper suspect George Hutchinson, though there is

44

no evidence they were acquainted. In the 1891 census he was still living at this address. Daniel Barnett died on 22 December 1906 from heart disease at the age of 57 he resided at 18 New Gravel Lane, Shadwell, London.

JOSEPH BARNETT

Joseph Barnett was named as the Ripper by authors Bruce Paley in the book: Jack the Ripper the Simple Truth, (1995) and by Paul Harrison in the book: Jack the Ripper the Mystery Solved (1991).

Born on 25 May 1858 at 4 Hairbrain Court, Blue Anchor Yard, Whitechapel. To John Barnett and Catherine, who had originated from Ireland, but like an estimated 1 million of their fellow countrymen, had fled the poverty and famine there to seek a better life for themselves in England and America. The Barnett's moved to the East End of London and lived first at 4 Hairbrain Court, and later at 2 Cartwright Street, Whitechapel. His father, John Barnett worked as a fish porter at Billingsgate market, and died from pleurisy at the age of 47, in July 1864. Joseph was the fourth child and third son, the other children were Denis born 1849 in Chalk, Kent, Daniel, born 1851 in Whitechapel, Catherine born 1853 in Whitechapel and John born 1860 also in Whitechapel. Shortly after her husband's death, Catherine Barnett, completely disappears from all the official records. It is speculated she may have remarried. Author and researcher the late, Christopher Scott, found a Catherine Barnett, (widow) aged 48 years, living at 4 Glasshouse Street, Whitechapel, in the 1871 census. Working as a servant, for Thomas Allman (widower), who was in occupation as a general labourer. In 1885 they married. Catherine died that year under the name Catherine Allman. It is not known if this is the correct Catherine Barnett. Dennis now took over as head of the family. This he was to do until 23 March 1869 when at the age of 20 he married a local girl, Mary Ann

45

Garrett. The couple left the East End and settled in Bermondsey, they would be married 32 years, and have four children, two daughters, Mary Ann, born 1870, died at 1-years-old in 1871. Elizabeth, born 1891. And two sons, Denis born 1872 died 1934. And John, born 1875 died 1936. Denis Barnet died in 1920 at the age of 71. His wife Mary Ann passed away in 1901 at the age of 52. The responsibility of being the new head of the family now fell to 17-year old Daniel. Life proved a struggle and in 1871 the family moved a mile north to Great Pearl Street, which had a reputation as one of the worst streets in the East End. Daniel, with the support of his sister Catherine, did their best in very difficult circumstances and made sure both Joseph and John attended school. Joseph was considered quite articulate and could read and write, though suffered from a speech impediment and a psychological disorder known as "echolalia." This disorder causes a person to repeat the last words spoken to them. Joseph, like his father before him, began working as a fish porter at Billingsgate market, and on 1 July 1878, along with his brothers Denis and John, received his market porters license. A steady worker could earn as much as £3 per week. Barnett was working at Billingsgate market, when on Good Friday 8 April 1887; he met a young prostitute named Mary Kelly. At the time Kelly was living in Thrawl Street and was known to walk the streets around Aldgate and Commercial Street, so it is quite likely his first meeting with her was as a client. They arranged to meet the following day, and quickly decided to live together, first on George Street, then at Paternoster Row, Dorset Street. Evicted for spending the rent money on drink, the couple moved again, first to Brick Lane then finally in February/March 1888 to 13 Millers Court 26 Dorset Street, where they rented a room at a rate of 4s 6d per week. Millers Court was a tiny room, about twelve feet square, with its own entrance. The room was so cramped that when the door was opened it would bang against the bedside table. It was classed as furnished, the furnishings consisting of little more than a small rug, a bed, a couple of small tables, a pail and washstand and two dining type chairs. Opposite the door was a fireplace, and to the left of the door, and at right angles to it, were two windows, one of which was broken, it was close enough to the door to be able to reach through it and unbolt it. Between numbers 26 and 27 Dorset Street, and opposite Crossingham's Lodging House, was a three-foot wide opening that was the entrance to Millers Court. There were six houses in the narrow court, and number 13 was the first door on the right. They were let by John McCarthy and were known locally as "McCarthy's rents." The other tenants of the court were Henry Maxwell, a night watchman and his wife Caroline. Lizzie Albrook, a friend of Kelly's, Julia Venturney also a friend of Kelly's, Elizabeth Prater, who lived in the room directly above Kelly, and Mary Ann Cox, a widow who was described by the Star newspaper as, "A wretched specimen of womanhood." John McCarthy denied to the newspapers any knowledge that Kelly was a prostitute or that his premises were used for immoral purposes. This is unlikely, however, as Cox and Prater were quite open about being prostitutes, therefore it is more likely McCarthy was fully aware of what his tenants got up to, but simply turned a blind eye to the situation as long as the rent was paid. Barnett and Kelly lived at Millers Court fairly comfortably, Barnett's wage, providing them with a fairly decent standard of living, comfortable enough so that Kelly did not have to walk the streets, Barnett forbade her from resorting back to prostitution. The Daily Telegraph, 12 November 1888, reporting Barnett's interview with the Central News Agency, "I was in decent work in Billingsgate Market when I first encountered her [Kelly], and we lived quite comfortably together" Despite appearing calm, their relationship was punctuated by frequent rows, often the result of Kelly's drinking. It was said of Mary Kelly that when in liquor, she was very noisy, otherwise was a very quiet woman. Neighbours who knew them spoke of a friendly and pleasant couple, who gave little trouble unless drunk. Barnett was described as, "A very inoffensive man." It was a drunken Mary Kelly, who smashed a couple of window panes in their room during a quarrel, it was these broken windows that Thomas Bowyer, sent by John McCarthy to collect what rent arrears he could, peered through and discovered her mutilated body. Barnett told the Daily Telegraph 13 November 1888 that, "Kelly was too tender hearted and would allow the poor miserable women whom she knew to share the room in which they lived." With other prostitutes allowed to occupy the small room, little in the way of privacy or intimacy would have been afforded the couple, putting untold stress on their relationship. According to the newspaper, the argument which caused him to leave was allowing a miserable creature named Harney (presumably Maria Harvey), to share their small bed for two consecutive nights. The reporter was informed that even after Barnett left Kelly, he had not given her up entirely and that they lived separately for reasons of incompatibility. When he had money, he used to call and share it with her and was on his way to see her on the morning of her murder to give her three pence. Barnett was described by the newspapers as, "A very wretched specimen of the human race." When Kelly's body was discovered the door was locked and had to be forced, leaving many to speculate that the killer either had a key and locked the door behind him on leaving, or was at least familiar with the geography of the room. Barnett claimed that the key had been missing for some time and a possible explanation is that it had simply been lost by either Kelly or Barnett perhaps when drunk. Entry was gained by reaching through the broken window, moving aside the dirty old muslin curtain and pulling back the bolt. Some have speculated Barnett took the key with him when he left, so he could gain access if and when he so desired. Elizabeth Prater, who lived in the room above Kelly, reported that Barnett and Kelly had an argument on the 30 October between 5 and 6:00 pm which caused Barnett to move out. It has been claimed that Barnett harboured a strong dislike of prostitutes in general and Kelly's friends in particular. Maybe he considered that they would tempt her back into prostitution. Kelly, much to Barnett's consternation, was still receiving visits from her ex-lover Joseph Fleming, who gave her money and made no secret of the fact that he wanted her back. In July/August 1888 after working at Billingsgate market for over 10 years, Joseph Barnett was sacked, for reasons that are not clear though was most probably theft. It has been claimed that Barnett liked giving Kelly gifts, so it is quite probable Barnett was stealing produce from work, which in turn helped save his wages to enable him to treat her and pay the rent. With Barnett's wage now gone, so had their comfortable lifestyle, Barnett began selling oranges, and Kelly resorted back to prostitution, as she was by this time seven weeks in arrears with her rent, the sum of 29s. Theorists have speculated that the reason her landlord, John McCarthy allowed Kelly to fall behind with her rent was that he was actually her pimp, there is, however, no evidence to support this. Though Barnett and Kelly were no longer lovers, he would continue to visit her almost daily and would give her money if he had it. She would ask him to read her the newspaper accounts of the Ripper murders (presumably Kelly could not read) and was anxious to learn if the Ripper had been apprehended. She appeared to be frightened of someone other than the Ripper, though would not say who. According to Julie Venturney, a friend of Kelly's, Mary said she could no longer bear Barnett and was fond of a man named Joe, presumably Joseph Fleming. It was said Fleming still visited Kelly and hoped they would get back together, even though she was at the time in a relationship. Barnett, despite the relationship ending, was still hoping for reconciliation and turned to his older brother Daniel for support and advice on winning Mary back. Daniel went to see Kelly on the night she was murdered, but it was to no avail, she was, according to the medical evidence murdered in the early hours of Friday 9 November 1888. Barnett was questioned by Inspector Abberline for four hours and had his clothing checked for blood stains. When he was questioned it was reported he was in an agitated state, though the police appeared to be satisfied that he had nothing to do with the murder, and he was subsequently released. Barnett told the police that he had visited Kelly at Millers Court about 7:45 pm on the night she was murdered, chatted for a while, apologised for having no money to give her then parted on good terms. He then went back to his lodgings at Bullers lodging house, 24-25 New Street, Spitalfields, where he played the card game "Whist" until half past twelve, before retiring to bed. Mary Kelly was murdered sometime between 4 and 5:45 am or according to some disputed eyewitness sighting of Kelly, much later. If Kelly was murdered later than Barnett's alibi is not exactly watertight. Barnett, at the mortuary, when viewing Mary's body, identified her by her hair and eyes, and not as some reports have claimed by her ears and eyes. At the inquest, Barnett was described as, "well-groomed with a neatly trimmed moustache, top hat, coat and cravat." His appearance prompted the Star newspaper to remark that, "He looked very respectable for someone of his class."

The theories that propose Barnett as Jack the Ripper are Barnett, after reading about the murder of Martha Tabram, killed the other prostitutes in a similar manner, in an attempt to scare Kelly off the streets, as he was losing control over her, and when this failed he killed her. Once he had killed her, there was no reason for him to kill anyone else. There is also some who believe that Barnett was not Jack the Ripper, but killed Mary Kelly during a quarrel, then mutilated the body in a way he believed, from the press reports, the Ripper mutilated his victims, thus disguising it as a Ripper murder. In 1888 at the time of the Ripper murders, Joseph Barnett was 30-years old, 5 ft. 7 inches tall, medium build with a moustache, fair complexioned with blue eyes. He died at the age of 68 in November 1926 at 106 Red Lion Street, Shadwell, London, three and a half weeks after his wife Louisa.

SAMUEL AUGUSTUS BARNETT

Not considered a suspect at the time of the Whitechapel murders; suspicion has focused on him more recently by television scriptwriter J Michael Straczynski. Barnett was an English clergyman and social reformer who spent his life preaching and working among the poor in the East End of London. He was known locally as the "Saint of Whitechapel." He used music, non-biblical readings and art to teach those with no education or religious leanings. He was particularly associated with the establishment in 1884 of the first university settlement, Toynbee Hall, 28 Commercial Street, Whitechapel. Toynbee Hall was founded in memory of Arnold Toynbee 1852-1881, the Balliol historian, and was the first university settlement for university men to live in close contact with their East End neighbours. Barnett was also instrumental in 1901 in founding the Whitechapel art gallery and the Whitechapel public library.

Samuel, Augustus Barnett, was born at 5 Portland Square, Bristol, on 8 February 1844 the son of Francis Augustus Barnett, an iron manufacturer, and his wife Mary (nee Gilmore). He was educated at Wadham College, Oxford. He then travelled to the United States and the following year was ordained to the curacy of St Mary's, Bryanston Square. He took priest orders in 1868 and in 1873 became the rector of St Jude's Church, Whitechapel. St Jude's had a notorious reputation for its squalid and overcrowded housing, and the Barnett's worked hard to improve the conditions for the poor of the parish. That same year he married Henrietta Octavia Weston Rowland 1851-1936, an English social reformer, author and philanthropist. Henrietta, was born in Clapham, London. They had no children. At their first Sunday service his wife, of whom it was said could not sing a note in tune, led hymn, singing with gusto to a congregation of six old women. Barnett wrote frequently to the press about the conditions in the East End, among his many complaints and suggestions were that street lighting and sanitation should be improved, the poor should treat their womenfolk better and that women should be stopped from stripping to the waist for fights. He also wanted the slaughterhouses removed because of the brutalising effect it was having on the health and morals of the locals. Barnett believed in vigorous self-help and made it plain that financial relief, often expected from the church, would not be forthcoming from him. He also believed in thrift and believed the poor should exercise better money management. He foretold of the murders:

The murders were bound to come, generation could not follow generation in lawless intercourse, children could not be familiarised with scenes of degradation and the end of all be peace.

He wrote Practicable Socialism in 1888 in conjunction with his wife, who wrote his multi-volume biography in 1918 and in 1924 became Dame Commander of the British Empire. Samuel Augustus Barnett died at 69 Kings Esplanade, Hove Sussex, at the age of 69 on 17 June 1913. His wife Henrietta, died 10 June 1936.

WILLIAM BARRETT

On 31 December, Harriet Sinfield, 21 years of age, who described herself as a maker of fiddle strings. Was charged at the Worship-street, police-court, with robbing William Barrett, a seaman, of a purse and £1 15s in money at a common lodging-house in George-street, Spitalfields. Barrett, who belongs to a ship called the Buckhurst, said he met the woman, yesterday and had been taken by her to a house. After some time she left him on the pretence of wanting a drink. When he examined his coat, which he had put on a chair, he discovered that his purse containing his money had been stolen. He ran after her and caught her in the street. She screamed, and he demanded his money, before giving her into custody. Sinfield denied the robbery, no purse or money was found on her. She said she ran away because the man had told her he was "Jack the Ripper." She was remanded for inquiries.

JOHN BATTERSON

John Batterson, a labourer, at the railway sheds at Balby Carr, living at 31, Victoria-street, Doncaster, was arrested on 28 January 1891, for assaulting Miss Edith Bellingham, governess to Sir William Cooke, of Wheatley Hall. The incident happened on 7 January. It is alleged that the man declared himself to be "Jack the Ripper," and that he brandished a knife and "Looked most alarming." Several young ladies were also assaulted, and seriously injured by blows, falls, and being dragged around. Some of them offered their purse and watch and chain in order to be allowed to go on their way. A woman named Priscilla Scholey, who lives at Levitt Hogg, was crossing Hexthorpe Flatts, when she saw Battison about 7 yards from the footpath. He was behaving indecently. When she had gone about 200 yards, Battison, overtook her, put his hands over both her eyes from behind, threw her down, and attempted to outrage her. She screamed and struggled, and the man ran away. Batterson, had been suspected by the police for some time, but had insufficient evidence to charge him. Bellingham, told the police that she should be certain to identify her assailant if she came face to face with him again. She was secreted not far from the spot where the labourers enter the works at the shed, after a short wait, she emphatically said to the police officer with her, "That's the man," pointing to Batterson. Despite her certainty in identifying Batterson, at his place of work, as the man who assaulted her. Bellingham when questioned shortly after her attack, was vague in her description of her assailant. He was discharged because the evidence against him was too weak. In some newspaper accounts he is named as John Edward Patterson and was referred to as the "Doncaster Jack the Ripper."

THOMAS VERE BAYNE

In the (1996) book: Jack the Ripper, Light-Hearted Friend, author Richard Wallace, put forward the suggestion that Lewis Carroll, real name (Charles Lutwidge Dodgson), author of the Alice in Wonderland books, was responsible for the Ripper murders, along with his lifetime friend Thomas Vere Bayne. Wallace believes Dodgson's work contained hidden confessions to the Ripper murders. Wallace offers us no evidence, for his claims, only a series of poorly constructed anagrams.

Thomas Vere Bayne was born in 1829. Student and Tutor at Christ Church, becoming Senior Student in 1858. He obtained his BA degree in 1852 and his MA in 1855. Junior Censor 1863, Senior Censor 1870. From 1861 to 1882 he was Curator of Common Room in Christ Church, a post in which he was succeeded by Dodgson. He was university Proctor in 1867, and became keeper of the archives in 1885. He died 1908. He was in

France from 1 September 1888 to the 5 October, when the Ripper murders occurred. He was also nearly sixty-years old, and as this entry in his diary shows, he wrote "Can barely move, great pain," was suffering from severe back pain.

WILLIAM BENJAMIN BELCHER

According to Dianne Bainbridge, and Norman Kirtlan, authors of the (2013) self-published book: Jack the Ripper in My Blood. Jack the Ripper was a milkman who lived in Hartlepool. Dianne Bainbridge, a mother of three who runs a wedding shop in Newcastle, says distant relative William Benjamin Belcher matches every characteristic of the profile for Britain's most infamous serial killer. Belcher was a milkman who could move around at odd hours without raising suspicion, had previous experience of butchery, lived in the middle of Whitechapel, and he had a history of violence against women. He also left London as the Ripper's murders appeared to end, moving to Hartlepool with his wife and young daughter and changed his surname to Williams. He also fabricated a past history of life in Devon and not London. The authors also claim he can be linked to two similar murders which occurred in the North of England, both near the train route between London and the town in County Durham. Forensic expert and ex-Northumbria police inspector Norman Kirtlan, who has spent years investigating the Ripper murders, says the new suspect is the most credible to date. He said: "My favourite suspect is the new one, a man called William who lived in Whitechapel and knew the area well, was a milkman so had access to the area at night and also had butchery skills. He also had a history of abuse and violence against women and children."

William Benjamin Belcher was born 21 June 1864 in Paddington, to Benjamin Belcher and his wife Ellen (née Percy). His parents married on 2 Nov 1863, at Christ Church, St Marylebone. His father was in occupation as a plumber. His mother died April 1880. The 1881 census shows William living at 20 Grove Street Marylebone. He married Annie Jenkins, Webber, a dressmaker, born in Devon, on 14 July 1884 at Christ Church Marylebone. His occupation is listed as a milkman. His address is still 20 Grove Street Marylebone. Their daughter Kate Ellen Belcher's was born in 1886.

NIKANER BENELIUS

Benelius, born in 1861, was a Swedish traveller; he lodged in a German lodging-house, 90 Great Eastern Street, Shoreditch, and had recently come to England from American. He was arrested on 17 November 1888 after walking into the parlour of a house on Buxton Street, Mile End, occupied by Harriet Rowe, a married woman, at half-past ten that morning. When asked what he wanted Benelius simply grinned at her, without speaking, alarmed by this she ran into the street, and found PC 211H Imhoff, and had him arrest Benelius. At the police station, he was searched, but nothing was found on him. Detective Sergeant Dew attended from Commercial-street station and stated that the prisoner had been arrested that morning under circumstances which rendered it desirable to have the fullest inquiries made of him. When questioned, Benelius, whose grasp of English was poor, said: "He went into the house whose door had been left open to ask directions to Fenchurch Street, as he was expecting some letters at the post office." Benelius was described In the Times newspaper 19 November 1888, as:

Foreign in appearance with a moustache, but otherwise, cannot be said to resemble any of the published descriptions of men suspected in connection with the Whitechapel murders.

His landlord said: "Benelius had been acting rather strange lately and had been preaching in the street," the landlord also claimed "that Benelius owed him 25s in rent." Benelius had previously been questioned and cleared of the murder of fellow Swede, Elizabeth Stride. Despite his rather strange behaviour, he was satisfactorily exonerated of any involvement in the murders and his innocence fully established. The City branch of the Charity Organization Society said that it would send him to America.

Police constable 211H Imhoff, who arrested Benelius, was born in 1856, in Baden, Germany, his full name was Henry Utto Imhoff. The son of Franz and Caroline Imhoff. He arrived in England, 1 January 1868 at the age of twelve, on the German registered ship The Alder. Joined the Metropolitan Police 1875 (warrant no. 59797. In the 1881 census, he is living at 11 Peabody's Buildings, Commercial Street. In the 1891 census, he is living at 23 Clarence Street, Bethnall Green, with his wife Mary, and his three sons, Henry Utto, Alfred, and Albert Edward. Resigned from the police 1893. He received his Certificate of Naturalisation 8 Oct 1906. He died in 1925 in Uxbridge.

CORPORAL BENJAMIN

On 7 August 1888, the body of Martha Tabram was found on the first floor landing of George Yard. She had been stabbed 39 times. Two different weapons had been used, most of the stabs appeared to have been inflicted with a penknife. One, which had penetrated the sternum, appeared to have been made by a dagger-like weapon, possibly a sword bayonet. The murder was believed to have occurred around 2.30 a.m. Tabram had last been seen in the company of a soldier at 12.45 a.m., by a friend, and fellow prostitute "Pearly Poll" Conolly. PC Barrett, had spoken with a soldier at 2.00 a.m., near George Yard. The soldier had told him he was waiting for a "chum" who had "gone off with a girl." Barratt, was taken by Inspector Reid, to the Tower of London Barracks, to see if he could identify the soldier. He was unable to do so. Reid arranged a parade of all the corporals and privates who had been on leave on the 6 August. Barrett, was told to take his time, a great deal depended on him picking out the right man and no other. He walked along the line, until he reached the centre, when he picked out a private wearing medals. Reid told him to be certain, and have another look, Barrett, promptly walked along the line of men again, this time stopping and picking out a different man. Reid, asked him how he came to pick out two men, Barrett replied, "The man I saw in George Yard had no medals and the first man I picked out had." The two men were taken to the orderly room, the soldier wearing medals was allowed to leave when Barrett, admitted he had made a mistake. The second man picked out by Barrett, gave his name as John Leary, when questioned he said he had been in Brixton with a Private Law, who corroborated his version of events. Leary was allowed to leave. Suspicion briefly fell on a Corporal Benjamin, who had been absent without leave since 6 August. When he returned, his clothing and bayonet, were inspected, nothing incriminating was found. He was asked to account for his whereabouts. Benjamin, explained that he had been staying at his father's hotel in Kingston upon Thames. His father confirmed his story, and he was allowed to leave.

MISS BIDWELL'S STALKER

The Cambridge Chronicle, 19 October 1888 Reported the story of a Miss Bidwell, of Milton Road, Chesterton, Cambridge, who was out walking with a lady friend one evening when a man came toward her flourishing his arms while exclaiming he was "Jack the Ripper," and would murder her. It is not known if he was brandishing a knife. The man made off before he could be recognised or apprehended. Since the incident, Miss Bidwell has received a letter purporting to have come from the Whitechapel murderer. The letter was badly written entirely void of punctuation and contained many spelling errors. Part of the letter reads:

Will lay in wait for you, I am master of the hart, take care of you selves, fat girl will cut nice. I have found your name. I am not sure whether it is Biddle or Bidwell, I am Jack the Ripper pal, oh so jolly fat are the best. I shall not be idle; I will have a look out for you. I shall not forget you.

The police regarded the letter as nothing more than a stupid practical joke, though Miss Bidwell unsurprisingly took a more serious view of the whole matter.

It is not known exactly which Miss Bidwell, received the letter and reported the incident to the police. Living at 18 Milton-road, Cambridge, in 1888, was Sarah Bidwell (née Cook), aged 73, and her two daughters. Sarah, Elizabeth Bidwell, aged 43, in occupation as a vest maker. And Ada Bidwell, aged 31 in occupation as a tailoress. Ada never married she died in 1936, in Cambridge.

THE BIRMINGHAM SUSPECT

The Morning Advertiser (London) 19 November 1888 reported the following story:

On Saturday afternoon a communication from the Birmingham detectives to the effect that a man suspected of being concerned in the Whitechapel murders had left Birmingham by train for London was at once acted upon by the Scotland-yard authorities. Detectives Leach and White, of the Criminal Investigation Department, proceeded to Willesden Junction and Euston respectively, and at the latter station, Inspector White, on the arrival of the Birmingham train, detained the suspected individual and conveyed him to Scotland-yard. It was stated that the man had been staying at a common lodging-house in Birmingham since Monday last, and the theory was that if, as was supposed by the police, he was connected with the East-end crimes, he left the metropolis by an early train on the morning of the tragedies. The suspected person was a medical man who was some years ago practising in London with another gentleman of some repute. He was of gentlemanly appearance and manners, and somewhat resembled the description given by the witnesses at the inquest as having been seen in company with Kelly early on the morning that she was murdered. Upon being minutely questioned as to his whereabouts at the time of the murders, the suspect was able to furnish a satisfactory account of himself and was accordingly liberated.

ALFRED NAPIER BLANCHARD

Alfred Napier Blanchard, a 34-year old canvasser, who resided at 2 Rowland Grove, Rowland Road, Handsworth, Birmingham, was arrested in the Fox And Goose public-house, Newton Row, Aston, Birmingham, on 5 October 1888 after being overheard describing how he had committed the Whitechapel murders. According to the landlord of the Fox and Goose, Richard King, Blanchard entered the pub on Friday morning at about 11 o'clock and commenced drinking until quarter past 8 at night. He consumed about five and a half pints of beer. While in the pub, Blanchard struck up a conversation with the landlord and asked him "what kind of detectives they had in Birmingham," the landlord replied "that he believed them to be very clever men," to which Blanchard replied, "It would be a funny thing if the Whitechapel murderer were to give himself up in Birmingham," to which the landlord agreed before declaring, "I am the Whitechapel murderer."

Someone asked him how he had done the murders without making the victims scream, to which he explained that this was done by simply placing the thumb and finger on the windpipe and cutting the throat with the right hand, another customer asked him if he had got the knife with him. To which he replied, "I've left that behind me." He also claimed he had done six of them in London. Blanchard said to the landlord "You are a fool if you don't get the thousand pounds reward offered for me, You may have as well have it as anyone else." Blanchard then attempted to leave the establishment, but was followed by several men and brought back. The police were sought and Detective Ashby being in the neighbourhood took him to Duke Street Police Station. When he appeared in court he told the magistrates "that after drinking heavily for a period of three days and reading about the inquest of the latest Whitechapel victim (Catherine Eddowes), he had become excited and foolishly claimed them as his own." Blanchard said, As he was proceeding towards the cells, the prisoner said he had a favour to ask. Would the press be kind enough not to mention this case? It was a serious matter for him, and should his employer get to hear about it he would lose his situation. He was told that neither the magistrates nor the police had any control over the press. The magistrates, last words on the matter where, "What a foolish man you have been. After police inquiry, it was proved he was in Manchester when the Whitechapel murders occurred, and had been there for some two months prior to his visit to Birmingham.

Alfred Napier Blanchard was born in Chorlton, Manchester in 1855, to William Edward Blanchard, a calico printer, and Marianne Ashby (née Cooke). In the 1881 census, he is living at 25 The Grove, Barton Upon Urwell. He is in occupation as a hardware traveller.

HELENA PETROVNA BLAVATSKY

Helena Blavatsky was born of Russian nobility in Ekaterinoslav (now Dnepropetrovsk) Ukraine, on 31 July 1831. Her mother, Helena Andreyna Fadeyev, was a novelist, whose writings concerning restricted Russian women consequently lead to her being called the George Sand of Russia. She died at the age of 28 when Helena was 12-years-old. With the death of her mother, and with her father Col. Peter Alexeivich Hahn being in the armed forces, Helena was sent, along with her brother, to live with her maternal grandmother, Helena Pavlovna de Fadeev, a famous botanist and a princess of the Dolgorkuov family. Helena's mother and grandmother were strong role models in her life, and she inherited from them the characteristics of a fiery temper and a disregard for social norms and did, therefore, mature into a nonconformist. At the age of seventeen she married forty-year-old General Nicephore Vassilievitch Blavatsky on 7 July 1849, the marriage was to last only a few months. She married her second husband, Michael C. Betanelly, on 3 April 1875 but also left him after only a few months, maintaining that neither marriage was ever consummated. Henry Steel Olcott called the marriage, "a freak of madness," and ridiculed her for marrying a man so much younger than herself and unequal to her mental capacity. She travelled the world, and in 1873, hearing of the enthusiasm for spiritualism spreading in the United States, emigrated to New York, where she impressed with her psychic abilities. In September 1875 she co-founded, with Henry Steel Olcott and William Quan Judge, the Theosophical Society, a new religious movement that took its inspiration from Hinduism and Buddhism. The Theosophical Society expounded the esoteric tradition of Buddhism, aiming to form a universal brotherhood of man, studying and making known the ancient religions, philosophies and sciences, and investigating the laws of nature and divine powers latent in man. In July 1878 Blavatsky became the first Russian woman to acquire United States citizenship. Described as a short, stout, forceful woman, foul of mouth with a fiery temper, it was said of her that she could swear fluently in three different languages. William T. Stead said of her "She was the very reverse of beautiful." A talented, gifted pianist and fine artist. In her later years, she suffered from heart disease, rheumatism, Bright's disease of the kidneys and obesity. Unable to walk, her dedicated followers took to pushing her around in a specially adapted bath chair. She died at her home in London 8 May 1891 during a severe flu epidemic. She was cremated with a third of her ashes remaining in Europe, and a third each going to America and India. Theosophists commemorate her death on 8 May, called "White Lotus Day." Blavatsky wrote Isis Unveiled (1877) The Secret Doctrine (1888) The Key of Theosophy (1889) and the Voice of Science (1889). Blavatsky is included as a Ripper suspect due to a remark by English oculist Aleister Crowley in an unpublished, untitled essay, he wrote:

It is hardly one's first, or even one's hundredth guess that the Victorian worthy in the case of Jack the Ripper was no less a person than Helena Petrovna Blavatsky.

This throwaway remark was, in fact, Crowley's way of saying that Blavatsky was in fact not Jack the Ripper.

BLOOMFEIN

The Nevada State Journal 22 June 1915, mentioned a man named Bloomfein, suspected of being Jack the Ripper. The man was being detained in the Philadelphia hospital for the insane for the murder of two children, 5 year old, Leonora Cohen, on 19 March, and two months later 5 year old, James Murray, on the East Side of New York. Cohen, was found with a strand of short grey heir clutched in her hand. Her Abdomen, had been slashed. Murray, had been stabbed, and strangled. The man, who is being investigated, told an incoherent story to Captain Lynch about cutting up people. Physicians at the hospital learned that he had delusions at intervals of about six weeks. Bloomfein stated that he lived on East Fifteenth Street.

BLOTCHY FACE

Blotchy Face was the name given to a suspect seen at 11:45 pm by witness 31-year old widow and prostitute Mary Ann Cox in the company of Mary Kelly shortly before she was murdered. Cox a resident of 5 Miller's Court, was on her way home to get warm after an evening soliciting when she noticed Mary Kelly, whom she had known for about 8 months with a male companion, they both appeared to be very drunk. Cox followed the couple down the passage into Miller's Court and wished Mary, Goodnight as she passed. Mary mumbled in reply "Goodnight" and said that she was going to have a song. Cox from the other end of the courtyard, heard Mary singing the popular Victorian music hall ballad "only a violet I plucked from my mother's grave when a boy." At 1 am Mary was still heard drunkenly singing. At three in the morning Cox, went out again, and the light from Kelly's room was out and there was no noise. At a quarter past six I heard a man go down the court. Cox due to the good light from the lamp opposite claimed she managed to get a good look at the man and described him as "about 36 years of age, 5 ft. 5 inches tall, stout, shabbily dressed, wearing dark clothing a dark overcoat around hard billy-cock hat and carrying a quart can of beer. He had a blotchy face, side whiskers and a heavy carroty moustache, and a clean-shaven chin." The suspect John Anderson has been tentatively mooted by some theorists as a possible name for the suspect Blotchy Face.

GEORGE BOLTON

At West Hartlepool Police-court, George Bolton, a grocer, was charged with being drunk and disorderly, in Mainsforth-terrace on the 24 November 1888. PC Iveson stated that shortly after half-past seven, he saw Bolton, rushing along the street, with a number of women in front of him and yelling out "I'm Jack the Ripper". Bolton denied the charge, but the officer's statement was corroborated by a woman. He was fined 5s and 9s and 6d costs.

CHARLES BOND

In April 1890, Charles Bond, alias John Doe, was charged with battery and disturbing the peace. Bond, was a hostler in the employ of C.G. Sayle, an attorney. A short time ago he called on Mrs. Monday, a cook employed by Mrs. Jennie Sweet, who keeps a boarding-house at 1531 K Street. He was there only a short time before he began quarrelling with Mrs. Monday. She ran into the yard and told Mrs. Sweet that she was afraid he would kill her. He was ordered from the house but refused to leave. Bond the struck Mrs. Sweet, and called her vile names, she went to fetch a policeman, but Bond caught up with her and struck her a blow to the head. He continued to strike her, and caught her by the throat and choked her, he said he would tear her heart, and windpipe out. He said he was a bad man and was "Jack the Ripper." In court, Sweet exhibited the bruises and scratches caused by Bond's fingers on her throat. Bond was said to have been drunk on whisky, when he committed the offence.

JOSEPH BONNY

On the 4 April, 1889, The Globe published an article about a robbery at the American Ambassador's country residence:-

At the Maidenhead County Police-court yesterday, Joseph Bonny, 47, a grocer and provisions dealer, of Tredegar-road, North Bow, was charged, on remand, with committing a burglary at Ramslade, near Bracknell, the Berkshire residence of Mr. H White, First Secretary of the United States Legation, on January 30th, and stealing a quantity of Jewellery valued at £4,000.

The accused was represented by Mr Dutton.

Fanny Bowerman, of Broad-lane, Bracknell, said her cottage was situated about a hundred yards from the carriage entrance of Ramslade.

She saw the prisoner on the Friday prior to the burglary, just before one o'clock.

He was going up the road towards Mr. White's, and he passed her as she was standing at her door.

She saw, him three minutes afterwards as he went by again.

By Mr. Dutton: The prisoner was about 20 feet away when she saw him.

He was respectably dressed, and he had on a long, black coat, a black handkerchief, black round hat, and dark trousers, and bools were clean, as if he had not walked far. He carried a stick with a silver knob, and white pocket-handkerchief in his left hand.

She took particular notice of him the second time, and she was afraid of him because she thought he was "Jack the Ripper.

WILLIE BOULT

A member of the public W.R. Collett of 104 Upland Road, East Dulwich, wrote to the City commissioner 6 October 1888 with his suspicions about a man he had met the previous July while staying with his wife in a boarding-house Portland House, Havelock Road, Hastings. Collett discovered that the man's name was Willie Boult and was described as about 30 years of age. 5ft 8 inches in height, slender build, dark brown hair, moustache and short side whiskers. Boult aroused Collett's suspicion when it was discovered he had left his employ with a firm of solicitors called Jacques in the WC district of London to move to the house in Hastings. Boult who in a few days, according to Collett became an alarming lunatic, always carried with him a small black shiny Gladstone bag which contained an ivory handled knife with a blade about 4 inches long. His friends were called to take him away to live with his mother in Fulham.

JOHN BRENNAN

In the hysteria immediately after the Annie Chapman murder, a 39-year old drunken Irishman named John Brennan, entered the White Hart public-house in Southampton Street, Camberwell. And proclaimed in a loud voice to everyone present that Leather Apron was a friend of his, and that he had the actual murder weapon in his pocket. Brennan's comments inevitably caused panic, and the customers almost tore down the door in their haste to depart the premises, while the terrified landlady barricaded herself in her parlour, leaving Brennan alone in the bar, where he no doubt helped himself to a drink, or two. When Constable Pillow 434P, arrived to arrest him, Brennan pointedly refused to leave. It was said Brennan treated the whole matter as a good joke. Brennan, who was described as having a very rough and strange appearance, with his coat split up the back.

JOHN BRINCKLEY

Daily News 14 November 1888 reported that John Brinckley, a 40-year old porter of Wilmington Place, Clerkenwell, was charged with being drunk and disorderly in Goswell Road, the incident happened on Monday of the previous night. Police Constable 192G confirmed seeing the prisoner drunk in Goswell Road wearing a woman's skirt over his other clothes. There were several persons round him as he cried out, "I'm Jack the Ripper, I'm going down the City Road tonight and I'll do another there." The Constable took Brinckley into custody. Brinckley, in his defence, stated that he did not remember putting on the skirt and suggested that someone must have put it on him for a lark and that he had worked hard all his life at Covent Garden market. The gaoler said "He knew the prisoner to be a hard-working man, but he often acted foolishly and had on more than one occasion been fined by this court." The prisoner was told, "You were not only drunk, but you played the fool under circumstances which might lead to serious mischief, there is a great deal of public excitement just now about a particular matter and I will send you to prison for fourteen days." The prisoner begged for a fine to be imposed, but the magistrate peremptorily refused and Brinckley was removed to the cells.

WILLIAM WALLACE BRODIE

On the 18 July 1889, the day after the murder of Alice McKenzie, William Wallace Brodie, described as respectably attired, though of no fixed abode and without occupation, walked into the Leman Street Police Station and gave himself up, claiming to be "Jack the Ripper." He said that having now committed eight or nine murders, only this latest crime bothered him. He appeared to be under the influence of drink, though made a full statement, and appeared in court on 20 July 1889 charged with the murder of Alice McKenzie. The police made a careful check into his background, which showed that he had sailed from Southampton on board the SS. Athenian for Kimberley, South Africa on 6

September 1888, and did not return to England until 15 July 1889, confirming that he could not have been Jack the Ripper. When he appeared in court for the second time, on 27 July, he was discharged, but rearrested for defrauding a jeweller, Peter Rigley Pratt of a watch, for which he received a six month sentence. Brodie had previously been sentenced in May 1877 to 14 year's imprisonment for larceny and was released on licence on 22 August 1888, after serving 11 years. Brodie resided at 2 Harvey's Buildings, Strand. On the night Alice McKenzie was murdered, Brodie, being very drunk, was assisted to bed by Mr Salvage, also of 2 Harvey's Buildings, and did not go out again until 10:20 am the following morning. In his lengthy, rambling and incoherent statement to the police, Brodie claimed, he walked from London to Cornwall and back in half an hour. He also claimed he went to seek out a prostitute who had given him a bad disorder 2 years earlier. He said he met a prostitute in Whitechapel whom he described as, "A fine woman dressed in a bright red dress, boots and hat." When she lay down under a barrow he cut her throat with his knife, which he whipped out from his outside coat pocket, before wiping it on a wisp of straw which was lying conveniently nearby. He left the knife which he claimed had been specially made for him in his red bag at the York Road Baths. In his statement, Brodie said, "This is the ninth murder that I have committed in Whitechapel, but none of them has caused any trouble to my mind except the last one, what with that, and a "worm" in my head that wriggles about, I cannot stand it any longer." While under arrest the police surgeon kept Brodie under observation and declared him, "now sane" which suggests that at some point he "was not," he was, however, suffering from acute alcoholism, causing hallucinations. When told he was charged with being a wandering lunatic Brodie said: "Do I look like one? I am as sane as any man in this court, I can assure you." When searched a razor was found in his possession, but no knife.

JOSHUA BROOK

Joshua Brook, a labourer, described as a stalwart, rough-looking man of 35 years, was charged with wandering abroad whilst of unsound mind, and breaking a glass window in the Masons' Arms public-house. At Leeds Police – court while standing in front of the dock Brook suddenly exclaimed "I'm Jack the Ripper it's right" while without warning violently struck the bench in front of him. After a violent struggle in which he struck a police officer two blows on the face, he said "is this murder or not?" Brook was led handcuffed out of court, examined by a doctor and declared of unsound mind. On 21 July 1892 he was admitted to Menston Asylum, formally The West Riding Pauper Lunatic Asylum. He remained in the asylum until his death on 4 November 1893 cause of death Syphilitic disease of the aorta. At the asylum his case notes describe him as surly in manner, he admits hearing voices, and seeing people in his room at night. He had earlier been charged with two counts of larceny in Leeds, Yorkshire, but acquitted. 8 December 1888. He had also been admitted to The West Riding Pauper Lunatic Asylum, Wakefield, 8 January 1891, where he remained until I October 1891.

GENERAL BROWN

A Home Office letter, 15 October, to Sir Charles Warren, mentions a General Brown, in connection with the Whitechapel murders. A letter to Jane Bromley had been addressed incorrectly, and she could not be located. Therefore, the letter was returned to the Post Office, where it was opened. The letter inside had been placed there by mistake and was a letter from a gentleman in Eaton Place to his son, who appeared to be an officer in the army.

The writer of the letter, who is not identified, went on to say that he could not help suspecting General Brown of being the Whitechapel murderer. The suspicious letter was passed on to the police, who interviewed and cleared General Brown. The source of the suspicion against General Brown appears to have been a lady who witnessed him operating on a racehorse and had jumped to the conclusion that he would not shirk at anything, presumably even murder. It is possible that she may have subsequently passed her suspicion regarding General Brown on to the unnamed letter writer.

THOMAS BROWN

The Daily Mail 27 April 1903 reported the following story:

Thomas Brown, aged 38, a general labourer, was sent for trial at the Thames Police Court on Saturday charged with attempting to murder by shooting four Germans William Mays, Bruno Weiss, Henry Mans, and Karl Adar, in a lodging-house in North East-passage, St. George's. The extraordinary letter read at the previous hearing of the case was re-read at the request of the magistrate. In this letter, Brown accused himself of committing one of the "Jack the Ripper" murders and made a rambling statement about mind reading and wireless telegraphy. Brown on Saturday said he wished to explain about the wireless telegraphy in his body, and it was not understood in this country. He gave himself up for the murder of Annie Austin in Dorset-street, Spitalfields, as he did not want anyone blamed for it. He was an Australian and had been charged with poisoning a woman in that country. In England mind-readers were different, and he would have to explain that before dealing with the shooting affair. In committing the prisoner the magistrate said he had no jurisdiction over mind-readers or wireless telegraphy. On the evidence of Dr. James Scott, the Medical Officer at Brixton prison, the Jury found the prisoner insane, and unfit to plead. To be detained during His Majesty's pleasure.

CHARLES BRUYN

In December, 1890, Charles Bruyn, a tobacco broker, of London, was committed to an insane asylum for a month at the insistence of his brother. Mr Bryun, was under the delusion that he was being hunted down by the London police as "Jack the Ripper." He has now been adjudged a lunatic, and is detained in Bloomingdale Asylum.

EDWARD BUCHAN

Suggested as a Ripper suspect by Roger Barber, in an article in Criminologist magazine autumn 1990,

DID JACK THE RIPPER COMMIT SUICIDE. Barber wrote:

The sudden cessation of the crimes after the murder of Mary Kelly is explained by the killer having committed suicide.

The East End News 23 November 1888 reported:

A determined case of suicide occurred in Poplar on Monday morning. A marine store dealer, named Edward Buchan, aged 29 years, cut his own throat with a knife. It appears that shortly after ten o'clock a sister of the man heard a strange noise, and on entering the back shop, saw Buchan in the act of cutting his throat. She raised the alarm and the father came to her assistance and attempted to take the knife from the man's hand, but failed, cutting his own severally in the attempt. Buchan ran round the room, slashing at his throat all the time, till he dropped down with his head nearly cut off. Dr Skilly was at once summoned, but Buchan died shortly after, he had nearly severed his head from his body.

Dr Skilly (some newspaper reports referred to him as Dr Skelly), said: "It was the goriest thing he had ever seen; the only thing not cut through was the bone."

Edward Buchan was born on 19 November 1859, to Horace David Mann Buchan, and Maria (née Griffiths), at 37 Robin Hood Lane, Poplar. Horace and Maria were married September 1851 in Stepney. They had four children, Horace, Maria, Edward, and Charles. Edward Buchan was said to have been a shoemaker, or store dealer, who killed himself on his birthday, 19 November 1888. The 19 November was also, co- incidentally, the day of Mary Kelly's funeral. His uncle committed suicide, in the same way, three years ago. It was said Buchan had been strange in his manner for some time. Apart from his suicide occurring on the day of Mary Kelly's funeral, there is nothing to link him to the Whitechapel murders.

WILLIAM BULL

William Bull was born in 1861, In Middlesex. He was 27 years of age at the time of the Whitechapel murders and lived at 6 Stannard Road, Dalton, London. Bull walked into Bishopsgate Street, police station on 5 October 1888 and confessed to the murder of Catherine Eddowes, and told the police he was a medical student at the London Hospital. He said, "I wish to give myself up for the murder in Aldgate on Saturday night last, or Sunday morning. About two o'clock, I think, I met the women in Aldgate, and I went with her up a narrow street. I promised to give her half a crown, which I did while walking along together, there was a second man, who came up and took the half-crown from her." Bull then began to cry and said, "My poor head, I cannot endure this any longer, I shall go mad, I have done it, and I must put up with it." When asked what he had done with the clothing he was wearing on the night of the murder he replied, "If you wish to know, they are in the Lea, and the knife I threw away," he declined to say anything more. Police made inquiries at the hospital, but could not find anyone of that name working there, in fact, Bull was found to be without employment and had made the confession while drunk. He later withdrew his statement saying that he could not do such an act. Inspector Izzard made inquiries into the man's background and found he came from a highly respectable family and bore an irreproachable character, though had recently given way to drink. The Inspector stated that he was satisfied that the man had made his statement out of pure mischief. After speaking to the man's father, it was proved he was actually in bed when the murder he confessed to had occurred. Bull said he had signed the temperance pledge.

HANS BURE

In October 1888, Hans Bure, a well-dressed German, was charged at Thames Police-Court with assaulting Elizabeth Jennings, of 37 Duckett-Street, Stepney. The assault happened at about 12:30 am on Saturday night. Jennings was walking along Harford Street, on an errand, when Bure caught hold of her arm and said, "Come along with me." She refused his request and made an attempt to escape, whereupon the man gave chase. She stood by a young man she knew, the man followed and she ran into the road. He ran after her, but saw another lady coming, and caught hold of her shawl. Jennings was frightened, her screams soon drew a crowd, who encircled the man and began calling him "Jack the Ripper." They detained him until Constable 150E arrived to take him into custody. Bure, who it is claimed could not speak English, talked through an interpreter, and said "He did not mean anything by his actions, he had been drinking and took the woman to be a prostitute." He admitted accosting her. Bure received a fine of 40s or one month's hard labour.

74

EDWIN BURROWS

Burrows, a vagrant, was arrested by Police Constables Bradshaw and Godley, on 8 December 1888 because he was wearing a peaked cap similar to the one described by Israel Schwartz, who had witnessed Ripper victim Elizabeth Stride being thrown to the ground by a man wearing such a cap shortly before she was murdered. Burrows resided at Victoria Chambers, a common-lodging- house, in Westminster, interspersed with periods of sleeping rough in public parks. Burrows was described as 45 years of age, 5 ft. 5 inches tall, with dark hair and whiskers, he wore a light brown tweed jacket. He lived on an allowance of one pound a week from his brother.

WILLIAM HENRY BURY

Bury was first suggested as a possible Ripper suspect by the New York Times in 1889 after a similarity was noted between the injuries he inflicted on his wife Ellen and the injuries inflicted on the first canonical Ripper victim Mary Ann Nichols. Bury would be forgotten as a Ripper suspect for nearly a century until rediscovered in 1988 by Dundee Liberian Euan McPherson, in an article, he wrote for the Scots magazine. McPherson would expand on his theory in the (2005) book: The Trial of William Henry Bury 1859-1889. Bury was also the subject of the (1995) book: Anatomy of a Myth, and the (2009) book: Jack the Ripper Unmasked, both by William Beadle.

William Henry Bury was born 25 May 1859 in Hill Street, Stourbridge, Worcester. To Henry Bury, official records state his surname as Berry and his wife Mary Jane (née Hendy), official records state her maiden name as Henley. The couple married 12 October 1851 at St Thomas, Dudley, Worcester. They had four children, of whom William was the youngest. The other children were, Elizabeth Ann, born 6 June 1852, who died at home on 7 September 1859, at the age of seven after a series of violent epileptic seizure, Joseph Henry, born 1854 and Mary Jane born 29 January 1857 in Stourbridge. In the 1871 census, Mary Jane, was residing at 97 Albion Street, Birmingham, with Joseph Henley, his wife Caroline, and family. She married jeweller Reuben Thomas Barnes, son of Thomas Collier Barnes, a China and glass-dealer, at St Pauls, Birmingham, 23 August 1880. The witness at their wedding was Joseph Henley. In the 1981 census they are living in Park-road, Dawlish, Devon. Mary Jane died in April 1881, of complications in childbirth, their son Percy Thomas, born April 1881, died the same day. Reuben remarried in 1885, and died in Australia, in 1925, at the age of 66.

Williams, father Henry was a hard-working fishmonger, whose work involved regular trips to Birmingham, to collect fish. On 10 April 1860, he was coming down Muckley's Hill near Halesowen, when there was a problem with the horse, jumping down to investigate, he lost control of the horse and it galloped off, crushing his body under the wheel. The heavy cart running over his body. This newspaper article from the Worcester Journal Saturday, 14 April 1860 gave a fuller account of the accident:

A fatal accident occurred on Tuesday last to a man named Henry Berry. The deceased was in the employ of Mr Joscelyne, fishmonger, and went to Birmingham to purchase some goods. While returning home, (as appears from the information of a man who was near), the horse he was driving became unmanageable when descending Muckles-hill. The deceased then attempted to get out but was thrown down, the wheel passing over his chest, killing him instantly. The horse still continued his furious career, until he arrived at the Shenstone Hotel, Halesowen, where he stopped as usual. The deceased had been in the employ of Mr

Joscelyne for five years, and has left an invalid wife and two children.

Henry's employer, was Abraham Joscelyn, born July 1813, in Black Notley Essex. The son of William Joscelyn a blacksmith, and Juliana (née Higham). He married Elizabeth Linnell daughter of Richard Linnell a bricklayer, on 10 August 1846. They had a son, Walter Linnell born 1861, died 1940. In the 1860 UK Trade Directory, Abraham is a fish, fruit, and poultry dealer, 53 High Street. In the 1861 census, he is living at 55 High Street, Stourbridge. He died 25 February 1862 at the age of 48 years. In his will he left effects worth a little under £450 to his widow. In the 1881 census, Elizabeth, aged 62 years, is living at 20 Heath Street, Stourbridge. Occupation retired fish merchant. The above newspaper report from the Worcester Journal regarding, the accident is in error they were three children, Joseph Henry, Mary Jane, and William. After the death of her husband and her eldest child, William's mother, sank into a state of severe postnatal depression and suffered a nervous breakdown, she was confined at the age of 29 to Worcester County and City Lunatic Asylum 7 May 1860, where she remained until her death at the age of 33, on 30 March 1864. She was admitted under the name Mary Berry, ID number 948, her maiden name was given as (Henley). Her hair was noted as black, eyes dark grey, status was given as a widow, her occupation was noted as a dressmaker. Her condition as very feeble and exhausted, with little disinclination to do any kind of work or to leave her bed. William it is speculated was not raised by his uncle Edward Henley, as some reports have claimed, but by a close family friend. She took pity upon the plight of the children and provided them with a home and a solid education, William attended the Blue Coat Orphanage in Hagley Lane, Stourbridge. At the age of sixteen, he found work as a factors clerk in a local warehouse in Horsley Fields,

Wolverhampton. In the 1881 census he is listed under the surname Berry, co-incidentally the surname of the man who would later hang him for murder in the city of Dundee. Bury then in 1884 found employment at Osbourne's a lock manufacturer in Lord Street, Wolverhampton though was sacked for theft. There are reports he was working for Mr. John Whitehouse & Son, brass founder, of Alexander Street. Bury was next making a precarious living hawking, selling items such as lead pencils and key rings on the streets in Snow Hill, Birmingham, he was seen by a former workmate Richard Swatman, looking shabby. He was arrested for vagrancy in Dewsbury, Yorkshire in 1884 and sentenced to 14 days in prison. His occupation was noted as warehouseman. His prison admission record, give his age as 25, his height as 5 ft. 2½ inches, and his hair colour as brown. He was recorded as having no previous convictions. A cut on his forehead and on the right side of his neck was noted. He arrived in London at the age of 28 in October-November 1887, and found work as a sawdust collector for James Martin, described as a general dealer. Bury contracted to pay Martin 16/- shillings a week in rent for a horse and cart. Martin ran what to all intent and purpose was a brothel, at 80 Quickett Street, Arnold Road, Bromley-by-Bow. He moved in with the Martin's, and slept in the stables and kitchen. It was at Quickett Street, that he met his future wife to be Ellen Elliot, a 32-year old barmaid and prostitute and the daughter of a London publican, George Elliot. Ellen was well known and respected among family and friends as a quite inoffensive woman, who had seemed very happy until she married Bury. She was described as a neatly dressed woman, fair-haired, slim and of genteel appearance. Ellen Elliot, was born 24 October 1855 at Stratford-le-Bow, East London. She was described as a sickly child who was often ill and rarely attended school. She had been left a legacy of bank and railway shares from an aunt, Margaret Barron, to the value of £300, worth in today's terms about £20.000. Ellen invested the money wisely, purchasing shares in the Union Bank of London. After a brief courtship of only one month the couple was married, at Bromley Parish Church on Easter Monday 2 April 1888. The newlyweds moved into Ellen's lodgings at 3 Swaton Road, Bow. The home of Thomas and Elizabeth Haynes. Elizabeth, was a witness at their wedding. On 7 April, only five days after they were married, Mrs Haynes, hearing Ellen screaming, rushed to her aid to find Ellen in bed and Bury kneeling on her attempting to cut her throat with a table knife which he was holding in his right hand. It was around this time Ellen confided to James Martin and his partner Kate Spooner that her husband often stayed out until the early hours, sometimes disappearing for a couple of days, before reappearing, worse the wear for drink, whereupon he would proceed to take his temper out on her. Exactly where he went and what he got up to she did not know. James Martin, on at least two occasions, witnessed William Bury assault his wife in public, and Ellen would often be seen displaying the facial marks resulting from a beating. Ellen also told the Martin's that her husband slept with a penknife under his pillow, and that he had infected her with a venereal disease, she also believed, prophetically, her husband would kill her. Bury was then sacked for stealing money from James Martin. With the help of Ellen's money (she agreed to sell some of her shares for cash) he bought a pony and cart, and became self employed as a sawdust and silver-sand merchant. He would purchase sawdust from various mills and sell it on to pubs in the East End and restaurants in the City. In August the couple left Swaton Road, and moved to 11 Blackthorme Street, Bow, and remained there for 8-10 weeks. In December they took up lodgings with William Smith, a builder/bricklayer, at 3 Spanby Road Bow. Bury stabled his pony and cart, at this address. The next we hear of their movements is 19 January 1889, when Bury told Ellen's sister, he had found manufacturing work for himself in Dundee at £2 per week, and Ellen at £1 per week, if she wanted it. He told his landlord, William Smith, a different tale, that they were emigrating to Brisbane, Australia. When asked by Smith which dock they were sailing from, Bury replied, "Ah, that's what you want to know, like a lot more." Bury asked Smith to build him a strong trunk to transport his belongings, and was very particular about the measurements of the box he wanted. Smith was surprised he wanted such a large trunk, as the only possessions he noticed the couple had where clothing, though he did notice Bury always appeared to have plenty of money and jewellery about his person. Smith later told the police that Bury had been lately, "Rather strange in his manner." On 19 January 1889 the Bury's travelled to Dundee on the London packet steamer Cambria, which was lying at London dock. The couple occupied a second class cabin and stayed on board overnight. During the crossing the other passengers noticed the couple appeared to be on good terms with one another, although were hesitant in revealing details about their past. During the trip it was noticed Bury seemed most anxious about a large, heavy whitewashed case he had taken on board. On first arriving in Dundee, the couple found accommodation with Mrs. Robinson, at 43 Union Street, for the sum of 40 pence per week, which was a little more expensive than other lodgings in the area. They, however, left after one week, claiming the rent was too high. It has been suggested that the real reason for their sudden departure was that Mrs. Robinson, the elderly landlady, had feared Bury, after he had looked at her wickedly, and thought him rather odd. Bury, it was said, had a tendency to walk rather quietly and often frightened people with his silent approach. They then moved into a two room, basement house at 113 Princes Street, formally a tailor's workshop, the basement being at the bottom of a four storey house. It was advertised to rent at 2s 6d a week. The building was squalid in appearance and the apartment dirty and cold with several broken window panes, though it was described as being in a quiet area. It was at this address, seven days later, that Bury murdered his wife. Neighbours at Princes Street rarely saw the couple, though on the occasions when they did, they noted they were often the worse for drink. Ellen was only spotted sporadically at night, whenever she would venture out to draw water from the communal pump. William Bury ran all other errands, such as replenishing candles, firewood and bread. The Bury's in conversation with their neighbours Alexander and Marjory Smith, began discussing Whitechapel and the murders, when Ellen remarked, "Oh Jack the Ripper is quite now." On 4 February, Bury went to Janet Martin's provisions store at 125 Princes Street, and asked if she had a length of rope, for what purpose she did not ask. Ellen Bury is not seen again. Her husband, however, is spotted on two or three occasions, always in a drunken state. David Duncan, a labourer lodging at 101 Princes Street, heard screams coming from the direction of number 113 though did not recall the time. At approximately 7:00 pm. Sunday, 10 February 1889, William Henry Bury walked into Bell Street Police Station and announced to Lieutenant James Parr, "I'm Jack the Ripper and I want to give myself up." Parr, not sure if he was dealing with a drunk or a madman, then asked the man why he called himself Jack the Ripper. "I'm him all right," Bury replied, "And if you go along to my house in Princes Street, you'll find the body of a woman packed up in a box and cut up." He gave officers the key to the property, telling them, "You will know it at once, because there are red curtains on the front window." He gave no further information, other than the number of his house, his name and occupation. Police officers visited

Princes Street and began a search by candlelight. The apartment was bare of possessions; the only items in the two rooms were a small bed piled high with clothing, and a large whitewashed packing case. Officers opened the box, by raising two loose boards on the lid and pulling back a piece of sheeting, to reveal the leg and foot of a female. Proceeding no further, they summoned doctors Templeman and Stalker, who proceeded to examine the contents of the 3ft 3in long, by 2ft 4in across, and 2ft 1in deep trunk. They discovered the naked and mutilated body of Ellen Bury, she had been strangled and her abdomen had been ripped open by a wound beginning 1½ inches from the pubis and extending upwards of 4½ inches, the wound was so severe that 12 inches of intestines were protruding through her stomach. Apart from the wound to the abdomen there were a total of nine other knife wounds to the body. The box, which was clearly too small to accommodate the body, had been packed tightly with books and clothing. Ellen's head had been forced to one side of the shoulder, the left leg was broken and twisted to such a degree that the foot rested on the left shoulder, the right leg had been smashed in order to fit it into the box, the body was lying on its back on a petticoat and a piece of cloth. A long-bladed knife, which had been used to commit the crime, lay nearby, along with a rope, complete with strands of hair still attached. It later transpired that Bury had lived with the box, and its contents, for several days, and along with some male friends had used it as a table to play cards upon. It became known while in court, that prior to his confession, he had gone to visit his friend and drinking partner, 29-year old Dundee-born painter and decorator David Walker, where the subject of Jack the Ripper had arisen several times during their conversation. In the days following the murder, he borrowed an axe from his neighbour, Marjory Smith, who joked to him light-heartedly, "Surely you're not Jack the Ripper are you," to which he replied, "I do not know so much about that." Police officers also discovered at Princes Street, two chalk-written messages, one behind a tenement door, stating, "Jack Ripper Is At The Back Of The Door," and one on a stairwell wall leading down to the flat, "Jack Ripper Is In This Seller." The newspapers attributed the handwriting to a small boy, though did not offer an explanation why they considered this to be the case. Presumably it was due to the poor grammar displayed. Bury received some education was literate, and at one time worked as a factors clerk, while his wife who rarely attended school, was not very well educated, because of this there is a suggestion that she wrote the message. The writing however was said to be old, and pre-dated the tragedy. Bury was detained on suspicion of having taken the life of his wife, by strangulation or stabbing, this information, it was noted, he received calmly. A search of his person revealed his wife's bank book, showing between £7 and £8 in credit, nearly £9 in silver in his pocket, a watch belonging to his wife, and some jewellery. Detectives from Scotland Yard, were sent to interview Bury and collect as much information as possible about him and ascertain his exact movements during the period he lived in London. The police discovered that he was in the habit of carrying a knife about his person, and that he was absent from his lodgings on the night's both Annie Chapman and Mary Kelly were murdered, and that his manner the following day was suggestive of a madman. Bury, while awaiting trial, told the police that on Monday 4 February 1889, he and his wife had been out having a good time, and could not remember going to bed. The following morning Bury awoke to find his wife dead on the floor, having been strangled with a cord. Having no recollection of whether he had committed the crime or not, and frightened and fearing he would be apprehended as Jack the Ripper, he was suddenly seized with a mad impulse, he picked up a large, sharp and finely ground knife, and plunged it into her abdomen, he then decided to conceal the body in the trunk. Detectives at this stage were sharply divided in their opinions as to the man's guilt in perpetrating the Whitechapel murders, many believed his Jack the Ripper confession was bogus, and that the real motive behind his wife's murder was to get his hands on her remaining money. They therefore concluded that the Dundee murder was a one off, and had no connection to the Whitechapel murders. The post mortem revealed that Ellen Bury had been dead for several days. Her body was formally identified by her sister, Margaret Coney, who had travelled up from London. She was later taken to the prison to identify Bury, much to his surprise. Bury, despite his initial confession, pleaded not guilty to his wife's murder and genuinely believed he had a chance of a reprieve. His solicitor asked for a second post mortem. Dr David Lennox, an experienced Dundee surgeon, carried out the second post mortem, assisted by Dr William Kinnear, and presented a comprehensive 14 page report. His conclusion was that Ellen Bury had committed suicide. This was a huge blow to the police, who now called in Dr Henry Littlejohn to perform a third post mortem, his findings were that Ellen had in fact been murdered, though he was unable to ascertain if the mutilations had taken place after death. Bury's trial commenced on 28 March 1889, the judge was Lord Young, Dill Kechnie led the prosecution case, William Hay appearing for the defence. During the trial, which lasted about thirteen hours, it was learned Bury had worked little over the last year or so, and constantly demanded money from his wife, when his requests were refused he would strike her. Little was said in Bury's defence throughout the trial, though his lawyer initially attempted to question the morals of Ellen Bury. Under the rules of evidence, Bury was not permitted to speak in his own defence. The jury returned a verdict of guilty, saying: "We strongly recommend him to mercy." Lord Young seemed to be staggered by their recommendation, "May I ask." He inquired, "On what grounds you recommend the prisoner to mercy." It was explained to the court that the jury viewed the medical evidence as conflicting. Lord Young refused to accept such a verdict and instructed the jury to retire once more. They soon returned, with a unanimous verdict of guilty, with no recommendation for mercy. Bury, throughout his trial, was said to have remained calm and slept soundly each night. The Dundee Advertiser 29 March 1889, described him as, "Brainless and heartless." On the morning of his execution, Bury had a breakfast of bread and butter, poached eggs and tea, and enjoyed a smoke. The magistrates then entered his cell, identified the convict, who thanked all present for their kindness. He said to the warder, "This is my last morning on earth; I freely forgive all who have given false evidence against me at my trial, as I hope God will forgive me." On his walk to the scaffold he was described as being, calm and collected, he was dressed in a pair of dark trousers with a vest and smart twill shooting coat, a white linen collar and a blue necktie, it was said "he looked as smart as if he was going to a wedding." He was hanged on 24 April 1889 at 8:00 am and was the last man to be hanged for murder in the City of Dundee. 5,000 people waited outside for the hoisting of the black flag, the body was buried within the precincts of the prison. Just before his execution, when the hangman, James Berry, tried to obtain a confession to the Whitechapel murders from him, Bury turned to the hangman and said: "I suppose you think you are clever to hang me," with the emphasis firmly placed on the word, "Me," before continuing, "I suppose you think you are clever because you are going to hang me, but because you are going to hang me you are not going to get anything out of me." The hangman James Berry, always remained convinced that Bury was Jack the Ripper. Suffolk journalist, Ernest A. Parr, in a letter to the Secretary of State for Scotland in 1908, stated that Berry had told him "explicitly that Bury was known to have been Jack the Ripper." According to Berry the detectives sent from London to investigate Bury's movements asked Berry for his opinion, he replied, "I think it is him right enough, and we agree with you," replied one of the detectives, "We know all about his movements in the past, and we are quite satisfied that you have hanged Jack the Ripper, there will be no more Whitechapel crimes."

In an article written in 1907 entitled, AFTER EXECUTING 197 CRIMINALS BERRY OPPOSES DEATH PENALTY, James Berry said:

He believed Jack the Ripper was John Henry Burey, the keeper of a cat's meat shop in the East End of London, people who knew him used to see him at work with his long knives'. Berry, in the article, went on to say, 'Behind this shop were rooms which he used to let to women on the streets, during his absence, one of these degraded women broke into his room and stole some of his savings, this made the man so mad that he swore an oath that if he could not find out who it was, he would murder every woman who had used his house, this threat he proceeded to carry out'. When in the cell and about to pinion him, I said, 'Well, Jack the Ripper, have you anything to say, if so, say it now, as you will have no chance later', 'No', was the reply, 'If anyone stole anything from me, I'd kill the lot to find the right one. I'm not going to give you any big lines, go on with your work, Berry, I'll not say anything'. Berry later recollected his first sighting of Bury, 'I confess that a strange feeling took possession of me, he was a peculiar looking man and undoubtedly he had the air of the uncanny about him, he was slightly over five feet in height with a haunted look in his eyes, there was a mysterious something about him which repelled me.

If the police told this information to Berry, there is no record of it. There is no evidence Bury was a suspect at the time of the Ripper murders. There is also no substantiated evidence Bury ever let rooms, had a cat's meat shop or was a butcher as some authors, and theorists have stated. They appear to be confusing him with fellow Ripper suspect James Hardiman. James Berry recollections should be treated with a fair degree of caution as he wrote the article 18 years after executing Bury.

At the time of the Ripper murders, William Henry Bury was 5ft 2½ inches tall, under 10 stone, with a stout build. He was described as good-looking, with sharp features, a dark complexion, a fair moustache a full beard and quite respectable in appearance. Another report described him as also having side whiskers.

One journalist gave the following description of Bury:

In his own clothes he was a fairly decent looking man but in prison garb... he strikes one as being minded. Bury, is of fresh complexion, his hair is dark brown, his moustache and whiskers being a shade lighter. He has a somewhat timid and excitable appearance. Viewed from the side he presents features somewhat of the Jewish or Semite type. He has dark but not heavy eyebrows and his eyes are keen and sharp. His nose is long and prominent, his cheeks thin, and his beard sparse and straggling... he appeared a diminutive and insignificant creature.

We know the couple went to Wolverhampton for a week, and stayed at a public house in Powlett-Street, possibly around the second week in August 1888. The exact date is still unknown. Martha Tabram was murdered 7 August 1888, Mary Ann (Polly) Nichols 31 August 1888.

On 3 February 2018, a mock trial of Bury, was held in the Dundee Sheriff Court, where the original trial was held. Bury's original conviction rested largely on medical evidence. The defence argued that the angle of the ligature mark supported Bury's claim that his wife took her own life by "self-strangulation" and the cuts to her body were made after her death. Evidence from his original trial will be presented based on modern forensic standards and the hearing will be overseen by a Supreme Court judge. In the retrial, Bury was acquitted of murdering his wife. Bones from his neck were displayed during the mock trial.

CALOR

The Bluefield Daily Telegraph 22 December 1903 reported the following story:

Jack the Ripper, who killed and mutilated prostitute, Sarah Martin, in a hotel in James Slip, in exactly the same manner as Old Shakespeare (Carrie Brown) twelve years ago, was "Calor." Detectives searched the transport ship the Kilpatrick, which was anchored in the bay ready to sail for Manila. The murderer, it was said, left many clues behind, including a letter which it is said may clear up the latest sensation.

A Finnish sailor and Jack the Ripper suspect named Emil Totterman, alias Carl Nielsen, was subsequently arrested and charged with the murder of Sarah Martin. There is, however, no evidence this murder was connected to the Whitechapel murders.

JAMES CARNAC

Alan Hicken, who runs the Montacute TV, Radio & Toy Museum in Somerset, acquired a lot from the estate of the late Sydney George Hulme Beaman, author, illustrator, puppeteer, and creator of Toytown and Larry the Lamb. Discovered amongst the photographs, books and artwork, once owned by Beaman, was an autobiography in which the author the one legged James Carnac, confesses he was Jack the Ripper. Carnac started writing the book in the 1920s, nearly 40 years after the Ripper murders, and bequeathed it to Beaman, with the instructions to have it published after his death. Beaman claims that after reading the book he was so horrified by its revolting content, that he removed certain passages from the book. Beaman expressed his personal opinion that Carnac, was Jack the Ripper. Beaman died prematurely in 1932 at the age of 43, from pneumonia. The book lay gathering dust for the next 80 years until discovered by Hicken. The book which is divided into three parts starts with Carnac's early childhood, born in Tottenham, circa 1859-1861, his father was a locally respected doctor, who took to drink. It is at school that Carnac's fascination with blood starts. As this following passage from the book shows:

Most people, I have found, harbour a strange dislike for blood, a dislike so strong that the sight and smell of it wells from a wound or a nose is sufficient to engender in them faintness and nausea. Even amongst my schoolfellows, I had observed this curious phenomenon. Such feelings puzzled me then and always have puzzled me. The colour of blood is very far from unpleasant; it is a fine, rich tint which is viewed without qualms in other objects. A person who shrinks from the sight of blood does not, for example, avoid looking at a bright red shawl. Nor can the smell be held responsible for the feeling that only in the presence of large quantities of blood is it perceptible at all. I can only assume that the dislike of blood is really due to some sub-conscious association of blood with the ideas of suffering and death. And on the matter of death, I shall expound my views later.

The author, explains to us his growing desire to cut a throat, how he failed his medical studies, and talks of a family tragedy, which shaped his formative years, it then recounts how each victim was selected, and how he committed the murders, before explaining the sudden cessation of the murders, was caused by a freak accident, Carnac was hit by a Hanson cab, which caused him to lose his right leg, the day after killing Mary Kelly. I have extensively searched the newspaper archives for details of such an accident, without success. Unfortunately, the book is littered with too many factual errors, to be taken seriously, as a historical document. As a work of detective fiction, it is highly recommended. Despite the best efforts of historians, James Willoughby Carnac has never been traced.

FRANK CASTELLANO

The Atlanta Constitution 22 March 1893, the Daily Northwestern 22 March and the Mountain Democrat 1 April 1893 reported that:

The police of New York is inclined to believe that they have in custody the elusive Jack the Ripper. A woman was ripped up the side on 19 March; the attack happened in New York, a big knife was left sticking in the wound. The knife was traced as belonging to Frank Castellano, an Italian barber, whose record the police has recently been examining. They have discovered that until recently he was a fireman on board one of the transatlantic steamers. There are several circumstances connected with the case that inclines the police to believe that Castellano is none other than Jack the Ripper, who has kept the fallen women of London in terror for the past two years. Some go as far as to say that Castellano will be found to be identical with the mysterious man who accompanied Carrie Brown (Old Shakespeare), to the East River Hotel on the night of her murder and for whose death "Frenchy the Greek" is now serving a term in the State prison.

Captain Doherty of the Fifth Precinct squad is much elated over the capture, and says that he will make every effort to secure a complete account of Castellano's travels and operations during the past few years.

FREDERICK RICHARD CHAPMAN

Dr Frederick Richard Chapman was identified in February 1972, by British civil servant and theorist Brian E Reilly, in an article, Jack the Ripper the Mystery Solved? In the City, the magazine of the city of London police force, as the only doctor whose death shortly after the murder of Mary Kelly, coincided with the cessation of the murders. Reilly used the pseudonym, Dr Merchant, when he referred to Chapman, to conceal his identity, believing Chapman was police Constable Robert Spicer's suspect. In 1931, ex-Constable Robert Spicer of Woodford Green, Essex, told the Daily Express, in an article under the heading, I caught Jack the Ripper:

I was on duty just after the double murder of Elizabeth Stride and Catherine Eddowes, on the night of 29th -30th September 1888, when I came across a well-dressed man with blood on his cuffs, carrying a brown bag, sitting on a brick dustbin in Heneage Court, off Brick Lane, with a prostitute called Rosy, who had in her hand 2s.

After evading the Constables questions, the man was arrested and taken to Commercial Street Police Station, where he told the station officer that he was a respected doctor, and gave an address in Brixton. Spicer further went on to say: "I was surprised the man was released without his bag even been opened, or explain what a respected doctor was doing at 3 o'clock in the morning with a prostitute." Spicer described the man as "about 5 ft. 8 inches tall, 12 stone, with a fair moustache, high forehead and rosy cheeks, wearing a high hat, a black suit and a gold watch and chain." Spicer claimed he had got into trouble with his superiors for this arrest and was ordered to leave well alone. He went on to say that this action so disappointed him that he left the police force the following year, adding: "The doctor was still accosting prostitutes years later in the vicinity of Liverpool Street station." On one occasion Spicer claims to have approached the man and said, "Hello Jack, still after them." Spicer's story, however, cannot be referring to Chapman, because by this time Chapman was already dead. Spicer's recollections, interesting though they are, should be treated with a degree of caution, for they were told to the press over 40 years after the last of the Whitechapel murders. It has also been noted that the real reason Spicer left the police force was that he had been caught drinking on duty in April 1889, and was dismissed.

Frederick Richard Chapman was born in Poona, Sulawesi Tengah, Indonesia, in 1851, the son of an Army NCO, Joseph Chapman, and his wife Elizabeth. His mother passed away in Sculcoates, Yorkshire in 1883 at the age of 61. He qualified as a doctor in Glasgow in 1874. Chapman was a medical officer in Hull for a smallpox hospital, during which time he wrote a number of medical pamphlets. He married Emily England 25 March 1876 in Sculcoates, Hull. They had two children, Lilian, and Ida. His address in the 1881 census is Clifton Villas Hessle Road, Hull. Moved to London in 1886, and lived at 4 Barrington Road, Brixton, where he died of septic tubercular abscesses on 12 December 1888 and was buried in a pauper's grave. He left effects to the value of £96.10s 9d in his will. His widow and youngest daughter later ran a lunatic asylum (Otto House) in Fulham. Apart from his death occurring shortly after the murder of Mary Kelly, there is nothing to link Chapman with Jack the Ripper.

WILLIAM LEONARD CHAPMAN

In January 1902, William Leonard Chapman, aged 50 years, formally in occupation as a commercial traveller, living at Hill Top Mount, Roundhay Road, Leeds, was charged with wandering abroad while of unsound mind. Inspector Ryall, told a curious story of the prisoner's conduct on Saturday night. About ten minutes to eight he engaged a hansom cab in Briggate, and asked to be driven to the Hotel Metropole. Arriving there, he requested to be taken back to Briggate, where he got into a second cab, but the driver refused to take him. He then engaged a four wheeler to take him into Trinity Street. The inspector deemed it his duty to remove the man to the Town Hall. Dr. Heald, police-surgeon, examined Chapman, and certified that he was a person of unsound mind. The family had him under surveillance for the past three months, it was said he went about in the night saying he was "Jack the Ripper." The magistrate ordered the man to be detained as a lunatic.

CHARLIE THE RIPPER

In the 12 March 1976 edition of the weekly publication Reveille, the question was asked, "Was the most notorious murderer in British criminal history a pasty-faced fish gutter that could not make love." Mrs. Carmen Rogers, a psychic medium, gave an account of a man she named, Charlie the Ripper, and believed he was a nondescript sort of man, with a thin face and pasty complexion, deceptively strong in the arms and hands, aged about 34, or 35, and who worked in the fish trade. He was unable to form normal sexual relations with women, hence took out his frustration by killing and mutilating them instead. He stopped killing, according to Mrs Rodgers out of a fear of getting caught.

FREDERICK NICHOLAS CHARRINGTON

Charrington was suggested as Jack the Ripper by M.J Trow in a short story in the (1999) book The Mammoth Book of Jack the Ripper. Trow built up a credible case against Charrington and suggested he was the right age, build, and knew the local area well. Also, being well known for his religious work, he could lure his victims into a false sense of security. Trow then went on to admit that there has been in fact no evidence against Charrington whatsoever, and did not believe he was Jack the Ripper, but had only used his name as an example to demonstrate how easy it is to build a case against any individual from that period, and claim them as a credible Jack the Ripper suspect.

Frederick Nicholas Charrington was born in Bow Road, Stepney, on 4 February 1850, and was the heir to the Charrington brewing fortune, until he turned his back on the family business as a result of what he had witnessed as a teenager, passing the Rising Sun, public-house Cambridge Heath Road, Bethnal Green. He had seen a man, worse the wear for drink; beat his wife to a pulp. Above the door was the name of the proprietor Charrington. He turned to religion and walked the streets at night lecturing against drink and vice in all its manifestations, and would interview prostitutes and their clients and keep little black books on brothel visitors. By 1888, despite being frequently beaten up for his efforts, Charrington, by his actions, was responsible for the closure of more than 200 brothels, though as the police Commissioner pointed out, this forced many vulnerable women to move on to the streets. Charrington founded The Tower Hamlets Mission at 31 Mile End Road, the centrepiece of which was the great assembly hall, capable of seating 5,000 people. Here the hungry would be fed for the price of signing the pledge. Charrington died in the London hospital in 1936, at the age of 86.

At the time of the Whitechapel murders, he was 38 years of age, tall with a slender build, dark brown hair and a drooping moustache.

ALMEDA CHATELLE

Jessie Keith, fourteen years of age, had been picking strawberries along the railroad track, close to her home, in Listowel, Perth, on 19 October 1894, when she disappeared. Hours passed and she did not return. Her worried parents after investigation learned she had not arrived at the grocery store. Search parties were organised, and tracking dogs brought in. The dogs led the local constabulary, to a pile of bush, close to a swamp. There lay Jessie Keith, her naked body covered over with moss and rotten wood. She had been raped, and dismembered. Cause of death was due to loss of blood. Her throat had been cut from ear to ear. There were also marks on the head, consistent with a blow from a heavy instrument. Jessie was the daughter of William Keith, a respectable farmer. Described as a beautiful, well developed, clever girl. A suspicious looking tramp was seen in the area. He was described as five feet nine inches in height, of dark, swarthy complexion, about 35 years of age, with a small moustache. He was wearing a black coat, and light coloured trousers. Almeda Chattelle, was arrested 44 miles from Listowel. He was found carrying a valise containing female undergarments, some of which he was alleged to have been wearing, and a bloodstained knife. In the (1904) book: Memoirs of a great detective, incidents in the life of John Wilson Murray.

Murray described his first recollections of Chattelle:

When I looked at him he reminded me of a gorilla. He was as hairy as Esau. As I studied him he seemed to look less like a gorilla and more like a donkey. He had huge ears and his face actually resembled the features of a jackass. He was very dark. He was not tall, but was broad and powerful, being under medium height, yet weighing one hundred and ninety pounds. He wore a woman's knitted jacket that had been stretched to bursting to cover his bulging muscles. On the back of his head was tilted a Glengarry cap. He walked with the peculiar swaying motion of a baboon when it rises on its hind legs and toddles across its cage. In fact, if the wild man of Borneo had been clipped close as to his hair, he would have been mistaken for this fellow's twin brother.

Chattelle said: "I was in a lunatic asylum in Massachusetts for a time. They sent me there from Boston. I thought there was no need to do it. After they had me there for some time they said I was all right and they let me go. I agreed with them, and I think I am all right now." Chattelle, after confessing in detail to the crime, said: "I am very sorry," he said softly. "I know it is too late to be sorry, but I am very sorry." One newspaper claims that Chattelle's picture was sent to the police in England because the manner in which Jessie Keith was disfigured had similarities to the Whitechapel murders perpetrated by Jack the Ripper. Chattelle claims he is not "Jack the Ripper." In Stratford gaol, the prisoner said that he did not know what possessed him, but that he was animated by an uncontrollable fiendish frenzy for the time. Chattelle, born in Quebec in 1847, was a sailor, sailing between Boston, and the ports of South America. He was executed 31 May 1895. The hanging attracted a large crowd.

RANDOLPH HENRY SPENCER CHURCHILL

Randolph Henry Spencer Churchill was born 13 February 1849 at Blenheim Palace and was educated at Eton, where he neither excelled in sport nor stood out academically. He was the father of British Prime Minister, Sir Winston Churchill. He married the American, Jennie Jerome, daughter of Leonard Jerome, in 1874.

Elected Conservative MP for Woodstock in 1874, his maiden speech in the House of Commons made no impression. He remained MP for Woodstock until 1885 then became MP for South Paddington from 1885-86. Made Secretary of state for India in 1885 in Salisbury's cabinet, a position he held until the following year when he was appointed Chancellor of the Exchequer and Leader of the House of Commons. When Churchill was appointed Chancellor of the Exchequer in 1886, Queen Victoria opposed the appointment, and described Churchill as, "So mad and odd." A disliked politician, who made many enemies, even among his own colleagues, there was often friction due to his rude and offensive manner. During the election, while campaigning in Woodstock, he complained that he had to shake too many unwashed hands and enter too many dirty cottages. A great orator, when due to speak in the House of Commons the cry would go out, "Randy's up," and the chamber would quickly fill. His speeches were described as often controversial, always brilliant. He tendered his resignation as Chancellor in 1886, without any expectation it would be accepted by Lord Salisbury, it was, and he spent the last eight years of his life in the political wilderness. He remained in the House of Commons, but his speeches had lost their effectiveness. He was dying of general paralysis, brought on by the disease syphilis. His last speech was in June 1894, during a debate on Uganda. He died on 24 January 1895. He was 45 years of age. His short political career was summed up best by Lord Roseby, Salisbury's successor as Prime Minister. Roseby said, "It consisted of a lot of noise and little in the way of achievement." There has been considerable speculation and many conflicting accounts about how Churchill became infected with syphilis. Some report it was during an encounter with a Blenheim housemaid, some say during a drunken episode as a student with an old hag. The source of this latter story was journalist Frank Harris in his autobiography, My Life and Loves, who was told the tale by Louis Jennings, a friend and political colleague of Churchill's. Jennings motive for telling the story, however, is dubious, and this episode may not, in fact, have actually referred to Churchill. Churchill's link with Jack the Ripper is tenuous. According to Author Melvyn Fairclough, Churchill, being the highest Freemason in the land and protecting the good name of the royal family and the position of the crown, gathered together a group, which consisted of Sir William Gull, John Netley, Frederico Albericci, and JK Stephen, in a plan to murder five prostitutes led by Mary Kelly, who had been using their knowledge of Prince Albert Victor's secret marriage to Annie Elizabeth Crook, for blackmailing purposes. This theory is without foundation, there is no evidence to support the claim that Churchill was ever a Freemason, and there is also no documentary evidence to prove such a marriage ever took place. The death certificate of Annie Crook clearly states she belonged to the Church of England and was not a Catholic as claimed. It has been speculated by theorists, that Churchill resembled George Hutchinson's extraordinarily detailed description of a man seen with Mary Kelly shortly before she was murdered. Hutchinson described the man as:

About, 5 ft 6 inches tall, 34-35 years of age, with a dark complexion and dark moustache turned up at the ends. Wearing a long Astrakhan coat, a white collar with black necktie, to which was affixed a horseshoe pin. He wore a pair of dark spats with light buttons over button boots and displayed from his waistcoat a massive gold chain. His watch chain had a big seal with a red stone hanging from it.

The Pall Mall Gazette, 28 June 1884, described Churchill as:

Of average height with a wide turned-up moustache, beautifully dressed, his gold chain has the solid appearance of real 18 carat.

If you believe Churchill was implicated in the murders, the following newspaper article may offer an explanation as to why the killer was inactive during the month of October. The Echo, Saturday, 20 October 1888:

Lord Randolph Churchill is in an unsatisfactory state of health. His medical adviser enjoins the utmost care, and his friends who have seen him lately are very disappointed with his appearance. Delicacy of the chest is the failing of this promising politician.

GEORGE CLARK

On 10 February, 1890, in Bishop Stortford, George Clark, aged 28 years, of no fixed abode, was charged with vagrancy. Inspector Penn said the prisoner begged on Sunday at two houses in Portland-road, and swore at children who were leaving Sunday school. The prisoner said the children shouted "That's Jack the Ripper," and this annoyed him. He was sent to prison for seven days with hard labour.

JOHN CLEARY

In the early hours of Sunday morning 8 September 1889, a man named John Arnold went to the London offices of the New York Herald. He said he had information on a new Jack the Ripper murder, which had occurred in Backchurch Lane. He said a mutilated body had been discovered by a constable. He gave his name as John Cleary, and his address as 21 Whitehorse Yard, Drury Lane. Reporters took the details of his story, hailed a hansom cab and hurried to the scene of the crime, to find nothing. Two patrolling police officers were questioned, by the reporters, but neither had heard of a murder. The matter was quickly forgotten, until two days later when a mutilated torso was discovered near Backchurch Lane, in Pincin Street. Cleary was now a prime suspect. A police search of the address he gave, proved fruitless as no one at that address had heard of a John Cleary. The New York Herald 11 September published a description of the man who had visited them:

He was between 25-28 years old. About 5 ft 4 inches tall, medium build, light complexioned, with a small fair moustache, and blue eyes. On his left cheek was an inflamed spot, which may in a previous life have been a boil. He wore a dark coat and waistcoat. His throat was covered by a dirty white handkerchief. He wore a round stiff black, felt hat, and walked with a shuffle, and a shake. in the usual fashion of the habitues of Whitechapel, whom he resembled in all aspects. He spoke with a local accent.

On 13 September a news vendor named John Arnold gave himself up to police. He said he was a resident of 2 Harvey's Buildings, Strand. He told the police he was approached near Fleet Street by "A man dressed as a soldier." This man told him "Hurry up with your papers, another horrible murder… in Backchurch Lane." Arnold said he gave the reporters a false name because he did not want his wife to know where he was staying. He described the soldier as: "35-36 years old. 5 ft. 6 or 7 inches tall, fair complexion, fair moustache, good-looking, wearing a black uniform and a cheese cutter cap. He was carrying a brown paper parcel about 6 or 8 inches long." Arnold was known to the police, as he had a reputation for drinking and gambling. He had deserted his wife, for which he had received a prison term. Chief inspector Swanson remarked in his report that:

I have never heard of him being dishonest. That he could be in any way connected with others or by himself in a murder is to me improbable.

100

DAVID COHEN

Author Martin Fido, while searching the London asylum records looking for a Polish Jew with the surname Kosminski, failed to find anyone of that name. He did find David Cohen, who seemed to match the information provided by Anderson, Macnaghten and Swanson. Aaron Davis Cohen was brought before Thames magistrates on 7 December 1888 by Police Constable J. Patrick 91 H, as a lunatic wandering at large. He was found rambling in the street, speaking little but Yiddish. The magistrate sent him to the Whitechapel Workhouse Infirmary, where he was given the name of David Cohen, which it is claimed was used as a John Doe for East End Jews without known identity, address or next of kin, or whose name was difficult to spell. He was born in 1865, his age in 1888 was given as 23, his description as brown hair, brown eyes and a beard, and his address as 86 Leman Street. At the workhouse he was reported as "violent, noisy and difficult to manage," he also attacked the other inmates. On 21 December 1888, he was transferred to Colney Hatch Lunatic Asylum, where his occupation was given as a tailor. At Colney Hatch, his violent behaviour continued and he had to be separated from the other patients, he refused and spat out food and had to be force-fed fed by a tube, and was described as "dirty, restless, aggressive spiteful mischievous and destructive." On 28 December he became physically ill, and over the next nine months, his condition steadily deteriorated. He died on 20 October 1889 from exhaustion of mania and pulmonary phthisis. (Consumption) Chief Inspector Donald Swanson's pencil notes written in his copy of Sir Robert Anderson's 1910 book The Lighter Side of My Official Life reveals that he suspected an insane Jew of the murders. He goes on to name the man as Kosminski, and says: "In a very short time the suspect with his hands tied behind his back, was sent to Stepney Workhouse and then to Colney Hatch

101

and died shortly afterwards." At no point is there any record of Kosminski needing to be restrained, it was Cohen who was violent and needed restraints. It has been suggested that as Kosminski did not die until 1919, Swanson's suspect, in reality, may have been Cohen, who fit's the criteria of having died soon after being sent to Colney Hatch. The drawback to this theory, however, and of Cohen being the Ripper, is that Swanson unequivocally names Anderson's suspect as Kosminski, as does Sir Melville Macnaghten in his memoranda. Also, it is noted that the CID were still on Ripper alert after Cohen's death. Swanson states: "After the suspect had been identified at the seaside home." As the first of the convalescent police seaside home's was not opened until March 1890, at 51 Clarendon Villas, West Brighton, this makes the suspect identified unlikely to have been Cohen, because by this time Cohen was already dead. Nevertheless, David Cohen is the only insane Polish Jew Committed to an asylum at the right time for the murders to cease, and the only registered lunatic-pauper admitted to Colney Hatch between 1888-1890, who fit's the extremely violent suspect described by Anderson, Macnaghten and Swanson. He, also, in contrast to Aaron Kosminski, died shortly after the canonical Ripper murders ceased. FBI profiler John Douglas, Stated: "If David Cohen wasn't Jack the Ripper, then it was surely someone very similar."

DR. COHN

In 1969 ex-Inspector Lewis Henry Keaton gave a tape-recorded interview, in which he proposed the theory that the Ripper was a doctor who was collecting specimens of infected wombs for research purposes. Unfortunately, just as he was about to name his suspect as either Dr Cohn or Koch or someone else whose name he could not quite recall, who used strychnine on his victims, the interviewer drowned out Keaton's words with interruptions and background noise. Keaton did not, in fact, join the police force until 1891, three years after the cessation of the Ripper murders, so, therefore, had no first-hand knowledge of the Ripper case. Keaton appeared to have confused his Ripper suspect with Dr Thomas Neil Cream, who used strychnine on his victims. Keaton, at the time of his interview, was almost 100 years old. Keaton was born in 1870, was 18 years of age at the time of the Ripper murders. He joined the Met in August 1891 (warrant Number 77010) and retired with the rank of Inspector in 1917. He died in 1970

JOSEPH COMPTON

On 3 November 1890, two young men named Joseph Compton and Frederick Hornsley, were charged with violently assaulting Alfred Bain, an accountant, of Shrubland Street. The defendants having left a public-house, decided to knock on the door of Mr Bain's house. When Bain came into the street to fetch a policeman Compton and another man, who has since absconded, attacked him. Bain was struck in the mouth, and knocked down. Compton shouted I am "Jack the Ripper," and offered to fight anybody in the street. The defendants were fined 21s each, or in default go to prison for a month with hard labour.

CLAUDE REIGNEIR CONDER

There is no evidence, Colonel Claude Reigneir Conder was ever suspected at the time of the murders of being Jack the Ripper, but according to research by crime writer Tom Slemen and criminologist Keith Andrews, they are convinced Conder, a 39-year old British intelligence officer, archaeologist, writer, map-maker and trained killer was Jack the Ripper, and have written a book: Jack The Ripper British Intelligence Agent (2010), naming him as such. They present the following points.

That Sir Charles Warren, a close friend of Conder, knew he was the Ripper, but kept quiet and took the secret with him to the grave.

That artefact's and rings excavated by Conder and Warren from King Solomon's temple in Jerusalem were stolen from his home by Annie Chapman when working as a cleaner for Conder.

That all of the Ripper victims knew each other and had all benefited from the stolen goods.

That he left cryptic messages carved on his victims' bodies.

That he became a devil worshipper, who collected human organs for satanic rituals.

Samples of Conder's handwriting Slemen claims matches the graffiti at Goulston Street.

There is no evidence to support the claim that Warren, suspected Conder of being Jack the Ripper, there is also no evidence that all or any of the victims knew each other. Presumably, the cryptic message Slemen is referring to are the marks on Catherine Eddowes face. If Conder was indeed leaving a cryptic message on a victim's body, why did he not leave it on all of them?

Conder was born in 1848 and was a descendant of the French-born Louis Francois Roubiliac, the most celebrated sculptor in 18th century Britain. He moved to Hackney, London, in the 1860's and served in the Royal Engineers alongside, pre-knighted, Charles Warren. They both became famous worldwide for excavating hundreds of sites, and Conder wrote an international best-selling book about his archaeological finds. He retired to

Cheltenham, where he died at the age of 62, from a stroke in 1910. His wife Myra died in 1934 and is buried in the same grave as her husband.

JAMES CONNELL

James Connell went for a walk in Hyde Park with Martha Spencer and alarmed her when he began to talk about Jack the Ripper and lunatic asylums. Connell said that when the Ripper was caught, he would turn out to be a lunatic. Spencer, of 30 Sherborne Street, Blandford Square, and described as married, spoke to PC Fountain 271A about her suspicions and Connell, was brought to Hyde Park Police Station at 9:40 pm 22 November 1888 and questioned. He was described as 36 years old, 5 ft. 9 inches tall, with a fresh complexion and a long dark brown moustache; he was wearing a soft felt hat, a brown check suit, an ulster with cape, red socks and Oxford shoes. Connell was able to prove the correctness of his address and respectability and was allowed to leave. Born 27 March 1852, in the village of Killskyre in Co Meath. Connell, an Irish political activist is best known for writing the socialist anthem "The Red Flag."

The people's flag is deepest red,

It shrouded oft our martyred dead,

And ere their limbs grew stiff and cold,

Their hearts' blood dyed its every fold.

Chorus:

Then raise the scarlet standard high.

Within its shade, we live and die,

Though cowards flinch and traitors sneer,

We'll keep the red flag flying here.

In an article which he wrote at the request of the editor of The Call in May 1920, Connell explained what inspired him to write The Red Flag. The strike of the London Dockers in 1889 was his first inspiration. Connell said that he wrote the first two verses and the chorus during a 15-minute train journey between Charing Cross and New Cross, and finished the rest that night. Connell was very emphatic that it should be sung to the air of "The White Cockade," which was in its original form an Irish military march but which through time deteriorated into little more than an Irish jig. That is probably why someone, somewhere changed the tune to Tannenbaum or Maryland as it is known in Britain and America. Connell once described himself as having been a "sheep farmer, dock labourer, navvy, railway man, draper, journalist, and a lawyer of sorts." He lived at 408 New Cross Road. He married Katharine Sarah (née Angier) in July 1882. In the 1891 census, he is in occupation as a draper. On 8 February 1929, at the age of 76, he suffered a stroke and was found unconscious on the stairway leading to his office in Chancery Lane. He died in hospital a few days later without regaining consciousness.

GEORGE COOPER

Lloyd's Weekly London Newspaper, 25 May 1890 reported the following story:

George Cooper, 21, was charged with assaulting Samuel Shenzon, a Russian Jew, of 9, Gun-street, Spitalfields. The prosecutor, whose evidence had to be interpreted, stated that at four o'clock on Friday afternoon he went to Helen-street, Whitechapel. The prisoner crossed the road, struck him twice, and knocked him down. The prisoner also 'tramped' on his legs, caught him by the throat, and blacked his eye. Cooper ran away, but was followed, caught, and given into custody. Witness's legs were very sore and were dressed at the London Hospital. He did not provoke the prisoner in any way. The prisoner said he remonstrated with the prosecutor for knocking a child down when he pushed against him. He (prisoner) pushed prosecutor, who then bit his thumb. He (prisoner) was then attacked by a number of Jewish men and women, who kicked and beat him, and shouted out that he was 'Jack the Ripper.' He was glad when the constable appeared. Prosecutor denied that statement. Constable 172H said when he was called to arrest prisoner, the prosecutor was bleeding from the mouth, and had a black eye. Prisoner did not complain at the station of his thumb being bitten. Mr Mead, having heard a witness for the defence, said. 'He believed the prosecutor bit prisoner's thumb, and he did all he could to make him let go his thumb. He had assaulted prosecutor, which he had no right to do, and he would be fined 5s. or five days.

BOSTON CORBETT

Mentioned as a Ripper suspect in the (2012) book: Jack the Ripper: American Hero: Was Lincoln's Avenger the Whitechapel Murderer? By Jacob Corbett (no relation).

Thomas Corbett was born 29 January 1832 in London. His family immigrated to Troy, New York in 1839. As a young man Corbett worked as a hatter, an occupation he would hold intermittently. The mental issues Corbett later displayed, it is theorised may be attributed to the regular exposure to Mercury nitrate, used in the treatment of fur to produce felt used on hats. Excessive exposure leads to hallucinations and psychosis. (Hence the expression as mad as a hatter). The death of his wife and child during childbirth left him despondent, and he turned to drink and became homeless. A street preacher pointed out the error of his ways, and he stopped drinking and joined the Methodist Episcopal Church, and became deeply religious. After being baptized, he changed his name to Boston, after the city in which he was reborn. While walking home from a church meeting it is claimed Corbett was propositioned by two prostitutes, deeply disturbed by the encounter, he went home and began reading chapters 18 and 19 in the gospel of Matthew ("And if thy right eye offend thee, pluck it out and cast it from thee and there be eunuchs, which have made themselves eunuchs for the kingdom of heaven's sake"). In order to avoid sexual temptation and remain holy, he opened his scrotum and removed his testicles, with a pair of scissors. He then ate a meal and went to a prayer meeting before seeking medical treatment. He was treated at Massachusetts General Hospital. In 1861 he enlisted in the Union army, but due to continued disruptive behaviour and refusal to take orders, Corbett faced a court-martial and was sentenced to be shot. His sentence was eventually reduced and he was discharged in August 1863. He later re-enlisted, this time in Company L, Sixteenth New York Cavalry, where he was promoted to corporal and later rose to the rank of sergeant. In 1865, Corbett was the first man to volunteer for service in the pursuit of President Lincoln's assassin, John Wilkes Booth. When the Union soldiers found Booth holed up in a barn, they flushed him out by setting it on fire. Boston Corbett shot the fleeing Booth in the neck. The shot paralysed Booth, and he died within two hours. As Corbett explained it: "I aimed at his body. I did not want to kill him....I think he stooped to pick up something just as I fired. That may probably account for his receiving the ball in the head. Corbett became widely known as "Lincoln's Avenger." Corbett was questioned about the shooting, but it was concluded Corbett had acted reasonably. With the war over, Corbett collected his share of the reward money for Booth's capture, and he went back to work as a hat maker and a preacher. His behaviour, though continued to be erratic, launching into prayer and waving his pistol when agitated. In January 1887, he was offered a job as an assistant doorkeeper at the Kansas State Legislature in Topeka. The job was short-lived, however – the following month, Corbett, brandishing a revolver, chased members of the House of Representatives out of the building. Corbett was arrested, and a judge sent him away to the Topeka Asylum for the insane. In May 1888, Corbett escaped from the asylum and claimed he was headed to Mexico, He was never seen or heard from again. One persistent rumour, about the fate of Corbett had him perishing in the Great Hinckley Fire of September 1, 1894. Although there is no proof, the name "Thomas Corbett" appears on the list of dead and missing. He was never seen or heard from again.

Was Thomas "Boston" Corbett, "Jack the Ripper. "?

Jacob Corbett certainly seems to think so, he says: "Of all the ripper suspects we've seen in the past 100+ years, none of them come as close as Boston Corbett does in fitting all the facts.

Even though Corbett's whereabouts, after his asylum escape in 1888, are unknown, the author offers us no evidence Corbett, was actually in London, at that time. He also offers us no evidence for his claim that Corbett knew Catherine Eddowes.

MARIA CORONER

Maria Coroner, 21 years of age, was charged on the 21 October 1888, with causing a breach of the peace by sending two hoax "Jack the Ripper" letters. One addressed to the local Chief Constable, the other to the editor of the Bradford Daily Telegraph. Declaring the murderer's intention of coming to Bradford "to do a little business." Her actions terrified the people of Bradford, after her letters were published in the newspapers. All Maria Coroner could say in mitigation was that the letters were intended as a joke. She was bound over to keep the peace for six months. She resided in Bradford, though, was born in Canada. Described as attractive, unmarried, and respectable. She was in occupation as a dress and mantle maker. When her possessions were searched a batch of newspapers containing reports of the Whitechapel murders, several written references to Jackson, the Manchester murderer, and a card of hangman William Bury, carefully wrapped in silk paper were found. It is speculated she later had a romantic friendship with Bury.

NATHANIEL COUSINS

On 30 September 1889, Nathaniel Cousins, a labourer, of Ide, near Exeter in Devon; was charged with unlawfully assaulting PC Coles. About 2:30, on the 13 September, the constable saw Cousins, coming towards him from the Bridge Inn. He used bad language and threatened him. He then took out a knife and said he was "Jack the Ripper," and would like to use it about the constable. He expressed a wish to meet the witness in the dark. Cousins denied the charge. However witnesses came forward to corroborate the constable's version of events. He was fined 7s 6d and costs £1 8s 6d, or a months imprisonment with hard labour.

Cousins, was next charged with poaching. PC Cole, said he saw the prisoner earlier that day, coming out a path field with two other men. He found a ferret on one of the men, and saw defendant had some nets in his pocket. He was fined 6d and 10s costs. All the money was paid.

DOUGLAS COW

At 12:40 pm 31 October 1888, Mrs Fanny Drake, of 15 Clerkenwell Green, London, went to Rochester Row Police

Station and made a complaint against a man she believed answered the description of the Whitechapel murderer. The man had caused her to become alarmed and frightened by grinning at her as they both walked over Westminster Bridge. Drake said, "The man gave such a grin, as I should always remember." At the police station, Fanny told the police she was convinced she had found the Whitechapel murderer. The man, Douglas Cow, when interviewed produced a number of letters and business cards proving he was a respectable businessman, who was in the employ of India Rubber Merchants, Cow And Company, 70 Cheapside, and 8 Kempshoot Road, Streatham Common. Drake apologised to Mr Cow for having caused him any inconvenience, and he was released without charge. He was 38 years of age at the time of the Ripper murders, 5 ft. 7 inches tall, with fair hair, fair complexion and a slight moustache, and was said to be very respectable in appearance.

Cow was born in 1850 in Deptford Kent. The son of Peter Brusey Cow an India Rubber Manufacturer, and his wife Sarah (née Hatfull). Douglas Cow in the 1881 census, is 31 years of age, married to Florence Amy (née Cox), his address is Norbury The Hermitage, Croydon. In the 1891 census he is aged 41, in occupation as an India Rubber Manufacturer, his address is Ryecroft House, Ryecroft Road Upper Norwood, Streatham Common. In the 1911 census, he is aged 61, retired India Rubber Manufacturer, living at Ryecroft House, Ryecroft Road Upper Norwood, Streatham Common. He died on the 25 March 1933 at the age of 83. He left in his will effects to the value of £159501 9s 11d.

FRANCIS SPURZHEIM CRAIG

Francis Spurzheim Craig, was named as Jack the Ripper, in the (2015) book: The Real Mary Kelly: Jack the Ripper's Fifth Victim

111

and the Identity of the Man that Killed Her by Wynne Weston-Davies.

Born in Acton, London in 1837. His father, ET Craig, was a journalist. Craig was a Victorian newspaper reporter and would enjoy success in his career, working in the United States of America between 1864 and 1866. In the 1871 Census he listed himself as a person of "No occupation". By 1875 he had been appointed editor of the Bucks Advertiser and Aylesbury News. Here, Craig's journalism career suffered an almost terminal blow when he was caught plagiarising reports from The Daily Telegraph, and was brutally exposed by a rival publication. On 24 December 1884, Craig married Elizabeth Weston-Davies in Hammersmith. According to Dr Wynne Weston-Davies, Craig discovered that his wife was engaging in prostitution and filed for divorce in 1886. On the 19 May, 1885 she was seen entering a private hotel near their marital home in Argyll Square, King's Cross, with a "young man at 10 o'clock at night". It was a crushing blow for Craig, who had been unaware of his wife's involvement in prostitution, the book says:

She left and went into hiding in the East End, under the pseudonym Mary Jane Kelly.

Craig followed her to Whitechapel, taking lodgings at 306 Mile End Road, in an attempt to locate her. As time passed his love for her turned to hatred. It was then that he plotted to murder her, disguising his involvement by killing a series of prostitutes beforehand, the book suggests. A few months after the murder of Elizabeth/Mary Jane, Craig left the East End and returned to west London as editor of the Indicator and West London News, a job he held until 1896. In 1903, while living in lodgings at Carthew Road, Hammersmith, Craig cut his throat with a razor, leaving his landlady a note which read: "I have suffered a deal of pain and

112

agony." He did not die until four days later, on Sunday, 8 March, 1903, at the inquest the coroner recorded a verdict of "Suicide whilst of unsound mind and when irresponsible for his actions." Craig was buried in the same grave as his parents in Margravine Road cemetery, Hammersmith.

Dr Weston-Davies plans to exhume Elizabeth/Mary Jane's body to carry out DNA analysis, which he believes will show the true identity of the Ripper's final victim and, therefore, prove Craig's motive for the murders.

THOMAS NEILL CREAM

Suggested as a Ripper suspect by John Cashman in the (1973) book: The Gentleman from Chicago. And more recently by Shirley Goulden in the (2011) book: I am Jack Confessions of the Whitechapel Murderer.

Thomas Neill Cream was born 27 May 1850 in Glasgow, Scotland. The oldest of eight brothers and sisters of William Cream and Mary (née) Elder. The family emigrated to Canada in 1854 when young Thomas was four years old. They made their home in Wolfe's Cove, Quebec. His father found employment and quickly became the manager of one of the provinces top lumber and shipbuilding firms, Gilmour & Company. He would later open his own successful lumber mill. In November 1872 Thomas registered at McGill College in Montreal, as a medical student, and graduated with honours on 3 March 1876. He wrote his Doctoral thesis on Chloroform. The title of the address given to the graduating class in medicine was, "The Evils of Malpractice in the Medical Profession." It was during this period he met and seduced a young woman named Flora Eliza Brooks, the daughter of a wealthy hotel owner. Lyman Henry Brooks. When Flora became ill her father had her examined by a physician who told him that his daughter had recently undergone an abortion. Cream was forced to marry Flora at gunpoint on 11 September 1876. Cream was allowed to leave the next day to continue his medical studies in England. Flora found a note from Cream on her pillow when she awoke the next morning, "A promise to keep in touch." He later wrote to Flora and enclosed with the letter some pills, which he advised her to take. Flora told Dr. Phelan, she had taken some medicine her husband had sent her. Flora contracted bronchitis and died of consumption (tuberculosis) August 1877. Her death would later be viewed with suspicion. After the death of his wife, Cream claimed a thousand dollars from his father-in-law by rights of his marriage contract, he eventually settled for two hundred. He boarded a ship bound for England, where he enrolled as a graduate student at St. Thomas's Hospital in London. St. Thomas's was located in the Waterloo-Lambeth area of the city, it was, here it is rumoured Cream contracted syphilis after consorting with the local prostitutes. He applied to the Royal College of Physicians and Surgeons in Edinburgh, where he earned a license in midwifery. He was next in Ontario, Canada, 1878, where he set up practice and earned an unsavoury reputation as an illegal abortionist. He was arrested after the body of a young hotel chambermaid Kate Gardener was discovered in a woodshed behind the store reeking of chloroform. Cream had performed an abortion on her which claimed her life. Cream in his defence claimed she had visited him to seek an abortion, which he had refused, she purchased the chloroform to commit suicide. A doctor testified that it would be impossible for a person attempting suicide to hold a chloroform-soaked sponge over her own nose long enough to cause death. The victim had scratches on her face as if she had been forced to take the chloroform against her will. Despite the overwhelming evidence against him, the coroner's jury ruled the death murder by persons unknown.

114

His reputation ruined, he moved on to Chicago, where he opened a practice on 434 West Madison. Close to the notorious red light of the city. In early 1880, a charge of murder was again brought against him. A young prostitute, Mary Ann Faulkner, died on his operating table. The police suspected Cream had poisoned her with strychnine, in the guise of a painkiller. Once more he escaped justice due to lack of evidence. The blame being deflected onto his sometimes assistant African-American midwife Hattie Mack. In court his defence team, claimed Faulkner's death was obviously caused by Mack "since it was a bungling piece of work and could not have been done by an experienced physician". Once again, he had evaded justice. Cream began to market his own Epilepsy and anti-pregnancy pills. In 1881 another woman, Miss Stack, died after taking his anti-pregnancy pills laced with strychnine. Once more Cream avoided arrest due to lack of evidence. Cream then began an affair with an attractive young woman, 33-year old Mrs Julia Stott, from Belvidere, Illinois, and murdered her husband, Daniel Stott. A 61-year old station agent with the North-Eastern Railway, when he became suspicious of the affair. Stott had sought treatment from Cream for his Epilepsy. Cream laced his pills with strychnine. Mr Stott died 14 June 1881. Fearing he would be apprehended, he wrote to the coroner and accused the chemist of adding strychnine to his formula. The sceptical coroner gave a sample of the prescription to a dog. Within fifteen minutes the dog was dead. The body of Mr Stott was exhumed and a warrant issued for Cream's arrest. He fled to Belle Riviere, Ontario, Canada, where he was captured 27 July 1881. Cream finally faced justice and was sentenced to life imprisonment. With one day of each year to be spent in solitary confinement. He was regarded as a model prisoner, and the only complaint against him was from the other prisoners, who complained of being awoken in the middle of the night by the sound of low hissing laughter coming from his cell. He could be overheard in his cell speaking to phantom women, promising them a slow and agonising death should he ever be released, "unfortunately," he was. Thomas with the help of his brother Daniel bribed prison officials, he served just ten years of his life sentence and was released from the Illinois State Penitentiary at Joliet on the 21 July 1891. His first port of call was to collect his inheritance from his father's estate, the remainder of $16.000. With revenge on his mind, Cream tried unsuccessfully to track down Julia Stott, even employing the Pinkerton Detective Agency in an effort to trace her. After a short stay with his brother, he left for England on 1 October 1891, where he settled at Lambeth. Over the next few months, he killed four prostitutes, 19-year old Ellen "Nellie" Donworth, 27-year old Matilda Clover, 18-year old Emma Shrivell and 21-year old Alice Marsh, with strychnine pills. Donworth, the daughter of a labourer, who lived at 8 Duke Street, off Commercial Road, was noticed by her friend Constance Linfield, emerging from a darkened court, in the company of a stranger with a peculiar look in his eye. A few moments later she was observed supporting herself with some difficulty against a wall. She then fell face-down into the street. At first it was assumed she was simply drunk. With assistance she was taken home, where she began to experience agonizing convulsions. The police were called when the doctor recognised the convulsions as systematic of strychnine poisoning. Before she died, she described the man who gave her the pills as, "A tall gentleman with cross eyes, a silk hat and bushy whiskers, he gave me a drink twice out of a bottle with white stuff in it." A week later, Matilda Clover, described as pockmarked, with protruding teeth, suffered the same agonizing death as Ellen Donworth. She was seen in the company of a man with a heavy moustache, wearing a tall silk hat who called himself "Fred." In the early hours

116

of the morning, neighbours hearing Matilda screaming rushed to her aid, between spasms she said "That man Fred has poisoned me... He gave me some pills." The doctor attributed her convulsions, and vomiting to alcoholic poisoning. He gave her some medicine which did little to alleviate her suffering. Her face turned black, and she died that morning. The cause of death was given as, primarily delirium tremens. No autopsy was carried out. The next day Lou Harvey (Louisa Harris), met a gentleman who said he was a doctor at St. Thomas's Hospital, the man said he wished to see her again, and would bring her some pills to improve her complexion. They met the next night as arranged, he led her to the darkened Embankment, where he produced two pills from his waistcoat pocket and gave them to her. Reluctant to swallow the capsules, he however was very insistent she takes them, once satisfied she had taken them, he suddenly announced he had to return to St Thomas Hospital, and could not continue with the rest of their plans for that evening. Harvey, who later testified in court against him, had a lucky escape, after deciding not to take the pills she instead tossed them into the River Thames. She was, able to furnish the police with a good description of the man who had given her the pills, and distinctly remembered his glasses and cross eyes. At 118 Stamford Street, (described as one of the ugliest and most sordid streets in London), lived two young women Alice Marsh, and Emma Shrivell. On 11 April 1892, they were entertaining a gentleman known as Fred, who claimed to be a doctor. Before he left, he gave each of them three long pills. In the early hours of the morning the landlady hearing screams rushed to their room. Both women twitched uncontrollably, Alice died on the way to the hospital, Emma six hours later. Cause of death was given in both cases as strychnine poisoning. Despite nothing to link Cream, to the crimes he, once again, could not resist incriminating himself

117

by writing to the authorities offering to name the Lambeth poisoner, for the reward money. He attempted to implicate two innocent doctors of the murder of Matilda Clover. Since Clover had supposedly died of natural causes, the case was reopened and Cream was arrested on 3 June 1892 and found guilty. While awaiting execution, Cream told his jailers that he was a great man and had killed far more than he was found guilty of. He was hanged at Newgate prison on the 15 November 1892. On the scaffold, he was, according to the hangman James Billington alleged to have said, "I am Jack the"… just as the lever was pulled and cut short his remark. This claim is unsubstantiated, the Police officials who attended the execution made no mention of it. Billington declared- "That he never hanged anybody with greater satisfaction than he did Dr Neill Cream." Billington believed to his dying day Cream to have been Jack the Ripper. Cream's claim to be Jack the Ripper, however, would appear highly unlikely as he was in Joliet Prison at the time of the Whitechapel murders. According to the Canadian author and theorist Donald Bell, Cream, having been left a legacy of $16,000 from his father, bribed his way out of prison to commit the murders, then returned to Joliet Prison before his official release. The records at Joliet however, show that Cream prisoner no. 4374, was imprisoned 1 November 1881 and was not released until 31 July 1891. Another theory by Sir Edward Marshall Hall, who defended Cream, suggests Cream may have had a double in the underworld and that both men used each other's terms of imprisonment as alibis for each other. None of these theories have any evidence to support them.

CHARLES CROSS

Charles Cross (His first name was erroneously given as "George" in some newspaper reports). Was born Charles Allen Lechmere 5

October 1849, in St Anne's, Soho, the son of John Allen Lechmere and his wife Maria Louisa (née Roulson). In 1858, Charles' mother remarried, to Thomas Cross, a policeman and Charles took his surname. Married Elizabeth Bostock the 21-year old daughter of Thomas Bay Bostock a lighterman. 3 July 1870 at Christ Church, Watney Street, St Georges's Parish East. Charles worked as a cart driver for Pickford's in Broad Street and was in their employ for 20 years. In the 1881 census, he is living at 20 James Street. In 1888 he was living at 22 Dovedon Street, Cambridge Heath Road, Bethnal Green. In the 1911 census, he is living at 24 Carlton-road. Cross claimed he left home for work at 3:30 am on the morning of 31 August 1888; at about 3:45 a.m. he was passing along Buck's Row when he saw what he originally believed to be a tarpaulin lying on the ground in front of the gates to a stable yard. On closer inspection, he found that it was the body of a woman and at that moment he called to Robert Paul a Carman walking down the street on his way to work at Covent Garden. As Paul approached the Board School building he saw a man (Cross) standing in the road ahead of him. His first reaction was one of wariness, after all, as he later stated: - "...Few people like to come up and down here without being on their guard, for there are such terrible gangs about. There have been many knocked down and robbed at that spot..." He, therefore, attempted to give the man a wide berth. But the man came towards him and spoke to him. "Come and look at this woman," he said. Paul, who was aware of the time as he was late for work did not reach the body of Polly Nichols until 3:45. Cross felt one of the deceased hands and finding it cold, said: "I think she is dead." Paul asked Cross to help move the woman, but Cross refused. Paul felt the woman's hand and face and found them to be cold. Not wanting to be late for work, the two men walked on and met PC Jonas Mizen 55H at the junction of Hanbury Street

119

and Baker's Row, and informed him of their find. Lechmere, gave the name "Charles Cross" to the constable. Cross said: "That the woman was either dead or drunk, though, at the time, he did not think the woman had been murdered."

Daily News report:

Charles A. Cross, carman, said he had been in the employment of Messrs. Pickford and Co. for some years.

On Friday morning he left home about half past three to go to work, and passing through Buck's row, he saw on the opposite side something lying against a gateway. In the dark he could not tell at first what it was. It looked like a tarpaulin sheet, but walking to the middle of the road, he saw it was the figure of a woman.

At the same time he heard a man about forty yards away coming up Buck's row in the direction witness had himself come. He stepped back and waited for the newcomer, who started on one side, as if he feared that the witness meant to knock him down. The witness said, "Come and look over here. There's a woman."

They both went across to the body, and the witness took hold of the hands while the other man stopped over her head to look at her. The hands were cold and limp, and the witness said, "I believe she's dead." Then he touched her face, which felt warm. The other man placed his hand on her heart, saying, "I think she's breathing, but it's very little if she is." He suggested that they should "shift her," meaning in the witness's opinion that they should seat her upright. The witness replied, "I am not going to touch her." The woman's legs were uncovered. Her bonnet was off, but close to her head.

The witness did not notice that her throat was cut, as the night was very dark.

He and the other man left the deceased, and in Baker's row, they saw Police Constable Mizen whom they told that a woman was lying in Buck's row. The witness added, "She looks to me either dead or drunk," and the other man remarked, "I think she's dead." The policeman answered, "All right."

The other man left witness soon afterwards. He appeared to be a carman, but the witness had never seen him before.

The Coroner: Did you see Police constable Neil in Buck's row?

The Witness: "No, sir. I saw no one after leaving home, except the man that overtook me, the constable in Baker's row, and the deceased. There was nobody in Buck's row when we left."

The Coroner: "Did the other man tell you who he was?"

The Witness: "No, sir. He merely said that he would have fetched a policeman but he was behind time. I was behind time myself."

Charles Cross, was not a contemporary suspect, attention has focused on him in more recent times by theorists Derek Osborne, Michael Conner and more recently in a documentary titled Jack the Ripper: The New Evidence, Swedish journalist Christer Holmgren. They proposed that Lechmere was the Ripper, and believe Cross was standing beside Nichols body when Robert Paul arrived because he had just murdered her. Cross, who claimed he left home at 3.30 lived at 22 Dovedon Street, a six minute walk to Buck's Row. He would have met Polly at about 3:36, leaving him an uninterrupted 9 minutes to murder her before the arrival of Robert Paul. Theorists have speculated his early route to work coincided with the other Ripper killing locations. It is speculated that the Pickford's branch he worked at dealt with the delivery of meat and that, therefore, it would have allowed his blood-splattered appearance to escape suspicion. He gave a false name to PC Mizen, and also at the inquest. He also stated he was not left alone with the body. He died 23 December 1920 in Poplar, London and was survived by his wife who passed away on 12 September 1940 in Stratford, London.

GEORGE CULLEN

George Cullen, alias Squibby, was a 25-year old muscular tattooed street gambler, he was charged with assaulting a young child Betsy Goldstein after a stone he threw at a policeman PC Bates 166H missed its intended target and hit the young girl. Squibby subsequently went into hiding, though, was spotted on the day of the Hanbury Street murder by Detective Walter Dew and Detective Thomas Stacey, a chase ensued, with Squibby diving between the legs of a horse and running as fast as his short legs would carry him along Commercial Street, in the direction of Aldgate. The sight of a man running from the police at great speed on the day of a Ripper murder soon attracted a crowd of hundreds, who followed hot on the trial of the man the police were pursuing, the cry quickly went up, "Jack the Ripper! Jack the Ripper! Lynch him!" Squibby, never one to hand himself over to the police quietly and without violent resistance was trembling and terrified of the howling mob when the police finally apprehended him. The presence of police reinforcements only appeared to confirm to the crowd that the man the police had apprehended was none other than Jack the Ripper. The crowd turned ugly, and even when Squibby was safely delivered to the Commercial Street police station, the mob proceeded to attack the police station repeatedly, in a desperate attempt to get their hands on him. The brave officers stood their ground, and eventually, the crowd dispersed. Squibby, much to his relief, was subsequently given a three-month prison sentence, believing he would be safer in Pentonville. Walter Dew, said: "After this experience "Squibby" was a changed man. Whenever he met me he never failed to thank me for " saving his life ", and as far as I know he never again gave trouble to police officers whose duty it was to arrest him."

GEORGE CURTEIS

The Birmingham Daily Post, 11 October 1888 ran the headline:

JACK THE RIPPER AT CHASETOWN

Great excitement was occasioned at Chasetown on Tuesday night by the strange conduct of a man calling himself 'Jack the Ripper.' He went about from house to house frightening and threatening the inhabitants. He entered the Chasetown institute and was soon ejected and the police communicated with. He had in his possession a black mask, and gave the name of George Curteis, describing himself as an acrobat. He said that he had been in Dudley Workhouse, and spent Saturday and Sunday in the casual wards at Cannock. He was an American, only having been in this country four or five years. A "live cat" was found in his coat pocket. Police-constable Houston took the man into custody, and he was brought before Messrs. A E. Manley and J. T. Godfrey Fausett, at Brownhills Petty Sessions, yesterday, charged with vagrancy. - The prisoner said that he had spained {sic} his ankle, and if the Bench would let him go he would return to the infirmary at Dudley Workhouse. The Bench dismissed the case on prisoner promising to conduct himself decently and to leave the neighbourhood.

THOMAS HAYNE CUTBUSH

Thomas Hayne Cutbush was accused of being Jack the Ripper by the Sun newspaper, first on 13 February 1894, and then subsequently in later editions. Though the newspaper never actually named their suspect, it was apparent in the articles that they were referring to a young man named Thomas Hayne Cutbush. Author A.P Wolf, in the (1993) book: Jack the Myth, also favoured Cutbush as the Ripper. As did David Bullock in the (2012) book: The Man Who Would Be Jack.

The Sun Newspaper article on 13 February 1894 stated:

The general impression for a long time has been that Jack the Ripper is dead. It was evident that the fiend who committed so many murders in such rapid succession with such extraordinary daring with such untiring ferocity would never cease his bloody work until death or detection. Just three years have now passed away since these murders ceased to take place; and such an interruption in the series of crimes points clearly to the disappearance in some form or other of the man who was guilty of them.

The article then went on to claim that Sun reporters had discovered the fate of Jack the Ripper

He was first brought to imprisonment on the charge of being simply a dangerous lunatic. And the evidence of his lunacy hopeless, abysmal and loathsome was so palpable that he was not permitted even to plead. In the brief of the counsel who prosecuted, in the instructions of the solicitor who defended, there was the same statement that he was suspected of being Jack the Ripper. In the case of both the one and the other, the very mention of this or any other dark suspicion was precluded; for, unable to plead, the wretched creature in the dock was saved from all indictments; was spared the necessity of all defence. He was sent forthwith to the living tomb of a lunatic asylum, and there he might have passed to death without mention of his terrible secret if a chance clue had not put a representative of

The Sun on the track. The clue thus accidentally obtained has been followed up by months of patient investigation, and has been thoroughly sifted. Today we lay before the world a story consecutive, careful, and firmly knit which we believe will offer the solution of the greatest murder mystery of the nineteenth century...' We know the Christian name and surname of Jack the Ripper. We know his present habitation; our representatives have seen him, and we have in our possession a morass of declarations, documents and other proofs which prove his identity. We have a facsimile of the knife with which the murders were committed, purchased at the same place. We are able to trace the whole career of the man who committed those crimes, we can give the names of his employers, their places of business, the terms of his service there, and the incidents of his connection with them incidents which clearly show that he was in the neighbourhood of Whitechapel at the time when the murders were committed; that he developed tendencies even in his employment of homicidal insanity; and finally he was at liberty and close to Whitechapel during all that period when the murders were committed; and that these murders immediately came to an end as well as other crimes of violence from the moment when he was safely under lock and key. But at this moment our readers must be satisfied with less information than is at our disposal. Jack the Ripper has relatives; they are some of them in positions which would make them a target for the natural curiosity..." His habits of life when he was out of employment were those one would imagine in such a creature as Jack the Ripper. He has spent most of his day in bed; it was only when night came that he seemed roused to activity and to interest in life. Then he used to go out, disappear no one knew whither, and never return till early on the following morning. And when he did return, his appearance was such as to reveal to any gaze but that of blind affection some idea of this bloody and horrible work in which he had been engaged. Even, however, to his relatives, his appearance suggested something terrible. His clothes were covered with mud; there were other stains which might suggest the nature of his work; but, above all things, there was the expression of his face. His face was so distorted as hardly to be recognised. Such is the description which has been given of him. The manner in which the creature spent the portion of the day in which he was not in bed, is also clear proof of his nocturnal occupations and of his identity. Persons who knew him declare that he always exhibited a strong love for anatomical study, and that this is most significant he spent a portion of the day in making rough drawings of the bodies of women, and of their mutilations, after the fashion in which the bodies of the women murdered in Whitechapel were found to be mutilated …

To disprove the newspaper claims, Melville Macnaghten, in 1892 penned his memoranda in which he not only disputed the likelihood of Cutbush being Jack the Ripper but named three alternative candidates; Montague John Druitt, Michael Ostrog and Aaron Kosminski, as more likely, in his opinion, to have been Jack the Ripper than Cutbush. Macnaghten went on to refute many of the newspaper claims. He stated:

Cutbush was unlikely to have been the Ripper, due to the fact that the knife used by Cutbush was different to that used by the Ripper, and was not purchased until February of 1891, some two years and three months after the cessation of the Ripper murders.

Macnaghten added:

That the frenzied killer of 1888 was unlikely to lie dormant for two years, then re-emerge and simply be content with stabbing women in the bottom.

Thomas Hayne Cutbush was born 29 June 1864 (His Broadmoor records state (1866) in Kennington, to Thomas Taylor Cutbush and Kate (née Hayne). His parents were married in 1864. He was brought up by his mother Kate and his sister who adored him. Thomas was said to have been a rather spoilt child. At the time of the Whitechapel murders, he was living with his mother and aunt at 14 Albert Street, Kennington, a distance of some three miles from Whitechapel. These ladies, it has been said, were of a nervous and rather excitable disposition. His aunt, Clara Hayne, says: "At times he has been violent or destructive, breaking glass and chandeliers. He has at times said he was poisoned and has refused all food except what she would prepare for him." Cutbush was unmarried, 24 years of age, was believed to be 5 ft 9 inches tall, slight build, with thin features, a high receding forehead, large dark eyes, a thick prominent nose a dark complexion and black hair. Cutbush was at one time employed as a clerk and traveller in the tea trade at the Minories, and subsequently as a canvasser for a directory. He abandoned his job and now led an idle and useless life. He studied medical books by day, and according to Macnaghten, wandered the streets at night, often returning home with muddy clothes. In some reports, it is claimed; "bloody clothes." Cutbush was detained as a lunatic on 5 March 1891, in Lambeth Infirmary, according to Macnaghten, suffering from syphilis and paranoid delusions. There is no mention in his Broadmoor records of syphilis. He wrote to Lord Grimthorpe, and others, believing that people were trying to poison him with bad medicines. He soon escaped, wearing only his nightshirt and was at liberty for four days, taking with him a knife which it is claimed he used to stab

127

16-year old Florence Grace Johnson in the buttocks, and also attempted to do the same to 18-year old Isabella Frazer Anderson in Kennington. Miss Florence Johnson, residing with her parents in Fentiman Road, Clapham Road, stated: "That while walking along Kennington-Park-Road on March 5 she suddenly received a blow from behind, and felt that she had received some injury. On turning round, she saw a man running away. Upon reaching home her garments were found to be cut through, and subsequently, at the police station, Dr Farr discovered a clean cut wound on the lower part of her back. Miss Johnson subsequently went to Peckham House Lunatic Asylum, and identified Cutbush as the man who had assaulted her." Another witness, Isabel Fraser Anderson, living in White Hart Street, Kennington, said: "On March 7 she was walking with a female friend in Kennington-Road, about a quarter past 10 o'clock. She felt her dress pulled from behind, and then heard a sound as if the dress was being torn. She saw a man run across the road. She complained to a Mr Smith, who pursued the man, but failed to catch him." These crimes appeared to be imitations of a criminal called John Edwin Colocott, erroneously referred to as Collicott, in press reports. Colocott, was 26 years of age, and lived at 43 Aldebert Terrace, Lambeth. A couple of months previously he had; according to newspaper accounts, stabbed at least six young women in the behind with a pointed awl, and may have been responsible for up to sixty assaults in total. Colocott was arrested, found guilty, but subsequently discharged on the arrest of Thomas Cutbush. When examined in prison, Colocott, was considered harmless and inoffensive. The St James Gazette 15 April 1891, wrote:

Juvenile Jack the Ripper Sent to a London Asylum

A companion fiend to Jack the Ripper, only on a somewhat lesser scale, was sent to Broadmoor insane asylum today, there to be confined during what is known as "Her Majesty's pleasure," and which practically means life. His name is Edward Colocitt, and he is the young son of a wealthy jeweler {sic} of this city. Some time ago the police authorities commenced to receive numerous complaints from young women in the western suburbs to the effect that while out after dark they were approached by a young man who came suddenly up behind them, and stabbed them in the back with a sharp instrument about the thickness of an awl. Extra detectives were put on duty in the districts from which the complaint came, but for some time without result. A couple of weeks ago, however, a furniture dealer noticed Collocitt standing behind a couple of young ladies in a suspicious manner, and determined to watch him. Suddenly he made a step forward, and gave one of the young women three stabs with his right hand in the back. Then he took to his heels, but was followed by Myers, the man in question, and arrested. After the fact of his incarceration was made known nineteen women identified him as their assailant. Six of these gave evidence in court, and the doctors testified that all of them had one or more clean cut, punctured wounds on portions of their anatomy immediately below the hip joint, and which had evidently been made by a very pointed awl. A weapon of this kind was thrown away by Collocitt while he was being pursued. It was testified that the total number of his victims was over sixty. The jury promptly found him guilty, but, on account of his wealthy connections, the plea that he was of weak intellect had its effect, and instead of going to the penitentiary he was committed to the lunatic asylum. One feature of his mania consisted of his selecting as victims plump young girls between the age of 14 and 18.

The newspapers appear to have confused the accounts of Cutbush with Colocott. Where Cutbush's crimes appeared to be imitations of Colocott, Colocott's crimes resemble a criminal from a century before Jack the Ripper called the "London Monster." The Monster would follow beautiful young ladies around the West End of London make obscene proposals; use filthy language, then cut or slash at their breasts and buttocks. It is claimed he attacked 50 women in total. Fashionable ladies, when out walking, resorted to strategically placing frying pans under their dresses, in case of an attack. In 1790 a 23-year old artificial flower maker and former ballet dancer named Rhynwick Williams, a native of Powys, Wales, was arrested. Despite many victims, assailant descriptions not matching Williams, and having seven alibi witnesses stating he had been at work at the time of some of the attacks, he was sentenced to six years in Newgate prison. The "gentleman" in the criminal register before Williams was sentenced to 2 years imprisonment for bestiality with a cow.

Thomas Cutbush was arrested on 9 March 1891, and charged with malicious wounding. Isabel Fraser Anderson said: - "that although she did not see the face of the man who stabbed her, his general appearance was like that of Cutbush." At his trial, drawings, found in his overcoat pocket were produced; these drawings depicted women in indecent postures. One represented the trunk of a woman with the walls of the stomach thrown open and the intestines exposed.

This interesting story appeared in Lloyd's Weekly News 26 April 1891:

His relatives are firm in the conviction that, had the prisoner been allowed to plead, they would have been able to convince the jury of his innocence. The circumstances, they freely admit, were suspicious, but they contend that they were not beyond explanation, and, as to the alleged stabbing of a young lady on Thursday, the 5th of March, they assert that they had evidence that would have shown it to be impossible that it could have been

130

committed by Cutbush. One strong point in their favour is the statement made by Mrs Dickinson, keeps a gunsmith's shop in the Minories, close to the Tower of London, and it was there that Cutbush purchased the dagger that was produced at the police-court. Mrs Dickinson appears to remember the transaction pretty clearly, and she expresses her conviction that the knife was purchased on Saturday, the 7th of March, two days after Miss Johnson was stabbed in the Kennington Park Road.

Cutbush was declared insane and committed to Broadmoor, where he died on 5 July 1903 from chronic kidney disease (Pyelitis). The recent opening of Broadmoor archive files to the public for the first time has shed new light on Thomas Hayne Cutbush. In the 26 documents that make up the records Broadmoor kept about him, he was described as having "brilliant blue protuberant eyes," and a limp. The medical notes accompanying his arrival in Broadmoor suggest that he was: "dangerous, is dazed and at times incoherent, strange and shifty in appearance." In letters written by Broadmoor staff, they detail Cutbush's rants against them; his using bad language, how he repeatedly threatened to rip them open with a knife, or stick a knife in them if he had a chance. A note dated 20 April '03 states that:-

Mrs Cutbush and her sister visited T Cutbush from 2.35 to 2.55. Mrs Cutbush tried to kiss her son and he tried to bite her face then commenced to swear at them.

Despite the threats, there is no record any of the medical staff suspected Cutbush of being Jack the Ripper. He was – to quote an entry in his medical records – "very insane."

David Bullock in his book, offers us an explanation of how and where the Ripper (Cutbush) disposed of the body parts removed from the victims.

"Whenever he would leave his house, he would always exit via the back window or via the door and he would walk through his garden into a mews behind his house."

"It is exactly the same way he would walk back. Whenever he returned via the garden, he would have to walk past an outhouse. It was this brick building outside in the garden."

"When he was arrested and suspected of being the Ripper, his family knocked down the outhouse. They did it before the police could inspect the outhouse."

"The family knew what he was doing, they knew how dangerous he was and I think they were looking to protect him. Why bulldoze the outhouse coincidentally just after his arrest?"

According to Sir Melville Macnaghten, Cutbush's uncle was Superintendent Charles Henry Cutbush, who in 1896 shot himself in front of his daughter; because it is claimed, he knew his nephew was the murderer. He had for some time been suffering from depression and mild paranoid delusions. Researchers, have discovered no family connection between Charles Henry and Thomas Cutbush.

Macnaghten did not state with absolute certainty Cutbush, was not the Ripper, only that he was unlikely to have been. Whoever Jack the Ripper was, he did not kill again after Thomas Cutbush was incarcerated.

Edwin Colocott, surprisingly never regarded as a Ripper suspect died 9 May 1930.

THE DARTMOOR SUSPECT

The Manitoba Daily Free Press, Winnipeg, Canada 8 March 1894 reported the following story:

A remarkable statement concerning the perpetrator of the Whitechapel murders has been made by an inspector of the criminal investigation department. He was, it appears, on duty near Mitre Court (sic) and the scene of the other murders throughout the time in which they were effected. The officer set himself to find out the criminal, and during the prosecution of his inquiries became possessed of an Oriental knife of a curious pattern of blade. Sometime later a man who manifested homicidal mania was arrested on a minor charge, and in him, the officer considered that he had found the perpetrator of the Whitechapel crimes. At first the man was placed in confinement near London; later on, the criminal was removed to Dartmoor (sic), where he went completely mad. All his conversation is about Whitechapel and about the women who were so mysteriously done to death within its precincts. Prior to this, however, the officer from whom this statement now emanates had made his report to his superiors. He had placed the whole of his information before them and received a bonus for his pains.

The Marion Daily Star Ohio, USA 10 March 1894 Reported:

Is he the Ripper? 'Jack the Ripper found. He is in the British Lunatic Asylum at Dartmoor the fact has developed, although so far it has been kept a profound secret that the authorities have got on the track of "Jack the Ripper". The information leaks out from Scotland Yard and has been guardedly confirmed by a leading officer of the metropolitan police. The atrocious criminal, it is said, is an inmate of the government lunatic asylum at Dartmoor, in which he was incarcerated within a few weeks after

133

the last Whitechapel horror, the authorities having no knowledge of his antecedents at the time of his committal as an insane pauper with homicidal tendencies. The Scotland Yard authorities have possession of the knife which is of Chinese make with which the Whitechapel murders were committed. They were also familiar with the Ripper's movements during the intervals between the murders, and have been able to trace him to the asylum after the last crime. Although pronounced incurable insane by the asylum physicians, the man has a clear recollection of the past, and all his conversations and remarks have reference to his crimes in the East End. Correspondence has passed between the government criminal department and the asylum authorities relative to the murderer's condition and as to whether now, or at any time in the near future, he is or will be likely to be sufficiently rational to be placed on trial. The result of these inquiries has not yet been disclosed.

JOHN DAVIDSON

In November 1888, John Davidson, aged 42, of Osborne Street, was summoned by his wife, Mary, for threatening to take her life. He said he was "Jack the Ripper," and had produced "knuckle dusters," he thought the best way to send her soul to peace would be to cut her throat. He repeatedly told her to get down on her knees and make preparations for a change from this world. They had been married six years, and had four children. Davidson was put under a rule of bail-himself in £20 and two sureties of 310 each-to keep the peace for twelve months, or, in default, go to jail for six months.

JOHN DAVIDSON

Davidson came to the attention of the police as a possible Ripper suspect, after a story appeared in the press entitled, The

Cabman's Shelter Incident. On the 1 October 1888, John Davidson walked into the cabman's reading rooms at 43 Pickering Place, Westbourne Grove, West London, at about four o'clock in the afternoon, and spoke to Thomas Ryan, who was in charge. After complaining about the cold weather Davidson asked if a chop could be cooked for him, which Ryan agreed to do with pleasure. While waiting for his meal to be prepared, several cabmen, who were in the shelter at the time, began talking about the Whitechapel murders. Ryan looked directly at Davidson and said, "I'd gladly do seven days and seven nights if I could only find the fellow who did them." Davidson looked directly at Ryan, and asked, "Do you know who committed the murders," before calmly declaring, "I did them." Ryan, a teetotaller, believing Davidson must be recovering from drink proceeded to give him a talk on the follies of alcohol, before requesting that Davidson signs the pledge book, which he duly did, signing the name J. Duncan and giving his occupation as a doctor. After signing the pledge book, Davidson said, "I could tell a tale if I wanted," Then he relapsed into silence. After a pause, he went on to speak of his experiences in India. He also stated that he was at Newcastle-on-Tyne before he went to India, before relapsing back into semi-somnolence. Ryan called his attention to the fact that he had not filled in his proper residence, and the man replied, "I have no fixed place of abode at present. I'm living anywhere." In answer to further conversation about teetotalism, Duncan accepted an invitation to go with Ryan to church that evening, and afterwards to accompany him to a temperance meeting which he was going to hold. For that purpose, he said, he would return to the shelter in an hour, but he never came back. Ryan said, "Davidson carried a stick, and looked a sinewy fellow, he looked like he was capable of putting forth considerable energy when necessary." He described Davidson as 5 ft. 6 inches tall, round-headed, wearing

135

an Oxford cap with a thick moustache, but no beard, with clean white hands, wearing a light check Ulster and a tippet buttoned to his throat, which he did not loosen.

Lieutenant William Wookey, governor of Newcastle prison wrote to the Home Office saying he believed the man in the cabman's shelter was a former convict John George Donkin.

John George Donkin, was born in Morpeth, Northumberland, 7 June 1853, son of Dr. Arthur Scott Donkin, and Mary (née Moor). He hoped to follow his father into the medical profession, he was employed as a locum for medical practitioners in the North of England, but failed to complete his formal studies. He then tried his hand at journalism before joining the army and serving for two years as an enlisted man in the 17th Lancers. Married Margaret Mason in 1874, the couple had two children. Declared bankrupt in 1876. In 1881 he served two terms of imprisonment in Newcastle prison for assaults upon women. On 7 July 1882, he was sentenced to one month's imprisonment for assaulting his wife. Donkin came home drunk and proceeded to strike his wife on the breast, then the nose, which caused it to bleed, he also struck his wife's mother who had been reading. She had given him no provocation. In 1884 he moved to Canada and joined the Mounted Police, where he remained until March 1888. On his return to England, he wrote a book: Trooper in the Far North West about his experiences which was published in 1889. It is speculated he later worked as a journalist for The Newcastle Chronicle. Donkin was believed to have been in London at the Time of the Whitechapel Murders. He died penniless in the Alnwick workhouse in Northumberland 3 January 1890 from inflammation of the lungs.

The police, at first believed they had a strong suspect, due to the fact that Davidson/Donkin had trained as a doctor, therefore, had the requisite anatomical knowledge, and had a prison record for assaults upon women. When questioned, he gave a satisfactory account of his movements on the dates of the murders and was cleared.

JOHN DAVIES

In 1891, at the Llanelly police-court, John Davies, a youth of about 19 years, employed as a boxer at the tinworks was charged with committing an indecent assault on Elizabeth Davies, a 24 year old woman, engaged as a servant at the Brecon Old Bank, Llanelly. Walking along the Great Western Railway, she saw the prisoner, walking in the same direction ahead of her, she quickened her pace and overtook him, and they then entered into conversation after he had bid her good night. Suddenly, he caught hold of her and she asked him to desist, after a violent struggle he committed the offence, of rape, upon her. She screamed several times, during the assault, but he told her if she did not stop, he would shoot her, with a pistol, which he had in his pocket. She asked him for his name and he replied "Jack the Ripper". The next morning she contacted the police. Davies, admitted the offence. Due to the seriousness of the charge, bail was refused.

JOHN DAVIS

On 30 June, 1889, John Davis, an 18 year old, Welshman was charged with being drunk at Clay Cross, Derbyshire. The prisoner had drawn a knife and threatened several women in the street, shouting that he was "Jack the Ripper." His conduct was so insane that he created a panic in the street, and seriously frightened several women. He was sent to prison for 14 days.

DR. MORGAN DAVIS

The 1881 and 1901 census state Morgan Davis was born in 1854, in Whitechapel. However, there is no record of a Morgan Davis, born 1854 in Whitechapel. The 1891 census says he was born in Llanwyrygan, Cardigan Wales. There is a record of a Morgan Davis registered in 1854 in Llandilofawr, in June 1890 he married Margaret Julian, born in Llanshipstead, Cardigan. They are living at 10 Goring Street, with three children, two boys and a girl. Dr. Morgan Davis retired to Aberystwyth where he died in 1920.

Davis lived at various addresses in London, Kings Street, Black Lion Yard, and Goring Street, Houndsditch. He trained in Aberdeen and was a house surgeon at the London Hospital. According to Roslyn D'Onston, while visiting one of his patients, Dr Evans, Davis began to discuss the Whitechapel murders, he then proceeded to give a graphic description, complete with a demonstration, of how the killer murdered then sodomised his victims. D'Onston, who shared a room with Evans, witnessed this demonstration and became suspicious when he learnt from the journalist W.T Stead, that Mary Kelly had been sodomised. He wrote to the police with his suspicions and accused Dr Davis of being the Ripper, claiming Davis was a man of powerful frame, and according to the lines on his sallow face of strong sexual passions and was a woman hater. There is no evidence however that Davis was ever questioned or suspected at the time of the Ripper murders by the police. There is also no evidence any of the victims were sodomised. In the book Uncle Jack, it is claimed Davis was a friend of a recent Ripper suspect Sir John Williams and was the Morgan addressed in the note saying Williams would be in Whitechapel on 8 September 1888.

DR. HAROLD DEARDEN'S BROTHER OFFICER

In the book: Great Unsolved Crimes (1935), Harold Dearden, wrote a chapter entitled Who Was Jack The Ripper, and told a story that on 9 November 1918 during the Great War (WW1) he was in the trenches at the Somme, when a fellow officer told him that this was the second time his birthday had been ruined. The previous occasion had been his tenth birthday party (9 November 1888) when a noisy and violent lunatic had been brought into his father's private mental asylum, on the outskirts of London. Disrupting the boys planned birthday party. The lunatic was said to be the son of one of his father's oldest friend's. As this event was supposed to have occurred on the same day as the murder of Mary Kelly, we are therefore expected to believe this lunatic was none other than "Jack the Ripper." The boy's curiosity getting the better of him peeped his head around the door and caught a glimpse of a gaunt and dishevelled figure surrounded by attendants. The story goes on to say that over a period of time the lunatic played with him in his father's garden and became a smiling and gently demented and constant companion for the boy, with a great talent for drawing animals which he deftly executed with both hands. No researcher has yet identified the brother officer or probably ever will.

FREDERICK BAILEY DEEMING

Frederick Bailey Deeming was born 30 July, 1853, in Ashby de la Zouch, Leicestershire. The youngest of seven children, to Thomas Deeming a brazier, and his wife Anne, (née Bailey) who was said to be a very religious woman. He claimed his father had been a lunatic and died in the Birkenhead asylum, having tried to commit suicide four times by cutting his throat, and that his mother whom he adored had also died in an asylum. He also claimed he had spent some time in an asylum when he was younger. All these claims are unsubstantiated, and may be fabricated. After his mother's death in 1873, he became emotionally disturbed and mourned for a considerable time after the event. He led a rather sheltered childhood and was considered as a young man, to have been rather lazy. It is suggested his father's cruelty drove him to sea. He found work at the age of sixteen as a ship's steward and was known as "Mad Fred" by his shipmates. He travelled the world, and made up different names and reputed occupations for each country he visited. During a trip to Calcutta, India, he suffered a severe attack of brain fever from which it is claimed he never satisfactorily recovered. Every so often he would commit some ludicrous act and infer that this was on the instruction of his dead mother. He said his late mother appeared to him at 2 am every night and told him to kill women. When he finally gave up his adventures at sea, he became a plumber and gas-fitter, and in 1881 married a young Welsh woman Marie James, who bore him four children. Shortly after, they moved to Australia. In 1889 he was lodging in Beverley, passing himself off as a retired sheep farmer named Harry Lawson. He entered into a bigamous marriage with 21 year old Helen Matherson, the daughter of his landlady. Shortly after he was sentenced to nine months imprisonment for swindling a jewellers shop in Hull. After his release, he was next in Liverpool, in July 1889, calling himself Albert Oliver Williams, a military officer on furlough from India, he took the lease on a cottage called Dinham Villa, in Rainhill, passing his wife off as his sister, and he began dating Emily Lydia Mather, the daughter of a local widowed shopkeeper, Mrs Dove Mather. Deeming then killed his wife and their four children by cutting their throats and crushing their skulls with a blunt instrument, he then proceeded to bury their bodies under a new floor he had just laid. On 22 September 1891, he married Emily at

St Anne's Church, Rainhill, and they travelled to Australia under the name, Williams. They rented a house at 57 Andrew Street, Windsor. It was here that Deeming killed Emily, with an axe and buried her body under the hearthstone in the bedroom. Her body was discovered when a tenant, shown around the property by the landlord noticed a powerful smell emanating from the bedroom. When Emily's body was found, it was discovered that her skull had been fractured and her throat had been cut. Deeming fled to Australia under the name Baron Swanston, but was apprehended on 12 March 1892, and brought back to England. While awaiting execution in Melbourne, Australia, it was rumoured Deeming boasted to fellow prisoners that he was "Jack the Ripper." He said it was his right to kill someone if he chose. He claimed he had syphilis and it had sent him insane. This confession was strenuously denied by his solicitor. The press had a field day and described Deeming as, "A monster in human form." On 8 April 1892, the Melbourne Evening Standard carried the headline, Jack the Ripper: Deeming at Aldgate on the Night of the Whitechapel Murders. He was subject to enormous, vilification, His counsel, sought a month's adjournment to allow the hysteria to abate. On the final day of his trial Deeming addressed the jury himself, making an attempt to gain public support and sympathy, he claimed the pre-trial publicity was against him, which it undoubtedly was, and that he had not been given a fair trial and had been declared guilty before he was even tried. He spoke for over an hour, and support appeared to be turning in his favour, when he unexpectedly suffered a fit, which left him kicking and thrashing about for over an hour, before finally returning to his senses. His speech, initially reasonable, soon gave way to anger, he made accusations against his own family and declared that the people present in the courtroom where the ugliest race of people he had ever seen; this outburst did little to help his cause.

141

He denounced women as the spreaders of disease and claimed he had contracted syphilis while in London, and spoke of receiving visitations from his dead mother. He was found guilty and hanged in Melbourne at 10:01 am on 23 May 1892. He weighed 143 pounds (65kg), a stone less than when he entered prison. He spent his last days writing his autobiography, which was later destroyed. His death mask, in the Black Museum, was exhibited as that of Jack the Ripper. In a 2011 documentary Robin Napper a former Scotland Yard detective claims that the display of Deeming's death mask showed that the police always considered him a prime suspect, for the Ripper murders. Deeming was 35 years of age at the time of the Whitechapel murders, fair-haired with a large, distinctive moustache, slight build and of medium height; his head was described as, "exceedingly small for a man of his size." In 1923 Sir William Colin Mackenzie, presented a paper to the Anthropological Society of New South Wales, his subject was Frederick Bailey Deeming, whose skull he said bore a resemblance to the male gorilla. At the time of the murders in London, it has long been accepted that Deeming was in South Africa, though Napper, believes he may have been back in England. Deeming used many aliases during his infamous life, including Bailey, Dawson Drew Druin, Duncan, Dunn, Lawson Swanston and Williams.

HENDRIK DE JONG

Crime historian Dr Jan Bondeson has named Hendrik de Jong as a prime suspect for Jack the Ripper.

Dr Bondeson, said: "It is impossible to know for certain if de Jong was Jack the Ripper but he is a more credible candidate than other names forward for the notorious murderer. We can't say for certain he was Jack the Ripper, but he is a credible candidate who until now has been ignored in England yet was seen as a prime suspect in the Dutch newspapers of the time."

Hendrik de Jong was born in Weesperkarspal, just outside Amsterdam, on 5 October 1861. His father, was a cattle farmer who died when he was seven years old. His mother Johanna died when he was fifteen years old. Due to poverty Hendrick, received very little formal education. He was forced along with his brothers to beg in the street or face starvation. After a few menial jobs, he enlisted in the Dutch army as a volunteer trumpeter, for a period of five years. In January 1888, he was arrested for theft. Declared insane, he was sent briefly to the Coudewater lunatic asylum. When released, he turned to a life of crime. Posing as a wealthy gentleman, he persuaded wealthy women to marry him. He wooed Sarah Ann Juett, a nurse from Maidenhead, Berks, while she cared for him in a hospital in Middlesbrough in 1892. He persuaded her to marry him and they moved to his native Netherlands. But months later she disappeared with de Jong telling her concerned parents, she had run off to America with another man. Shortly after dispersing of Juett, de Jong seduced Maria Schmitz, a wealthy Dutchwoman, and after a whirlwind romance they tied the knot before she too vanished. De Jong, had murdered both his wives. Since their bodies were never found it could not be proved de Jong killed them. Instead, he was jailed for just three years for a separate lesser offence of swindling a Dutch hotel keeper. Upon his release from prison in 1898, de Jong crossed over the border to Belgium where he bludgeoned to death Philomene Wauters and Jeanne Pauwels in Ghent. After committing the murders, he attempted to set their bodies on fire. A huge manhunt was launched, but he successfully fled to the United States, never to be seen again.

Dr Bondeson, further states:

"He was active at the same time as Jack the Ripper, spoke good English and roughly fits the rather rudimentary contemporary descriptions of the Ripper. He was familiar with England in general, and London in particular. Since he worked as a ship's steward on a ship between Rotterdam and London, he was in an ideal position to commit the Ripper murders, and his visits to London coincided with the various atrocities of the autumn of terror."

HARRY DENKER

In December, 1889, Harry Denker, aged 34 years, was charged at the Thames Police Court with assaulting Thomas Taylor and a constable. The prisoner had a crowd round him, when the constable asked him for his name and address, he replied "Jack the Ripper." He would not give his name, and became violent and assaulted the officer. He was sentenced to 7 days hard labour.

JOSEPH DENNY

Denny came to the attention of the police on the 28 December 1888 because he matched the description George Hutchinson gave of the Ripper. Hutchinson had described a man seen with Mary Kelly shortly before she was murdered, wearing an Astrakhan trimmed coat. Denny was arrested by PC 177A Wright and taken to Old Street Police Station, after being seen by Thomas and John Robert Hardy accosting women in Kings Cross while wearing a long Astrakhan trimmed coat.

Denny was born 1864 in Islington, to William and Mary Denny. In the 1871, census he is aged 7 living at 20 Bryan Street, Islington. His father, William, was a Hackney Carriage Driver. His mother a dressmaker. At the time of his arrest, Denny lived at 64 Myddelton Square, Clerkenwell, Islington. Was described as 20 years of age, 5 ft. 6 inches tall, with a fair complexion, slight moustache and very curly hair. Denny was able to prove he was elsewhere at the time of the Whitechapel murders and was released. In the 1891 census he is aged 22 years, in occupation as a Carman and is living at 31 Freeling Street, Islington. He was admitted to St John's Road Workhouse Infirmary 12 December 1895 and discharged 17 December 1895. In 1895 he is living at 57, Elwood-street, Islington. In the census his year of birth is variously given as 1864, 1867, and 1869.

LOUIS DIEMSCHUTZ

Louis Diemschutz, also referred to as "Deimschitz" or "Lewis Diemschitz". Born c. 1862 in Russia. A salesman of cheap jewellery, who lived on the premises and was the steward of the International Working Men's Educational Club at 40 Berner Street (now called Henriques Street). He resided there with his wife. He was returning from Weston Hill Market, Crystal Palace, when he entered Dutfield's Yard with his pony and cart. Immediately at the entrance, his pony shied to the left and refused to proceed any further. Diemschutz suspected something was in the way, but could not see since the yard was utterly pitch black. He probed forward with his whip and came into contact with a body, whom he initially believed to be either drunk or asleep. Thinking it might be his wife, he entered the International Working Men's Educational Club to get some help in rousing the woman, he went into the club by the side entrance and finding his wife safe inside, told several club members: "There's a woman lying in the yard, but I cannot say whether she is drunk or dead." upon returning to the yard with Isaac Kozebrodski and Morris Eagle, the three discovered, by candlelight that she was dead, her throat had been cut. Diemshutz and Kozebrodski headed south towards Fairclough Street shouting "Murder" and "Police." Eagle ran north to Commercial Road. They encountered Police constable Edward

Spooner, who accompanied them back to the yard. As the constable tilted the women's head back Diemshutz got his first glimpse of just how terrible the wound to her throat was. He told a journalist later that day: "I could see that her throat was fearfully cut, there was a great gash in it over two inches wide." All the people in the yard were then interrogated and their names and addresses taken. Once they had given a satisfactory account of themselves and their movements, and their hands and pockets, had been inspected and searched, they were allowed to leave. It was believed that Diemschutz's arrival frightened the Ripper, causing him to flee before he had the chance to mutilate the body. Diemschutz himself stated that he believed the Ripper was still in the yard when he had entered, due to the warm temperature of the body and the continuing odd behaviour of his pony. In March 1889 Diemschitz was sentenced along with Isaac Kozebrodski to three months hard labour, and a fine, for his part in an affray when local residents in Berner Street attacked the Club. The club members fought policemen whom they had summoned, believing them to be reinforcements for their assailants.

A private investigator Randy Williams, author of the (2016) book: Sherlock Holmes and the Autumn of Terror, believes Jack the Ripper was three men, and an accomplice 26 year-old, Louis Deimschutz, 17 year-old Isaac Kozebrodski, a tailor, 41 year-old Samuel Friedman, a hat maker, or tailor, aided by a fourth Prince Pyotr Kropotkin, a member of the Russian aristocracy. Williams claims Deimschutz orchestrated the killings; Kozebrodski helped carry out the crimes; Friedman acted as their lookout and bodyguard, and Kropotkin was the organizer, as well as the driving force behind the murders, Williams also believes the men murdered Emma Elizabeth Smith. Smith claimed she was brutally attacked by three or four men. Williams discovered the men were connected through a society known as the International Working Men's Education Club (IWMEC). Williams uncovered documents which shed greater light on the agenda of the organization and its political motivations. The organization championed a socialist-communist agenda that aimed to topple the socio-political system in England—by any means necessary.

MICHAEL DEVINE

On 9 October, 1888, a young man from Govan, Scotland named Michael Devine knocked down a Mrs Westwood and stood over her brandishing a penknife while foolishly declaring he was "Jack the Ripper." He also knocked down a man named M'Quade, and his wife. He was ordered to pay three guineas or go to prison for thirty days by the magistrate.

CHARLES LUTWIDGE DODGSON

Charles Lutwidge Dodgson is better known by the pseudonym, "Lewis Carroll," the author of Alice's Adventures in Wonderland (1865) and Through the Looking Glass (1872). He concocted the pseudonym Lewis Carroll by translating his first two names, Charles Lutwidge, into Latin, as, Carolus Lodovicus, and then anglicising and reversing their order. As well as being a writer of children's books, Dodgson was also a famous photographer, mathematician and illustrator.

Born on 27 January 1832 in Daresbury, Cheshire, his parents, Charles Dodgson, and Francis Jane, (nee Lutwidge), were clergyman, and he grew up in a strict Christian household, with his early education provided by his parents. He was the oldest son and the third of eleven children. On his fourteenth birthday, he enrolled at Rugby the public school, immortalised by the novel Tom Brown's Schooldays. He remained at Rugby for three deeply unhappy years. Described as a "shy, sensitive boy with a stammer," he was also somewhat deaf in his left ear as a result of having contracted mumps in the autumn of 1848. While at Rugby he suffered bullying from the older boys and wrote afterwards of his time there:

I made some friends there, but I cannot say that I look back upon my life at a public school with any sensation or pleasure or that any earthly considerations would induce me to go through my three years again, I can honestly say that if I could have been... secure from annoyance at night, the hardships of the daily life would have been comparative trifles to bear.

The last passage it is suggested, implied that Carroll endured some form of sexual abuse at night. Educated at Oxford, he graduated with honours in mathematics and in 1855 taught mathematics at Christ Church, Oxford, and would continue to do so until 1881. Among his hobbies was photography, and he excelled at photographing young women, which was his greatest pleasure. One of his photographic subjects was Alice Liddell, daughter of Henry George Liddell, the Dean of Christ Church. Alice became the model for the fictional Alice. In 1932 she recalled how:

She and her sister's used to sit on the big sofa on each side of him, while he told us stories, illustrating them by pencil or ink drawings as he went along. He seemed to have an endless store of these fantastical tales which he made up as he told them, drawing busily on a large sheet of paper all the time. They were not always entirely new, sometimes they were new versions of old stories, sometimes they started on the old basis, but grew into new tales owing to the frequent interruptions which opened up fresh and undreamed of possibilities.

In 1862 Dodgson wrote down the stories at Alice's request. Author Henry Kingsley visited the Liddell's and happened to pick up Dodgson's stories and persuaded him to publish his writings. In 1865 he published his first Alice book under the title, Alice's Adventures in Wonderland. He also wrote a number of books on mathematics. Dodgson has been suggested as a Ripper suspect by author Richard Wallace in the (1996) book: Jack the Ripper Light-Hearted Friend. Wallace claims deleted passages from Dodgson's diaries contained comments on the murders. Wallace using an anagram takes this passage from Dodgson's "Nursery Alice":

So she wondered away, through the wood, carrying the ugly little thing with her. And a great job it was to keep hold of it, it wriggled about so. But at last she found out that the proper way was to keep tight hold of itself foot and its right ear." And turns it into:

She wriggled about so! But at last Dodgson and Bayne found a way to keep hold of the fat little whore. I got a tight hold of her and slit her throat, left ear to right. It was tough, wet, disgusting, too. So weary of it, they threw up – Jack the Ripper.

Other theorists have Dodgson committing the murders with his Oxford colleague, Thomas Vere Bayne. At the time of the Ripper murders, Vere Bayne was nearly 60-years old and was suffering from acute back pain. An entry in his diary dated 16 August 1888, simply said, "Can barely move great pain." Vere Bayne was actually in France from 1 September to the 5 October. Dodgson, in 1888, was 56 years of age. He spent the autumn of 1888 at his summer cottage in Eastbourne in the company of his actress friend, 14-year old Isa Bowman. He was there on 31 August and 30 September and stayed until 3 October. Dodgson died of pneumonia 14 January 1898. Dodgson stood about six feet tall, slender with a soft face, and curly brown hair. He walked with a jerky gait and tended to tilt backwards when he stood. He ate frugally, disliked tea, and sometimes talked to himself. He mentions the Ripper only once in his private diary, entry 26 August 1891, when he makes reference to talking with Dr Dabbs, while in the Isle of Wight, about his very ingenious theory about Jack the Ripper, though disappointingly never reveals what this ingenious theory was.

PETER DONALD

In November, 1888, Peter Donald, a well-dressed, respectable-looking man, aged 35, an engineer on the steamship Nepaul, lying at the Albert Docks, was charged with being drunk and disorderly and terrorising the public by terming himself "Jack the Ripper." PC David Bostock 298 H, was on duty in Commercial-road, Whitechapel, when a hansom cab drove up to him. The prisoner who was seated inside drunk, hailed him and said, "I am Jack the Ripper." As his conduct was likely to cause alarm, Bostock took him into custody. On the way to the station the prisoner said, "What a fool I must have been to act like this." He was advised not to be so foolish as to identify himself with "Jack the Ripper." He was fined 2s. 6d. Peter Donald, was born in Scotland, and was married to Harriet, in the 1901 census, they lived in Poplar. He died in 1921.

TIMOTHY DONOVAN

Donovan was suggested as a possible Ripper suspect by Donald Rumbellow in the (2004 edition) of the book: The Complete Jack the Ripper.

Donovan, it is claimed, was 28 years of age at the time of the murders, lived at 7 Russell Court, St George's in the East, Stepney. And was a labourer, who also worked casually as the deputy manager of Crossingham's Common Lodging House, 35

Dorset Street. He died from cirrhosis of the liver, phthisis and exhaustion at the London Hospital on 1 November 1888. Donovan, who was described as thin, pale-faced, and sullen said at the inquest that at about 1:45 am on the 8 September he saw Annie Chapman, eating a baked potato in the kitchen of Crossingham's, she was, in his opinion, the worse for drink. He had known her for about sixteen months, the last four months while she resided at the lodging house, she was a quite woman, who gave no trouble, Donovan said. He asked her for her doss money, which she said she had not got as she was weak and ill and had been in the infirmary. Donovan refused Chapman's request to let her stay on trust and so she left, saying she would be back soon, asking him to save her bed. Donovan, it has been claimed in his statement's to the police and press, appeared to soften the severity in which he originally dealt with Chapman on the night she was murdered, in an attempt not to appear too unkind in turning an ill woman out onto the streets where she was subsequently murdered. Chapman was malnourished and suffering from advanced and chronic diseases of the lungs and the membranes of the brain. Rumbellow, in his book, makes the suggestion that Donovan almost certainly knew Catherine Eddowes and Mary Kelly, and that they both knew who Jack the Ripper was, and perhaps this is why they were murdered. It is speculated that Eddowes had claimed that she knew who the Ripper was, and intended to collect the reward money. There is no evidence Mary Kelly at any time said she knew who the Ripper was, only that she was afraid of someone, though would not say who. While it is true Donovan knew one of the victims, (Chapman) there is no evidence he knew Eddowes or Kelly, this is again pure speculation. If Eddowes and Kelly were murdered because they suspected Donovan of being Jack the Ripper and were going to reveal him, who killed Mary Kelly, because by this

151

time Timothy Donovan was already dead. The theory of Donovan being the Ripper is only credible if you believe Mary Kelly was not a Ripper victim and was murdered by someone else and disguised as a Ripper murder. An alternative suggestion is that Rumbellow's suspect is the wrong Timothy Donovan, for there is a second Timothy Donovan, who, more importantly, was alive when Mary Kelly was murdered. Aged 30 years, a labourer. He has a long history of violence, at the age of sixteen he assaulted a woman with a "sheep's head." He repeatedly appeared before Thames Magistrates Court during 1887-88 on charges of assault, and in 1904, at 27 Lucus Street, Stepney, and while under the influence of alcohol murdered his 36-year old wife Mary with an old worn table-knife.

The Times Wednesday 1 April 1903 gave a fuller account:

TIMOTHY DONOVAN, 40, labourer, indicted for the wilful murder of Mary Donovan, his wife. Mr. R.D. Muir and Mr. Bodkin prosecuted; Dr. E. P. S. Counsel defended. The prisoner and his wife lodged in Shadwell. He was of intemperate habits, but his wife was a sober woman.
On the evening of Saturday, March 7, the prisoner returned home at 9 o'clock. Soon afterwards he went to the landlady, who was in the kitchen, and said, "I think I have done something; I think I have done it." The landlady asked him what he had done, and he replied, "Go upstairs and see." The landlady went to the room occupied by the prisoner and his wife, and saw his wife lying on the floor with a wound in the neck. A doctor was fetched by the prisoner, and he found that she was dead. The prisoner, who was under the influence of drink, was arrested the same night in Shadwell, and made statements to the effect that on his return home his wife threw something at him, and he in a moment of passion picked up a knife from the table and stabbed her. He

added that he did not mean to do it, and that it was all done in a moment. It was stated that the prisoner always appeared on very affectionate terms with his wife, and it was only when he was drunk that quarrels took place. For the defence it was contended that there was a drunken brawl, in the course of which the prisoner struck his wife, forgetting that he had the knife in his hand. The jury found the prisoner Not Guilty of murder, but Guilty of manslaughter. It was stated that there were 20 summary convictions against the prisoner for assaults on the police, drunkenness, & c. Mr. JUSTICE KENNEDY, in passing sentence, said that the jury had found themselves enabled to take a less severe view of the case. He assumed from their finding that they were of the opinion that there was in fact, not merely drunkenness on the prisoner's part, but that there was a drunken brawl, in which he used the knife on his wife. In any view the prisoner had taken the life of the woman with a knife, and it was a very serious crime that he had committed. He sentenced him to 12 years' penal servitude.

There is no evidence to suggest that either of these two men are Timothy Donovan the deputy of Crossingham's.

ERNEST DOWSON

Writer Robert Thurston Hopkins, included a chapter on Jack the Ripper, entitled "Shadowing the Shadow of a Murderer" in his (1935) book: Life and Death at the Old Bailey. Author Simon Webb in the (2017) Kindle E-book: Absinthe Jack: Was Ernest Dowson Jack the Ripper, examines the possibility that Dowson's consumption of epic quantities of absinthe may have turned him from a woman-hating brawler into the terror of Whitechapel.

Hopkins proposed a suspect who fitted the description of the man described by eyewitness George Hutchinson, seen with Mary

Kelly shortly before she was murdered. He used the pseudonym "Mr Moring" for this suspect and went on to describe him as a drug-addicted poet. Martin Fido identified decadent English poet and novelist, Ernest Dowson as the suspect, Mr Moring. The relevant chapter from Hopkins book is reproduced here:

One of Mary Kelly's friends was a poor devil-driven poet who often haunted the taverns around the East End. I will call him "Mr. Moring," but of course that was not his real name. Moring would often walk about all night and I had many long talks with him as together we paced the gloomy courts and alleys. Of externals Moring was utterly heedless. He wore a blue pea-jacket, baggy trousers (much like the modern Oxford bags) and pointed button boots. His collar was, I distinctly remember, tied together with a bow of wide black moire ribbon, and like his boots, seemed to be crumpled into folds of sympathetic irregularity. He was what the Victorians called a ne'er-do-well, and a decadent. He had black, lank hair and moustache, and the long, dark face of the typical bard. It was said that his father a prosperous tradesman in the East End-had disowned him because he had become a drug addict. Occasionally he returned home and begged money from his parents, and on his return to old haunts lie would enjoy a short period of luxury and sartorial rehabilitation. Moring, who knew every opium den in the East End, although at that time they were not counted in with the sights of London, often gave himself up to long spells of opium smoking.

Ernest Christopher Dowson was born 2 August 1867 at the Grove, Belmont Hill, Lee, Kent. To Alfred Christopher Dowson and Annie Chalmers (née Swan). He was educated at Queen's College, Oxford, though left in the spring of 1888 without taking his degree to help in his father's failing boat – fitting business. In 1891 he met 12-year old Adelaide "Missie" Foltinowicz, a Polish restaurateur's daughter. He courted her for two years, but when she came of age, she instead married a waiter, who lived above her father's business. Much of his poetry would be influenced by his infatuation with her. "You, who are my verses." He joined the Rhymer's Club, a society of poets, whose philosophy was that art in any form should be produced merely for the sake of artistic value, and whose membership included William Butler Yeats, Lionel Johnson and Arthur Symons. Dowson frequently contributed poems to, literary magazines The Yellow Book, and, The Savoy and is considered as one of the finest poets of his generation. Dowson wrote 120 poems, in his lifetime. Dowson was a man of febrile sexual energy: when he could afford it, he would have a woman (mainly prostitutes) each night. Arthur Symons, his friend said of Dowson when drunk he was "almost literally insane, certainly quite irresponsible... A vocabulary unknown to him sprang up like a whirlwind; he seemed always about to commit some absurd act of violence." In 1895 both his parents died within a few months of each other. His father, who lived a good deal of his life in France, on account of his delicate health, he was in the advanced stages of consumption (tuberculosis) died of an overdose of chloral hydrate. His mother, who was also consumptive committed suicide, by hanging herself. From this period onwards he wandered aimlessly around Europe. Never robust, his health had been steadily getting worse for some years. As disease weakened him more and more, he hid himself away, and refused to see a doctor. He died at 26 Sandhurst Gardens, Catford, in relative obscurity, from alcoholism 23 February 1900 at the age of 32 and was buried in Lewisham cemetery. In his will, he left effects to the value £1119 18s 7d.

His friend, W.B Yeats, described him as: "Timid, silent and a little melancholy," others who knew him described him as, "Shy, frail and timid." Arthur Symons, who knew Dowson and his poetry intimately, said that he was: "Undoubtedly a man of genius. One of the very few writers of our generation to whom that name can be applied in its most intimate sense."

Was Dowson, Jack the Ripper? He did reside in Whitechapel at the time of the Ripper murders, though, was not drug addicted as Hopkins described. He also had no history of violence, and none of his poems could be considered misogynistic. He may have been considered melancholy, but this description could equally be applied to many of the poets from this period.

BETTY DOYLE

Sarah Doyle, while preparing to move house, came across in the attic an old dusty suitcase containing a hitherto unknown newspaper article. It was written by her great-great-grandfather Dudley Doyle, a newspaper reporter for Weekly Old World News, and a previous occupant of the Kensington mews flat. According to the article, Dudley's parents were the victims of an unsolved homicide when the boy was nine-years-old. They were slain in their beds while they slept. The intruder also killed the family cat, a bird and a few house plants. Dudley moved in with his adoring grandmother. Despite her being a little controlling and overprotective, they had a close relationship until he left school and went to work as a junior reporter for Weekly Old World News. Due to the demands of his job, he began to see less and less of his grandmother. One of his frequent companions was a lady named Mary Ann Nichols, whom he met at a bar. When he learnt that Mary Ann had been murdered, he went to the crime scene to investigate. He noticed something familiar about the wounds the killer had inflicted, though, couldn't quite put his finger on it. A week later, another one of his companions, Annie Chapman, was murdered near Dudley's favourite pub. He had spent the previous night in her company at a dinner and a dance hall. He visited the crime scene and once again the injuries were very familiar, he still didn't know why, however. Three more women died, each one he had dated the night previously. Once again, he visited each crime scene, and as before the injuries reminded him of something. A week later the elusive answer he had been seeking finally came to him. After running out of women to date, he went early home after work. His grandmother was cooking a meal for him. After watching her carve the roast, he noted that she was a master carver with a unique method of slicing the meat. He suddenly came to the realisation that his beloved old grandma was "Jack the Ripper." Dudley confronted the elderly lady, who broke down in tears and confessed she had followed him each night, and in her own words, "Murdered those unworthy trollops." She couldn't allow those women to dirty her grandson and get away with it. Torn between his love for his grandma and his natural reporting instincts, he decided to give up reporting and look after his old grandma. The pen used by Dudley to write the article was found in the pocket of Betty's dress. According to some accounts, neighbours swore that for decades, they could see the ghost of Betty Doyle through the windows, other locals suspected it was Dudley himself, dressed as her, driven insane by the knowledge of what his grandmother had done.

SIR ARTHUR IGNATIUS CONAN DOYLE

Doyle was born in Picardy Place, Edinburgh, on 22 May 1859, to an affluent family of Irish Catholic descent. The third of ten children, his mother, Mary, (née Foley) ran a boarding house, and his father, Charles Altamont Doyle, was an artist, who in 1879 entered a nursing home suffering from alcoholism, he died there in 1893. After the death of his father, the burden of supporting his large family fell on him. Doyle studied medicine at Edinburgh University from 1876-1881 and received his MD in 1885. One of his teachers, Dr. Joseph Bell, was a master at observation, logic, deduction, and diagnosis. All these qualities were later to be found in the persona of the celebrated detective Sherlock Holmes. The year before, he worked as a ship's surgeon on a Greenland whaling ship on a seven-month tour of the Arctic, where it is claimed in letters he wrote home to his mother, that he took a sadistic pleasure in the killings. He began writing to make some money while he waited for his medical practice at 1 Bush Villas in Elm Grove, Southsea, Portsmouth to grow. In 1885 he married Louise (née Hawkins), known as "Touie" Louise died from tuberculosis on 4 July 1906. They had two children, a son, Alleyne Kingsley, 1892-1918, who was wounded at the battle of the Somme and died in the 1918 flu pandemic, and a daughter Mary Louise 1889-1976. He married Jean Elizabeth Leckie, in 1907, and they had three children, Denis Percy Stewart, 1909-1955. Adrian Malcolm, 1910-1970, and Jean Lena Annette, 1912-1997. In 1887 Doyle wrote A Study in Scarlet and created Sherlock Holmes. By 1891 six Holmes novels had been published in the Strand magazine. In 1893 tired of writing short stories and believing the Holmes stories beneath him, and wanting to be remembered more for his historical novels, he decided, in the story The Final Problem, to kill off Sherlock Holmes by dispatching him over the Reichenbach Falls with his nemesis Moriarty. The outcry from his fans, however, was so great that he was reluctantly forced to resurrect his creation. He originally based the character Sherlock Holmes on Edgar Allan Poe's Detective C. Auguste Dupin, and Holmes physical appearance on Professor Dr Joseph Bell, a criminal psychologist and surgeon he had worked with in university. Some fans actually came to believe that Holmes was real and not fictional, and sent letters and parcels to him at Doyle's home address. He ran, unsuccessfully, for parliament as a Liberal Unionist, in 1900 and again in 1906.

He served as a doctor in a field hospital in the Boer War and was knighted in 1902. When World War One broke out in 1914 Sir Arthur Conan Doyle tried to enlist in the military stating, "I am fifty-five, but I am very strong and hardy, and can make my voice audible at great distances, which is useful at drill." His offer was refused. A physically powerful man, he was 29 years of age at the time of the Whitechapel murders, stood 6 ft. 2 inches tall, and weighed 16 stone. A keen sportsman, good cricketer and founding member of Portsmouth football club, he was also a Freemason, joining the Phoenix Lodge in July 1887. He died on 7 July 1930 at the age of 71 at his home in Windlesham, Sussex, from heart disease. His last words were directed toward his wife: "You are wonderful." In 1888 it is theorised that when asked his opinions on the Whitechapel murders Doyle suggested that:

"The killer may have disguised himself as a midwife or an abortionist, thus avoiding suspicion, escaping while being heavily bloodstained."

Doyle was proposed as a suspect by a woman incensed by what she considered witchcraft, shouted out that he was Jack the Ripper, during a spiritual tour of Australia by Doyle. At the time of the Ripper murders, Doyle was a general practitioner in Southsea and did not relocate to the capital until 1891. In later years he sought solace in spiritualism, believed in the existence of fairies, and was a follower of the theosophy cult founded by Madame Helena Blavatsky. Best known for his Sherlock Holmes mysteries, he was a prolific writer and also wrote historical romances and several books on spiritualism including The New Revelation (1918) The Coming of the Fairies (1921), and The History of Spiritualism (1926), though apart from the Sherlock Holmes novels, none of his other work made serious money. The Sherlock Holmes expression, "Elementary my dear Watson"

159

though synonymous with the character, never actually appeared in any of Doyle's stories, and was, in fact, the creation of Hollywood script writers.

MONTAGUE JOHN DRUITT

Montague John Druitt was first named as a Ripper suspect by Sir Melville Macnaghten in his 1894 memoranda as:

The man most likely to be Jack the Ripper.

Macnaghten referred to Druitt in the following quote:

I have always held strong opinions regarding him, and the more I think the matter over, the stronger these opinions become. The truth, however, will never be known, and did indeed at one time lie at the bottom of the Thames, if my conjectures are correct.

Macnaghten went on to describe Druitt as:

A doctor, about 41 years of age, of good family, who was alleged to be sexually insane and whose body was found floating in the Thames on the 31 December 1888.

He further goes on to say:

A rational and workable theory to my way of thinking is that the Ripper's brain gave way altogether after his awful glut in Millers Court and he then committed suicide and that from private information, I have little doubt that his own family suspected this man of being the Whitechapel murderer.

Druitt was proposed as the Ripper in the (1987) book: The Ripper Legacy: The Life and Death of Jack the Ripper Martin Howells & Keith Skinner. And the (2004) book: Montague Druitt: Portrait of a Contender D.J. Leighton.

Montague John Druitt was born in Wimborne, Dorset, on 15 August 1857, the second son of seven children, to William Druitt and Ann (née Harvey). His father William was a doctor, as was his brother Robert and also his nephew Lionel. Montague was educated at Winchester, and at New College, Oxford, where he graduated in 1880 with a third-class honours degree in the classics. While at Winchester he became heavily involved in the debating society, choosing political topics for his speeches. That same year he took up a teaching post at a boy's boarding school at 9 Eliot Place, Blackheath, run by Mr George Valentine. Druitt a keen sportsman, began playing for the Morden Cricket Club, Blackheath and was described as one of the best players in the history of the Blackheath Club. Talented at fives, he won the double and single fives titles at Winchester and Oxford. He was noted to have had formidable strength in his arms and wrists. In 1882 he started a second career in law and was admitted to the Inner Temple on 17 May. On 29 April 1885, he was called to the bar and rented chambers at 9 King's Bench Walk. The law list records him as a special pleader for the Western Circuit and Hampshire, Portsmouth and Southampton Assizes. Druitt is often described as a failed barrister, yet left behind an estate valued at some £2,000, a not inconsiderable sum for the day, and one which he was not likely to have accrued by teaching alone. He was successful until 1885 when things started to go wrong in his life. First, his father died, at the age of 65, from a heart attack on 27 September 1885. Then his mother began to show signs of mental instability and became suicidal and delusional, she would later attempt to take her own life with an overdose of Laudanum. She was admitted to the Brook asylum in Clapton, London, where she remained until 31 May 1890, when she was sent to the Manor House Asylum, Chiswick, she died there from a heart attack on 15 December 1890. Suicidal urges appeared to be a

161

trait in Ann Druitt's family; her sister had also spent some time in an asylum after attempting suicide, and her mother committed suicide while insane. On, or about, the 30 November 1888, Montague John Druitt was dismissed from his teaching job at the school, for what the press described as, "Serious trouble," what exactly this serious trouble was, is unknown, but has led to speculation that it was due to a homosexual act with one of the pupils. While there is no direct evidence to support this, it does remain a possibility. Druitt was considered a successful, handsome man, yet there is no record of any female companions during his life. When his eldest brother William, learnt that Montague had not been seen for over a week and had been dismissed from his teaching job, he went to investigate, and found a suicide note amongst his brother's possessions which read: "Since Friday I felt I was going to be like mother, and the best thing for me was to die." Montague John Druitt's body was fished out of the Thames, around 1:00 p.m. on Monday, 31 December 1888, by Henry Winslade, a Waterman; the body was believed to have been in the water for about one month. The body, which was fully dressed and bore no injuries, was brought ashore and searched by PC George Moulson, who found four large stones in each pocket of his overcoat, 2 and 17 shillings two pence in coinage, two cheques, one for 50, and one for 16, a first class season rail ticket from Blackheath to London, a second half return Hammersmith to Charing Cross, dated 1 December, a pair of kid gloves, a white handkerchief and a silver watch with a gold chain, no papers or letters were found. The date on the return half ticket suggests Druitt committed suicide in Hammersmith or Chiswick on 1 December 1888. The inquest was held at the Lamp Tap, Chiswick before Dr Thomas Diplock. His body was formally identified by his elder brother, William. It was concluded that

162

Druitt had committed suicide whilst of unsound mind. He was buried in Wimborne Cemetery on 3 January 1889.

Was Montague John Druitt-Jack the Ripper? On almost every point relating to Druitt, Macnaghten is in error. Druitt was not, as Macnaghten described, 41, but 31 years of age. He was not a doctor, but a barrister and schoolmaster. He did not commit suicide straight after the last murder, but some three weeks later. Records show Druitt lived alone at 9 Eliot Place and did not reside with his family as Macnaghten claimed in his memoranda. Macnaghten told the Daily Mail on 2 June 1913 that he joined the yard six months after the Ripper committed suicide, saying:

I have a very clear idea who the Ripper was," adding, however, that he would never reveal it, saying, "I have destroyed all my documents and there is now no record of the secret information which came into my possession at one time or another.

Unfortunately, the "secret information" Sir Melville Macnaghten claimed to possess, which caused him to favour Druitt, above all the other suspects, is unknown. In 1903, Inspector Abberline, gave an interview to the Pall Mall Gazette in response to a claim made in a Sunday newspaper that the Ripper was a young medical student who had drowned in the Thames. Abberline said:

Yes, I know all about that story, but what does it amount to, simply this, soon after the last murder in Whitechapel the body of a young man was found in the Thames, but there is nothing beyond the fact that he was found at that time to incriminate him.

WILLIAM HARVEY DRUITT

Montague John Druitt's elder brother, and witness at his inquest, William Harvey Druitt, was forwarded as a Ripper suspect by

163

Andrew Holloway, who proposed that William murdered Montague to gain control of the family estate.

Born on 3 June 1856, in Wimborne, Dorset. Educated at Clifton. A solicitor resident in Bournemouth. Died 1909. Left in his will Effects £19456 0s. 9d. worth over £1 million in today's value.

Stated that he had heard from a friend on 11 December 1888, that his brother had not been seen at his chambers for over a week. Enquiries, in London by William revealed that Montague had been dismissed from the school by Mr Valentine, the Headmaster. A search of his brother's possessions produced a note which reads: "Since Friday I felt I was going to be like mother and the best thing for me was to die!.." At the inquest William said, Montague had never made an attempt on his life before. He also claimed Montague had no other relatives, this claim was untrue, and he had numerous other living relatives.

DR THOMAS DUTTON

Dr Thomas Dutton was born in 1855, in St Georges, Pimlico. The second of nine children born to George Dutton and his wife Barbara. He allegedly wrote a three-volume book entitled "The Chronicle of Crime," which consisted of his handwritten notes and comments on all the chief murders of the past sixty years, including Jack the Ripper. The book was shown in 1932 to writer Donald McCormick, (1911-1998), who would take notes. It was from these notes that he would draw upon when he wrote his own book: The Identity of Jack the Ripper (1959). McCormick named the Ripper as Dr Alexander Padachenko. Dutton's book, however, has not seen the light of day since his death in 1935 and is now believed to be lost. Dutton, said: "Jack the Ripper was a middle-aged doctor who had become embittered by the death of his brilliant son." Though Dutton does not, in fact, name the suspect,

164

it does appear to have echoes of the Dr Stanley, son contracts fatal disease from prostitutes and extracts revenge theory. Unfortunately, there is no actual evidence Dutton's book ever existed. Some of Dutton's other claims are also a little dubious. He claims that Inspector Abberline suspected Severin Klosowski (George Chapman) as early as 1888, of being the Ripper, Abberline later denied this. He claims that he took micro-photography of the Goulston Street, Graffiti. Made micro-photographs of 128 specimens of the alleged correspondence of Jack the Ripper, and concluded that at least 34 were in the same handwriting. He also claimed he assisted with the post mortems on the Ripper victims. Dutton wrote to the Daily Mail newspaper 14 May 1929, and told the story of going home one night carrying a black bag which contained a Masonic apron, he was accosted by two women, who shouted out "Jack the Ripper." He was taken into protective custody when harassed by a mob. He told the newspaper, he believed, the murderer was a ship's butcher. According to author Donald McCormick, Inspector Abberline at the time of the murders discussed the possibility that the Ripper may have in fact been a woman, with his friend and mentor Dr Thomas Dutton, after Mrs Caroline Maxwell reported seeing and speaking to Mary Kelly hours after she was supposedly murdered. Maxwell was quite adamant that it was Kelly she saw and not someone else. Abberline cross-questioned Maxwell, but failed to prove she was lying or perhaps mistaken. Abberline asked Dutton,

"Do you think it could be a case of not Jack the Ripper, but Jill the Ripper, and was it possible that the killer may have dressed up in Kelly's clothes to disguise herself, and when spoken to by Maxwell pretended to be Mary Kelly?

Dutton replied:

"He believed it was doubtful, but if the killer were female the only kind capable of perpetrating such an act would be a midwife, for they might just possibly possess enough surgical skill and knowledge of anatomy to carry out these diabolical crimes."

Dutton was listed as living at 130 Aldgate High Street, from 1879-1891. He died at the age of 79, in November 1935 from heart disease. It was said Dutton had died alone in abject poverty, and if it had not been for the kindness of a friend, he might have been buried in a pauper's grave, for £2.00 was all he had to his name.

W H EATON

Shortly after the murder of Mary Kelly, idle curiosity got the better of a 22 year old, clerk named W. H. Eaton, of Fonthill-Road, Finsbury. Having perused the newspapers and finding little in the way of information on the latest Ripper murder, he decided to take a closer look at the actual location of the crime scene himself. He took himself to Dorset Street, and once there quickly realised that he could not get close enough to Miller's Court, due to the entrance being blocked by two stalwart policemen. He therefore instead began to question the bystanders, hoping to gain additional information not mentioned in the newspapers, and asked in an anxious manner if the bloodhounds had arrived yet. His inquisitive behaviour, soon alerted the crowd's attention. Convinced that he was none other than "Jack the Ripper," the howling mob began to follow him, causing him to run to Bishopsgate Police Station for his own protection. Eaton was questioned at the station, though quickly established his innocence and was allowed to leave.

FRANK EDWARDS

In 1959 George Henry Edwards, an 82-year-old, retired blacksmith, told a story to the Reynolds News that in 1888,

166

shortly after the double murder of Elizabeth Stride and Catherine Eddowes, he paid a visit to see his cousin 35 year old, Frank Edwards, who was an accountant in Chichester, West Sussex. 11 Year-old George after reading about a sighting of a suspect carrying a shiny black bag seen by Fanny Mortimer of 36 Berner Street, passing by, shortly before the discovery of Elizabeth Stride's body. Believed Frank matched the description and thus was Jack the Ripper. The man spotted was in fact Leon Goldstein, of 22 Christian Street, innocently on his way home after visiting a coffee house in Spectacle Alley, his black bag contained empty cigarette boxes. George became further suspicious about Cousin Frank when he noticed a bloodstained shirt collar and razor in his attaché case, on the night a woman was murdered in Whitechapel. He remained silent about his discovery, and it was more than 70 years later before he revealed that his cousin was none other than "Jack the Ripper." George Edwards explained his long silence was because he feared that he might be done in two. Unfortunately, Cousin Frank may have come under suspicion from George for nothing more than cutting himself while shaving.

BLACK ELK

Born 1 December 1863, in Little Powder River, Wyoming. Hehaka Sapa, or Black Elk, was a medicine man, a confidant of Crazy Horse, a warrior at Wounded Knee, and, in between, a performer in Buffalo Bill Cody's Wild West Show, and while touring Europe, briefly a Jack the Ripper suspect. In 1886, he joined Buffalo Bill Cody's Wild West show. On 6 May, 1888, Black Elk and four Sioux companions missed the steamship taking Cody's Wild West back to the United States. And were left stranded in Salford, Manchester. Speaking only rudimentary English, they made their way to London. The newspapers pointed the finger of suspicion

167

towards these stranded "Savages." On the third day, in the capital, they were arrested, and asked to give an account of their movements. What they were questioned about is not specified. The arrest took place before the commencement of the Ripper murders, but after the murder of Emma Elizabeth Smith. The men were later released. They joined Mexican Joe's troupe, and for the next year toured Europe. Black Elk married Katie War Bonnet, a Catholic and had 3 children (Benjamin, John and Lucy Looks Twice) in later years Black Elk became a Catholic missionary. In 1930 Black Elk met the poet John Neihardt, a meeting that resulted in the book: Black Elk Speaks (1932). Controversy swirled around the book. How much of the book is Neihardt and how much is Black Elk? The book fails to mention his arrest in 1888. He died 19 August 1950, at the age of 87 in Pine Ridge, South Dakota.

JOHN MOSES EPPSTEIN

Proposed as a Ripper suspect by author Peter Fisher In the (1996) book: An Illustrated Guide to Jack the Ripper. Fisher pondered the question of how the Ripper was able to escape bloodstained through the streets of Whitechapel without attracting undue attention. He came to the conclusion that the Ripper wore a cassock over his bloodstained work clothes and was, in fact, a clergyman. Fisher believed the suspect seen by eyewitness George Hutchinson, with, Mary Kelly shortly before she was murdered carrying a parcel contained not a knife, or knives, as some theorists have believed but in fact a cassock. Fisher also concurred with the press reports at the time which stated that the murders, by their very bestiality, could not have been the work of an Englishman. Fisher looked to Turkey and reports that Turkish troops had committed, "The most heinous crime that had stained the history of the present century." Fisher began a search of the relevant records for a clergyman with a Turkish connection, and discovered John Moses Eppstein, in the Crockford's Clerical Directory for 1888.

Eppstein was born John Moses Levi, in 1827 in Memel, Prussia. His parents were Elijah Levi and Rose. His father died shortly after his birth. He was brought up by his grandfather, Rabbi Benjamin, in Jerusalem, who made him take the name Eppstein. He became a Deacon in 1858 and a priest in 1862. He was a missionary in Turkey between the years 1867-1885. In 1885, he was appointed head of the Society's mission in London. He knew English, German, French, Hebrew, Yiddish, Spanish, Greek (both modern and classic), Latin, Syriac, Chaldee, Felachi (the Nestorian dialect of Chaldee), Persian, Italian, and Turkish. In 1893 he removed to Bristol, in charge of the "Wanderers" Home." He married Sarah Perkins in 1857. His son William Charles Eppstein was the curate at St Mary's Spital Square Whitechapel, between the years 1887-89. Fisher theorised that with Epstein's son working in the district it gave his father the perfect opportunity to acquaint himself with the area using the pretext of visiting his son. When his son moved to a new position in Stowmarket the opportunity to prowl the East End no longer presented itself. This Fisher believes explains the sudden cessation of the murders. John Moses Epstein, died 10 May 1903, Bristol, Gloucestershire, at the age of 76 years in his will he left effects to the value of £470 0s 3d.

JAMES FARLEY

In August 1893, James Farley, described in newspaper accounts as an old pensioner, though, was actually only in his forties, was a powerfully-built ship's stoker, one who had travelled the world. He lived in John-street, Dudhope-crescent, Dundee, Scotland. Farley looked after his young son and kept house while his wife and daughter went to work in the mills. Described as a strange, erratic man who believed he was being persecuted by his neighbours. His peculiar habits in the locality in which he lived earned him the nickname of "Jack the Ripper." One afternoon he snapped and wreaked a terrible revenge on those whom he felt had slighted him. As he descended the stairs with his son, he encountered three women in conversation on a landing. Suspecting they were talking about him, he dashed into his house and fetched a pistol, he shot Mrs Norris a neighbour and her daughter a woman called Maudie, in the face, before locking himself and his son in the house. The assistance of the police was sent for. From the window, revolver in hand, he defied the officials. An attempt to force the door resulted in two constables, Anderson, and Dickson, being shot, one in the right shoulder, one in the face. Police reinforcements were called for, and a further attempt to force the door, resulted in inspector David M'Bey, being stabbed in the abdomen by Farley. He was eventually apprehended. While being taken to the police-station, a crowd had gathered and become so excited that Farley would have been lynched, but for the presence of a strong force of police. Farley seemed unconcerned with the agitated crowd and shouted several times in a defiant manner, "God save Ireland." He resisted all efforts to staunch the blood flow from a deep wound to his head. Farley had been heard muttering to himself earlier that day "I will do it, I'll kill two or three of them yet." Farley's wife stated, that if she had been at home yesterday afternoon she could have quietened her husband, and saved all the serious trouble. Police Inspector David M'Bey, died six days later from his injuries. Farley was declared insane, he spent almost 20 years in the hospital wings of Peterhead, and Perth prisons, before being transferred to Westgreen asylum in Dundee. He was released May 1913. Thousands lined the streets for the Inspectors funeral.

FATHER OF GWB

In 1959 Daniel Farson author of the (1972) book: Jack the Ripper presented a television program on Jack the Ripper. Shortly after the programme aired a 77 year old Australian, using only the initials "G.W.B" wrote to him and told him the story that one day in 1889, at the age of six, while playing in the London streets at 9:00 pm his mother called out to him, "Come in Georgie, or Jack the Ripper will get you." The boy's father overhearing this remark patted the boy on the head telling him, "Don't worry, you would be the last person Jack the Ripper would touch." Years later, after an argument, when the boy challenged his father to stop beating his mother, the boy's father confessed to his son that he was, in fact, "Jack the Ripper." During this confession, the father explained that at the time he did not know what he was doing, but his ambition was to get drunk and kill every prostitute that accosted him. He also claimed that when he committed the murders he wore two pairs of trousers, the outer bloodstained pair he would dispose of in the pile of manure which he sold from his cart. He told his son the story of how he once came close to being captured, he had just killed a woman, and was keeping warm, hiding in his pile of manure when a policeman came by and started asking about Jack the Ripper, he felt scared to death he was about to be apprehended. The father was born in 1850 which would make him 38 at the time of the Whitechapel murders. He married in 1876 and by all accounts was a violent drunkard, who would come home each night and beat his wife and children. He explained to his son that he pined for a daughter, but his first child, a girl was, born an imbecile. When all his subsequent children born were male. He took to drink and suffered severe mental problems, which resulted in him killing prostitutes. According to the son, the father told him to change his name because he was going to confess to the murders before he died.

The son, who claimed his father died in 1912 at the age of 62 constantly, scanned the newspapers awaiting the great revelation, which never came. As the child was 6 years of age in 1889 and was 77 years of age, when he wrote the letter, we can deduce the letter was posted around 1960. Unfortunately, the story sounds a great deal like what the father sold from his cart.

COLLINGWOOD HILTON FENWICK

26-year old Collingwood Hilton Fenwick was charged at the Southwick police-court with stabbing 19-year old Ellen Worsfold described as an "unfortunate" (Victorian euphemism for a prostitute). Worsfold in the newspapers was described as a good-looking girl. The incident happened at about one o'clock in the morning on Thursday 15 November 1888. Worsfold met Fenwick in Westminster Bridge-road, and he accompanied her to her lodgings at 18 Ann's-place, Waterloo-road. After giving her half a crown presumably for her services, he proceeded to stab her in the lower abdomen with a small penknife. Her cries for help alerted a young man named Jim Peters, who lived in the next room Peters came to her aid and they both chased after Fenwick who had rapidly fled the scene of the crime. Peters managed to catch up with Fenwick in Tower-street, Waterloo-road, and confiscate his knife, a small pearl-handled one-sided blade. Peters refused a bribe of a sovereign to let Fenwick go, and bravely held him, until the arrival of plain-clothes-constable Bettle 95L, who took the man into custody. Jim Peters told the court that upon hearing the girls screams he came out of his room without stockings or boots and gave chase. When he confronted the man he was afraid to go too near him because from what the girl had told him he believed he was encountering "Jack the Ripper." When Worsfold was examined by Dr Frederick W. Farr, at Kennington-road police-station a half inch long wound was

172

discovered which had caused a great loss of blood. Though the wound was not believed to be serious, or life threatening, it would be a long time before it healed. When Fenwick was taken into custody it was said he had been drinking. He appeared to show genuine remorse for what he had done and nearly fainted when the doctor gave his evidence as to the extent of the injury caused to Ellen Worsfold. He said: "I have made a great fool of myself. I have made a mistake which will be a warning to me for a long time to come." The details of the trial were found unsuitable for publication. It is possible the wound inflicted on Worsfold, may have been to her genitals, which was deemed too shocking for Victorian sensibilities, to put into print. It was stated Fenwick gave his address as 34, Methley-street, Kennington-road. He had previously been of good character and though in no occupation at that time was a man of independent means, the son of a member of the firm of solicitors, Aspinall & Fenwick. There is confusion over his sentencing, some newspaper reports state he was found not guilty, others report he was sentenced to 12 months imprisonment for the crime.

Collingwood Hilton Fenwick was born in Liverpool, Lancashire, in February 1861 to Henry Fenwick, a solicitor and his wife Sarah, who was born in Montego Bay Jamaica. In the 1871 census, Sarah is now a widow. In the 1911 census, Collingwood Hilton Fenwick is 45 years of age, living at 37 Newcastle-road, Wavertree, Liverpool, with his 24-year-old wife, Annie, who was born in, Umborleigh, Devon, She may have been his common law wife as there is no record in England of them ever having married. His occupation is listed as private means (derived from house property). He was committed to Bodmin Asylum in 1916. He died there 21 July 1917, at the age of 55 years. He left in his will effects to the value of £3239 12s. 7d.

173

CARL FERDINAND FEIGENBAUM

Feigenbaum was proposed as a suspect by former British murder squad detective Trevor Marriott, in the paperback edition of the (2007) book: Jack the Ripper the 21st Century Investigation. Carl Ferdinand Feigenbaum, who was also known by the aliases Karl Feigenbaum, Anton Zahn, Karl Zahn and according to Marriott, possibly Strohband. Feigenbaum was executed by electric chair at Sing Sing prison on Monday the 27 April 1896, for the murder of 56-year old widow, Juliana Hoffman. The murder had occurred in a two-room apartment above a store at 544 East Sixth Street, New York. On 1 September 1894 at 1.00 am Mrs Hoffman's son, 16-year old Michael, who shared a room with his mother was awoken by a scream, and witnessed Feigenbaum, who had recently taken a room there, standing over her, a large knife, in his hand. Feigenbaum lunged at the boy, but Michael fled through an open window. Feigenbaum cut Mrs Hoffman's throat, before fleeing out of the rear window, throwing the knife away as he fled, he was arrested later that night. Feigenbaum told his lawyer: "I have for years suffered from a singular disease which induces an all-absorbing passion, this passion manifests itself in a desire to kill and mutilate every woman who falls in my way, I am unable to control myself." The lawyer, William Sanford Lawton, on hearing this, at once thought of the Whitechapel murders, and suspected that his client may be Jack the Ripper. The lawyer put forward the question of the Whitechapel murders to Feigenbaum, whose reply was: "That the lord was responsible for my acts, and that to him only could I confess." The lawyer drew enough from this to convince himself that the prisoner was not only Jack the Ripper, the man who had murdered twelve? Women in London, but was also the man who had murdered an elderly prostitute, Carrie Brown, in New York on 24 April 1891. Feigenbaum was said to have been German, about 53-54 years old. 5 ft. 4 inches in

174

height, 126 pounds in weight with a medium complexion, dark brown hair (thin on top), small grey, deep-set eyes, a high and heavily arched forehead and a Large red nose with pimples. Some reports state Feigenbaum may have had at some point a moustache and beard. Feigenbaum claimed to be a gardener or florist and had previously been a seaman aboard passenger ships. In his Will, Feigenbaum, left everything to his sister, Magdalene Strohband, a widow, in Ganbickelheim, Germany.

There is no firm evidence that he was in London at the time of the Whitechapel murders, or that he was suspected at the time. At no point did Feigenbaum, confess to the Whitechapel murders, or admit he was Jack the Ripper. There is also no evidence he was responsible for any murder other than that of Juliana Hoffman Feigenbaum's candidacy rests purely on the hearsay of William Sanford Lawton. A few months after the execution of Feigenbaum. Lawton, committed suicide on 13 February 1897, in Lincoln Park, Chicago, by shooting himself in the right temple.

WILLIAM ALFRED FIELD

William Alfred Field, a 60-year old gardener, was charged with being drunk and disorderly between 1 and 2 o'clock on the morning of Saturday 24 November 1888. He had scared various women in the Westminster-Bridge road, by chasing them while shouting," I'm Jack the Ripper." He was sentenced to fourteen days hard labour.

JOHN FITZGERALD

John Fitzgerald, a plasterer bricklayer's labourer, confessed to a member of the public that he was responsible for the murder of Annie Chapman. The information was then passed on to the police who did a search for the man and discovered him at a common lodging house in Wandsworth. He is known to have previously been living in Hammersmith and made the confession after drinking heavily for several days. He could not give the date of the murder, so the authorities are disinclined to place much reliance on his statement. His story was investigated and proved to be untrue, as he had an alibi for the night Chapman was murdered. He was released on 29 September 1888.

JOHN ALEXANDER FITZMAURICE

La Presse, 20 March 1889 reported the following story:

London, 18th March Last Thursday, an individual who identified himself as John Alexander Fitz-Maurice, was taken prisoner at the prison in Wicklow. This man declared that he was Jack the Ripper and told the story of several murders committed by him in London and elsewhere. Yesterday the prisoner retracted his initial statements and has admitted to a murder committed by him in 1888 on the person of Mary Jane Wheeler. An inquiry has been opened on this matter.

Fitzmaurice claimed to be a native of Cardiff. Information from Cardiff Police that he could not have been involved in the Ripper murders, led to his release. Author Trevor Marriott, believes Fitzmaurice, was an alias of Ripper suspect. James Wilson.

JOSEPH FLEMING

Fleming was first proposed as a Ripper suspect in the early 1990s by researcher Mark King. He discovered that a lunatic named Joseph Fleming had died in Claybury Mental Hospital in 1920. This Joseph Fleming, also known as James Evans, has never been proved to be the Joseph Fleming that Ripper victim Mary Kelly knew. Fleming was born in 1859 in Bethnal Green and was 29 years of age at the time of the Whitechapel murders. He was, according to Joseph Barnett, a Mason's plasterer, and Mary

Kelly's former lover, he had lived with her first in Pennington Street, and later in Bethnal Green Road, prior to her meeting Joseph Barnett. Her relationship with Fleming appeared to be serious, since there was talk of marriage at one time. It is not known why the relationship ended, but Kelly's drinking may have been a contributing factor. Despite their relationship having ended, and even though Kelly was now living with Joseph Barnett, Fleming would, according to Julia Venturney her friend and neighbour, still visit Kelly and give her money and made no secret of his desire to win her back. It is, therefore, feasible, they were still lovers. Kelly confided in her friend that she could no longer tolerate Barnett, and was fond of a man named Joe (presumably this was Joseph Fleming). Fleming, according to Venturney, often ill-treated Kelly because she now lived with Barnett. If Fleming murdered Kelly and his motive was jealousy, this does not explain the other Ripper murders. Apart from the fact Fleming knew Mary Kelly and still visited her, there is nothing else, it would seem, to connect him with the Whitechapel murders, nor lead us to suspect he was Jack the Ripper.

FOGELMA

In an article in Empire News, 23 October 1923 a student of criminology wrote:

Every head of police knows that Jack the Ripper died in the Morris Plains lunatic asylum in 1902. He was sent there from Jersey City in 1899, and was for a time, employed in the infirmary of the institution. He was not a "permanent':, he had fits of insanity, and I, who knew him as a patient, gave information to the Mulberry Street authorities concerning the patient's identity. He was not wanted in the United States, so the Detective Department of New York took no steps in the matter. A letter giving the facts in the case was sent to Scotland Yard, and as

177

nothing further was heard of the matter, it was allowed to lapse. The man was not a Russian. He was a native of Norway and had no knowledge of surgery. He was just a simple sailor suffering from an incurable and terrible disease. During the three months before his death, two women called to see him. One was known to the patient as Olga Storsjan, and the other – who said she was his sister – gave her name as Helen Fogelma. As Fogelma the patient was entered in our books. He was subject to fits of terrible depression, and before his death became a fearful coward. He had all the weird superstitions of his race, and on one occasion I heard him scream out in the night, calling on God to have mercy upon his soul. But during the intervals when his brain worked, he muttered of scenes and incidents that connected him clearly with atrocious crimes of 1888. His sister, to whom I mentioned these muttered facts, became fearful for his life, but when I assured her that, being now a certified lunatic, he was immune from the death penalty, she told me that he had done some terrible things in London. She showed me cutting [sic] from the Press of New York and from the London papers. These she had found in the trunk of her brother, who after he landed in New York lived with her at 324, East 39th Street. Many of the passages were underscored, and marginal notes, in a sarcastic vein, gave an insight into the working of the madman's brain. His sister told me that in his native town of Arendal he was known as a good-living youngster. His passion was for the sea, and he came to London with no idea of staying there. Then for a year or so, she lost sight of her brother, and heard no more of him until in 1898 he came to see her and the other girl, both of whom had come to New York to seek a living. When he appeared in their flat at the above address, the girls did not know him. He was worn to a skeleton and in rags. They kept him for some months, and all the time he had to spare he would read over again the cuttings relating to the

Ripper crimes. Olga Storsjan was the old-time sweetheart of this awful wreck of a man, and soon after his coming to their flat she decided to leave it. She went to Jersey City, but the man followed her, and it was upon her information to the police that he was arrested and committed to the asylum. Before he died this man sent for the Rev. J. Miosen, the pastor of a Nestorian church in New York. To him, the dying man told enough to connect him with the crimes committed in London.

The article in Empire News was written to refute claims made by William Le Queux's in his book: Things I Know about Kings, Celebrities and crooks (1923). Le Queux stated that the identity of Jack the Ripper was known and that he was a Russian criminal named Dr Alexander Pedachenko, sent by the Secret Police to annoy and baffle Scotland Yard. Unfortunately, we do not know enough about Fogelma to say with any certainty how much truth, there is in the story relating to him. The author of the newspaper article omits to identify himself or offer us an explanation why, he waited 21 years from the death of Fogelma, to the publication of his article to reveal his suspicions. Neither does he provide us with a physical description of Fogelma. Research has failed to discover Fogelma's name in the Morris Plains asylum records. There is also no record to prove the Rev. J. Miosen, or Fogelma's sister, Helen or former girlfriend Olga Storsjan, ever existed. Though the name Fogelma is rare and often credited as Norwegian in origin, there is a possibility it may actually be Scandinavian. Morris Plains Lunatic Asylum still exists. Today it is called Greystone Park Psychiatric Hospital.

WILLIAM JOHN FOSTER

On the 11 October 1888, William John Foster was arrested at 11 Memel Street, Belfast, on information received. Foster was in bed when constable Carland called. Foster gave his occupation as a watchmaker, though added that he did not need to work, as he lived off an allowance from his father, who was a brewer in London. A search of his room revealed a clasp knife in his coat pocket, a purse containing £19, a watch bearing the monogram, A.M.R, which Foster claimed was his own, and a bag containing a table knife, a number of watchmaking appliances and three razors, one of which had blood on it. Foster said he had no fixed abode and had arrived in town on Sunday from Greenock, where he had stayed for two days, prior to that he was in Glasgow, and before that Edinburgh. His clothes were examined, and it was noted the boots he wore were similar to those worn by military men. He was remanded in custody for a week. It is not known what information the police received, or from whom, which, caused them to become suspicious of Foster. According to the Star newspaper, he was described rather unflatteringly as 30 years of age, 5 ft. 8 inches tall, of slight build, shabbily dressed with a fair complexion and a short cut sandy moustache, his hair was described as flaxen, crispy and hedgehog-like, his head was remarkable for its length rather than breadth or height, his eyes, his most characteristic trait, appeared to protrude somewhat, and his ears, which were said to be cocked and projected outward.

JOHN FOY

On the 21 October 1888, John Foy, an Irish labourer, was charged at the Court House, Broxton, with throwing stones at people, as he walked around Tilston village in Cheshire. Simon Rowland a labourer, said Foy, came up to him, and picked up a handful of stones, and threw them at him, while using bad language to all who passed. A nurse from Tilston Rectory was passing with a bassinet with a child in it, when Foy, who was drunk, picked up a stone and deliberately threw it at her, nearly striking her, and the child. PC John Hunt, observed the incident, followed and apprehended him. Foy had previously had several complaints against him. He had stopped women in the street, terrified them by proclaiming he was "Jack the Ripper," at the same time using filthy and abusive language. The prisoner continued being abusive all the way to the station, brandishing a clasp-knife, and saying he would not mind giving the officer a "dig." He also threatened to break the windows of several houses as they passed if he could get stones, he also made two or three attempts to strike the officer. When searched 7s 8½d and a knife were found on him. The magistrate ordered him to pay costs.

ROBERT FULLERTON

On 27 November, 1888, at the Belfast police-court, a man named Robert Fullerton was fined 20s for shouting in a leading thoroughfare that he was "Jack the Ripper."

PATRICK GALLAGHER

On 12 October 1888, Patrick Gallagher, a young man living at 3, Allen's-court, was charged with being drunk and riotous in Boughton on the previous night. PC Stokes, said the prisoner was making use of very obscene language and calling himself "Jack the Ripper". Gallagher it was stated had been before the court on a previous occasion. He was fined 16s and costs, or in default 14 days imprisonment with hard labour.

GAVIN

The Trenton Times and the Ogden Standard 6 March 1891, reported the story of a man named, Gavin, who had made a ferocious assault with a knife upon fellow passengers in a railway carriage in Castlerea, Dublin. The man, it was said, has been declared of unsound mind, and had previously served two prison terms for stabbing people without any motive. The police are impressed with his likeness to the descriptions of Jack the Ripper and are making further inquiries.

ANDREW JOHN GIBSON

Is Toowong Cemetery, Brisbane, Australia the final resting place of Jack the Ripper? That is the claim of two men Ripperologist James Tully, and Steve Wilson. Wilson is the great-grandson of convicted killer rogue impostor, bigamist backwater quack and man of a thousand identities Walter Thomas Porriott, who's legally acknowledged name was Andrew John Gibson. Porriott was buried amid family shame beneath his ever-faithful last wife Eliza "Bessie." His name does not appear on the gravestone, just the words 'Bessie and her husband.' His exact date of birth is unknown, though was believed to have been about 1870. He would have been around 18-years old at the time of the Whitechapel murders. In 1951 he married 58 year-old spinster Eliza 'Bessie' O'Leary. He died in 1952, at the age of 82. In 1997 Wilson, publicly claimed he had little doubt his late relative was the infamous serial killer and cites the following points as supporting evidence.

Porriott was in England when all five confirmed murders were committed.

He sailed from England to Australia on 9 November 1888, the date of the Mary Kelly murder.

When he sailed to Australia in November 1888 the murders stopped in England.

He married a Francis Mary Scally (or Skelly) in 1891. He would later marry another woman named Kelly in the United States.

On 13 February 1940 he was charged with unlawfully killing a pregnant woman, Gladys Ada Elizabeth Higginbotham, in

182

England while impersonating a medical practitioner, Dr Harry Cecil Rutherford Darling, he was sentenced to 10 years in prison. His age was given as 72.

JOHN GEORGE GIBSON

Gibson was named as Jack the Ripper by Robert Graysmith author of the Zodiac, in the (1999) book: The Bell Tower. Graysmith makes the claim that Theo Durrant, a 24-year old Sunday school teacher, who was executed for the murder of two women, Blanch Lamont 18, and Minnie Williams 21, in San Francisco's Emmanuel Baptist Church, in 1895 was, in fact, innocent of the crime and that the real culprit was John George Gibson, the church pastor. Durrant who was studying to be a doctor, was described as Intelligent, hard-working and generous, and was highly regarded by everyone who knew him. He often worked about the church, fixing pews, plastering cracks in walls, and sealing leaky pipes. Graysmith in his book states that Gibson was also responsible for the Whitechapel murders, and had an assistant Jesse Gibson (no relation). Graysmith claims Gibson was unable to give the precise date when he arrived in New York, so might have been in London when the Ripper murders occurred, and left shortly after. Graysmith also adds that Gibson preferred to be called Jack, and matched the suspect description of witness Mary Ann Cox. Cox, who lived at 5 Miller's Court, had known Kelly for about nine months. At around 11:45 pm. She saw Kelly in the company of a man she later described as 36 years of age, 5 ft 5 inches tall, stout, build with a fresh complexion but blotches on his face. He had a thick carroty moustache and was dressed in dark clothes and a black billy-cock (derby) hat. He was carrying a quart can of beer. At the time of the Whitechapel murders, Gibson was 29 years of age, 5 ft 9 inches tall, fair-haired with a small sandy moustache, well-built

183

and broad shouldered. Described as nervous, easily excited, eccentric, and extremely effeminate both in speech and manner, unmarried, though popular with the women in his parish. He preferred dealing with women in groups and went out of his way to avoid spending time with them individually. It was said he did not handle adversity well, and tended to fall apart when things did not run smoothly. When the newspapers reported the murders of Lamont, and Williams, Gibson almost suffered a nervous breaking. Gibson's peculiar behaviour after the tragedy caused some to view him with suspicion and believe he may have been guilty of the crime himself or as an accomplice of Durrant. Many believed a terrible mistake had been made with the arrest of Durrant, who was described as a quite and nice boy. When the mutilated body of Minnie Williams was discovered in the library, Gibson was asked to assist. Before doing so Gibson enquired "Is the clothing, er disarranged? Are the limbs exposed?" Instead of immediately contacting the police, he locked the church door, and went to the Golden Gate Undertaking Company. "Someone has died at the Emmanual Baptist Church". Gibson said, "And we need to have the body removed please do not tell anyone about this as it will disturb the congregation". "The Undertaker asked was it a sudden death? "No, I shouldn't think so," was Gibson's response. Gibson hid away from reporters and refused to answer any questions. Gibson sent a telegram to a young man he had known for some time, 19 year old Robert Newton Lynch, asking him to become his personal secretary and press spokesman. Lynch accepted. They had been intimate friends despite the 20 year age gap. From that moment Lynch When the second body of Blance Lamont was discovered in the belfry of the Church, police inquires revealed she was last seen in the company of a young man Theo Durrant. He was arrested, charged and executed for the crime. The brutality of the murders led people to believe that

184

Durrant dubbed "The Demon of the Belfry" was also responsible for the Ripper murders.

John George Gibson was born in Edinburgh, Scotland on 14 August 1859, and educated at Spurgeon's College, London. Pastor of St Andrews Baptist Church, South Street, St Andrews, Scotland from 1881-87. Emigrated to America, December 1888. Pastor of San Francisco's Emmanuel Baptist Church from 1894, he delivered his first sermon on 11 November. According to the San Francisco News, Gibson confessed on his death-bed to Charlie Floyd, in the spring of 1912, that it was he, and not Theo Durrant, who murdered Blanch Lamont and Minnie Williams. Unfortunately, the person Gibson supposedly confessed to, Charlie Floyd, never actually existed and appears to be an amalgamation of several different people. There is no evidence Gibson was in London at the time of the Ripper murders. While Graysmith produces no evidence that Gibson was responsible for the Whitechapel murders, he also provides no evidence that Gibson perpetrated the murders in San Francisco's Baptist Church either, or that Theo Durrant was actually innocent of the crimes for which he was convicted. When Durrant climbed the scaffold on 7 January 1898 he was given an opportunity to speak, he began a long-winded ramble declaring his innocence, which showed no signs of abating, when he paused for breath, the hangman seized the opportunity and pulled the lever. According to San Francisco historian Herbert Asbury, Durrant was known to San Francisco prostitutes at the time for a strange fetish. "For a year or so during the early eighteen-nineties Durrant visited the brothels in San Francisco's Commercial Street several times a week. He always brought with him, in a sack or a small crate, a pigeon or a chicken, and at a certain time during the evening's debauch, he cut the bird's throat and let the blood trickle over his body."

185

WILLIAM GILBERT

On 3 August 1889, William Gilbert, described as a rough looking fellow, was charged at Marlborough Street Police Court, with being drunk and riotous in Piccadilly, at a quarter to one in the morning. Gilbert, who had drawn a large crowd around him, told several women that, he, was "Jack the Ripper," and it had frightened them greatly. On the way to the police station, he pulled out an old table knife. PC Sheppard, said, the prisoner called the women very bad names, and would not go away when told to so. Gilbert in his defence, said that he was not drunk. He had tramped from Watford, and when in Piccadilly that morning was cutting up some cigar ends when some women struck him on the back, and said, "What yer, old Jack the Ripper", at that moment a police constable took him into custody. Due to Gilbert's insistence he was not drunk, the case was adjourned, until the inspector, who took him into charge could testify to his drunken condition on Friday night, was present.

GEORGE ROBERT GISSING

English novelist, born in Wakefield, Yorkshire, 22 November 1857. The son of Thomas Waller Gissing, pharmaceutical chemist, and Margaret (née Bedford). He was educated at the Quaker boarding school of Alderley Edge, and at the age of fifteen, encouraged by his father, won a scholarship to Owens College, Manchester, where he was considered a star pupil destined for a brilliant academic career. He excelled in history, literature and art. His prospects were ruined, however, in 1875, when he was caught stealing money from the student's cloakroom. The money was for Marianne Helen "Nell" Harrison, a young prostitute with whom he had become infatuated and attempted to reform. Gissing was expelled, found guilty and sentenced to one month's hard labour in Bellevue Prison

Manchester. Ashamed, and humiliated, he went to America and attempted to support himself teaching, and writing articles for a Chicago newspaper. Friendless and penniless, he returned to London in October 1877 and two years later, 27 October 1879, entered into a doomed marriage with Nell. The marriage was unhappy and lasted only five years. His wife being a drunkard, who intermittently returned to prostitution. Eventually, he paid her to live apart from him, which she did, and she died at the age of 30 from drink (and possibly venereal disease) 29 February 1888 in Lambeth. Gissing's first novel Workers in the Dawn was self-published in 1880 and was paid for by a small legacy left him. The book, a naturalistic study of the most desperate levels of poverty-stricken London life was semi-autobiographical (an idealistic young man tries to save an alcoholic prostitute) and was a complete failure, selling less than 50 copies in the first six months of publication. Gissing never knew neither wide fame nor prosperity and was compelled to sell the copyright for most of his novels outright to publishers, which meant that even his occasional successes were often financially unrewarding. H. G. Wells once advised him to lighten his style in order to win a larger audience, but Gissing said: "Never have I tried to please the public." From 1884 he earned a modest and precarious living from his novels and tutoring work. He lived alone during this period and was often desperately lonely. The following exert is from (London and the Life of Literature in Late Victorian England the Diary of George Gissing 24 Jan 1893:

On my way home at night an anguish of suffering in the thought that I can never hope to have an intellectual companion at home. Condemned for ever to associate with inferiors and so crassly unintelligent. Never a word exchanged on anything but the paltry everyday life of the household. Never a word to me, from. anyone, of understanding, sympathy or of encouragement.

He had few literary associates, or friends of any kind, and spent punishing hours every day at his desk. With loneliness slowly killing him, desperate for company he went for a walk and addressed the first female he saw, Edith Alice Underwood, of Camden Town, an uneducated stonemason's daughter. They were engaged within a fortnight, and married 25 February 1891 and moved to Exeter. They had two children, Walter Leonard, and Alfred Charles. The move to Exeter was Gissing's plan for a deliberate exile from the metropolitan literary world. Gissing was convinced that, Edith, was "so gentle and pliable that, once she had got used to country life and been trained out of her working-class accent, she would make an ideal wife." Once again, this marriage was not a happy one. Gissing refused to be seen in public with his wife, or invite people to his home. They returned to London in 1893 and after many fearsome scenes, Gissing parted from his family, in 1897. Edith was a violent and mentally unstable woman, who was committed first to Hoxton Asylum in 1902, and later to Dorset County Asylum in Dorchester, where she remained until her death from organic brain failure in 1917, at the age of 50. For the first time, he acquired literary and educated acquaintances, including H.G Wells, whom he met in 1897, and became a close friend. Wells said:

Gissing was no longer the glorious, indefatigable, impracticable youth of the London flat, but a damaged and ailing man, full of ill-advised precautions against the imaginary illnesses that were his interpretations of a general malaise.

In the (1963) book: 'George Gissing: A Critical Biography,' Jacob Borg remarked:

In later years when he became intimate with H. G. Wells and his wife, Gissing had told them flatly that he could not invite them to his home. "Impossible," he is quoted as saying, "quite impossible." I have to dismiss any such ideas. I have no home.

Misery seemed to feed Gissing's genius, and the prevailing tone of his novels during the mid-1890 is that of the struggling life of the shabby-genteel, and the conflict between education and circumstances. His themes were struggling authors and their financial and marital difficulties, his masterpiece novel was New Grub Street, written in 1891. Gissing gives the reader a unique insight into the world of the Victorian hack-writer, and creates a protagonist Edward Reardon, a gifted scholar, Reardon must decide between writing long-form literary novels to satisfy his soul or "selling out" and writing shorter commercial fiction to provide for his wife and child. Reardon finds some initial success in writing fiction. He gives up his job as a clerk and spends most of his earnings from writing on a European trip. He then marries the socially ambitious Amy Yule, who is dazzled by his apparent literary talent. Under pressure to produce, and unwilling to compromise his artistic ideals to meet the demands of the market, he struggles. Eventually, both Reardon's health and his marriage collapse. Like much of Gissing's work, his depiction of Reardon betrays a degree of self-portraiture. Gissing made no attempt at popular writing and for a long time, the sincerity of his work was only appreciated by a limited public. Diagnosed as suffering from emphysema, he moved restlessly from place to place as a semi-invalid, always sure that happiness was to be found elsewhere. On his return to England in July 1898 he rented a house in Dorking and was introduced to young author Gabrielle Marie Edith Fleury at the home of H G Wells. Later she and Gissing became partners in a common-law marriage at a ceremony in France. The marriage was kept secret from his wife Edith who had refused him a divorce. They moved to France. First to Paris, then later to Ispoure near Saint-Jean-Pied-de-Port. Gissing

189

returned only briefly back to England on the advice of his doctor for a six-week stay in a sanatorium in Suffolk, his emphysema had caused his health to decline. Gissing died at the age of 46, on 28 December 1903, of double pneumonia. He is buried in the English cemetery at Saint-Jean-de-Luz. His disastrous marriage to a prostitute, plus the fact that some of his novels were considered rather gloomy, has led some to speculate that he may have been Jack the Ripper. However, this is highly unlikely as he left for France and Italy on 16 September 1888, and was still there during the period that the later Ripper murders occurred. The first occurrence in print of Gissing's involvement in the Ripper murders appeared in Richard Whittington-Egan's (1975) book: A Casebook on Jack the Ripper. The original source is believed to be Pat Pitman.

WILLIAM EWART GLADSTONE

William Ewart Gladstone was born on 29 December 1809 at 62 Rodney Street, Liverpool. He was the fourth son, and fifth child, of a family of six, born to Sir John Gladstone (1764-1851) a sugar plantation owner, and Anne Mackenzie (née Robertson). William was educated at Eton 1821-1827 and Christ Church, Oxford 1828-1831. He initially favoured a career in the church; however, his father persuaded him that he could do as much good in politics. He entered parliament as the Tory MP for Newark in December 1832 and in his maiden speech defended his father against allegations that he had mistreated his slaves on their West Indian plantation. He married Catherine Glynne, the daughter of Welsh landowner and Conservative politician Sir Stephen Glynne (1807-1874) and they had eight children, four boys and four girls. Appointed Vice President of the Board of Trade in 1841, and later President of the Board of Trade in 1843. When the Tory Party broke apart in 1846, Gladstone, now believing strongly in free trade, followed Peel in becoming a Liberal-Conservative. He returned to Parliament in 1847 as MP for Oxford University, having lost his Newark seat, and in 1853 was appointed Chancellor of the Exchequer in Lord Aberdeen's coalition government. As Chancellor, Gladstone abolished many tariffs and lowered others; one of his first acts was to order the Foreign Office to stop using large thick sheets of double notepaper when thinner sheets would do. He also reduced income tax, though the costs of the Crimean War forced him to raise it again. He was Chancellor again under Palmerston, between 1859- 1865, and again under Russell 1865-66. Four times Prime Minister 1868-74, 1880-85, February-July 1886, 1892-94, his total time as Prime Minister was 12 years and 126 days. Gladstone was both the oldest ever person to form a government – aged 82 at his appointment – and the oldest person ever to occupy the Premiership – being aged 84 at his resignation. Nicknamed "Grand Old Man," he was still in the House of Commons as late as 1895 at the age of 86. As Prime Minister, he was an active legislator and reformer, his government passed the Education Act 1870 that established school boards and made elementary education compulsory for children between the ages of five and thirteen. In 1873 he passed laws restructuring the High Courts. In later years his ministry became dominated by Irish affairs, a supporter of home rule for Ireland the Irish home rule bill-1892, which he had first championed in 1886 never made it through the House of Lords, he resigned as a result and left office in 1894 ending a long political career. More than most parliamentarians of the time he proved an ability to connect with the Victorian working classes. Famous for his spirited debates with Disraeli, there no friendship between them throughout their long political lives. He also endured a frosty relationship with Queen Victoria; the Queen once famously

191

remarked: *"He speaks to me as if I was a public meeting."* Physical relations with his wife appeared to have ceased after she had conceived nine times in fifteen years, he relieved his sexual frustration by tree-felling on his estate. Gladstone in his attempts at fighting the social evil of prostitution would invite prostitutes home for tea, in the hope of persuading them to change their ways. Gladstone recorded in his diaries that he found himself having to risk sexual temptation. He began to flagellate himself as a punishment after his encounters with prostitutes. This practice caused him much ridicule and the risk of possible scandal throughout his political career. Some writers have suggested that he took this reforming zeal a little further than he perhaps should, and was, in fact, Jack the Ripper. In 1888 at the time of the Whitechapel murders, Gladstone was 78-years-old and half-blind from an unsuccessful cataract operation. Gladstone died from cancer at the age of 88 on 19 May 1898 at Hawarden Castle, Flint, and is buried in Westminster Abbey.

JAMES GLEN

James Glen, 29 years of age, a cabinet maker, described as a quite-looking man, of small stature, about 5ft 6 inches in height, with a small dark moustache. Was charged with having on the 10 or 11 November 1889, in his house at 245 High Street, Glasgow, known locally as "the Green Close", murdered his wife, Elizabeth, (née Clinton) by beating, cutting, and stabbing her. He had been married about six years, and had three young children. (Some newspaper accounts state four children). Elizabeth was described as a sober, industrious woman, stoutly built, about 5ft 4 inches in height, and 30 years of age. At eleven o'clock the neighbours distinctly heard screams and cries of "murder!" as this was an everyday occurrence in Green Close, one of the poorer districts of the city no one paid any attention. Shortly after Glen came out of the house in an excited state, and said to one of his neighbours that he "Had done for her now." He went to visit his father, James Glen, at 26 Duke Street, Glasgow, and the two proceeded to Dr Chalmers house in George Street. He had previously visited his father in one of his mad fits, and was taken to the doctor and given some medicine, which had soothed him when in a similar state. Glen told the Dr, he had done something to his wife, the Dr, went into the street, whistled and summonsed two policemen. Glen was taken into custody. The police on reaching the small apartment, discovered the fearfully mutilated body of Elizabeth. They were forty wounds upon it, the most serious, injuries being upon the neck and abdomen, through which the bowels protruded. The neck had evidently been mutilated with a hatchet, which was found near the body, covered in blood, with pieces of hair still attached. Two bloody knives were also found. One a white handled pocket knife, the other a table knife. She was wearing only a chemise and stockings. When questioned by the newspapers, neighbours said the couple lived happily enough together. Mary Hoey, the next door neighbour at 245 High Street, said Glen and his wife did not quarrel. On the night of the murder she heard something being pulled up and down the house, then a heavy fall, then Mrs Glen squealing, it went quiet after that. Another neighbour Patrick Rocke, heard fearful wild cries by Glen, the likes of which he had never heard before. The prisoner's father, said his son had been delicate for the past 12 months, and always complained of pain through his body. He suffered from delusions, one such delusion was that his wife was trying to poison his beef-tea. He offered the tea to his wife and the cat, both refused. He said he had frequently killed fellow-workmen, and hid them in boxes. He was under the delusion that he was "Jack the Ripper" and other murderers. Dr J. F. Sutherland, kept Glen under observation, and prepared a report

193

on his mental condition, the conclusion he arrived at initially was at the time of the commission of the murder, he was of unsound mind. His opinion now is that Glen is sound of mind. His symptoms and past history seemed to point to delirium tremens as the cause of his mental state. The plea of not guilty, was supplemented by one of insanity. Glen was found guilty of murder while insane, and detained at her majesty's pleasure.

BENJAMIN GRAHAM

Benjamin Graham, a 42-year old glass-blower, of Fletcher's Row, Clerkenwell, was arrested on the 17 October 1888 and taken to Snow Hill Police Station, after confessing to the Whitechapel murders while drunk. A doctor's certificate was produced which showed the defendant had suffered from excessive drinking, though no trace of insanity. The police said that his foolish conduct had caused them a great amount of trouble and was sorry that they could not punish the prisoner in some way. He was later released.

Graham was born in Great Yarmouth, Norfolk, in April 1848. Son of Richard Graham, a carpenter, and his wife Jane. Benjamin married Susannah Rose 10 December 1871, they had five children. In the 1881 census, they lived at 1 Tysoe Street, Clerkenwell, Holborn. He is still in occupation as a glassblower in the 1891, and 1901 census. On 17 October 1888, he was admitted to the Homerton Workhouse, his previous address was given as 14 Fletcher's Row. He died January 1909, in London, at the age of 60. His wife died in 1914.

WILLIAM GRANT

Grant was apprehended by PC Frazer 352H about 2 am on 16 February 1895 in the Spitalfields area, after he had inflicted a 1½ inch wound on prostitute Alice Graham's abdomen, after a quarrel over the price of her services. The newspapers gave further details of the attack:

Alice Graham later testified: "That she had never encountered the man before seeing him in a public house on Tenter-ground, Spitalfields, on the evening of Saturday the 9 February 1895 where, she stated, he was treating women.."At 10 o'clock that night she encountered him again, on one of the Spitalfields Streets, and this time he approached her and spoke to her. They went to a public-house, and from there to two others in turn. It was while on the way to a coffee-house in White's-row that prisoner dragged her down "some yard," as she described it, threw her on the ground, and ripped her in the stomach. She was quite sober, she asserted, and although prisoner had been drinking he was not drunk. She struggled and resisted, and he cut her. She did not see the knife, but she felt it inside her. At first, she thought she was only scratched, but by the time she had got up and walked a little she found the blood flowing and presently sank down. Then she got a "swimming," and scarcely remembered any more till she was at the station Her wound caused by a pocket–knife with a sharp-pointed blade was considered serious, though not life-threatening. Grant told the police that she was being extortionate. Sentenced to ten years imprisonment, he was released in 1902 after serving seven. The newspapers immediately seized upon the fact that a prostitute had been attacked in Whitechapel with a knife and began the inevitable speculation that Grant might be Jack the Ripper. Police checks were made to ascertain his whereabouts in 1888.

An Australian newspaper, The Port Philip Herald 12 February 1895 reported:

JACK THE RIPPER CAUGHT RED HANDED

195

A notorious assassin seized by the police while mutilating a woman, the police confident. The London police are of the opinion that at last they have got safely under lock and key the long sought after assassin known as Jack the Ripper, whose series of atrocious murders and mutilations, principally at Whitechapel, extended over a period of years. At an early hour, about 2 o'clock this morning, a quick succession of piercing screams were heard by Constables on duty in Butler's Street, Spitalfields, and several of them ran at once to the spot whence the sounds proceeded. The first Constable arrived just in time to catch a dark stalwart looking man stooping over a young woman, who was lying on the pavement and struggling for her life. Armed with a long knife, the man was cutting and hacking at the unfortunate woman in merciless fashion. The assassin was smartly seized and disarmed, and on being taken to the police station gave the name of Grant and his occupation as a ship's fireman. The woman, who was terribly wounded and is not likely to recover, is of the unfortunate class.

His own solicitor, Mr George Kebbel, let it be known that Grant had admitted he was Jack the Ripper but believed Grant had died in prison. In a letter to the Pall Mall Gazette, Kebbell wrote:

In reply to claims in Sir Robert Anderson's memoirs that Jack the Ripper was a Polish Jew, the Ripper was not a Jew, but an Irishman, educated for the medical profession, and for reasons not known disowned by his relatives. This man was caught in the very act, in an alley in Spitalfields.

In 1910 theorist L Forbes Winslow issued a denial of this claim, agreeing with Mr Kebbel that Grant had trained as a medical student and had sunk to the position of fireman on a cattle boat, but knew Grant could not be Jack the Ripper, as he did not fit with

196

what perceived evidence he had discovered about G. Wentworth Bell Smith, who was his favoured Ripper candidate.

William Grant was born in Cork, Ireland. The exact date is unknown, various newspapers and census records claim a date of 1860, 1861, and 1865, his Banstead Asylum records, named him as William Granger described him as widowed, and give a date of birth of 1865. In 1883 he joined the Cork City Artillery but was dismissed in 1889 as being of bad character. He spent the next few years wandering back and forth between workhouses in Cork and London, it is claimed that while he was in London, he frequented the company of loose women, and was frequently stripped, robbed and cheated by them. In February 1891 he spent a month at Banstead Asylum, Surrey, and also spent time in prison for drunkenness. At the time of his arrest, he said he was working as a fireman on a cattle boat, though could not identify any ship he had served on. A story appeared in the Pall Mall Gazette dated 7 May 1895, which reported that Grant had been unhesitatingly identified by the one person whom the police believe, saw the murderer with a woman a few moments before her mutilated body was found. If this witness was Joseph Lawende, he told the police in his original statement that he had only noticed the man's height, and did not think he would recognise him again. It is, therefore, curious as to why he was expected to positively identify the suspect seven years later. Grant was described as 5 ft 9½ inches tall, gaunt looking with a slim build, grey or blue eyes, pale complexion, a black moustache, scars on his cheek and neck, and several tattoos of dancing girls, anchors and crowns, and dots on his arms and hands. Grant, in his favour as a Ripper suspect, possibly had some medical training, he did attack a prostitute with a knife and may have held a grudge against them on account of him being frequently robbed and cheated by them. Grant's whereabouts are

197

unaccounted for at the time of each of the Whitechapel murders. Against him being the Ripper, is the gap of almost seven years between the last canonical Ripper murder, Mary Kelly, in November 1888, and the attack on Alice Graham in February 1895. The time gap shortens if you believe Frances Coles murdered 13 February 1891, was a Ripper victim. Graham was also allowed to scream out, which differed from the method of attack by Jack the Ripper. There is no record of Grant being investigated or suspected at the time of the Ripper murders. It is not known if Grant was in London in 1888, he may well have been in Cork. He was admitted to the City Road Workhouse 22 December 1891. The Stepney Workhouse 14 October 1894. In the 1901 census, he was listed as a convict in Parkhurst Prison on the Isle of Wight. Grant was admitted from the infirmary to the Hackney Workhouse 15 December 1902, his date of birth is listed as 1860, and his occupation is given as ship's fireman. He was admitted to The City Road Workhouse 26 December 1902. The Poplar Union Workhouse 24 September 1904. And the Fulham Road Workhouse 20 December 1913 aged 53. He was discharged 23 February 1914.

ALFRED GRAY

In 1889, in Tunis, Alfred Gray, an English vagrant, was arrested along with a band of Tunisian robbers, and assassins, on a charge of murder, similar in manner to the recent Whitechapel crimes. He was briefly suspected of being Jack the Ripper, when he revealed he came from Whitechapel. He lived with an Italian woman and was said to extraordinarily resemble the description of the Whitechapel murderer that had been published in the newspapers. His height and age, as well as his moustache and hat, correspond with the description given. A box in his possession was searched and a razor was discovered amongst

198

his clothing. While being interviewed by the police a tattoo was noticed on his chest and back of different emblems. Both his arms were also tattooed, one bearing the figure of a naked woman. The other representations of guns and ropes, with the letters "M and P" which he declares, stood for Mary and Polly two women whom he formally knew. Gray it was stated was 24 years of age at the time of his arrest. The first Ripper victim was Mary Ann Nichols known as "Polly." The last Ripper victim was Mary Kelly. The prevailing theory at Scotland Yard is, Gray facing serious charges in Tunis, attempted to implicate himself into the Ripper investigation, in the hope he would be brought back to London, where it shall be discovered that he is neither "Jack the Ripper" nor any other criminal wanted by the London police. Gray was sentenced to three months' imprisonment as a vagrant. His real name was Boxall, he deserted from the 3rd Battalion, Rifle Brigade in 1887, he was arrested and went abroad with his regiment the same year, and it is surmised that he deserted again.

JAMES GREEN

Green was mentioned as a possible Ripper suspect after a link was spotted between James Green, who washed the blood from the street after the murder of Mary Ann Nichols, and James Green who appeared at the inquest of Annie Chapman. Unfortunately, these were two different men. The first, James Green, who washed the blood from the street, after the body was removed, was the son of Emma Green, and lived at New Cottage 2 Bucks Row. On the night Mary Ann Nichols was murdered, he went to bed at 9.45 pm. He slept in the back room which he shared with his brother who had gone to bed at 9 pm. His mother, had gone to bed at 11 pm in the upstairs front room with her daughter who occupied the same room. She had slept through till

199

4 am when a knock on the front door, woke them up. She opened the window and saw three or four constables and two or three other men. She saw the body of the deceased lying on the ground, but it was still too dark to clearly distinguish exactly what had happened. Her bedroom window was barely 20 feet from the murder scene, yet Mrs Green who was a light sleeper heard nothing unusual, such a noise as a scream would be sure to wake her.

The second, James Green, who attended the inquest of Annie Chapman, lived at 36 Acton Street, Burdett-road, Poplar. He worked for John and Thomas Bayley packing case manufacturers, located at 23a Hanbury-street. Green had arrived at work about ten minutes past 6, when an elderly man named John Davis, came out of his house at 29 Hanbury-street, and said, "Men, come here." Green accompanied James Kent, whom he worked with, to the back of number 29, where they saw a woman lying in the yard by the side of the steps. Green, then left the premises with Kent. He did not see anyone touch the body, or enter the yard until Inspector Chandler arrived. At the inquest, Green was described as of medium height with short neatly plastered down hair.

WILLIAM GRIFFITHS

William Griffiths was charged at Dalston Police-Court Hackney, London, with being drunk and disorderly. The incident occurred in Essex Road at about one o'clock on the morning on 10 October 1888. Police Constable 200J, stated that he was on duty in Essex Road when the prisoner, Griffiths, came up to him and said, "I want to be taken to the police station. If you do not take me, I shall murder somebody tonight. I am Jack the Ripper." He then produced a large pocket knife, which he attempted to open. The Constable then told the man to go home. Griffiths then entered a public house, and on leaving fell down. Finding the man to be drunk the Constable, with assistance, took him to the police station. Griffiths apologised for his actions, saying, "It was a drunken freak, and that he had no intention of injuring anyone." The Magistrate passed judgement, saying, "It was a very foolish act," and concluding that the prisoner must find one surety in £5, to keep the peace for three months or go to prison for twenty-one days. Griffiths, a general dealer, lived at 1 Mildmay Avenue, Islington, and was described as young and wearing a velvet cord suit.

PETER GULAURA

On 25 October 1888, at the Borough Police Court, North Shields. Peter Gulaura, described as a tramp, belonging to the West Indies, was charged by Sergeant Charlton with being drunk and disorderly in Frost Street, Tynemouth. The officer stated that when taken into custody, the defendant had in his possession a lady's waterproof mantle and a boy's overcoat. He had the mantle wrapped round his head, and was shouting and making a great deal of noise. He was being followed by a group of boys shouting "Jack the Ripper." The defendant denied being drunk, and complained of the boys shouting after him "Jack the Ripper." He was fined 2s 6d and costs or in default go to prison for seven days. Inquiries would be made with regard to ownership of the mantle and overcoat.

DR WILLIAM WITHEY GULL

Gull was first mentioned as a possible Ripper suspect by Dr Thomas Stowell in the November 1970 issue of the Criminologist, and again in 1973 by Joseph Gorman Sickert in the BBC drama-documentary Jack the Ripper. Authors, Stephen Knight in the

(1976) book: The Final Solution, and Melvyn Fairclough in the (1991) book: The Ripper and the Royals, also suspected Gull.

In one story which implicates William Gull as the Ripper the medium R.J Lees, having had a psychic impression of the murderer, follows a psychic trail throughout the night, which leads him and the police, to the home of an eminent physician. The physician had trained at Guys Hospital, was married with a son, and when questioned admitted that he suffered from an occasional loss of memory and had once come round to find blood on his shirt. Proof of his guilt as Jack the Ripper was found in the house, and he was committed to an asylum under the name Thomas Mason 124.

A second, alternative scenario which implicates Gull has him involved in a plot to silence five prostitutes, led by Mary Kelly, who were attempting to blackmail the government with their knowledge of the secret marriage between Prince Albert Victor and commoner Annie Elizabeth Crook.

William Withey Gull was born aboard the barge "The Dove" which was moored St Osyth Mill, in St Leonard, Colchester, on 31 December 1816 and was the youngest of eight children, two of whom died in infancy. His father, John Gull, (1778-1827) was a barge owner, and wharfinger who died of cholera. His mother, Elizabeth (née Chilver) raised the six children to the best of her abilities and taught them the old adage that, "If something is worth doing, it is worth doing well." The children were given a strict Christian upbringing, and in 1832 moved to Thorpe near Thorpe-Le-Soken. Young, William made up his mind to enter medicine, and in 1837 entered Guy's hospital as a pupil, determined to succeed. He graduated with a BA in medicine at the University of London in 1841, obtaining honours in physiology and comparative anatomy in surgery and medicine. In 1843 he was appointed lecturer on natural philosophy at Guy's hospital. In 1848 he married Susan Ann Dacre Lacy, daughter of Colonel J. Dacre Lacy, of Carlisle. They had three children, a daughter Caroline, a son Cameron, who died in infancy, and a son William Cameron. In 1871 he treated the Prince of Wales for typhus and was created a Baronet the following year, and appointed the Prince's regular physician. He later became the physician in ordinary to Queen Victoria. It was said of Gull that he was a man of firm and outspoken views, and could be blunt to the point of rudeness, to one patient he replied when asked if there was any hope, "There is very little life left in you, in fact, you are heart dead now." Gull while walking at his home in Scotland, suffered a minor stroke in the autumn of 1887, which left him slightly paralysed on the right side. Over the next couple of years, he suffered three further epileptiform attacks, and a further two strokes. Friends who visited him said they noticed little difference in his looks and manner. Gull, however, claimed that he felt like a different man and gave up his practice. He died at the age of 73 on 29 January 1890. His death certificate was signed by his son-in-law, Dr Theodore Dyke Acland. Unethical though not illegal behaviour. William Gull lived at 74 Brook Street, Grosvenor Square, and was 71 years of age at the time of the Whitechapel murders. He was buried at Thorpe-le-Soken. In his will he left the not inconsiderable sum of £344,022 19s 7d.

ELIZABETH HALLIDAY

Born Eliza Margaret McNally, in 1864, in County Antrim, Northern Ireland. Known as "Lizzie Brown." Over a 14 year period, she married six times. She married Charles Hopkins, also known as "Ketspool" Brown in 1879. He died 2 years later. Shortly after she marries pensioner Artemus Brewer, after less than a year of marriage, he was also dead. She next marries veteran George

Smith. After her attempts to murder him with a cup of poisoned tea fails, she flees, to Vermont. She then marries Charles Playstel, despite still being legally married to George Smith, the marriage would last only two weeks. Lizzie, turns up next in Philadelphia, and stays with the McQuillan family, her parent's former neighbours in County Antrim. She opened a small shop, which she quickly burnt to the ground for the insurance money. Arrested she served two years in prison for that crime. After her release from prison, she headed for Newburgh in Orange County, where she met Mr Paul Halliday, a 70-year old widower, whom she would later marry, despite being 40 years his junior. She had initially worked for him as a housekeeper. It was said he married her purely to save paying her wages. Lizzie unfortunately, suffered from a mania, and when seized by this mania committed a succession of crimes. First, she burnt down the house of Mr Halliday, then the barn, finally the old mill, killing Mr Halliday's half-witted son in the process. She then went on to kill and mutilate Mr Halliday. She also shot and killed Margaret J. McQuillan and her daughter Sarah J. McQuillan, on 30 August and 2 September, and hid their bodies under a pile of manure. The murders occurred in the Shawangunk Mountains, in the hamlet of Burlingham in Walker Valley. Halliday gave an interview in the "World" on 5 November, in which she revealed that she was 28-years old, had been married six times and had been drugged by a gang of people she knew, but could not identify in fear for her life. Also, that they had forced her to witness the killings of her husband and the McQuillan women. For a long time after her arrival, at the Sullivan County jail she refused to eat, and it became necessary for the jail physician to force liquid food through her nostrils, the Times reported:

In November, she tried to strangle the Sheriff's wife. A few days later, she set fire to her bedclothes. In December she tried to hang herself with the binding torn from the bottom of her dress. On December 15, she came near ending her life by gashing her throat and arms in a terrible manner with glass broken from her cell window. For the last three months it has been necessary to keep her chained to the floor.

The reporter was able to confirm all six of Halliday's marriages. While awaiting trial, Lizzie was linked to the Ripper murders by Sullivan County Sheriff Harrison Beecher. The Marion Daily Star 19 December 1893 reported:

Recent investigation shows that Mrs Halliday is in all probability connected to the Whitechapel murders, for it has been proved that she was in Europe at the time of the murders, and often refers to the murders when she is in possession of her mental faculties, and when she is "raving." Mrs Halliday constantly speaks of the murders. Sheriff Harrison Beecher, who is in charge of the Sullivan County jail, in Monticello, New York, where Mrs Halliday, the murderess, is held, said to Mrs Halliday, "You are accused of the Whitechapel murders, are you guilty," to which she replied: "Do they think I am an Elephant that was done by a man."

Monticello, N. Y., Sheriff Harrison Beecher, whose name is familiar to the readers of newspapers in connection with his office as Sheriff of Sullivan County during the trial of Lizzie Halliday, the triple murderess, is suffering severe pain from a swollen hand, the result of a bite from that notorious prisoner. The case of a peculiar one, inasmuch as nearly two months have elapsed since it occurred. On June 27, as the Sheriff was taking her from the courtroom after the sentence had been pronounced by Judge Edward she turned upon him with tigress ferocity and planted her teeth in his hand. Anticipating an attack of a similar nature, the Sheriff had provided himself with gloves, which he wore all the time. The teeth entered the glove and produced abrasion of the akin, but nothing was thought of it at the time. Three or four weeks since the scratch began to itch and burn. A few nights ago the Sheriff was awakened by a severe pain in the injured member, since then he has suffered acutely and now the swelling is extending toward the elbow. Should it continue to swell, it is thought that it will result in the loss of the arm.

Convicted of first-degree murder, she was sentenced to die by electrocution, though this was later commuted to life imprisonment, on account of her insanity. She ended her days in Matteawan State Hospital for the Criminally Insane, though not uneventfully as the following reports show:

Aug. 30, 1895: attempt to strangle Catherine "Kate" Ward, attendant at the Matteawan State Asylum.

Matteawan, N. Y Oct. 17, 1906- Mrs. Lizzie Halliday, upon whose head rests the guilt of slaying six men and women, added a seventh victim to her list the other day in the Hospital For Insane Criminals at Matteawan, N. Y., when she stabbed her nurse, Miss Nellie Wicks to death.

For ten years this strange and diabolical woman, once a gypsy queen, led a career of murder, theft, and arson, but of all her crimes this was perhaps the most fiendish.

Miss Wicks, a graceful and pretty young woman, had been in the asylum is nurse a little more than a year. Mrs. Halliday manifested for her a peculiar fondness. The girl, touched by the woman's apparent affection, did all in her power for the unfortunate creature.

Lizzie Halliday had no object, so far as could ever be learned, for the previous murders she had committed. For this one she had a reason. Miss Wicks was going away from the asylum. She had arranged to take a course at the New York hospital to fit her as a trained nurse, and Mrs. Halliday, in her insane affection, had determined that the girl should not go.

A peculiar feature of the tragedy is that for days Mrs. Halliday, wandering about the "harmless ward," a room 40 by 60 feet in size, had been whispering threats against Miss Wicks to the other patients. These threats came to the ears of the superintendent, but he did not think them serious.

Miss Wicks had the utmost faith in the crazed Lizzie Halliday. She felt sure the woman had a genuine affection for her and that she would not harm her. Passing through the ward, she nodded kindly to Mrs. Halliday and others of the inmates. She did not see that the woman was following her noiselessly.

Miss Wicks unlocked a door leading to a retiring room and entered. With a quick spring Mrs. Halliday was beside her, wrenched the keys from her and locked the door on the inside. Before a word could be uttered by Miss Wicks the maniac sprang at her and bore her to the floor. The nurse fell face downward, and the woman fell astride her shoulders as she reached down and plucked away a pair of small scissors that were banging at Miss Wicks' girdle.

With these she began stabbing her victim to death. In all she inflicted more than 200 wounds on the face and body of the girl, and yet she struck no vital part, and the suffering victim lived until by purest accident rescue came, but too late to save her life.

It was fully fifteen minutes after Miss Wicks had entered the retiring room when Miss Mary Doyle, another nurse, found the door locked. She listened at the keyhole and heard groans and chuckles and muttered words. Looking about the ward, she missed Mrs. Halliday, and, suspecting that something was wrong, she called Dr. Bearn, an intern.

The doctor tried to open the door with his own key, found there was a key in the lock on the other side. With the aid of other attendants he tried to break down the door and, failing, went through a corridor and then through the linen room, which communicated by another door with the retiring room.

A fearful sight met his gaze. The nurse was still lying on the floor and upon her was seated Mrs. Halliday, still using the scissors with terrific effect. She was furious at being interfered with and fought the doctor and attendants with the utmost ferocity. It was not until she was felled to the floor that she gave up the battle. She was at once placed in solitary confinement, and the unconscious form of the nurse was hurried to the emergency ward, where all that was possible was done for her. But she lived only twenty minutes.

Lizzie Halliday, was 58 years of age when she died of chronic Bright's disease (kidney disease) at Matteawan State Asylum, 27 June 1918.

FRANK HALL

In October 1888, Sarah Brett, 53 years of age, of 66 Hornby-road, Camberwell, London, had been found in the gutter with her throat cut. She lived with her common law husband, 62 year old Carman Thomas Onley. On the 3 October, a sailor friend of her son, 19 year old Frank Hall, came to live with them. She gave him board and lodgings without payment, and treated him like her own son. On the 15 October, the three had been out drinking heavily, when they returned an altercation arose, the woman said, "We'll give Frank 10s if he'll get rid of me". Thomas retired to bed, to sleep off the drink, leaving Frank, alone with Sarah. The moment they were alone Frank, took a large carving knife from the table and cut the woman's throat. She rushed into the street where she staggered and fell. Inspector Taylor (P Division) and several constables arrived on the scene. He asked her who had done it, and she said "Frank the Sailor." In a back bedroom at No. 66, he found Hall lying on a bed with his trousers on, and endeavoured to arouse him. He appeared to be drunk. In the front bedroom, he found the other prisoner Onley, sitting on the side of the bed, also in a drunken state. Constable Bennett found a knife in the bed of Onley, and produced a large carving knife with wet blood upon the blade. Onley, and Hall were taken into custody. Hall appeared to be the more drunk of the two. On the way to the station Hall said he was "Jack the Ripper." and wanted to know if they thought he was the "Whitechapel bloke." Hall, had initially tried to pin the blame on Onley, by placing the knife on his bed. Onley, was later released without charge. Dr. Munyard who had a practise in Southampton Street, Camberwell, was called, and stated it to be a dangerous wound extending from ear to ear. Dr. Munyard said:

"The wound was about four to six inches long, none of the large vessels were severed; it was a clear cut wound such as might be caused by a knife; it was not dangerous in itself".

Sarah, remained in the workhouse infirmary till the 31 October. The jury found Frank Hall, Guilty of unlawfully wounding, he was sentenced to six months hard labour.

Thomas Onley was born in 1828, in Newington, Surrey. He died in 1897. Sarah, was born in 1835, in Stockbury, Kent. They had four children, two sons, William, born 1868, in Camberwell, and Thomas, born 1881, in Camberwell. And two daughters, Ada, born in Newington in 1869, and Henrietta, born 1875 in Camberwell

EDWARD HAMBLER

On Saturday 12 October 1889 Edward Hambler, a ship's joiner, aged 61 and described as respectably dressed, was charged at the Thames Police Court with disorderly conduct and been dressed in women's clothes. Inspector Arthur Ferrett, H Division, stated that on Sunday night he saw a crowd of some 600 people in Bromley Street, Ratcliff. He went to investigate and found Hambler being detained by two men. Hambler was dressed in female attire and was wearing a woman's hat, veil, black jacket, print, dress, two flannel petticoats and a large dress improver. Hambler was arrested and taken to the police station. It was revealed that the assembled crowd suspected that he was Jack the Ripper, and there was much excitement as a consequence, indeed if the police had not arrived, there was a very real danger that he would have been torn to pieces. Hambler, who gave no explanation for his strange behaviour, said only that it was a freak. Hambler was told that he had acted very foolishly, and much to the amusement of the court was told he did not make an attractive woman. Hambler was bound over to the sum of £10 and told to keep the peace for six months.

Inspector Arthur Ferrett, who arrested Hambler, was, born in 1844 in Coaley, Gloucestershire, England. In the 1911 census, he is a police pensioner aged 67, living at 3 Rose Hill Terrace, Larkhall, Bath, with his wife of 46 years, Harriett, Elizabeth.

THEOPHIL HANHART

On 21 December 1888, Constable Whitfield, was on duty in Dustan-row, which runs on to the bank of the Regent's canal, when he saw a man walking up and down in a strange manner. The constable asked him what he was doing there, the man replied, "I have a very bad mind about these affairs in

Whitechapel." Constable Whitfield asked him, "Did you do them?" the man replied, "Yes." Thereupon he was taken into custody. The man was Theophil Hanhart born in Switzerland in 1864 and was the son of a German pastor. At the time of the Whitechapel murders, he was a 24-year old French and German teacher at Rudloe College, near Bath. Hanhart was interviewed by Inspector Reid, who satisfied himself that Hanhart could not have committed the crimes. The Rev W. Mathias, stated that Hanhart, had been in his employment since 16 September that year. And had not been out of his sight until the night before last. Hanhart was certified as suffering from mental derangement and not fit to be at large. He was sent to the Shoreditch infirmary. The Sunday Times 23 December 1888 said: *The prisoner corresponded in description exactly with the man wanted in connection with the Whitechapel murders.* Hanhart was admitted to Bethnall Green, Lunatic Asylum 24 December 1888, till 29 December 1891. He was admitted to Hanwell Asylum 29 December 1891, he remained here till his death 11 July 1900 at the age of 35 years.

ROBERT HANSOM

At Jarrow, in the North-East of England a young man named Robert Hansom was charged with drunkenness. Hansom was shouting out to a crowd that he was the Whitechapel murderer while throwing a pocket knife about the street, which he claimed he committed the outrages with. When sober, however, he denied all knowledge of his conduct. He was fined 5s with costs.

JAMES HARDIMAN

In an article in True Detective December 2004 entitled: Jack A Knacker? Robert Hills put forward the name of James Hardiman as a possible Ripper suspect. Hills suggests that as all the victims were middle-aged, with the exception of Mary Kelly, who was more his wife's age, Hardiman was driven to murder by a hatred of mothers in general. He then proposes an alternative motive that Hardiman was avenging his daughter's death and that he suffered from pre-crime, stress, and may have contracted a venereal disease.

James Hardiman was born 8 October 1859, at 31 The High Street, Mile End New Town, London. The oldest son of Edward Hardiman a slipper maker and Harriet Sarah (née Stockton). In the 1861 census, the family is residing at 2 Well Street, Mile End New Town. In the 1871 census, the family is now living at 24 Preston Street, Mile End New Town. On 2 October 1876, at St Thomas, Church, Bethnal Green, 16-year old James Hardiman marries 17-year old Sarah Ann Scott. Sarah was born 25 February 1859 at Bishop Street, South Birmingham. In 1876 they are living at 1 Union Street, Bethnal Green. In I881 they are living at 29 Hanbury Street. In the 1881 census James Hardiman is a prisoner at Wandsworth Common. He served 12 months hard labour for stealing the sum of £45 and embezzling the sum of £5. It is noted he is 23 years of age, 5 ft 4 inches tall, with a fair complexion, light brown hair, and blue eyes. In 1885 James and Sarah, are now living at 38 Cudworth Street, Bethnal Green. In June 1887, they are living at 60 Corporation Row, Goswell St, Holborn. In July 1887, they are living at 20 Heneage Street, Brick Lane. A daughter Harriet Maria was born 9 June 1887. But dies aged 1-years old, 18 June 1888, from emaciation arising from nerve damage, caused by untreated congenital syphilis contracted from her mother. His wife dies at the age of 29 on the 13 September 1888, at the Royal London Hospital. Cause of death was Phthisis Pulmonalis (tuberculosis of the lungs with progressive wasting of the body) and exhaustion. Her education was noted as illiterate. In the 1891 census, he is listed as a widower, living with his mother, Harriet, and his younger brother

William. James Hardiman died 22 December 1891 at 29 Hanbury Street, from tuberculosis at the age of 32. His occupation was given as a Dealer in Horse Flesh; Cats Meat Dealer. (A cat's meat man sold meat for cats, not meat from cats). His education was listed as Illiterate. An anonymous alleged Ripper letter, which pre-dates the "Dear Boss" letter and is dated 24 September 1888 States:*"I am a horse slaughterer."*Another alleged Ripper letter is signed, "Joe the cat's meat man."

WILLIAM HARDIMAN

In an article for Ripperologist magazine, Stan Reid presents the case for William Hardiman as the Ripper. And cites the following, that Hardiman lived at 29 Hanbury Street, where Annie Chapman was murdered. He had some skill with a knife cutting up meat in the cat meat shop where he worked, and could easily explain away bloodstains on his person, and may have been the youth who attacked Emma Elizabeth Smith.

William Hardiman was born 14 April 1872 at 24 Preston Street, Mile End New Town, London. The youngest child of Edward Hardiman, a slipper, and shoe maker, and Harriet Sarah (née Stockton). The other children were Sarah 1857-1885. James 1859-1891. Harriet 1862-1915. Edward 1864-1939. Samuel 1867-1873. John 1869-1919. William was 16 years of age at the time of the Whitechapel murders and lived with his 50-year old mother, Harriet described as a well-proportioned woman, who sold cats meat (pieces of horseflesh unfit for human consumption on a skewer for a farthing or halfpenny) from the ground floor front room of 29 Hanbury Street. On the night of Annie Chapman's murder, she said: "she went to bed at half-past ten, slept very soundly and did not wake until about six the next morning." She was awoken by the sound of people tramping through the passage, and thinking there was a fire, sent her son to have a look. When he returned, he said, "Don't upset yourself mother, it's a woman been killed in the yard." Harriett said: "She heard nothing that night and that people often went through the passage of the house without her seeing who they were; she also said that to her knowledge she had never seen the deceased woman in her life before." At the inquest, Mrs Hardiman was described as, "Dressed in keeping with her position in life." William was the younger brother of fellow Ripper suspect, James Hardiman. In the 1881 census, William is aged 9 residing at 27 Hanbury Street. In the 1891 census aged 19, he is living at 29 Hanbury Street, his occupation is listed as Moulder in clay. In the 1901 census, he is listed as aged 29, unmarried lodging at 8 Morgan Street, Mile End Old Town, and his occupation has now changed to Metal Worker. He died 29 December 1905 at the Royal London Hospital, at the age of 33, after drinking Hydrochloride Acid. A verdict of suicide was given at the Inquest. His residence was 73 Cheshire Street, Bethnal Green. His mother Harriett Hardiman died in Hackney in 1910. Her brother Joseph Stockton 1835-1896, died in the London County Lunatic Asylum, Ilford.

PETER J HARPICK

Historian and true crime writer Jonathan Goodman, in the (1984) book: Who He, put forward a previously unknown candidate for the Ripper, Peter J. Harpick a transvestite sculptor innovative in the use of plasticine. The suspect was taken seriously and Goodman received a number of letters from Ripperologists asking for more information concerning Harpick. Goodman later revealed that he had in fact invented Peter J. Harpick and that the suspect's given name was, in fact, an anagram of Jack the Ripper. Goodman's intended purpose was to show how easy it is for Ripper writers to convince its readers into accepting the

214

validity of their suspect, while supplying little biographical detail, and even less in the way of actual evidence. Goodman had no wish to discover the identity of the Ripper, and treated the subject with mild disdain.

JOHN HARRIS

On 20 July, 1889, a man named John Harris, confessed to the Last murder, (Alice McKenzie), and appeared at Worship-street, charged with being drunk and disorderly in Commercial-street. The newspapers reported, him as "Sixty-four years of age, and so decrepit and miserable in appearance, that the notion of him killing a woman in such a manner was laughable. He had got a crowd around him, and shouted out he was the Shah. Earlier in the day, while drunk, he had been picked out of the Thames. Harris had many previous convictions for drunkenness. He was sentenced to 14 days hard labour.

JOHN HARVEY

On 14 September 1891, John Harvey, a 38 year old costermonger, of no fixed abode, was charged with being drunk and disorderly. PC Henry Smith, said that on Saturday night he saw the prisoner running like a madman along Kingsland, High street, shouting out that he was "Jack the Ripper". Harvey, was arrested and taken to the police station, where he was found to be very much the worse for drink. The prisoner said he remembered nothing of the incident, and was very sorry. He was fined 10s or in default of payment seven days imprisonment.

THE HAVENT RIPPER

A retired police officer, Gavin Maidment, senior assistant at Havant Museum, uncovered documents which connect the Ripper to the killing of 9 year old Percy Knight Searle, who was found stabbed to death in Havant, Hampshire in 1888 has discovered archives which mention that a magistrate received a letter bearing a Portsmouth postmark, days before Percy's killing, signed "Yours, Jack the Ripper." The letter told police not to bother looking for him in London because "I'm not there," suggesting he had moved his activities to the south coast. Robert Husband, 11, the only witness to the killing, said in a statement that he saw a man stab Percy. Husband himself was eventually charged with the murder after a pocket knife found at the scene, believed to be the murder weapon, was found to belong to his brother. He was acquitted at Winchester assizes and the case remained unsolved.

GEORGE HAWKES

In October 1888, George Hawkes, of Ladywood Road, Birmingham, was charged with being drunk and disorderly and using bad language. His noisy behaviour, and announcement that he was "Jack the Ripper," had drawn a crowd. He expressed regret and stated that some years ago he had suffered a sunstroke while serving in the army in Africa and when he has a little drink it takes away his mind. Case adjourned for 6 weeks.

WILLIAM HAYDAY

William Hayday a 59-year old well-dressed labourer, living at Little Park Street, Dorset Square, St Marylebone. Was charged with maliciously inflicting grievous bodily harm upon Mrs Ethel Weekley, the wife of a labourer, living at Brunswick Street, Blackfriars.

The incident was reported in the Manchester Evening News 23 October 1914:

Mrs Weekley, whose face was terribly disfigured said she met the prisoner a total stranger to her, on Thursday, in Drury Lane. He remarked that she looked "rough" she replied "So would you if you had a man out of work" He asked her if she would like to earn a shilling by going home with him and cleaning his place in preparation for the return of his wife from Hove. She agreed and drove with him in a cab to a house. There he locked the door and threw her upon a bed. "For God's sake," she cried, "let me off, I went to benediction last night, I didn't think this was going to happen." He then punched her in the face, and when she attempted to scream he forced pieces of wet rag up her nostrils and into her mouth. He also tied her feet together to stop her from struggling. You didn't think when I brought you here that I was Jack the Ripper," he remarked. He had a silver handled knife in one hand, she said, and with the other continued to punch her. Then he took her by the throat and threatened to strangle her. He was a carver, he said, and had cut women up and done "Ripper" murders. Afterwards, he promised to give her untold gold. Eventually, he took the wet rag from her mouth and asked if he should make her a cup of tea. She nodded assent, and immediately he left her, she screamed "murder" and "police." A policeman knocked at the door, and the man untied her and opened the door. As the police entered the prisoner suggested she take some money and remarked that he was Jack the Ripper. In reply to the magistrate she said she did not think he was drunk, but he seemed like a madman.

DAN HAYES

In August 1889, Patrolman Lewis, of the North End police, arrested Day Hayes, of Liverpool. PC Lewis found Hayes very drunk and noisy in Commercial Street, and took him into custody. On the way to the station, Hayes declared himself the real "Jack the Ripper," and claimed he had killed nine women, and had visited Boston intending to kill nine more. After the prisoner had sufficiently sobered up, he was told he will pay £5 to the court for his little joke.

WILLIAM HAYNES

On 21 October 1892, at Birmingham Police Court, 21 year old William Haynes, of 4, Bacchus Road, Winson Green, in occupation as a gun-maker, was charged with being drunk and disorderly. On Thursday night, a person, apparently a woman, was seen running and shouting and behaving in a most singular manner. In a short time a crowd of over a hundred people had gathered. The person was dressed in an unusually large Gainsborough hat, corsets, over which were a light-coloured bodice, a black dress, and coloured skirt, and a cape jacket, which was tied at the neck with a length of pink ribbon. To make himself more convincing the eccentric individual had carefully pencilled his eyebrows and eyelashes. A veil covered his elaborately "made-up" face. He also wore a lady's macintosh and hood. Underneath all this female clothing he was wearing his ordinary male attire, with the exception of a jacket and waistcoat. In this disguise he paraded up and down Broad Street, he soon became the centre of observation by a large crowd, who designated him "Jack the Ripper." When it was discovered that the "woman" was a man, the crowd became more aggressive towards him. His large hat was torn from his head and ripped to pieces, there is no doubt he would have been completely stripped of his whole female attire, had it not been for the timely intervention of the police. Police-constable Ward, seeing the man was drunk, escorted him to Moor Street police station. When asked where he got his female attire from, the prisoner replied: "It belonged to my sister." He was not sure why he dressed as he did. He was advised to stay away from drink and your sister's clothing. He was fined 2s. 6d. And costs. As the prisoner was led away he was handed a bundle of clothing from a relative.

JAMES HEAP

In October 1888, James Heap, appeared in court on a charge of drunkenness. He told the constable he was "Jack the Ripper". Due to his drunken condition he had to be taken to the police station in a cart. Heap was fined 10s, including costs.

THOMAS HEFFERON

In November 1889, Thomas Hefferon, described as a rough-looking fellow, was charged with being drunk, and with annoying females in the public streets. Constable 367 H was on duty in Cannon-street-road, when he saw the prisoner, stopping respectable women and saying he was "Jack the Ripper". Women appeared to be very frightened of him. He was sentenced to 7 days imprisonment with hard labour.

GEORGE RICHARD HENDERSON

Henderson, who was described as a person of rather a singular appearance, was charged on 9 October 1888 at Bow Street Police Court with being a suspected person loitering about the streets. Considerable excitement was raised in Covent Garden when at about 3:30 am it was rumoured Jack the Ripper was in the area and going about threatening people. Henderson was carrying a black bag and was himself wandering around aimlessly, and it was claimed that his strange behaviour had alarmed several people. Police Constable 411E arrived and took Henderson to the station, where he was questioned and searched. Henderson was unable to give a satisfactory account of himself and was thus detained. When searched, 54 pawn tickets were found in his possession, also found upon his person was a rough draft of a letter which had recently appeared in print suggesting to the Home Secretary that those who were harbouring the Whitechapel murderer felt that they were equally guilty as accomplices after the fact, and could not come forward and give him up, no matter for what reward until a free pardon was offered to them. In court, witnesses came forward on Hendersons' behalf and spoke of him as a respectable man. He was summarily discharged, though, was cautioned to refrain from walking the streets at such an hour behaving in an alarming manner. He was also advised that at such an early hour of the morning he would be better at home.

STEPHEN HENDERSON

On 16 July, 1896, in Oakland, San Francisco, Stephen Henderson, who has made himself obnoxious to the authorities of this city, and San Francisco of late by addressing erratic letters to the coroners in which he claims to be "Jack the Ripper" has been quietened for the present by being committed to an asylum. He was sent to Ukiah today, after admitting he had spent seven of his life in an asylum in Germany. Henderson had panicked the women of San Leandro and West Oakland, by chasing and threatening them. The Mendocino State Asylum for the Insane, in Ukiah, was established in 1889, the hospital was closed in 1972.

WILLIAM HENLEY

In June 1889, at the Chepstow police-court, William Henley, a young man of 19 years, was charged with being a lunatic wandering at large. Henley had only just arrived in the area from a reformatory in Worcestershire. He laboured under the idea that people believed him to be "Jack the Ripper" and that gangs of men were after him to take his life. In order to escape from his foes he lay concealed in mud of the river Wye. He was remanded to the workhouse for a week.

HENNELL

A young butcher named, Hennell, committed suicide by cutting his throat from ear to ear. The incident happened at his parents' home at 76 Enfield Buildings, Ashford Street, Hoxton. He had repeatedly expressed a fear that they were after him for the Whitechapel murder. His parents, worried about his behaviour, had begun to watch him closely for the last few days. The first instance, his mother left the room, he cut his throat. The date of his suicide 17 September 1888 rules him out of any involvement in the murders, of Stride, Eddowes, and Kelly.

John Thomas Hennell, was born 17 November 1858, in Shoreditch, to John Hennell, a butcher, and Emma (née Smith). In the 1881 census, he is living at 23 Copenhagen Street, Islington. His son John William was born 1881, died 1922, in Australia. His wife Louisa Doie (née Smith) died 1884.

THOMAS HENRY

On 9 July, 1914, Thomas Henry, a 25 year old porter, was found guilty of stealing a bicycle at Rillington on 25 May, and was found riding it the next day at Scarborough. During the hearing the prisoner behaved in a curious manner, and showed signs of becoming violent. When referred to as the prisoner at the bar he said: "If I'm at the bar fetch me a pint. I have had no blooming ale for six weeks." He handed in a long letter, in which he said if he was not in prison he was in an asylum. He alleged that his mother was put in an asylum and killed at night, while she was asleep and had her money taken. He said he would murder a man for a penny and two for twopence. Give me 20 years if you like. I can

221

and do all the murder. "Jack the Ripper am I." Prisoner finished by pleading for work.

CHARLES Y HERMANN

The Daily Mirror, 10 April 1905 reported the following story:

AMAZING CONFESSION.

British Subject Charges Himself with Committing "Jack the Ripper" Crimes. "Jack the Ripper," who spread terror in the East End of London by a series of fiendish murders many years ago, is said to have confessed to his crimes in New York. Reuter's correspondent says A man giving the name of Charles Y. Hermann has confessed to having committed a series of barbarous murders in Whitechapel, whither, he says, he went fifteen years ago. He states that his parents were a non-commissioned officer in the British Army and a Cairo woman. The police believe that the man is suffering from hallucinations. Between 1888 and 1891 nine women were foully murdered in the Whitechapel district, and judging from the nature of the wounds inflicted the crimes were evidently perpetrated by one man. Scotland Yard made no arrests, and although several similar "confessions" have been made the police authorities believe the real murderer died in a lunatic asylum.

The Daily Express, London, Wednesday, 12 April 1905 reported the following story:

The confession in New York by a man named Hermann to the "Jack the Ripper" murders in Whitechapel, in 1888 and 1889, ought not, in the opinion of Dr Forbes Winslow, the famous lunacy expert, to be regarded as hallucination."I am convinced," he said to an "Express" representative yesterday, "that this may be the real criminal the mysterious lodger, whose movements I

222

traced, and who was undoubtedly the culprit when I was investigating the outrages."I traced this man, who was a homicidal, religious monomaniac, to his several lodgings, and until recently I had some pairs of his boots in my possession. These boots were made in Canada, and I believe that their original owner was a Canadian. 'In all probability, the criminal crossed the Atlantic, and the fact that similar murders were subsequently committed in New York supports this view. 'It has been stated that "Jack the Ripper" was confined in a Government lunatic asylum. But in that case, he would have been brought to trial. A criminal, though mad, must take his place in the dock."

JOHN HEWITT

Suggested as a Ripper suspect in 1985 by accountant and researcher Steward Hicks, after discovering his name in the records of the Lunacy Commission in London.

Hewitt was born in 1850 and was a Manchester physician and surgeon. Who had become mentally ill and in 1888 was confined as a voluntary patient to Coton Hil Asylum, Stafford. Due to his voluntary status he was allowed to come and go as much as he wished. The records show he was safely incarcerated at the time of the Whitechapel murders. Upon his release Hewitt married a nurse from the asylum, Lily Louisa (née Whitehouse), on 31 March 1889, at Parkstone in Dorset. And they later lived in the seaside town of Bournemouth. He died 27 February 1892 at Kings Norton from paralysis of the insane. Defined in the 1844 lunacy act, the condition paralysis of the insane is the result, almost uniformly, of a debauched and intemperate life. Its duration is scarcely ever longer than two or three years, after which it generally takes its sufferer to the grave. He left in his will effects to the value of £300.

THOMAS HEYWOOD

In September 1888, an electrician named Thomas Heywood, in the employ of Lord Burton, at Rangemoor Hall, became suddenly mad, he rushed off into an adjoining wood, and declared that he was "Jack the Ripper". A party was ordered to search the woods for Heywood. In the meantime Heywood had stripped himself of all his clothing, and travelled some miles before he was captured. He was found attempting to swim in the middle of the road. He was temporarily lodged in Burton Workhouse.

JOHN HILL

A 31-year old ship's fireman, John Hill, was charged with assault and intent to ravish Elizabeth Tilley, a widow of respectable appearance who earned her living as a laundress. The incident occurred on Old Brunswick Road, 10 March 1891, at about 9:00 pm Tilley was returning from a house near the East India Docks, where she had been working and was making her way home to Bromley when from a darkened passageway appeared Hill. He seized her and threw her to the ground, which was covered in snow. She made two attempts to stand, but was thrown back onto the ground on each occasion. On her third attempt, he fell with her, and proceeded to place his fingers inside her mouth to stop her from screaming; telling her that, "Jack" (meaning Jack the Ripper), had got her. He then threatened to use his knife against her if she was not quite. After a struggle, Tilley managed to escape his clutches and ran down the street, until she, fortunately, encountered Police Constable 61KR, who immediately began a search of the area, and quickly located Tilley's attacker in a courtyard near to where the assault had occurred. Hill was found in possession of a parcel that Tilley had dropped. After much violent resistance, Hill, was taken to the police station. The officer was praised for his swift action, and the jury found Hill guilty, and sentenced him to 1 year in prison with hard labour.

WALTER HILL

On 15 January 1889, a respectable looking man named Walter Hill, who resides in the Archway-road, was charged at Dalston Police Court, with being drunk and disorderly, at Highbury. He went up to a policeman and shouted that he was "Jack the Ripper". The constable summoned assistance by means of the American alarm (An American alarm was the call box found on telephone poles). An ambulance cart was brought from the station, and the man conveyed there within a few minutes. He was sentenced to fourteen days imprisonment with hard labour.

BENSON HILTON

On 18 October 1888, in Church-street, West Hartlepool, a man caused a considerable commotion, when stood in the middle of the thoroughfare, shouting at the top of his voice that he was "Jack the Ripper". A crowd had gathered round, but noticing the man was evidently drunk, his ravings excited nothing more serious than ridicule. PC Taylor, came upon the scene and took him into custody. He gave the name Benson Hilton, his occupation as an artist, and his home town as Bradford. The following morning he expressed regret for his conduct, and was fined 2s 6d and 2d costs, or seven days imprisonment. The money was paid. Benson Hilton was certainly an artist.

ALFRED HINDE

In January 1936 Alfred Hinde, a 67-year old watchmaker and repairer, of Winstanley Road, was knocked down and killed by an omnibus at Wellingborough. Hinde was briefly suspected at the time of the Whitechapel murders of being Jack the Ripper. In

1888, Hinde went to assist a woman calling for help and fought with the woman's assailant, who subsequently made off. A passing detective thought it was Hinde who was the woman's aggressor and took him to the police station where he was detained. Witnesses soon came forward to clear him. Hinde, who was injured in the struggle with the man, had his hospital treatment paid for by the police.

HANS HOCHKISS

In a squalid, sordid hotel room in the backstreet's of Bombay, India, an old emancipated man by the name of Hans Hochkiss told a deathbed confession to three of his neighbours, of having committed the Jack the Ripper murders while in London. Hochkiss also confessed, while working as a boatman to having committed a further series of murders, (at least seven women, mostly servant girls were brutally murdered 1884-85 in Austin, Texas). Hochkiss told a rambling tale of how his compulsion to murder was driven by the bad behaviour of a woman whom he had loved in his youth. Unfortunately, two of the witness's grasp of the English language were so poor that they failed to understand the severity of what Hochkiss was actually telling them. The third man, an English sailor named Johnson, was an extremely dubious character who had no intention of giving a statement to the police. Before he fled, Johnson told the tale to another shady customer, the hotel owner, who in turn passed the story on to the police. All efforts to find Johnson to corroborate the truth of this story were without success.

H H HOLMES

Born Herman Webster Mudgett 16 May 1861 in Gilmanton, New Hampshire, to devout Methodists, Levi Horton Mudgett, a farmer and Theodate Page (née Price). Holmes was the third born child, he had an older sister Ellen, an older brother Arthur and a younger brother Henry. It is claimed he was unusually intelligent from an early age and had a privileged childhood. It is also claimed he was obsessed with death and had begun dissecting animals, from an early age. After graduating high school, he changed his name to Henry Howard Holmes, and would later be known as H.H. Holmes. His life of crime started out with frauds and scams. As a medical student at the University of Michigan, he stole corpses from laboratories, burned or disfigured them, then planted the bodies, to make it look as if they had been killed in an accident. Not before taking out insurance policies on them. Holmes may have also used the bodies for experiments. Credited to have killed at least 27 people and possibly as many as 200. He ran a virtual murder factory in his hotel in Chicago. He has also been linked to deaths in other parts of the United States and Canada. Holmes had a keen interest in human anatomy which led him to become a medical student before he embarked on an amazing career combining hotel-keeping with robbery and murder. In 1888 he worked as a drug store, chemist and took over the business when the proprietor mysteriously disappeared. He lived above the store and shared the accommodation with a jeweller and his wife, Icilius and Julia Conner. Mrs Conner worked as Holmes's secretary. Using the proceeds from numerous frauds, Holmes built a Gothic-style hotel in Chicago at 63rd street which was completed in 1891. During its construction he would repeatedly hire and fire the construction crews, so nobody became suspicious of exactly what he was designing. The hundred-room building, known locally as "Holmes's Castle," welcomed many guests, but they did not all survive the experience? Among the visitors who disappeared was Julia Conner. Some were locked in soundproof bedrooms fitted with gas lines that let him asphyxiate them at any time. Some victims were locked in a huge soundproof bank vault near his office where they were left to suffocate. The victims' bodies were dropped by secret chute to the basement, where some were meticulously dissected, stripped of flesh, crafted into skeleton models, and then sold to medical schools. Holmes also cremated some of the bodies or placed them in lime pits for destruction. Holmes had two giant furnaces as well as pits of acid, bottles of various poisons, and even a stretching rack. Through the connections he had gained in medical school, he sold skeletons and organs with little difficulty. Holmes picked one of the most remote rooms in the Castle to perform hundreds of illegal abortions. Some of his patients died as a result of his abortion procedure, their corpses also processed and their skeletons sold. Chloroform was his weapon of choice. It is an anaesthetic, he didn't want any evidence that these people came to their demise in anything other than a natural way. But the need to have that much chloroform is certainly significant. You wouldn't be buying that much chloroform if you weren't killing a lot of people and using it to subdue your victims. During the 1893 Columbian Exposition, Holmes opened up his home as a hotel for visitors to the world's fair. Unfortunately, some of his guests did not survive his hospitality. Many of these victims—no one knows for certain the total number—were women whom he seduced, swindled, and then killed. Holmes had a habit of getting engaged to a woman and then for his fiancée to suddenly "disappear." Others were lured there by the offer of employment. All the while, Holmes continued to work insurance scams and it was one of these scams that led to his undoing. He joined forces with Benjamin Pitezel to collect $10,000 from a life insurance company. The two travelled around for a time committing other frauds. Landing in jail in Texas, Holmes brought fellow inmate Marion Hedgepeth—who knew Holmes as H. M. Howard—in on the life insurance scheme with Pitezel. When Holmes failed to deliver Hedgepeth's share of the deal, Hedgepeth tipped off the authorities. While they eventually identified Howard as Holmes, the authorities did not catch on to Holmes soon enough to stop his final murders. He killed Pitezel and then convinced Pitezel's widow that her husband was still alive. Becoming concerned that the five Pitezel children might expose him, he went away with three of the children, eventually killing them. At first, Holmes was charged with insurance fraud. He later stood trial for the murder of Benjamin Pitezel. During his time in custody, Holmes gave numerous stories to police, admitting to killing 27 people. The final tally of his victims was estimated between 150 and 230 but no one is quite sure. After his conviction, Holmes appealed his case, but lost. He met his end on 7 May 1896 when he was hanged for the Pitezel murder in Philadelphia. There is a legend that as Dr H. H. Holmes stood on the gallows, several spectators in the crowd heard him cry out "I am Jack the..." before the gallows silenced him forever. This account, however, appears to be confused with fellow murderer and Ripper suspect, Dr Thomas Neil Cream, who it is also claimed cried out "I am Jack the"... before the trap door opened. A recent TV documentary, entertaining though it was ultimately failed to prove the link between Holmes and the Ripper.

WILLIAM HOLT

Holt was a doctor at St George's Hospital, who also thought of himself as a bit of an amateur detective, he donned various disguises and went patrolling the East End hoping to capture Jack the Ripper. On 11 November 1888, two days after the murder of Mary Kelly, when fear of the Ripper was at an all-time high, Holt, dressed in one of his disguises, stepped out of the shadows wearing spectacles and with his face blackened with burnt cork. His strange appearance frightened a woman called

229

Humphrey's in George Yard, almost at the exact spot where Martha Tabram had been murdered. When she asked him what he wanted he simply laughed and ran away, her screams of, "Murder," drew a crowd, who quickly encircled Holt close to the Princess Alice public-house. He was rescued just in time by the police as sticks were brandished and cries of, "Lynch him," could be heard coming from the angry crowd. He was arrested, and taken to Leman Street Police Station but was released the following day after he was able to satisfactorily prove his innocence. Described by the press as about 35 years of age, 5 ft. 7 inches tall, with a dark complexion and dark moustache, he wore no waistcoat, but had an ordinary jersey beneath his coat, in his pocket he had a double peaked light check cap and was bareheaded. In press reports, his spectacles were described as, White painted rings around his eyes, and thus was referred to as the "white-eyed man."

William Holt, was born in 1835 in St Martins, London. He married Julia, Mary (née Laundy) 6 January 1878, at St Mary's Church in Lambeth. In the 1881 census, he is living at 46, Goldstone Villas, in Hove, East Sussex, with his wife Julia, son William St George, and daughter Ethel Marguerite. In the 1891 census, he is living in Ashford, Kent. In the 1901 census, he is a boarder, living in Chesterfield, Derbyshire.

MIRIAM HOWELLS

At Aberdare police-court, Miriam Howells, a married woman, of Penrhiwceiber, was charged, with sending threatening letters, claiming to be from "Jack the Ripper." on the 15 November, 1888, to Elizabeth Magor, and Margaret Smith. The letter received by Mrs Magor, reads:

Dear Mrs Boss, I mean to have your life before Christmas. I will play a - of a trick with you, old woman. I played a good one on the last, but this will be better. Ain't I clever? Believe me to remain yours for ever, Jack the Ripper, Beware.

When asked why she had wrote such letters, Howell's, replied: "That she meant no harm, and only did it for a lark, and hoped nothing would come out of it." The magistrate, Mr North, said she had made a joke of crimes of a revolting character, and hoped she was thoroughly ashamed of it, and that it would be a lesson to her. The defendant was then dismissed.

HENRY HUMPHREY

The Courier, 24 November 1888 reported the following story:

WAS HE JACK THE RIPPER?

Henry Humphrey, 36, a professional billiard player, was brought up on Monday for behaving in a disorderly manner and threatening Ann Vaughan, of Malvern Road, Kilburn. - The prosecutrix, a young woman, said the prisoner came up to her and said "Good evening, miss," but she took no notice of him, and walked towards her cousin, another young woman, who was approaching her. The accused followed and said something about them being nice young women and other foolish talk. Humphrey then raised his arm, and from his sleeve produced a long dagger with a sharp curved point, and said, "This will do for you." She and her cousin screamed at the top of their voices, and the defendant told them not to do that. He went away, and they told a policeman what had happened. Police-constable 332 X arrested the prisoner in the Chippenham public-house, and when told the charge he said it was only a stupid joke. The man was in drink but knew what he was about. He had actually been into a shop and sharpened the knife on the counter. - Mr. de Rutzen

231

said this sort of thing must be stopped. He remanded Humphrey for a week and refused bail.

GEORGE HUTCHINSON (AMERICAN)

In 1881 George Hutchinson (not to be confused with the Mary Kelly witness, George Hutchinson), was an inmate of Elgin Asylum. Not considered dangerous, he was granted a great deal of freedom, and took a particular interest in the process of killing animals at the asylum slaughtering house, occupying his time by skilfully fashioning toothpicks out of animal bones. He escaped and murdered a prostitute in Chicago, mutilating her in a manner similar to the later Whitechapel murders. He was recaptured, at Kankakee and placed in an asylum there. He escaped and was at liberty at the time of the Ripper murders, though there is no evidence he was in London at that time.Author and researcher Simon Wood discovered the following articles.

New York Times of 16 May 1888—A DANGEROUS CRIMINAL ESCAPES Joliet, Illinois, 15 May:Billy Hutchinson, one of the worst desperadoes that Chicago has yet turned out, made his escape from the Kankakee Asylum yesterday morning. Hutchinson has been a habitual criminal for 20 years past. He has served three terms at Joliet Prison for such crimes as burglary, robbery, and murder. In June 1885, he slaughtered his mistress, an Iowa girl named Kitty Hall, in their rooms in a house on Pacific Avenue, Chicago. He escaped with a sentence of 17 years at Joliet. He became insane soon after and was taken to the asylum at Kankakee. Hutchinson is subject to epilepsy, and while in his fits will commit murder. He is a dangerous criminal to be at large, and every effort is being made for his recapture.

The following day, 17 May 1888, this story appeared in the Chicago Daily Tribune— BILLY HUTCHINSON RECAPTURED

An Escaped Murderer Arrested in Chicago and Returned to Kankakee. Joliet, Illinois, Billy Hutchinson, the Chicago convict and murderer who escaped from the Kankakee asylum last Monday, was recaptured in Chicago today and returned to the asylum. "[Billy Hutchinson, an escaped lunatic from Kankakee, was captured about 1 o'clock yesterday afternoon by Lieut. Backus of the Harrison Street Police Station in a saloon on Clark Street near Harrison. The lunatic was locked in a cell and immediately made an attempt to hang himself to the bars with his suspenders. His position was discovered in time by the lock-up keeper and a close watch was kept on him. He made two more efforts to end his life, and was finally sent to the lunatic department of the jail. Hutchinson, about two years ago, murdered his paramour, Kittie Hall, in a disreputable house at No. 126½ Pacific Avenue. He was captured and sentenced to seventeen years in Joliet. Soon after his arrival at the penitentiary, he gave unmistakable signs of insanity and was sent to the asylum at Kankakee. He escaped a few days ago and made his way to Chicago, it is supposed on foot. Billy was taciturn and refused to say how and when he arrived in the city.

GEORGE HUTCHINSON

George Hutchinson was named as Jack the Ripper by the following authors. Bob Hinton, in the (1998) book: From Hell the Jack the Ripper Mystery. Stephen Wright, in the (1999) book: Jack the Ripper an American View. Garry Wroe in the (2002) E-book: Jack the Ripper Person or Persons Unknown? Chris Miles in the (2004) book: On the Trail of a Dead Man: The Identity of Jack the Ripper. And Stephen Senise in the (2017 book: Jewbaiter Jack the Ripper: New Evidence & Theory.

Hutchinson first came to our attention with his detailed account of a suspect seen with Mary Kelly shortly before she was murdered.

233

The description Hutchinson gave has caused some to view him with growing suspicion. Hutchinson made the following statement at the Commercial Street Police Station:

About 2:00 am, 9, I was coming by Thrawl Street, Commercial Street, and just before I got to Flower and Dean Street I met the murdered woman Kelly and she said to me, "Hutchinson, will you lend me Sixpence," I said, "I can't, I've spent all my money going down to Romford," she said, "Good morning, I must go and find some money." She went away towards Thrawl Street, a man coming in the opposite direction to Kelly tapped her on the shoulder and said something to her, they both burst out laughing. I heard her say, "Alright," to him, and the man said, "You will be alright for what I have told you," he then placed his right hand around her shoulders. He also had a kind of a small parcel in his left hand, with a kind of strap round it. I stood against the lamp of the Queens Head public house and watched him. They both came past me, and the man hung down his head with his hat over his eyes. I stooped down and looked him in the face, he looked at me stern. They both went into Dorset Street, I followed them. They both stood at the corner of the court for about 3 minutes. He said something to her, she said, "Alright my dear, come along, you will be comfortable." He then placed his arm on her shoulder and gave her a kiss, she said she had lost her handkerchief. He then pulled his handkerchief, a red one, out and gave it to her. They both then went up the court together. I then went to the court to see if I could see them, but could not. I stood there for about three-quarters of an hour to see if they came out, they did not, so I went away.

Hutchinson described the man he saw as:

About, five ft six inches in height, and 34 or 35 years of age, with A dark complexion and dark moustache turned up at the ends.

234

Wearing a long Astrakhan coat, a white collar with black necktie, to which was affixed a horseshoe pin. He wore a pair of dark spats with light buttons over button boots and displayed from his waistcoat a massive gold chain. His watch chain had a big seal with a red stone hanging from it. He had a heavy moustache curled up, and dark eyes and eyelashes, he had no side whiskers and his chin was clean shaven. He looked like a foreigner. He carried a small parcel in his hand, about 8 inches long and it had a strap round it, he had it tightly grasped in his left hand, it looked as though it was covered in dark American cloth. He carried in his right hand, which he laid upon the woman's shoulder, a pair of brown kid gloves. One thing I noticed and that was that he walked very softly. I believe that he lives in the neighbourhood and I fancied that I saw him in Petticoat Lane on Sunday morning, but I was not certain.

An exceptionally detailed statement, not only did Hutchinson visually observe every detail, despite the poor light, but he also appeared to have heard every word that was exchanged between the couple. There are several possible scenarios to explain the statement he made.

He was telling the truth about what he saw and heard that night, and remarkable as it may seem gave us the best eyewitness description we have of Jack the Ripper.

He was telling the truth, but his statement was exaggerated to please both the press and the police.

His statement was a total fabrication to cover up the fact, he was Jack the Ripper, and had been seen by Sarah Lewis. Hutchinson by his own admission, admitted he was broke, took notice that the man was well dressed and appeared wealthy, so hung around waiting for the man to appear on his own, with the intention of robbing him.

Perhaps the real reason he hung around so long was that it was Mary Kelly he was keeping an eye on possibly even stalking her. She had said that she was frightened of someone other than the Ripper, though, did not say who; was it Hutchinson who was making her feel uneasy?

Possibly the reason he hung around for so long was because he had no money for a bed and was just idly passing time until morning, sheltering from the weather, it was, after all, a particularly unpleasant night.

Maybe he was just concerned for Kelly's safety and was looking out for her, he had known her for a period of three years, and was aware there was a killer of prostitutes prowling the streets, and Mary, was in the company of a stranger whom Hutchinson knew from his attire was not from the local area.

Hutchinson elaborated on his statement a little more to the press, saying that his suspicions were aroused by seeing the man so well dressed, though had no suspicion the man was the Whitechapel murderer. And that he reported what he had seen on Sunday morning to a policeman. Despite Hutchinson claiming to harbour no suspicion against the man, and maintaining his curiosity was aroused by seeing such a well-dressed individual in the area, he immediately contradicts this statement by saying, "I believe he lives in the area."

Little is actually known about Hutchinson beyond the newspaper reports at the time. He was described as a former groom, now employed as a labourer. Tom Cullen In the (1965) book: Autumn of Terror, describes him as a night watchman. This occupation, if correct, would certainly account for Hutchinson's remarkable powers of observation.

Was George Hutchinson, Jack the Ripper? We know he knew one of the victims, Mary Kelly, and by his own admission occasionally gave her money, so was possibly an occasional client of hers, and was one of the last people to see her alive. He lived at the Victoria Home for Working Men 39-41 Commercial Street, which was right in the heart of the Ripper's hunting ground, and waited three days before coming forward to give his important statement to the police, a statement many believe could not be true, for it described, amongst other things, the colour of the suspect's eyelashes. This has led many to speculate that his whole statement was a fabrication to cover up the fact that he was spotted by Sarah Lewis, hanging around outside Millers Court waiting for a client of Mary Kelly's to leave, before killing her. He later told the press that he, in fact, had later gone to Millers Court and stood outside Mary Kelly's window. This account differs from the story he had earlier told the police. Why was this discrepancy not spotted at the time? Also, why did he not notice Sarah Lewis going into Miller's Court. After the murder of Frances Coles, there were no more Ripper style murders, yet there is no record of a George Hutchinson committing suicide, dying or being committed to an asylum. One newspaper described him as, "A man of military bearing" which, along with what he said to Mary Kelly about having spent all his money going down to Romford, may point to a family connection with the town. We do know there was an army barracks there, so he may possibly have been a former soldier. In the (1991) book The Ripper and the Royals, Melvyn Fairclough interviews a man named Reginald Hutchinson, who claims his father, George William Topping Hutchinson, was the man who knew Mary Kelly. He claims that his father was born on the 1 October 1866 (which would have made him 22 at the time of the murders), and described him as an honest and hardworking plumber, who rarely, if ever, went without work. He said his dad took careful note of details and could remember things accurately. If this is the correct George Hutchinson, it would explain his excellent observational skills. His father mentioned to him several times that he knew one of the women, and was interviewed at the time by the police. When asked by his son who he thought Jack the Ripper was, his father replied, "It was more to do with the royal family than ordinary people," and believed the Ripper was someone like Lord Randolph Churchill. Reginald also claimed that his father had been given 100 shillings, though would not reveal why. The suspect described by Hutchinson did possess more than a passing resemblance to Lord Randolph Churchill. Hutchinson described the man as:

Having a dark moustache turned up at the ends. And displayed from his waistcoat a massive gold chain. His watch chain had a big seal with a red stone hanging from it.

"The Pall Mall Gazette, 28 June 1884, described Churchill as:

Having a wide turned-up moustache, beautifully dressed, his gold chain has the solid appearance of real 18 carat.

In 1895 George William Topping Hutchinson married Florence Jervis, at Trinity Church, Stepney. They met when she tripped over his cane after coming down the steps from the stage of the music hall, where he sat in the front row, having watched her performance as a yodeller and skipping rope artist. They became keen ice skaters, and George was an accomplished violinist. He was still working when he died from a heart attack at the age of 71 in 1938.George Hutchinson was in fact not the only witness to give a detailed description of a suspect despite the poor lighting

238

conditions. J. Best, 82, Lower Chapman-street, describing a suspect seen in the company of Elizabeth Stride on the night she was murdered, said:

*I was in the Bricklayers' Arms, Settles-street, about two hundred yards from the scene of the murder on Saturday night, shortly before eleven, and saw a man and a woman in the doorway. They had been served in the public-house and went out when me and my friends came in. It was raining very fast, and they did not appear willing to go out. He was hugging her and kissing her, and as he seemed a respectably dressed man, we were rather astonished at the way he was going on with the woman, who was poorly dressed. We 'chipped' him, but he paid no attention. As he stood in the doorway, he always threw sidelong glances into the bar, but would look nobody in the face. I said to him, "Why don't you bring the woman in and treat her? But he made no answer. If he had been a straight fellow he would have told us to mind our own business, or he would have gone away. I was so certain that there was something up that I would have charged him if I could have seen a policeman. When the man could not stand the chaffing any longer he and the woman went off like a shot soon after eleven. I had been to the mortuary, and am almost certain the woman there is the one we saw at the Bricklayers Arms. She is the same slight woman, and seems the same height. The face looks the same, but a little paler, and the bridge of the nose does not look so prominent.*John Gardner, labourer, 11, Chapman-street, corroborated all that Best said respecting the conduct of the man and the woman at the Bricklayers' Arms, adding:*Before I got to the mortuary today (Sunday), I told you the woman had a flower in her jacket, and that she had a short jacket. Well, I have been to the mortuary, and there she was with the dahlias on the right side of her jacket. The man was about 5ft. 5in. in height. He was well dressed in a black morning suit with a morning coat. He* *had rather weak eyes. I mean he had sore eyes without any eyelashes. I should know the man again amongst a hundred. He had a thick black moustache and no beard. He wore a black billycock hat, rather tall, and had on a collar. I don't know the colour of his tie. I said to the woman, "that's Leather Apron getting round you." The man was no foreigner; he was an Englishman right enough.*

Another witness, Edward Spooner, a horse-keeper, at the inquest of Elizabeth Stride, stated:

I could see that she had a red and white flower pinned to her jacket and cachous in her hand.

Spooner made these observations by the light of a match.

Therefore, the detailed description statement George Hutchinson gave may not be quite as suspicious as it first appears to be. The inquest into Mary Kelly's death opened and closed on 12 November 1888 and the press expressed their surprise at the sudden termination of the proceedings before all the witnesses had a chance to come forward, So once again, there was nothing suspicious in Hutchinson not coming forward sooner with his statement. Some Ripper authors have suggested Abberline knew Hutchinson was lying, but just could not prove he was the Ripper, and that the detectives sent to accompany him around the following morning, hoping to spot the suspect he described, were actually keeping an eye on him to stop him killing, or even better, catch him in the act. I personally do not believe an experienced detective like Abberline doubted Hutchinson's statement for one moment. For Hutchinson described exactly whom the police and the press at the time thought the Ripper was, "A foreign-looking Jew." Swanson, Macnaghten, Anderson and even Abberline with his favoured suspect, George Chapman, all believed the Ripper

240

was foreign and Jewish looking. Abberline stated that he believed Hutchinson's statement was, "Important and true." If the police did not believe Hutchinson's statement, description, why did they subsequently arrest two foreign-looking gentlemen Joseph Denny and Joseph Isaacs, wearing long Astrakhan trimmed coats exactly as Hutchinson had described? In his original statement to the police, Hutchinson stated the man he had seen was, "Jewish in appearance," this was later changed to, "looked like a foreigner," in an attempt to avoid stirring up anti-Semitic feelings, as hostility and anger against the local Jewish population was already running high.

The Evening Star (Washington, D.C.) Wednesday, 14 November 1888, interestingly viewed, Hutchinson, with a degree of suspicion.

Unless the story told by the man Hutchinson is made out of whole cloth-a question which it ought not to take a competent detective two hours to settle-there is now a shadow of hope of capturing the miscreant who has been committing so much butchery. But, in the meantime, it would be just as well to keep a sharp eye upon Hutchinson himself. He may be a convenient person to have about at a critical stage of the investigation which is soon to follow. The man popularly known as "Jack the Ripper" is full of devices, and it would not be surprising if it were found necessary later to put Hutchinson in his turn on the defensive.

Hutchinson it is speculated was paid the equivalent of a month's wage by the police for his help in searching for his Ripper suspect; he was also paid by the press for his story. One report claims he was paid substantially for his assistance. Could this be the real reason why he was so keen to help? Until new research discovers more about the eyewitness George Hutchinson there will remain only the possibility of a genuine Ripper suspect. In all

241

probabilities, Hutchinson was nothing more than a man seeking his 15 minutes of fame.

Journalist and political researcher, Stephen Senise in Ripperologist #146 suggests the witness George Hutchinson may have fled justice on 29 October 1889, on the ship Ormuz, bound for Sydney, Australia. He was imprisoned for two years for the indecent assault of two boys, aged 11 and 8. Upon his release, his records state his trade as labourer, his date of birth as 1861, his height as 5 feet 5 ½, and his weight as 154 lbs. He was described as having "blue or brown eyes, brown hair, and a moustache." "If" this is the correct George Hutchinson it would certainly account for why no researcher has been able to trace and identify him in England. It would also explain why after the death of Mary Kelly he appeared to simply vanish off the face of the earth.

HYAM HYAMS

Hyam Hyams was first suggested as a Ripper suspect by Mark King in an article for Ripperologist Magazine issue #35 June 2001.

Hyam Hyams was born in Aldgate, London on the 8 February 1855, to Solomon Hyams and Fanny (née Levy) Solomon was listed in the 1871 census as a cigar maker. In the 1881 census, Hyam Hyams aged 26 is listed as living at 29 Mitre Street with his mother, brothers Barney, George, Morris, two sisters, Clara and Jane, and Jane's husband John. There is no mention in the census of Solomon. Fanny is listed as the head of the household, Hyam's occupation, like his mothers, is listed as a fruiterer. In April 1888, Hyam married Rachel, and they lived at 36 New Street, Gravel Lane London. They had two children, a boy named William, and a daughter Kate, born in 1888. In the 1891 census,

242

Fanny Hyams is listed as living at 24 Mitre Street; this was the former home of Amelia Lewis, wife of Ripper witness Joseph Hyam Levy.Levy along with Harry Harris and Joseph Lawende, saw a man and woman, probably Catharine Eddowes and the Ripper, standing next to the entrance to Church Passage, which led into Mitre Square, only minutes before Eddowes' murder. Levy stated in his inquest testimony that he remarked to Harris "I don't like going home by myself when I see these sort of characters about. I'm off." The newspapers suggested that Levy "knows something, but that he is afraid to be called at the inquest."This had led to speculation that Levy, knew Hyams?On 29 December 1888 at 6:00 am Hyam Hyams was arrested by PC E. Walker, 75 H, in Leman Street charged with being a wandering lunatic and taken to the Whitechapel Workhouse Infirmary, suffering from delirium tremens. (Psychosis brought on by excessive and habitual consumption of alcohol). His address was given as 217 Jubilee Street, Mile End. He was released on 11 January 1889 only to be re-admitted on 15 April 1889, described as "weak in mind," Hebrew, aged 34 years, married and in occupation as a general dealer. He was sent to the Colney Hatch Lunatic Asylum under restraint and in a noisy condition. He was discharged on 30 August 1889 as recovered. On the 9 September 1889, he was delivered to the city of London Lunatic Asylum at Stone, Kent, as an insane person after attacking and stabbing his wife and seriously injuring his mother after striking her about the head with a hatchet. Labelled the "Terror of the City of London police." His wife stated that she had suffered four miscarriages and that in the past for the past 9 years her husband had suffered from periodic epileptic attacks, whereupon he became progressively more violent and delusional; one delusion being that his wife was unfaithful to him. He was sent back to Colney Hatch on 4 January 1890 as patient #10757. His case notes record that he suffered

243

from very frequent epileptic fits, was described as a "crafty and dangerous maniac" who "destroys his bedding and paints his walls with filth, shouts the most obscene language and practices self-abuse." Self-abuse–masturbation otherwise referred to as 'solitary vices.' Hyams throughout his incarceration, was described as, "Violent, threatening, noisy and destructive." Otherwise "quiet, but bitter against his wife." He continuously threatened other patients and members of staff, and on one occasion, when a medical officer was passing through the ward, crept up behind him and stabbed him in the neck with a makeshift knife. Hyams, appears twice in the 1891 census, he is listed as an inmate at Colney Hatch, and also as living at 40 New Street, Gravel Lane. His wife, living in hope he would return to her one day cured. He remained at Colney Hatch until his death at the age of 58 on 22 March 1913 from exhaustion and cardiovascular degeneration.Hyams, it is noted by theorists fits many of the criteria of Anderson's Swanson's and Macnaghten's suspect. He practised self-abuse, was violent, male, Jewish and the date of his committal to Colney Hatch, fits with the dating of Kosminski's committal. Hyam was described as 5 ft 7 inches tall, medium build with brown hair and a large brown moustache. There is no evidence that he was suspected at the time by the police of being Jack the Ripper.Research by Tracy Ianson, on Hyam Hyams, suggests that, Hyam Hyams of Mitre Street, mother and father Fanny and Solomon, may not be the person held in Colney Hatch. In the 1901 census, he is living at 27 Floreston Street, with his wife Rosa Hyams (née Aarons) still in occupation as a fruitier. He died in 1933.

JACK IRWIN

Irwin was mentioned as a possible Ripper suspect by A.H.Skirving, of the Canadian police. Skirving mentioned the prisoner, Jack Irwin, in Chatham, Ontario, whom he believed was the Whitechapel murderer. After an investigation, it was shown Irwin was not in England at the time the murders occurred.

BENJAMIN ISAACS

An omnibus conductor in the employ of the London General Omnibus Company told the strange story of a man who boarded the omnibus at Highgate. The man, who was wearing a green handkerchief round his neck and holding a green umbrella in front of his face, immediately began conversing with himself. When the man arrived at London Bridge he suddenly pronounced that he was Jack the Ripper and threatened to rip a lady who was seated on the omnibus. When the conductor asked him if it was true that he was Jack the Ripper, Isaacs replied, "Yes, I am Jack the Ripper." He was promptly ordered to leave the omnibus, whereupon he was arrested. The man was later identified as 40-year old Benjamin Isaacs. He was later charged with disorderly conduct.

JOSEPH ISAACS

Isaacs, born in 1858 was a 30-year old Polish Jewish cigar maker, who had taken accommodation at Mary Cusins lodging-house at 6 Little Paternoster Row, Spitalfields on the 5 or 6 of November 1888. Cusins and a lodger Cornelius Oakes became suspicious of Isaacs after he was heard pacing the floor of his room all night, it was noted that although he had a violin and several other musical instruments he was never known to play any of them. Oakes stated that Isaacs often changed his clothing, sometimes he would wear a hard felt hat, at other times a double-peaked cap. He heard him threatening violence to all women over the age 17, and his conduct was, according to Oakes "frequently strange." When he suddenly vacated his room after the murder of

Mary Kelly, Cusins became even more suspicious. She took her suspicions to the police, who searched his room and found he had left behind a violin bow. The police, assuming Isaacs would return for the bow, asked Cusins to keep a look out for him. On 12 November, he was charged at Barnet Police Court with petty larceny and was sentenced to 21 days in prison. Upon his release, on 5 December, Isaacs returned to Paternoster Row to retrieve the bow, whereupon Cusins followed him. Isaacs went to Julius Levenson's pawnshop, and after distracting Levenson stole a gold watch worth 30 shillings, and ran away. Isaacs was arrested the next day in Drury Lane (co-incidentally on the same day as Ripper suspect, Aaron Cohen), and taken under strong escort to the Leman Street police station. The newspapers believed the police had arrested Jack the Ripper and overheard Inspector Abberline saying to one of his officers, "Keep this quiet, we got the right man at last, this is a big thing." Isaacs was interviewed by Abberline and must have given a satisfactory account of himself, as he was subsequently only charged with the theft of the watch. He pleaded guilty and was sentenced to three months hard labour. Isaacs was described as short in stature, with a black moustache, wearing an Astrakhan trimmed coat. He appeared to fit the suspect description of eyewitness George Hutchinson, who saw a man with Mary Kelly, shortly before she was murdered, wearing such a coat. This would offer a possible explanation as to why the police paid such attention to Isaacs, and why they believed initially they had such a strong suspect.

Joseph Isaacs was born in Whitechapel, London, in 1858. His father was David Isaacs, a tailor, born in Poland. In the 1881 census, they are living at 144 Wentworth Street, Whitechapel. On 26 September 1887 in Barnsley, Yorkshire, Isaacs stole a valuable clarinet, from the shop of Mr. Job Walker, musical instrument dealer, Sheffield road, Barnsley. And was sentenced to

3 months imprisonment at Wakefield. He was described as 29 years old, 5ft 3¾ tall, with dark hair, had three small red moles on left cheek. His occupation was listed as a cigar maker. His religion as Jewish. In the 1891 census, he is married to Alice, and has 2 sons, 2 year-old Joseph H and 1 year-old William S. He is still in occupation as a cigar -maker, living at 13 Cayton Street, Islington, London.

JACOB ISENSCHMID

Jacob Isenschmid, (sometimes referred to as Joseph in contemporary accounts) was a butcher from 59 Elthorne Road, Holloway. He came under suspicion after the murder of Annie Chapman, by Dr Cowen of 10 Landseer Road, and Dr Crabb of Holloway Road. Cowen and Crabb went to the police on 11 September 1888 and informed them that Mr George Tyler, of 60 Mitford Road, (also erroneously referred to as Milford Road in some reports) had become suspicious of his tenant, Joseph Isenschmid, Swiss-born and known locally as the "Mad Pork Butcher." Tyler told the police that he had met Isenschmid on 5 September and provided him with accommodation. Tyler also told the police that Isenschmid often stayed out late at night, and had been absent from his lodgings since Annie Chapman's murder. A visit by Inspector Styles to Isenschmid's estranged wife Mary his spouse for the past 21 years, who resided at 97 Duncombe Road, Upper Holloway, revealed that she had in fact, only seen her husband once in two months, since an argument, when he had called a few days previously to collect some clothing. Even though she had hardly seen her husband, she "helpfully" told the police that he was in the habit of carrying large knives around with him, saying: "I do not think my husband would injure anyone but me, I think he would kill me if he had the chance." She also told the police that her husband had not been right in his head

247

since a fit in 1882-83. According to the Star newspaper, his behaviour during this period of insanity was frequently violent, and he was often seen sharpening a long knife. He also began to suffer delusions, one being that everything belonged to him. He also styled himself the "King of Elthorne Road." The address of which he had at one time kept a pork butcher's shop. A watch was promptly put out for this promising suspect. Isenschmid was arrested at 6.50 am, on 12 September and taken initially to Holloway Police Station, then to Islington Workhouse, whereupon he was judged to be insane. On the same day he was taken to the Fairfield Road Infirmary Asylum in Bow. Sergeant Thick, made inquiries at the asylum and learned from the medical superintendent, Dr William Mickle, that Isenschmid had told him a number of girls in Holloway, had called him "Leather Apron." Thick examined Isenschmid's clothing, but, could not find any incriminating evidence on them such as blood. On the 18 September, Inspector Abberline, was eager to conduct an identity parade with the witnesses from the Prince Albert public house, only to be told by Dr Mickle this, was not possible due to the poor health of his patient. Inspector Abberline reported that:

Although we are unable at present to procure any evidence to connect him with the murders, he appears to be the most likely person that has come under our notice to have committed the crimes.

It is not known if Isenschmid was ever formally identified as the man Mrs Fiddymont, wife of the proprietor of the Prince Albert public house, 21 Brushfield Street, otherwise known as the "Clean House" had seen entering the pub at 7 am on the 8 September, shortly after the murder of Annie Chapman. The man's rough appearance had frightened her. Fiddymont was in the pub talking to a friend, Mary Chappell when she noticed the man's light blue check shirt was badly torn and that he had blood splashes on his hand and below his ear. He was wearing a dark coat and a brown stiff hat pulled over his eyes. The man ordered, and quickly drank his half-pint of ale, and left the pub, whereupon he was followed by Joseph Taylor, a builder who lived at 22 Stewart Street. Taylor, who was described as a perfectly reliable man, well known throughout the neighbourhood, said:"The man walked very rapidly with a peculiar springy walk that I would recognise again, he carried himself very erect, like a horse soldier. His neck was rather long, and he was holding his coat together at the top. He had a nervous and frightened way about him and his appearance was exceedingly strange."Taylor watched the man go as far as "Dirty Dicks" in Half-Moon Street. He described the man as:

Thin, about 5 ft 8 inches tall, 40-50 years of age with a ginger coloured moustache, curling at the ends, short sandy hair, his eyes, "wild like hawks" and dressed shabby genteel, with a loose-fitting pair of trousers and a dark coat.

As Isenschmid was described as early 40's about 5 ft 7 inches tall, very ferocious looking with ginger hair and a normally powerful build, now shrunken with starvation, it would be a fair assumption to say that Isenschmid was the man who called into Mrs Fiddymont's pub. The importance to the police of identifying the bloodstained man who called into the Prince Albert public house was significant because of its location only four hundred yards from 29 Hanbury Street, where Annie Chapman had been murdered.

Jacob Isenschmid was born 20 April 1843 in Buch, Buempliz, Bern, Switzerland. His father Bendicht Isenschmid, was a farmer. His mother was Catharina (née Pfaffli). Jacob married Mary Ann (née Joyce), the daughter of a farmer, Richard Joyce, on Boxing

Day, 26 December 1867, at St Barnabas Church, Finsbury. Mary Ann at the time of her marriage resided at 98 Old Street. Jacob at 41 Bath Street. They had seven children, John Richard, Catherine Annie (Kate), Ada Mary, Annie Edith, Minnie Jane, Jessie, and Amy Magdalen. In the 1871 census they are living at 4 Baldwin Street, Finsbury. In the 1881 census they are living at 52 Kingsbury Road, Islington. In 1886 Ada, Annie, Minnie, and Jessie are admitted to Islington Workhouse. On 24 September 1887 Isenschmid had become depressed and mentally unstable following the collapse of his business, and was admitted to the Colney Hatch Lunatic Asylum. Dr John Gray noted Isenschmid suffered delusions. In one such delusion he threatened to blow up the Queen with dynamite, and in another threatened to kill his wife, children and his neighbours. Isenschmid was described as a very powerful built man, not epileptic, suicidal or a congenital idiot, but dangerous to others. Supposed cause: Unknown (Drink). After ten weeks he was discharged as cured on 2 December 1887, and attempted to make a fresh start with his wife. They moved to Duncombe Road, and he found a new job as a journeyman butcher at Mr. Marlett's High Street Marylebone. Unfortunately, it was not long before he began to act strangely once more. His wife told the Star newspaper that, "He got so bad that I got an order to have him put in the asylum again." He was committed to the Bow Infirmary Asylum, Fairfield Road, Bow. 12 September 1888, where he remained until 4 February 1890, when he was discharged to Banstead Asylum 4 February 1890, he remained here until 19 May 1890. He was admitted to Colney Hatch, 26 September 1891, until 15 October 1891. On 5 June 1899 he was again admitted to Colney Hatch, where he remained until 6 January 1900. He was admitted once more to Colney Hatch 4 November 1902 where he remained until 31 July 1903. His daughter stated she had seen little of her father since 1903,

250

though surprisingly recorded that she had never heard of any insanity in the family. Since the separation from his wife, Isenschmid resided at the St John's Road Workhouse, Islington, and earned his living by going to the East End markets where he would buy cheap cuts of meat, which he would then take back to his lodgings, dress and resell to restaurants and coffee houses in the West End. On 7 September 1908, he was once again admitted to Colney Hatch, his notes describe him as "excited talkative, and destructive." He threatened to murder those around him and used filthy language. He remained here until his death on 8 March 1910. The cause of death was noted as recurrent mania, lobar pneumonia, and exhaustion. This initaly promising suspect was safely incarcerated in an asylum when Elizabeth Stride, Catherine Eddowes, and Mary Jane Kelly were murdered. Their daughter Jessie was admitted 15 October 1912 to the Colney Hatch Lunatic Asylum, she was discharged 19 December 1913. She died in Islington in 1959, at the age of 76. His wife Mary Ann died in 1929 in Edmonton, London, at the age of 88. The Edinburgh Evening News 17 July 1890. Reported the following story:

DEATH OF 'JACK THE RIPPER

For about two years past there has been a man whose name has never been ascertained, but who has been termed 'Jack the Ripper', living in the neighbourhood of Upper Holloway, London. He was a tall, very thin, and strange individual, and was in the habit of walking at a very fast pace. It appears that a short time ago he was sent to the Islington Infirmary as a wandering lunatic, and died two days after. He was frequently asked why he walked at such a pace and in such a manner, and always replied that he did so for the benefit of his health and that the doctor had told him he must expand his lungs.

251

JACK THE FLASHER

On the night of Wednesday 26 September 1888, a young girl named Duffy, had gone to a field in the suburbs of Warrenpoint to fetch home the cows for the night, when she was startled by a strange partially dressed man who leapt out of a hedge and chased her through the field while proclaiming he was Leather Apron, and the murderer of the Whitechapel victims. When the girl reached home she was almost breathless and in a very excited state. The girl resided with her parents in Chapel-street Newry. The girl's father informed the constabulary who searched the area but failed to find the mysterious stranger. The man's behaviour caused great panic for several days amongst the female portion of the community, and not one could be induced to venture out on the Newry road after dark. The police believe the man is a half-crazed individual.

JACK THE RIPPERS

Various stories appeared in the newspapers connected to Jack the Ripper.

On the 14 November 1888, a City constable was quietly walking along Commercial-road, when suddenly some persons called out that he was "Jack the Ripper." The constable who was in mufti (in plain or ordinary clothes), was wearing a low broad-brim hat, and was of rather singular appearance. Hundreds of people quickly surrounded the constable. He tried to avoid them by increasing his pace, but the quicker he went the faster the mob followed, until he was hemmed in on all sides. The situation was looking serious until some constables of H Division came to his assistance. He informed them of his identity, and was escorted safely away from the mob.

In November, 1888, A woman, from Clapham, who obtains her livelihood at the wash-tub, and whose name and address, the newspapers thought it not prudent to give, told a story, that one afternoon she had to take one of her children to Guy's hospital. The child was suffering from a complaint that required particular attention. She was told by the doctor not to leave the hospital for a while. It was not until late evening before she left the institution to walk home. After stopping at a friend's house on the way, it was now past 10 in the evening before she arrived at the Albert Embankment. Suddenly a man of respectable appearance, about 45 years of age, accosted her, saying: "You look ill, my poor woman. It's late for you to be out with a child. Have you far to go home?" The woman replied that she had a mile and a half still to cover before she reached her destination. The stranger then said, "Why don't you ride then?" The poor woman exclaimed that she could not afford it, whereupon the stranger put his hand in his pocket and gave the woman half-a-crown, saying at the same time, "This will enable you to get home, and when you arrive there tell your friends that you met Jack the Ripper." The stranger then hurried away. The woman naturally frightened by this, was taken very ill with shock, on reaching home.

In 1889, in Manchester, a young woman about 19 years of age, whose name is suppressed, informed the police that she had received a threatening letter signed "Jack the Ripper." Further letters continued to arrive, some by post others being put under the door. Nineteen letters in total were received, threatening to take the girl's life and that of a companion. Some of the letters were stained with blood, others had coffins rudely drawn upon them. A man who had followed them, was questioned about the affair, but turned out to be innocent. On 21 December, the girl reported to the police that she had been stabbed. She stated that she went into the backyard at home to empty a jug, and saw a man on the wall with a knife in his hand. He struck at her cutting her near the wrist. She screamed and her father ran out, but could see no one. She was taken to the hospital, to have a severe cut stitched. The matter caused great alarm and fear in the neighbourhood. After the report of the stabbing the police kept a close watch on the house. Recent information received caused the superintendent to question the girl, under questioning she confessed that she had written all the letters herself. As to the alleged attack, she stated that she never went into the yard, and never saw any man. She cut her own arm herself. The only explanation she gave for her actions was "she was unhappy at home."

In August 1889, William Brown, of Tay Street, Edinburgh, was on his home when he was accosted by a man in a lane near Dairy Cemetery. The man thrust at him with a large sheath-dagger, remarking at the same time "I am Jack the Ripper." Brown, knocked the man down. The man pleaded "for god's sake" to be liberated, Brown allowed the man to go, but retained possession of the curved dagger. Brown described his assailent as a bearded man about 5ft 8 inches in height.

In October 1888, the female residents of Thurles, workhouse county Tipperary, were greatly panicked when at about three in the morning an intruder, a respectably dressed young man, had entered the ward and approached the bed in which a young girl was sleeping. She awoke, and upon seeing the stranger screamed loudly, and cried out that he was "Jack the Ripper." All the inmates then commenced an uproar, and could be heard shrieking and shouting in a most extrordinary way. The intruder became alarmed, and made his escape through the window. A search was made through the workhouse, but no person was found.

254

JACOBS

In the (1934) book: Lost London the Memoirs of an East End, Detective, ex-detective Sergeant Benjamin Leeson writes:

A story circulated that the 'Ripper' was a butcher, who wore blue overalls and a leather apron. An English Jew named Jacobs, a slaughterhouse butcher, and a perfectly harmless man, who always wore such an apron on account of his occupation, came under suspicion. People would point Jacobs out in the street as the suspected man, and he had to be rescued on several occasions by the police from angry street mobs and taken to the police station for protection. The thing so preyed on the poor fellow's mind that it finally caused him to lose his reason.

On his first night on duty as a 19-year-old copper, Benjamin Leeson came to the assistance of PC Thompson, 240, "H " division, who discovered the body of Frances Coles, an alleged victim of Jack The Ripper.

HENRY JAMES

At the adjourned inquest of Mary Ann (Polly) Nichols, on the 17 September, Thomas Ede, a railway signalman, said he saw a man behaving suspiciously, close to the Foresters Arms public house on Cambridge Heath Road, on the day Annie Chapman was murdered, 8 September 1888. The coroner was of the opinion that this incident could have no reference to the present inquiry, as the 8 September was the day of the Hanbury-street murder. He would, however, accept the evidence. Ede stated:

His peculiar appearance made me take notice of him, he was moving oddly and one of his arms appeared to be wooden, as it was hanging at his side.

He also claimed to have seen four inches of a knife protruding from the man's pocket, though could not say what type of knife it was. "I followed him, but as soon as he saw he was followed, he quickened his pace and I lost sight of him under some railway arches." He described the man as 5 ft. 8 in. high, about thirty-five years of age, with a dark moustache and whiskers. He wore a double-peaked cap, a short dark brown jacket, and a pair of clean white overalls over dark trousers. The man walked with a slight limp as though he had a stiff knee, and he had a fearful look about the eyes. He seemed to be a mechanic. The suspect, Henry James was questioned, but soon cleared of any suspicion of being Jack the Ripper because according to the press reports: "He was a well-known local lunatic."

WILLIAM JAMES

William James, 33-years old, and variously described as a hawker, or labourer, in newspaper accounts, was indicted for the manslaughter of William Hall. The incident occurred on 7 December 1888. Hall, a sorter in the general Post Office was walking home along Marshalsea Street with a female companion when suddenly a woman approached them crying. Her male companion also came up to the couple and spoke to the woman who was crying, James then proceeded to strike the man. Hall and his companion walked away and approached a Constable about the event which had just occurred. The Constable then approached James, who claimed he was "Jack the Ripper." The Constable appeared not to take the matter further, and James subsequently followed Hall and knocked him to the ground with a blow, the force of the blow being such that it caused the man's head to come into violent contact with the ground. The thud of the fall was heard by a Constable standing some distance away. Hall was removed to Guy's hospital where he died as a result of suffering an injury to the right side of his head. In court, James denied striking Hall and said he only pushed him in self-defence because he was making improper overtures to the woman he was with, who was a married woman. James, who had a previous conviction for assault, admitted he was guilty of manslaughter by a shove. He was sentenced on 7 January 1889, to 18 months imprisonment.

JILL THE RIPPER

William Stewart, in the (1939) book: Jack the Ripper a New Theory, suggested that the Ripper was a woman abortionist or midwife who might have been betrayed, perhaps by a woman she had helped. The midwife was then sent to prison; whereupon her release had sworn revenge on her own sex. Stewart believed the abortionist-midwife would be able to pass through the streets with bloodstained clothing without attracting undue attention and would explain why, when Mary Kelly was murdered; she was laid on the bed unclothed with her clothes neatly folded on a chair, awaiting an abortion from the midwife she had contracted. William Stewart, was not the only theorist to believe that the Ripper may have been a woman. Sir Arthur Conan Doyle, the creator of Sherlock Holmes, had earlier suggested that the killer might have disguised himself as a midwife when making his escape through the crowded streets while heavily bloodstained. According to author Donald McCormick, Inspector Abberline at the time of the murders discussed the possibility that the Ripper may have been a woman, with his friend and mentor Dr Thomas Dutton, after Mrs Caroline Maxwell reported seeing and speaking to Mary Kelly, outside the Britannia public house, wearing a dark shirt, velvet bodice, and a maroon-coloured shawl, hours after she was supposedly murdered. Maxwell was quite adamant that it was Kelly she saw and not someone else. Abberline cross-questioned

Maxwell again and again but failed to prove she was lying or perhaps mistaken. Abberline asked Dutton,:

"Do you think it could be a case of not Jack the Ripper, but Jill the Ripper. And was it possible that the killer may have dressed up in Kelly's clothes to disguise herself, and when spoken to by Maxwell pretended to be Mary Kelly."

Dutton replied:

"He believed it was doubtful, but if the killer were female the only kind capable of perpetrating such an act would be a midwife, for they might just possibly possess enough surgical skill and knowledge of anatomy to carry out these diabolical crimes."

William Stewart was pre-dated in his belief that the Ripper was a woman by Lawson Tait, an eminent surgeon, who suggested in 1889 that the Ripper was: "A big strong woman who worked in one of the local slaughterhouses, who concealed her bloodstains by rolling up her skirt, and walking through the streets covered by a heavy petticoat." Lawson also believed the murderer was an epileptic maniac, who committed the murders while the fit is on, being unconscious of the crime afterwards.

JILL THE SAILOR

On 8 September 1955, the London Evening News reported the story of an ex-convict prison number SYF 45 (name not revealed), who eighteen years previously was told by a fellow prisoner in Parkhurst that his wife was Jack the Ripper. The man, who was Roman Catholic, wished to unburden his conscience. He told a tale of how he had been a steward on board a liner, and on his very last trip, picked up a prostitute. His wife found out about his indiscretion and refused to live with him, they, however, continued to occupy the same house. One morning the husband found a bloodstained pair of his trousers hanging out to dry. When he confronted his wife about this, she broke down and confessed that she had been killing prostitutes because one of "their kind" had ruined their lives and seduced her husband. She was determined to see that as many as possible did not ruin other people's lives. When she committed the murders she borrowed her husband's knife, which had been a wedding present, and claimed she dressed as a sailor, and kept her nurse's cloak and bonnet in her bag ready to change into when the deed was over, thus avoiding any suspicion, as the police were looking for a man. Her husband at first disbelieved her story, until she told him the name of her latest victim "Mary Kelly." The very woman who had picked him up. She stopped killing after hearing that a man had been arrested for the murders, and claimed that she would give herself up if the man was actually charged.

JAMES JOHNSON

James Johnson was charged at Dalston Police Court with assaulting a well-known prostitute, Elizabeth Hudson, at the corner of Richmond Road, Dalston. Hudson described as, "A woman of loose character," told how at 2 am the accused approached her and threw her to the floor, at the same time pulling from his coat pocket a long knife about eight-ten inches long, with a sharp point and attempted to stab her. Hudson's screams of murder alerted the police, who apprehended Johnson as he attempted to flee the scene. However, when searched, no knife was found on him. Johnson, in his defence, said: "Everything the female has said is entirely the other way round. They used dirty insulting language to me, one of them put her hand in my pocket and I gave her a shove and she went down. She was so drunk; she did not want much force. I have never been in a court of justice before in my life, I work for a living. I had

259

no knife in my possession and I never carry one."Hudson's friend, Alice Anderson, a feather curler, (curled feathers to prepare them for use in hat making, etc.) who resided at the same address as Hudson, also made the claim that the man had previously accosted her in Kingsland Road, near the Lamb public house. James Johnson was described as aged 35, respectable, well set, clean shaven with a pale complexion and spoke with a strong American accent. He gave his occupation as a waiter and resided at 18 Bridhurst Road, Wandsworth. His landlady, Mrs Seaton, had known him as a respectable man for a long time. The magistrate discharged him, remarking: "that he had got himself into a very awkward scrape by his own folly." The police claimed that Hudson was the worst and most troublesome prostitute in the neighbourhood.

JOHN JOHNSON

In January 1901, John Johnson, aged 24, of no fixed abode, and well know to the police, was brought before Sheffield Court House, on three charges.The first was of breaking into the warehouse of Arthur Lambert, razor manufacturer, of 29, Norfolk Lane, and stealing 22 or 23 dozen razors, a leather bag, three spoons, four folks, and 5s in money. Mr. Lambert said he had left his warehouse secure on Saturday, 20 October, and on the following Monday, found that it had been broken into. The back window had been forced and the items worth £11 or £12 stolen. Johnson left the razors at the house of Thomas Hurt, 6 court, 3 house, Gilpin Street. Hurst's wife said she knew Johnson as "Jack the Ripper."Johnson was next charged with stealing a till containing £2 17s 7d, the property of Frederick Jeckells, decorator, of 244, West Street. The theft occurred on 21 June. Johnson went into Jeckell's shop, asked some questions about the price of a bucket, the pushed the assistant aside, seized the till and made off. He was seen putting the contents of the till in his pocket and throwing the till away. The third offence was the theft of a suit of clothes value 17s. From the shop of James Henry Hall, second-hand clothes dealer, 218, Bramall Lane. Johnson when arrested admitted stealing the clothes, but denied the other two charges.

JOHN SOLOMON JONES

John Solomon Jones, a slate merchant, was fined 10s, and costs in Liverpool, for being drunk and disorderly. He was running about the streets in a drunken condition, followed by a mob, yelling that he was the Whitechapel murderer, and threatening to have the lives of those following him. The incident happened in October 1888. When he had sobered up, he said he knew nothing about it. He was fined 5s for being drunk and disorderly.

NATHAN KAMINSKY

Nathan Kaminsky was born in 1865 and was 23 years of age at the time of the Ripper murders. He was a Jewish boot maker, who resided at 15 Black Lion Yard. Diagnosed as suffering from syphilis, 24 March 1888, he was treated in Ward BB, at the Whitechapel Workhouse Infirmary and was discharged as cured six weeks later. 12 May 1888. Martin Fido, in the (1997) book: The Crimes Detection and Death of Jack the Ripper, suggests that Kaminsky was, in fact, the real Leather Apron and that John Pizer was identified in error. This hypothesis is based on the fact that Kaminsky's age, race and occupation are identical to David Cohen, and therefore they must be one and the same. Fido suggests that following the hunt for Leather Apron, Kaminsky changed his name and occupation prior to his attack of raving mania. Therefore, when he was arrested it was under the incorrect name of David Cohen. Fido surmises that Kaminsky

261

was the real second suspect named in the Macnaghten Memoranda and that the name Kosminsky was used in error.

JAMES KELLY

Named as Jack the Ripper by authors James Tully in the (1997) book: The Secret of Prisoner 1167 Was This Man Jack the Ripper, and by John Morrison in the (1988) book: Jimmy Kelly's Year of Ripper Murders.

James Kelly was born 20 April 1860 at 43 St Mary's Street, Preston, to Sarah Kelly, an illiterate 15-year-old Liverpudlian, and John Miller a clerk. Miller deserted Sarah upon finding out that she was pregnant, and fearing shame having a child out of wedlock, Sarah allowed the boy to be brought up by her mother Teresa, in Southport. In 1870 Sarah met John Allan a master mariner, who had a share in his own ship. They soon married and went to live at 95 Manchester Road, Southport. Sarah did not reveal to her husband that she had a son and their marriage was short lived. Allan died on 16 May 1874 at Pisagua in Peru. He left everything to Sarah, who now wanting to make some form of recompense to her son, made a will on 22 July 1874, leaving everything to him. The money £25.000 was to be held in trust until he reached the age of 25. Sarah, who had been unwell for some years with a disease of the liver, died on 29 July 1874 at the age of 29, two months after her husband. James Kelly was therefore raised believing his grandmother was his real mother. He left school at the age of thirteen and was apprenticed to the firm of upholsterers Ray & Miles of London Road, Liverpool. At the age 17, a position was found for him at Isaac H. Jones pawnbrokers, 102 West Derby Road, Liverpool. In 1878 at the age of 18, he moved to London. In 1881 he met his future wife to be Sarah Ann Brider, who was known as "Titty" to her family. Sarah was born in Islington 18 June 1861, to John Charles Brider,

262

a bricklayer, and Sarah Ann (née Booker). She was described as a very reserved good living girl, modest and proper, who was employed as an Indian envelope folder by Thomas De La Rue at 107-115 Bunhill Row. Kelly paid regular visits to see Sarah and her family at 21 Cottage Lane, which was just off City Road. Sarah's parents thought him a serious and religious young man with good prospects. In March 1882 Kelly moved in as a lodger. The conditions for the young courting couple were far from ideal and provided little in the way of privacy, for also living at 21 Cottage Lane were Sarah's mother and father, her sister, her three brothers and a lodger, whom Kelly had to share a room with. Kelly frustrated at the lack of intimacy with Sarah, began to seek the company of prostitutes, which resulted in him contracting a venereal disease, fearful of doctors, he decided to treat himself with a syringe. His mood and behaviour had begun to change, and he was suffering from a nasty discharge from both ears and became convinced he had abscesses in his head. Despite their problems, and Kelly's deteriorating mental state the couple married on 4 June 1883 at St Luke's Parish Church, Old Street. James Kelly was 23, Sarah 21 years of age. There was to be no honeymoon, and the couple did not sleep together on their wedding night, they simply went home from the church, changed clothes before going off to work. From the outset the marriage was described as stormy, and the fact that the couple were now married made little difference to their living arrangements, and they still did not have a room of their own. Kelly's mood and behaviour were now getting much worse and he became jealous and suspicious of Sarah talking to people, claiming that she is cheating on him with men on the street. After being confronted by his mother in law and wife about his self treatment (after they found the syringe and drugs when cleaning his shared room) he flew into a rage, and accused Sarah of being a prostitute who has infected him. On 21 June during a violent argument, Kelly stabbed his wife in the throat with a pocket knife. They had been married a little over 2 weeks. The following report is from The Clerkenwell Press, Saturday, 30 June 1883:

James Kelly, 23, an upholsterer, of 21, Cottage-lane, City-road, St. Luke's, was charged before Mr Barstow, at Clerkenwell Police-court, on Friday, with attempting to murder his wife, Sarah Ann Kelly, by stabbing her in the neck at the above address, on the previous night. Police-inspector Maynard said the prosecutrix was lying at St. Bartholomew's Hospital and was too injured to attend. Mrs Sarah Brider, the mother-in-law to the prisoner, said that Kelly had only been married to his wife a little over a fortnight. She lived in the same house with them. On the previous night, they were all in the parlour, and the prisoner accused his wife of keeping the company of girls of loose character at Islington. There had for a day or two previously been a slight quarrel between them. She said, in reply, "I won't live with you any longer; you are unkind and cruel." The prisoner said, "You won't leave me; I'll stop you from doing so," and added that he would "knock her down." Nothing further was said at the moment, but after a few minutes, he asked her to forgive him, and sit by his side on a couch. She said she could not forgive him, and the witness saw him put his arm around her neck and drag her head down to the floor. He then ran out of the room, and his wife fell down on the carpet in a swoon, bleeding very much at the neck. A doctor was sent for, and she was conveyed to the hospital. Dr Raynor said that on the prisoner's wife being admitted to the hospital she was in an unconscious state. She had a puncture wound below the left ear nearly three inches deep. Her life was very much in danger. The prisoner was taken into custody by the police on returning to the room. A pocketknife was found on the floor with the blade broken sharply off from the handle. Mr

264

Barstow remanded the prisoner. Police-inspector Poule, of the G division, reported to Mr Barstow, on Saturday afternoon, that the young woman was in a dying state, almost all hopes having been given up for her recovery. Mr Barstow, accompanied by the inspector and the chief clerk, at once drove to St. Bartholomew's Hospital, in order that the injured woman's depositions might be taken down in writing. When the prisoner, James Kelly, who has only been married to his wife for a fortnight was charged with the attempted murder on Friday, evidence was given by his mother-in-law, that in consequence of a quarrel with his wife, he stabbed her under the left ear with a pocket-knife, inflicting a deep wound. The prisoner stands remanded till next Friday. On Monday morning Police-inspector Maynard, of the G division, reported to Mr Hosack, the sitting magistrate at the Clerkenwell Police-court, that the woman had died at half-past ten on Sunday night. Yesterday morning Mr Langham held an inquiry at St. Bartholomew's Hospital relative to the death of Sarah Ann Kelly, aged 22, late resident in Cottage-lane, City-road, St. Luke's, who is alleged to have died from injuries inflicted upon her by her husband, James Kelly, who is now under remand at Clerkenwell Police-court, charged with the offence. The Jury, after a short deliberation, returned a verdict of Wilful Murder against James Kelly. When asked if he had anything to say for himself Kelly replied:- "I don't know what I am, I must be mad."

Sarah died on 24 June 1883 Found guilty and sentenced to hang. His execution date was set for 20 August 1883. His impending execution didn't seem to unduly concern him as he believed he was on a "mission from god" and would be saved from death. A petition of clemency was lodged by his lawyers and among the signatories are Sarah's parents. On the 17 August Kelly is certified insane, and his sentence is commuted. He was sent to Broadmoor, from where he subsequently escaped on 23 January

1888 using the keys he had made from an old piece of metal he had unearthed whilst digging in the kitchen garden. He remained at liberty for a remarkable 39 years. Heading to London, then to France and America, he found work as a coach trimmer in various motor works, and on at least two occasions while at large, decided to give himself up. First on the 27 January 1896 and again in 1901, before having a change of heart, after authorities failed to meet his ship to apprehend him. In 1917 he went totally deaf and was now beginning to find life a struggle. He worked until he was 65 years of age, but fearing old age was closing in decided to give himself up. On 11 February 1927 at the age of 67 James Kelly, after claiming to have wandered around the world, voluntarily returned to Broadmoor, saying he wanted to die among friends. He also claims that:"I have been on the warpath since I left Broadmoor."The News of the World described him on his arrival at the gates of Broadmoor as, "A wizened little man with grey hair and wrinkled face, footsore and half starved." Kelly's mental condition had also begun to deteriorate and he was full of petty grievances and felt he was not receiving the attention due to him. At the beginning of 1929 he tried to escape again, but this time both his age and health were against him, and he could not repeat his feat of 1888. He died at the age of 69 on 17 September 1929 of double lobar pneumonia. He is buried in an unmarked grave in Crowthorne. In 1888, James Kelly was 5 ft 7 inches tall, with an olive-dark complexion, black hair, a heavy black moustache, spare build and a thin pale face. On the 10 November 1888, the day after the Murder of Mary Kelly, detectives raided 21 Cottage Lane and questioned Mrs Brider as to the whereabouts of James Kelly. According to author John Morrison, Kelly is supposed to have confessed to being Jack the Ripper on his return to Broadmoor. Morrison, however, offers us no evidence to support this claim.

JOHN KELLY

Proposed as a suspect by Terry Lynch, in the (2008) book: Jack the Ripper the Whitechapel Murders.

Common law husband of Ripper victim, Catherine "Kate" Eddowes. John Kelly was described as of a very pleasant demeanour. A quiet and inoffensive though peculiar looking man, with a fresh-coloured face, fine features, sharp and intelligent eyes, a head of thick black hair, moustache, and a somewhat low forehead. He was medium height, and described as a hard-working fellow. A labourer who also jobbed around the markets, for more than twelve years and had been employed fairly consistently by a fruit salesman named Lander. According to the newspaper reports is familiarly known as "Jack Kelly." He was a sick man, having a kidney complaint and a bad cough. Eddowes moved into Cooney's a common lodging house at 55 Flower and Dean Street, it was here she met John Kelly, and they lived together at this address for several years. On Sunday 9 September 1888, short of money the couple tried their luck hop picking at Hunton, Kent. They remained in Kent for over two weeks, though having had little success in finding work or earning any money, they made their way back to London on foot in the company of a woman named Emily Birrell and her husband (some newspaper reports state companion). They arrived back in London on Thursday 28 September 1888. Before the couples went their separate ways Emily gave Catherine a pawn ticket in the name of Birrell for two pence for a flannel shirt. Birrell and her man were on their way to Cheltenham. According to the Superintendent of the Casual Ward at Shoe Lane, Catherine told him, "I have come back to earn the reward money offered for the apprehension of the Whitechapel murderer. I think I know him." The Superintendent warned her to take care she was not murdered, to which she replied "Oh, no fear of that." Theorists have speculated that it was her lover John Kelly, whom she believed was the Ripper. Her remark "Oh, no fear of that," when warned to take care not to be murdered suggests, she felt safe enough in her belief that she would not become his next victim. If she did make these claims, and we have only the Superintendents word she did, she only said "I think I know him," leaving an element of doubt. On the morning of 29 September, Catherine and John agreed to pawn a pair of his boots; at Jones pawnbrokers, 31 Church Street, for 2s 6d, she received a ticket in the name of "Jane Kelly." They were seen having breakfast in the kitchen at Cooney's lodging house at around 10:00 am By 2:00 pm they were broke again, Kelly claimed he last saw Eddowes at 2:00 pm, in Houndsditch, when they parted company on good terms with Catherine saying she was going to Bermondsey to borrow money from her sister Annie, claiming she would be back by 4:00 pm. Other reports claim it was her married daughter, she was visiting. Kelly stated:

"I didn't want her to go that night, somehow. I was a bit afraid because of the Hanbury-street affair. However, she said she'd go, because she could get some help there, and the last words I said to her as she went out of the door were, "Don't be late, Kate, because of the knife!'"

By 8:30 pm she was drunk and causing a disturbance in Aldgate High Street. Taken to Bishopsgate Police Station where she was locked up to sleep off the effects of the drink. At 1:00 am, she was released, departing with the words "I shall get a damn fine hiding when I get home." At 1:45 am her mutilated body was found in Mitre Square by Police Constable Edward Watkin's. John Kelly under oath stated he was told by two women that Catherine had been locked up at Bishopsgate Police Station, for having a little drop of drink. John Kelly on reading in the newspapers of the pawn tickets in the name of Birrell and Kelly found in a tin box, beside the body, presented himself to the police and stated that from what he had been reading in the newspapers, he believed the murdered woman was his "wife." He then identified the body at the mortuary in Golden Lane, as his common law wife. Kelly appears to have an alibi on the night Eddowes was murdered, in Deputy Lodging House Keeper, Frederick Wilkinson, who spoke at the inquest: "I saw Kelly in the house about ten o'clock on Saturday night. I am positive he did not go out again." John Kelly was admitted to the Whitechapel Workhouse Infirmary on 29 November 1888, suffering from laryngitis.

To the newspapers, he spoke fondly of Catherine:

"Kate and me, he added, have gone through many hardships together; but while she was with me, I would not let her do anything bad." We lived very well together, and we never had a quarrel all the seven years we knew each other."

When taken to the mortuary last night he was very much affected and was completely broken down. In spite of the ghastly nature of the wounds in the face, Kelly at once recognized the woman as "his Kate,"

THE KENNINGTON SUSPECT

The Evening News, 10 November 1888 reported the following story:

THE SUPPOSED MURDERER SEEN AT KENNINGTON

A reliable correspondent informs us that on Friday morning, about 11.45, a respectably dressed man, a stranger to the locality, was observed to stoop and wash his hands in a puddle at the corner of Clayton street, nearest to the Kennington Oval. He wore a dark

269

suit, black coat, black billy-cock hat and had a small black leather bag with him. He was about five feet six inches in height, under 30 years of age; broad shouldered, and wore a thick dark brown moustache. The person who saw him wash his hands in this singular place declares that he noticed marks of blood on one hand. This, of course, occurred at a time when the news of the murder in Dorset Street had not reached Kennington. He further describes this mysterious individual as having a sallow complexion and a thin, clean shaved face.

CONSTANCE KENT

Constance Emilie Kent was born 6 February 1844 in Sidmouth, Devon. One of nine children, four of whom died within a few months of birth, to Samuel Saville Kent, an inspector of factories for the Home Office, and his wife Mary Ann. Constance was said to have been an unpleasant child, sulky, rude and morose. Her mother Mary Ann began to display signs of mental instability and died of an obstruction of the bowel on 5 May 1853. Her father, Samuel, within a few months of his wife's death married Miss Pratt, who was the governess of the children, and they moved to Road, near Frome in Wiltshire. Constance was said to have taken her father's remarriage rather badly, and became a nuisance to them, so much so that she was sent off to school in London. When she returned it was to discover the news that Mrs Kent had given birth to a boy named Francis Saville, whom the Kent's doted upon. On 29 June 1860 three-year-old Francis Saville, was found murdered, his throat cut by a razor, so deeply, his head, was almost decapitated from the body. There was also a wide, deep wound to the chest, which was said to have been caused by a weapon, other than the razor. Suspicion for the crime immediately fell upon Constance now sixteen years old. Scotland Yard was called in, and Detective Inspector Jack Whicher, quickly centred his attention on Constance. After questioning, and despite pleading her innocence, she was charged with the child's murder. The evidence against her, however, was weak and she was summarily discharged into the care of her father Samuel. Following her release through a lack of evidence for the murder of her stepbrother, Constance was sent away to a convent in Dinan, France for two years. Upon her return, she attended a religious school in Brighton. The school encouraged confession and sometime between 1863 and 1865 she confessed to the Rev. Arthur Wagner, the murder of her stepbrother and requested the confession be made public. In 1865 Constance appeared before Bow Street magistrates and confessed publicly to the murder. In a detailed confession she told how she had obtained a razor from her father's wardrobe a few days before, waited until everyone was asleep, then took the child from his cot to the shrubbery outside and proceeded to cut the child's throat, she then thrust the razor-like knife into his chest. This version of events, however, conflicts with the autopsy report, which stated that the wound to the body could not have been caused by a razor. Her motive for the crime she claimed was revenge against her stepmother, whom she felt slighted the children of her mother. Constance was sentenced to death, though due to public sympathy her sentence was commuted to imprisonment. One theory circulating was that she had confessed to the crime in order to protect her father a known adulterer, who had been having an affair with the dead child's nurse. Another theory is that Constance Kent's confession was indeed false and merely an act to shield another person, it was not for the benefit of her father, but for the benefit of her brother, William Saville-Kent, with whom she shared a very close brother-sister relationship. Constance spent 20 years in Millbank Prison, where she trained to be a nurse and was released in 1885 at the age of 41. She emigrated to Australia with her half-brother

William, and took up nursing, adopting the name Ruth Emilie Kaye.

E J Wagner speculated that due to her skill with a knife, and having already committed one savage murder, she was further responsible for the Ripper murders. She died at the age of 100 on the 10 April 1944.

MICHAEL KIDNEY

Michael Kidney, a waterside labourer, was born c. 1852 and was the lover of Elizabeth Stride and a witness at her inquest. Kidney was nine years Strides junior, and at the time of the murders resided at 36 Devonshire Street. He had been in a relationship with her, for about three years. Stride, when not living with Kidney, intermittently inhabited a common lodging house at 32 Flower and Dean Street, and would often disappear for days or weeks drinking. Her absences totalled about five months over the course of those three years. On 6 April 1887, Elizabeth was due but failed to appear in court to lay charges against Kidney for assault, her failure to appear would result in the charges being dropped. At the time of her murder Kidney said that he had not seen her for five days, though, was not concerned unduly by her absence as he still expected her home, when he got back from work. He stated she was sober when they parted. He did not believe she was seeing anybody else because in his own words, "she liked me better than anyone else" and it was usually the drink that made her go off. Stride was seen at about 12:45 am by Israel Schwartz, being assaulted in the street by a man he described as about 30 years old, 5 ft 5 inches tall, with dark hair, a small brown moustache, broad shouldered, wearing a cap with a peak. The man tried to pull her into the street, but instead turned her round and threw her down onto the foot-way, she screamed three times, but not very loudly. On the opposite side of the street stood a man lighting his pipe, the man who threw the woman down called out, "Lipski," it is not clear if this was directed toward the man lighting his pipe or at Schwartz. As Schwartz was of "Jewish appearance," the police decided the term Lipski was being used as an ethnic slur.

The previous year, a Polish Jew named Israel Lipski murdered Miriam Angel, a fellow lodger, at 16 Batty Street. Angel, who was also Jewish, was killed on 28 June 1887. Nitric acid had been poured down her throat. Israel Lipski confessed and was hanged at Newgate on 22 August.

Schwartz, who spoke little or no English, then walked away, whereupon he was followed by the second man for a short distance. Schwartz could not say if the men were together or knew each other, or if the second man was following him or fleeing the area as well. He described the second man as 35 years of age, 5 ft 11 inches tall, light brown hair, brown moustache, dressed in a dark overcoat and an old black hard felt hat. On 1 October 1888, Michael Kidney turned up drunk at Leman Street Police Station, announcing that if had been the policeman on whose beat Stride's body had been found, he would have killed himself. He also boasted that he could catch the killer if he had the men at his disposal; "If I was to place the men myself I could capture the murderer. He would be caught in the act." He had no further information to give. Michael Kidney was treated for syphilis 11 June 1889 at the Whitechapel Workhouse Infirmary, on 17 August for lumbago and 11 October for dyspepsia (upset stomach or indigestion), his age was given as 40 years.

A P Wolf, in the book: Jack the Myth (1993), suggests that Stride was not a Ripper victim, but was in fact murdered by Kidney

273

during a drunken quarrel. Wolf, does not state Kidney was Jack the Ripper.

SEVERIN KLOSOWSKI

A suspect since 1903 when he was identified as the Whitechapel murderer in the Pall Mall Gazette by Inspector Frederick George Abberline.

Born Severin Antoniovich Klosowski, on 14 December 1865, in Nagornak, Poland, to Antonio Klosowski, a carpenter and Emilie (née Ulatowski). He trained as a junior surgeon under Moshko Rappaport in Zvolen, from December 1880 until October 1885, then later studied at the hospital of Praga in Warsaw. His passport described him in 1886 as, age 21, height medium, hair of a dark shade, eyes blue, nose and mouth medium, chin and face longish. There is some uncertainty as to exactly when Klosowski arrived in England, though documents show he was still in Poland up until February 1887, therefore the best estimate Klosowski emigrated to London is June 1887. Roman Catholic by birth, he spoke Yiddish, but little or no English upon his arrival in London. He found employment as an assistant hairdresser for Abraham Radin at 70 West India Dock Road, and later took up employment, first as an assistant and later as proprietor of a basement barber shop 89 Whitechapel High Street, below the White Hart public house. On 29 October 1889, he married Lucy Baberski. The couple lived at various addresses in London, including 126 Cable Street, Commercial Street and Greenfield Street. In September 1890 a son, Wohystaw was born, but died on 3 March 1891. Soon after the loss of their son, the couple moved to New Jersey, America. The census taken in April 1891 lists the couple as living at 2 Tewkersbury Buildings, Whitechapel, so it is likely they moved to New Jersey around April 1891. Klosowski soon found work at a barber shop in Jersey City, while there, and during a quarrel, Klosowski held his wife down on the bed, pressing his face against her mouth to prevent her from screaming. When a customer entered the shop Klosowski calmly got up to attend him. Lucy then noticed a handle protruding from under the pillow and discovered a sharp and formidable knife. Klosowski later told her that he had intended to cut her head off, and pointed to a place in the room where he would have buried her. Lucy asked, "But the neighbours would have asked where I had gone to," which Klosowski calmly replied, "I should simply have told them that you had gone back to New York." In February 1892 Lucy would return to England alone to live with her sister at 26 Scarborough Street, Whitechapel, she later gave birth to their second child Cecilia, on the 12 May. Severin returned to England in the spring-summer of 1892 and the couple reunited for a short while before the relationship ended for good. In the winter of 1893 Klosowski met a woman named Annie Georgina Chapman (no relation to the Ripper victim Annie Chapman) and took her surname, henceforth he would be known as George Chapman. In 1893-95 he was working at Haddin's hairdressers 5 West Green Road, South Tottenham High Road, and later, in 1895, was working at William Wenzel's barber's shop 7 Church Lane, Leytonstone. Chapman, ended the relationship with Annie Chapman and met Mary Spink, who had been left a legacy of £500. Spink was an alcoholic and had recently separated from her husband. The couple moved to Hastings in March 1896 and opened a barber shop in George Street, which was by all accounts a great success. Mary played the piano while George attended the customers. It is claimed Mary would often be seen with bruises to her face and marks about her throat and neighbours would often hear her crying out in the night. On 3 April 1897, Chapman bought an ounce of Tarter Emetic from William Davidson's chemist shop 66 High Street, Hastings.

Tarter Emetic is a white powder often hidden in food, though has a slightly bitter taste. It contains a metal called Antimony a colourless, odourless and almost tasteless poison, administered in small enough doses it causes a slow and painful death. Antimony poisoning was often misdiagnosed as gastric fever, as the symptoms were similar. In larger doses, Antimony is likely to be expelled, and one of its characteristics is that it preserves the body many years after death.

In September 1897 Chapman and Mary returned to London and took the lease of the Prince of Wales public-house, which was situated off City Road in Bartholomew Square. Around this period Mary began suffering from severe stomach pains and nausea and died on Christmas day with her husband by her side. The cause of death was given as phthisis (consumption). In April 1898 Chapman appointed a new barmaid Elizabeth Taylor, known to her friends as Bessie. They became lovers and Chapman undertook yet another bogus marriage. In March 1899 they took over the Monument public house in Union Street, however, Bessie soon began to suffer the same symptoms as Mary Spink, and died on 13 February 1901. On this occasion, the cause of death was given as intestinal obstruction and exhaustion. Within a few short months Chapman was on the lookout for a new barmaid, and in August he employed Maude Marsh. She soon became his lover and his next victim. In October yet another bogus marriage was entered into, despite Chapman still being officially married to Lucy Baderski. In 1902 the couple moved to the Crown pub 213 Borough High Street. The same pattern ensued, Maud soon falls ill, though this time the victim was admitted to hospital on the insistence of her mother. While in the hospital her condition quickly improved, though she soon fell ill again on her return home, she died on 22 October 1902. An investigation into her death resulted in the exhumation of the bodies of Mary Spink and Bessie Taylor. Both showed signs of Tarter Emetic poisoning and both bodies were remarkably well preserved. Chapman was arrested, found guilty of three murders and hanged at Wandsworth prison on 7 April 1903. According to Hargrave. Lee Adams in the book: The Trial Of George Chapman (1930), when Chapman was arrested Inspector Abberline is reported to have said to the arresting officer George Godley, "I see you've got Jack the Ripper at last." Adam also reported that Abberline questioned Lucy Baderski about Chapman's movements at the time of the Whitechapel murders. Abberline retired from the police force in 1892 and therefore would have had no authority to question Baderski in 1903. This, plus the fact that there is no evidence Baderski knew Chapman before December 1888 makes this story highly unlikely. Abberline, in the Pall Mall Gazette 24 March 1903 said of Chapman:

I have been so struck with the remarkable coincidences in the two series of murders that I have not been able to think of anything else for several days past. Not, in fact, since the attorney general made his opening statement at the recent trial, and traced the antecedents of Chapman before he came to this country in 1888. Since then the idea has taken full possession of me and everything fits in and dovetails so well that I cannot help feeling that this is the man we struggled so hard to capture fifteen years ago.

The article goes on to say:

There is a score of things which makes one believe that Chapman is the man and you must understand that we have never believed all those stories about Jack the Ripper being dead or that he was a lunatic, or anything of that kind.

Was Klosowski/Chapman, Jack the Ripper?

We know Chapman had some medical skill, though to what degree is debatable. We also know he resided in London at the time of the Ripper murders and possessed a violent and misogynistic nature. Chapman does appear to fit, apart from his age, which was described as somewhat older the remarkably detailed physical description of a suspect seen by George Hutchinson with Mary Kelly shortly before she was murdered. Hutchinson described the man as 35 years of age, while Chapman was 23, though from the photographs of him appeared older than his years.

The main drawback against Chapman being the Ripper is that would a frenzied serial killer lay down his knife and be simply content to slowly poison his victims?. Chapman's victims were also dissimilar to the Ripper's victims in age and class. If Chapman was the Ripper how did he suppress the urge to kill again for over nine years, between the murder of Mary Kelly in 1888 and the murder of Mary Spink in 1897?

KARL KNAPPE

The Daily Telegraph, 10 September 1895 reported the following story:

In the Stipendiary Magistrate's Court this afternoon, F.H. Von Schoenberg appeared on information charged with libelling Mr E. Jellicoe, a solicitor, in a letter written to Mrs Chemis. The defendant, who has appeared both in the Supreme and Magistrate's Court lately as an interpreter in various cases brought by Knigge, restaurant keeper, versus his wife, all of which ended in a fiasco, asked for a remand, as he could not get a solicitor to act for him. He made a rambling statement accusing persons of being desirous to injure him and said that he had been twice accused of shooting persons, while all the time he was trying to bring "Jack the Ripper," whom he knew all about, to justice. He gave a description of "The Ripper," who he said had been stopping in his house in Timaru for some time. Jack's real name was Karl Knappe. He was an artist - "a spoilt artist" - of no means and no trade; a countryman of his and was, in addition, a cannibal. Defendant said he had seen him take pieces out of the bodies of his victims and eat them, "when he was hungry." At this stage, Mr Martin decided to adjourn the libel case until Friday, and in the meantime, Schoenberg agreed to substantiate the charges re the "Ripper in private to the magistrate.

BERTRAM KNUTSON

The Manchester Guardian 8 October 1888 reported the following:

For some days past the inhabitants of Eltham, in South-East London, especially the female portion, have been alarmed at a strange looking man sleeping in the woods and fields, and occasionally emerging into solitary places to beg. Complaints were made to the police, many people thinking he was the Whitechapel assassin. The police turned out in force to find him. Inspector Harris, on Friday night, found him asleep covered in grass in a field abutting on Nottingham Lane Eltham. He was taken to the police station and charged with being found wandering abroad and sleeping in the open air without visible means of subsistence. He gave the name of Bertram Knutson, his age as 23 and said he was a Norwegian sailor. He was arraigned before Mr Fenwick at the Woolwich Police Court on Saturday and was told that he must not go about in the present disturbed state of public feeling alarming people in the woods and fields. He directed the police to take Knutson to the workhouse.

There is a record of a Bertram Knudsen, born 1866, a sailor admitted to the Hackney workhouse, 29 July 1888. Discharged 31 July.

VASSILY KONOVALOV

Konovalov was born in 1857 in Torshok, Tver, Russia, and was supposedly a junior surgeon who in 1887 murdered a woman in Paris, five prostitutes in London during 1888, and a woman in Russia in 1891, before being finally caught and confined to an asylum. Konovalov was described as of medium height with broad shoulders and a curled and waxed black moustache. There is, however, no actual evidence Konovalov ever existed. The stories about him appear to be nothing more than another variation of the Russian secret agent sent to discredit our police force/government theory.

AARON KOSMINSKI

A self-described "armchair detective" and a Finnish molecular biologist have claimed to have discovered the identity of Jack the Ripper, A report in the Mail on Sunday names the killer as Aaron Kosminski. Molecular biologist Dr Jari Louhelainen used a technique called "vacuuming" to remove DNA from a stained shawl purportedly belonging to one of the victims, Catherine Eddowes. Businessman Russell Edwards had bought the shawl at an auction in 2007 and had asked Louhelainen to help him find any clues that may be connected with the Ripper case.

The scientist said that infrared imaging revealed that the stains on the shawl were blood stains and were consistent with arterial blood splatter caused by slashing. Louhelainen claimed that the DNA from the blood stains found on the shawl was a match for Eddowes. Other stains found on the shawl were fluorescent and had the characteristics of semen. Louhelainen said that a second

280

set of DNA tests was carried out on the stains after cells from the epithelium a tissue that lines cavities and organs were discovered in the stains. Two strands of DNA were tested against a descendent of Kosminski's sister. The first was a 99.2 percent match, while the other strand was a perfect match. Louhelainen wrote that the DNA extracted from the shawl enabled him to specify Eddowes's killer as being of Russian Jewish ancestry with dark hair."I'm excited and proud of what we've achieved," Louhelainen told the Mail, "and satisfied that we have established, as far as we possibly can, that Aaron Kosminski is the culprit."However, scientists and scholars of the Ripper case have already cast doubt on Edwards and Louhelainen's specific claims, alleging that the evidence on the shawl is so compromised that any positive identification may be impossible.

Aaron Kosminski was named in the Macnaghten Memoranda, along with Montague John Druitt and Michael Ostrog, as more likely to have been Jack the Ripper than Thomas Cutbush. Macnaghten, in his draft memorandum, described No.2: Kosminski:

A Polish Jew, who lived in the very heart of the district where the murders were committed. He had become insane owing to many indulgences in solitary vices. He had a great hatred of women, had strong homicidal tendencies and was, and I believe still is, detained in a lunatic asylum about March 1889. This man in appearance strongly resembled the individual seen by the City PC near Mitre Square. There were many circumstances connected with this man, which made him a strong suspect.

Sir Robert Anderson had first dropped a hint in 1901 that the police knew the identity of the Ripper in an article entitled Punishing Crime, he wrote:

Jack the Ripper was safely caged in an asylum.

He repeated this claim once again in 1907 in his book: Criminals and Crime. Anderson expanded on this a little more in 1910 in his memoirs The Lighter Side of My Official Life, he wrote:

I will merely add that the only person who ever had a good view of the murderer, unhesitatingly identified the suspect the instant he was confronted with him. In saying that he was a Polish Jew, I am merely stating a definitely ascertained fact.

In 1987 Chief Inspector Donald Swanson's personal copy of Anderson's book appeared, complete with Swanson's handwritten notes in the margins and endpaper, he wrote:

After the suspect had been identified at the seaside home where he had been sent by us with difficulty in order to subject him to identification, and he knew he was identified. On suspects return to his brother's house in Whitechapel, he was watched by police city CID by day and night. In a very short time the suspect with his hands tied behind his back was sent to Stepney Workhouse, and then to Colney Hatch where he died shortly afterwards, Kosminski was the suspect.

Aaron Kosminski, it would appear, was suspected of being Jack the Ripper by not only Sir Melville Macnaghten but also Sir Robert Anderson and Chief Inspector Donald Swanson.

Aaron Kosminski was born 11 September in 1865 in Klodawa, in the Province of Kalish in central Poland. The son of tailor Abram Josef Kozminski and his wife, Golda Lubnowski. He may have emigrated to England in about 1880/81 with two of his three his sisters and their husbands. He was a hairdresser, though one who had not worked for years. On 12 July 1890, he was admitted to the Mile End Old Town workhouse infirmary, from his brother

Wolf's Kosminsky's residence at 3 Sion Square, Commercial Road East. It was noted that he had been insane for two years. He was discharged three days later into the care of his brother, whose address is given as 16 Greenfield Street, this was the address of his brother- in-law, Morris Lubnowski. He was readmitted on 4 February 1891 from 16 Greenfield Street, and three days later was committed to the Colney Hatch Lunatic Asylum where he remained until 13 April 1894, when he was transferred to Leavesden Asylum for imbeciles. He remained there until his death at the age of 54 on 24 March 1919, the cause of death was reported as gangrene of the left leg. He was buried on 27 March at East Ham cemetery; his address was given as 5 Ashcroft Road, Bow, which was the home of Morris Lubnowski and his family. When Kosminski was admitted to Colney Hatch, it was said that:

He goes about the streets and picks up bits of bread from the gutter and eats them, he drinks water from a standpipe and refuses food at the hands of others. He took up a knife and threatened the life of his sister. He is very dirty and will not be washed.

When he was readmitted to the Mile End infirmary, Dr Houchin, who examined Kosminski, stated:

That the patient believed he was guided and controlled by an instinct that informed his mind, that he claimed to know the movements of all mankind and compulsively self-abused himself.

Let's look again at what Anderson and Macnaghten wrote. Macnaghten referred to a city P.C near Mitre Square, which was the night of the double murder 30 September. Except, there was no policeman who saw Catherine Eddowes with her killer, the only witness who saw a man with Catherine Eddowes and give a description was Joseph Lawende, except, Lawende was not a policeman. The only policeman who saw one of the victims with a man on the night she was murdered was Constable William Smith, except, Smith was not a city PC. Anderson wrote that the only person who ever had a good view of the murderer identified the suspect the instant he was confronted with him, but refused to give evidence against him because the suspect was also a Jew Constable Smith, however, was not a Jew. This only leaves Joseph Lawende as our witness. Lawende claims he only got a glimpse of the man he saw with Eddowes that night and doubted if he could identify him again. The first Seaside home where the identification was alleged to have taken place, did not open until March 1890 in Hove, and Kosminski was not incarcerated until February 1891. Therefore, the earliest the identification could have taken place was February 1891. If Lawende only got a glimpse of the man and doubted he would recognise him again, how was he able to identify him with such certainty some 15 months later? It is therefore quite reasonable to assume that Lawende was not Anderson's witness, so who was? Lawende was in the company of two men that night, Harry Harris and Joseph Hyam Levy, who saw Catherine Eddowes with her likely killer. Harris took no notice of them, and was unable to supply any description, and was not called at the inquest. Levy, who for reasons not known, became distressed by the couple, this has led to speculation that he recognised and knew the man seen with Eddowes, and that it was he who was Anderson's witness. Levy was called to the inquest, but was unable to supply a description, though the press remained suspicious as to the extent of what Levy actually saw or knew. On 9 October the Evening News reported-

Mr. Joseph Levy is absolutely obstinate and refuses to give us the slightest information. He leaves one to infer that he knows something, but that he is afraid to be called on the inquest. Hence he assumes a knowing air.

It was Joseph Hyam Levy, who supported the naturalisation application of fellow Ripper suspect Martin Kosminski. Despite the scarcity of the name, Kosminski, no connection has yet been established between Martin Kosminski and Aaron Kosminski.

Was Aaron Kosminski, Jack the Ripper?

He did not die soon after being sent to Colney Hatch as Macnaghten and Swanson have claimed, but some 30 years later. He was not removed to a lunatic asylum in March 1889 but February 1891. Even though few records of Kosminski's health have survived, in 1915 he was described as, slight in stature and light in build, his weight was given as under eight stone and even though his weight had slowly decreased he was described as in good health, which suggests that he was always slight of build. Aaron Kosminski was 23 years of age at the time of the Whitechapel murders. Kosminski was at liberty for nearly two years after the murder of Mary Kelly, so why did he stop killing? There is no evidence he possessed any anatomical knowledge or had violent, homicidal tendencies, toward prostitutes, and was not considered a danger to other people. The Mile End Workhouse Infirmary declared that he had been insane for two years, therefore the onset of his illness started before the Ripper murders commenced. In later years Macnaghten began to favour Montague John Druitt.

MARTIN KOSMINSKI

Martin Kosminski first came under suspicion by theorists after researchers noticed a link between Martin Kosminski and Joseph Hyam Levy. It was Levy who supported Kosminski's naturalisation application in 1877 and was also one of the witnesses who saw a man with Catherine Eddowes shortly before she was murdered. Levy became distressed by reasons which are not clear, this has led to speculation that he may have recognised the man he saw with Eddowes that night, as a relative of Martin Kosminski., or perhaps what caused Levy such unease was he spotted Martin Kosminski, with Eddowes.Martin Kosminski was born 1845 in Kalisch, Poland, in 1872, at Duke's Place Synagogue, he married, Augusta Barnett. The couple had three children, a son Charles born 1873. And two daughters, Jessie born 1875, and Katie born 1877. On 17 December 1877 he became a Freemason initiated into the Lodge of Tranquillity. In the 1911 census, he is aged 69 years, living at 50 Berners Street. Like his father, he was a furrier and was still in business at various addresses until 1922, when the business continued under his son's name.

H C KROMSCHROEDER

W. Cunliffe of 33 Harcourt Road, Brockley, SE, wrote to the City authorities on 8 October, 1888. About his suspicions of a German man, H.C. Kromschroeder of St John's Wood, who had been employed as a draughtsman at Woodhouse & Rawson's electrical engineers, Cadby Hall Works, West Kensington until 1888. Just prior to leaving his employment Kromschroeder showed his fellow workers a large & dangerous looking "Bowie" type knife which he had buckled to his waist. He was also according to Cunliffe in the habit of associating with women of loose character, and spoke of vengeful & bitter expressions of hate & violence toward them, he also spoke of "ripping them up." He spoke very good English without a German accent. His accent according to Cunliffe, was said to hail more from Birmingham, or the North or Lancashire. He was described as wearing a diagonal cloth coat, and a stiff brown billy-cock hat. Cunliffe believed Kromschroeder resembled the first of the two suspect sketches reproduced in the Daily Telegraph, newspaper.

Henry Christian Kromschroeder Crompton, was born in St Georges, Hanover Square London 13 March 1859. His parents were Herman Heinrich, Kromschroeder born Osnabruck, Germany, and Elizabeth Charlotte, (née Brown) in the 1881 census, Henry is living in Edgbaston, Birmingham, in occupation as a gas meter maker. He married 25 year old, Harriet Mary (née Reynolds) 7 August 1888, at St Marks, Church, Regents Park London. Harriet was born in Scotland, c 1863. She died at the age of sixty in 1923. His daughter Hilda Florence was born 17 August 1889. In the 1891 census, He is 32 years of age, living at 133 Charlton Lane, Greenwich, in occupation as an electrical engineer. His son, Eric Alwyn was born on 30 December 1892 in Charlton, Kent. In the 1901 census, he is living at Hoole, Cheshire, under the name Henry Crompton. He died 19 September 1923, at the age of 64, of heart disease, his address was 28, Redland Grove, Bristol, Gloucestershire. In his will he left effect to the value of £909 11s.

ARBIE LA BRUCKMAN

Proposed as a Ripper suspect in 2003 by Mike Conlon in an article "A Tale of Two Frenchys." for' Ripperologist: #32.

Arbie La Bruckman, was born c. 1860 in Morocco. He was 28 years of age at the time of the Whitechapel murders. He and his family arrived in New York around 1870, and he worked as a cattleman for the National Steam Navigation Company, sailing between the ports of Liverpool, London and New York. In 1891 he was described as about 31 years of age, 5 ft 7 inches tall, weighed about 180 pounds, with black hair a dark brown moustache and was said to possess a remarkably strong physique. La Bruckman in an interview to the press said:

My name is Arbie La Bruckman, but I am commonly called John Francis. I was born in Morocco twenty-nine years ago. I arrived here on the steamer April 10 from London." The reporter asked, "Why were you arrested in London?" La Bruckman replied, "About 11 o'clock one night a little after Christmas, 1889, 1 was walking along the street I carried a small satchel. I was bound for Hull, England, where I was to take another ship. Before I reached the depot, I was arrested and taken to the London Headquarters. I was locked up for a month, placed on trial and duly acquitted.

By way of compensation for his wrongful arrest, he was given a suit of clothes, and £100, in other reports he claimed he received £500. However, no record exists of such a trial having taken place.On the 24 April 1891 an elderly 60-year old prostitute named Carrie Brown, was strangled and horrifically mutilated. At about 11:45 pm Brown, entered the East River Hotel, New York, in the company of a man half her age. Mary Minter a prostitute and frequent visitor of the hotel assisted the night-watchman Edward Fitzgerald, and helped the couple procure a room, they were assigned room #31. The murder was discovered by Fitzgerald the following morning at 10:00 am. A trail of blood was noticed leading from room, 31 to room, 33. Amer Ben Ali was identified as the man who had rented room 33, that night. Minter remembered the woman as drunk, and the man as silent and grim. The police led by Inspector Byrnes felt they had a good witness in Mary Minter, who was certain she could recognise the man again. She described him as "being about 5 ft 8 inches tall, about 30-years old with a long, sharp nose, light-brown moustache and light-brown hair." She thought from the few words he spoke, that he was a foreigner. He wore a light overcoat a

288

black derby hat and impressed her as fairly well dressed. Arbie La Bruckman was arrested on the 29 April 1891. He told the police that he was at his lodging house, 81 James Street, at the time Carrie Brown was murdered and that persons there could vouch for his whereabouts, they presumably did so, and he was subsequently released without charge. Despite protesting his innocence, and the evidence against him largely circumstantial, Amer Ben Ali was convicted of second degree murder and sentenced to life imprisonment. He served 11 years in prison, before he was released.

JAMES DAVID LAMPARD

James David Lampard a brick mould maker was born in Stepney in 1850. The son of James Lampard and Elizabeth (née Link). His father was also a brick mould maker, as was his grandfather James Leonard. His father filed for bankruptcy in 1882, and died in 1890. The family lived first at 27 Carter Street, Stepney, Bethnal Green, London and later at 27 Weaver Street. On 9 October 1888. J J Beckett, a barge owner and contractor of Union Wharf, East Greenwich, wrote to the police and informed them he believed he knew the identity of the Whitechapel murderer. He told them of his suspicions about a man named James David Lampard. He explained that he had visited Greenwich police station on Friday, 5 October 1888 and saw a copy of the letters said to have been written by the Whitechapel murderer. The writing and language in the letters struck him as familiar, Beckett, pondered the matter over and came to the realisation that the man he believed responsible for the recent crimes was a former frequent customer of his when he was the proprietor of the Ram & Magpie, Public-house, 1&2 Fleet Street, Bethnal Green. He came to know Lampard well and spent a great deal of time in his company. He told of how in former years Lampard was in affluent

289

circumstances, but had led a life of great profligacy and this had brought him to a condition little better than beggary. He further told that Lampard had travelled both the European and American Continents and often used slang American terms like "Boss" when addressing him. He also claimed Lampard had an interest in anatomy and dissection, having dissected and stuffed different animals and birds. Beckett made further inquiries about the man in Whitechapel, among people who knew him well. He learnt that Lampard had been "out of his mind" and had recently been a patient at the London Hospital. On 8 August 1888, he was admitted to the London Hospital suffering from "Nervous Disease." He was released on 25 August deemed cured. His address was 28 Thorold Street, Bethnal Green, and his occupation was Commission Agent. Beckett believed Lampard fitted the description given by a doctor in the Chronicle, as an educated man who had been insane but had been discharged and supposedly cured. Also, he knew the Whitechapel area well, having lodged in most of the lower-class lodging houses. Lampard was 38 years of age at the time of the Whitechapel murders. About 5 ft 8 inches tall, well built, and broad-shouldered. He had the appearance of a military man and was an enrolled militiaman (East Kent Militia) with a very authoritative tone of voice. He had a red face, pointed moustache, no whiskers, dark hair, a high forehead and was bald in front. Often wore a high hat and frock coat, sometimes a peaked cap. He always maintained a gentlemanly appearance even when badly dressed.

JOHN LANGAN

E.W. Bonham of the British Consul in Boulogne wrote to the police with his suspicions about a man named John Langan, who had asked the Consul for some assistance in enabling him to go to Cardiff, South Wales, with the intention of obtaining work in the coal mines. Bonham thought Langan fitted a recent drawing of the Ripper which had appeared in the Daily Telegraph 6 October 1888. Langan, who was described as an American, had no papers about his person or means of subsistence, and was detained as a vagrant and interviewed. He told police that when in America, he was employed in an ironworks and when last in England, lodged with John Richmond at 47 Castle Street, Hamilton near Glasgow, Scotland, before that he lodged with Mrs Davis, in Dufferin, a village two miles from Merthyr, Glamorganshire. He was subsequently cleared of any involvement in the Whitechapel murders.

JOHN LANGHORN

On 17 December 1888, In Montreal, a man named John Langhorn, was arrested after assaulting Miss Florrie Newcomb. The attack happened in La Gauchetiere, a dark quarter of the city. The man darted out of a gateway as she was walking along a darkened street, and caught her by the arm, exclaiming! "You must come with me." Her screams alerted two men who apprehended him on the corner of Montcalm Street without a struggle. The two men handed him over into the charge of two constables who also alerted by the woman's screams were hurriedly making their way to the scene. When he was taken into custody, he told the police, "I am Jack the Ripper. All Whitechapel is looking for me. I have just arrived. I intended to give myself up, as I have already killed fifteen, and I'll yet complete the number if you let me go. You had better hang me by the neck until I am dead." He then began to laugh uproariously. When he was searched, a letter in his handwriting and signed, Jack the Ripper, was found in his possession, along with 25 cents and a very large murderous-looking knife. He also wrote a letter to the chief of police in which he claimed to be Jack the Ripper, and stated that he wanted an investigation, and wished to be hung. The newspapers stated: He is a great liar. Langhorn was described as 25-years old, a diminutive individual about 4 ft 6 inches in height, wearing the latest London fashion and who spoke with an unmistakable cockney accent. The police say the man is a crank.

EDWARD LARMONTH

In November 1888, Edward Larmonth, a pauper and vagrant, terrified the inmates assembled in the Auckland Workhouse dining-hall by declaring himself to be "Jack the Ripper," while using extremely bad language. He was committed to hard labour for three weeks.

JOSE LAURENCO

Laurenco, born in 1862 was suggested as a Ripper suspect by Edward Knight Larkins, a clerk in the British Customs Statistical Department. Larkins believed that the injuries inflicted on the Ripper's victims were similar to the injuries inflicted by Portuguese peasants on their enemies during the peninsular war against France, and therefore concluded that the Ripper had to be a Portuguese sailor. Larkins diligently searched the shipping logs and found three men, Manuel Cruz Xavier, 37 year old cattleman, described as a short man, with black hair. Jose Laurenco and Joao de Souza Machado, cattle boat seaman, described as 41-years old, medium height, with a black moustache. Sailors from the three ships, The City of London, The City of Cork and The City of Oporto, whom he believed had taken it in turns to commit the murders, depending on which ship was in dock on the relevant night in question. When it was pointed out that none of the three men was in town the night Alice McKenzie was murdered, Larkins added a fourth suspect, Joachim De Rocha. Larkins theories were investigated by the police and the

British consul in Oporto, and shown to be without foundation. Larkins remained unsatisfied, feeling the police had failed to recognise the overwhelming evidence that the murderer was Portuguese. Dr Robert Anderson perhaps summed up best the official police view of Larkins theories in a memo to the Home Office, describing Larkins as, "A very troublesome busybody." Laurenco had not sailed with the ship The City of Cork when it docked on 8 November 1888, therefore there is no evidence that he was in London when Mary Kelly was murdered. Larkins concluded that Laurenco must have been a stowaway on the night Kelly was murdered.

Edward Knight Larkins was, born June 1840, in Dover Kent. He married Isabella (née Clarke), June 1863 in Lambeth. He died 19 May 1895 in Kent. His father, Richard Larkin, in the 1871 census is listed in occupation as a pilot. (A person who conducted vessels along the coast).

HENRI DE TOULOUSE LAUTREC

In the (2015) book: Jack the Ripper: The Case Solved, author Greg Alexander, suggests the artist Henri de Toulouse Lautrec, was implicated in the Ripper murders. Alexander, in his book speculates that:

Lautrec had relations with Ripper victim Mary Kelly, and may have painted her when she worked in a brothel in Paris. That the artist had an obsession with redheads, and it was possible Kelly at some point may have had red hair, on account of her nickname "ginger".A letter from Lautrec to his mother reveals that one of his girlfriends in Paris was English and that her first name had been Jeanette. Since Lautrec was in the habit of placing the extra name "Marie" in front of the first name, this English lady would therefore have been called "Marie-Jeanette." This is the very

293

name Kelly had picked up while staying in Paris and which had appeared on her death certificate.Lautrec had contracted syphilis from a notorious prostitute and also that one of Lautrec's girlfriends had come to a rather unfortunate end.Alexander is not of the opinion that Lautrec committed the murders in person or even that he knew they had happened, due to his physical handicap which meant he couldn't walk very far even with a walking stick. But that his chaperone/doctor Henri Bourges (1860-1942) was responsible, aided by some dubious unnamed accomplice, financed by Lautrec, father.

Lautrec was born 24 November, 1864, in Albi, France. He began drawing at a young age, when ill health kept him bedridden. Due to a genetic weakness Lautrec's legs ceased growing after he broke both his femur bones in separate, minor accidents during his adolescence. Lautrec had a normally proportioned upper body, but the stubby legs of a dwarf; his mature height was barely five feet, and he walked with great difficulty using a cane. Lautrec eventually established himself as the premier poster artist of Paris and was often commissioned to advertise famous performers in his prints. Toulouse-Lautrec is among the best-known painters of the Post-Impressionist period, with Paul Cézanne, Vincent van Gogh, and Paul Gauguin. He died at the age of 36 on 9 September 1901 due to complications from alcoholism and syphilis.

JAMES LEADBEATER

On 26 October, 1888, James Leadbeater, a labourer of Cinderford, was charged at Littledean police-court, with unlawfully and indecently assaulting and ill treating Catherine Abberly on the 23 October. When the case came up the charge was reduced to robbery. Abberly, an old woman, said the prisoner came to her house in the afternoon. She was sitting in the kitchen. He handed her a letter, but as she could not read she gave him it back, and asked him what it contained. He said it was an appeal for relief, as he was bad off. He had up till then stood at the door, but advanced into the kitchen, and placed his head near to her, and said, as he was very deaf, she must speak into his ear. He then took her round the waist. She screamed as loud as she could. He tried to put his hand into his pocket, but she prevented him from doing so. She managed to get him out of the house, closed the gate, went back into the house and shut the front door. The man waited outside a moment, then came back into the house and seized her again. She exclaimed, "Good god, its Jack the Ripper! He'll kill me." He then behaved in a grossly indecent manner towards her. She succeeded in preventing him from effecting his purpose. He then left the house. The prisoner had nothing to say in answer to the charge.

JOHN LEARY

Police Constable, Thomas Barrett 226 H was on routine patrol duty in George Yard on the night Martha Tabram was murdered, 7 August 1888, when at 2:00 am In Wentworth Street, he saw and spoke to a soldier. The Constable asked the soldier "why he was loitering around," to which the soldier replied, "that he was waiting for his mate who had gone with a girl." As Martha Tabram was estimated to have been murdered at about 2:30 am the identification of the soldier became vitally important. An identification parade was held at Wellington Barracks, Tower of London in August 1888, and Constable Barrett was told to be careful as to his actions as many eyes were watching him, and a great deal depended on him picking out the right man, and no other. Barrett walked along the line and picked out a soldier, who gave his name as John Leary. The soldier was able to provide the police with a satisfactory account of his movements on the night of the murder. It transpired that he had been in the company of Private Law, who corroborated Leary's statement and neither had been anywhere near Wentworth Street. Constable Barrett described the soldier he saw that night as 22-26 years of age, about 5 ft 9 inches tall, with dark hair and a small brown moustache, turned up at the ends. Inspector Reid concluded that Barrett had made a "great mistake."

HENRY EDWARD LEEKE

Leeke, an oil and colour-man, (manufactured paint, responsible for mixing the required colouring), of Gilbert-Street. Was accused by two men, William Avenall, 26, a chimney sweep, of Adam and Eve-court, Oxford-Street, and Frederick W. Moore, 28, a carver and gilder of Carlisle-Street, of being Jack the Ripper. On the 10 November 1888, shortly before 5 o'clock in the evening, Leeke described as a man of small stature, went into a public house in the neighbourhood of Berners Street, Oxford Street, when someone shouted- "Here's a funny little man, perhaps he's Jack the Ripper." Upon leaving the man was seized violently, hit repeatedly with a stick and dragged along the street in a brutal manner by Avenall and Moore, who said they were detectives in private clothes and were taking him to the police station. In court the two men, who were described as hard working and respectable, said in their defence that they first encountered Leeke sitting in a corner of the public-house with his head down and mumbling to himself, his strange manner alerted their attention, they asked the man "what was the matter," he replied- "Don't bother me, I'm in serious trouble." When they asked the man where he lived and he replied "62 Berner-Street," they knew this was not true as they did the chimney sweeping at that address and knew only females lived there. Avenall and Moore really believed the man was Jack the Ripper, and therefore believed they were justified in their actions in taking the man along to the police station. The magistrate said that to drag a man along the street saying he was the Whitechapel murderer in the present highly excited state of public feeling was a highly dangerous thing to do, and such conduct might actually lead to the loss of life. On the charge of impersonating a detective, the evidence was conflicting and was dismissed. On the charge of assault, the magistrate said the accused men would each have to pay a fine with the alternative one month's imprisonment, as there was no reasonable excuse for acting as they had. It was said that though Avenall and Moore did not beat the man, they so frightened him as to cause him to become ill and to get into such a state of nervous depression that he had taken to his bed.

CHARLES LE GRAND

Charles Le Grand, born c. 1853, used various aliases throughout his long criminal career. Le Grand, Grant, French Colonel, Captain Anderson, Mr Ohlsen, George Jackson, Charles Colnette Grandy, and Charles Granday. His probable real name was Christian Briscony, and is believed to be Danish in nationality. Le Grand, was one of two private detectives "Grand and J.H. Bachelor" hired by the vigilance committee treasurer and several newspapers. They promoted the candidature of Matthew Packer as a witness. Packer, an elderly greengrocer, who lived at 44 Berner Street, initially when questioned by the police, had no useful information to give. When Sergeant White, took his statement, when asked if he had seen anybody at the time he replied,

"No. I saw no one standing about neither did I see anyone go up the yard. I never saw anything suspicious or heard the slightest noise and know nothing about the murder until I heard of it in the morning".

Two days later the visit of the two detectives at his small shop and home, prompted Packer's memory to greatly improve, he now remembered selling black grapes to Ripper victim Elizabeth Stride and her companion on the night she was murdered. Le Grand and Bachelor, took Packer, to the morgue where he identified the body of Elizabeth Stride as the woman he had sold the grapes to. Later that day they escorted Packer in a Hansom cab to Scotland Yard to make his statement. Dr. Phillips was convinced the deceased had not swallowed grapes within many hours of death. However, he did say that on one of the handkerchiefs found on the body, he found stains believed to be fruit. Le Grand was a convicted crook, blackmailer, pimp and con man, in 1877, he was sentenced to seven years in prison, for a series of thefts. In 1888, he reinvented himself as Charles Le Grand private enquiry agent, with offices at 283 Strand. He was again in trouble in 1889, for sending threatening letters, to a Harley Street surgeon, and demanding money. For this he received a sentence of two years imprisonment with hard labour. On 6 October 1891, he was charged with extortion and possessing a forged cheque. All the recipients were ladies of some wealth and position. In the letters he made the most horrible threats as to what he would do unless his demands were complied with. Interestingly, all the letters were written in red ink. He was sentenced to a total of 27 years in imprisonment. He served 15 years in Portland and Parkhurst prisons, he was released on 5 January 1907. In 1908, he was sentenced to two years imprisonment for forgery. Le Grand was a member of the vigilante groups during the ripper scare, and it is speculated may have used the knowledge of where exactly the police patrols would be, and was Jack the Ripper himself. The Times newspaper described Le Grand in 1891 as a "tall, well dressed man of military appearance". His age in 1888, would have been 35. He died in Copenhagen 6 December 1935.

KING LEOPOLD II

Suspected of being Jack the Ripper by the writer Jaquemine Charrot-Lodwidge, while undertaking research for theorist and author Daniel Farson. Lodwidge noticed the following points about Leopold and became suspicious. That he led a scandalous life. That during his reign Belgium retained possession of the Congo and during these visits to the Congo may have developed a sadistic nature, after observing Congolese customs and rituals. And whose house in London may have been the one, medium Robert Lees, led the police to after he had received a psychic impression of the murderer.

Louis Marie Philippe Victor was born in Brussels on 9 April 1835 and was a member of the Saxe-Coburg family. Leopold II was a first cousin of Queen Victoria. His mother, Louise, was a descendant of Empress Maria Theresa of Austria, as was his future wife. He ascended the throne at the age of 30 on 17 December 1865; on the death of his father Leopold I. He took the name Leopold II and married Marie Henriette of Habsburg-Lorraine Archduchess of Austria, on 22 August 1853, and they had four children. He greatly admired his father's attempts to increase Belgium's influence in the world, ideas he shared. His long-held belief was that Belgium should become a colonial power; he wanted to give Belgium an Empire which was consonant with those of Great Britain and France. He also wanted a Merchant Navy, and outlets for his country, his speeches in the Senate were indicative to his ideas, and he proclaimed that "All I desire is to leave Belgium larger, stronger and more beautiful." He was instrumental in launching several major public works aimed at improving the country's economic

299

infrastructure, such as the modernization of Antwerp Harbour, and the building of the Gileppe dam. He wanted to turn Brussels into a real capital city and commissioned the mapping-out of broad thoroughfares and parks, and invested a major part of his income in public works. His life, however, was not without scandal, as he amassed a personal fortune by exploiting free slave labour. Belgium gained recognised possession of the Congo in April 1884 and did not relinquish control until 10 August 1908, shortly before his death, during which time the Congo was exploited and stripped of much of its natural resources. The writer Mark Twain called Leopold, "The slayer of 1.5 million Congolese, and a greedy, grasping, avaricious, cynical, bloodthirsty old goat." Sir Arthur Conan Doyle published The Crime of the Congo, an account of how under Leopold's rule the Congolese had been robbed of all they possessed on such a scale that "Has never, to my knowledge, occurred before in the whole course of history." Over the time of Leopold's rule, the population of the Congo declined from an estimated 20-30 million to less than nine million. Leopold married his lover, Blanche Delacroix, on 12 December and died five days later at the age of seventy-four from a stroke, on 17 December 1909. There is no evidence Leopold II was in London at the time of the Whitechapel murders. The London residence identified by Lees was clearly described as belonging to an eminent Physician. Charrot Lodwidge is incorrect when stating that Leopold observed Congolese rituals, Leopold never visited the region, but instead ruled by decree from Belgium.

ARTHUR LEVENDON

The Hull Daily Mail 3 July 1908. Reported the following Jack the Ripper story:

For some days the pretty Surrey town of Kingston-on-Thames has been terrorised by the report that "Jack the Ripper" was

300

about, and meant to kill some of the school children. The description of a man with a naked bayonet chasing the children has caused panic. The description given of him was that of a man with a face of many colours. PC. Church was on duty at the foot of Kingston Bridge, when three little boys complained that a man had been chasing them in some gardens with a naked bayonet. On going to investigate PC Church found a 16 year old youth named Arthur Levendon, (newspapers incorrectly spelt his name as Lewendon) who had in his possession a sword bayonet and four pieces of rouge. His face was coloured red, blue, and green. Levendon had terrified a young schoolboy George Swaish by jumping out from behind some bushes and asking him if he was a nigger-headed Riddie? When the boy replied "no" Levendon replied "Well, I will let you go." Don't forget that I am "Jack the Ripper." In court respectably dressed Levendon a bricklayer, of Richmond-road, Kingston, said it was all a joke, his sweetheart was always talking about "Jack the Ripper" and he thought he would frighten her, as Jack the Ripper. He was fined £1 or 14 days imprisonment.

WOLF LEVISOHN

Wolf Levisohn was suggested as a possible accomplice of Jack the Ripper, alias Severin Klosowski, alias George Chapman, in the (2001) book: Alias Jack the Ripper by R Michael Gordon. Levisohn was described as a Jewish travelling hairdresser salesman, living at 135, Rosslyn Road, South Tottenham. At Chapman's trail Levisohn spotted him and said, "There he sits, that is his description, he has not altered since the day he came to England, he has not even a grey hair, always the same la di da." Levisohn also revealed that Chapman had asked him about a certain medicine, and whether he could procure some for him. Levisohn replied, "No, I do not want to get 12 years." Levisohn, while on business in Whitechapel at about 11:30 on the 15 November 1888, was accosted by two well-known prostitutes, Mary Ann Johnson, aged 30 and Christine De Grasse, aged 33, who solicited him, when he refused their advances they shouted, "You are Jack the Ripper." Their cries quickly drew an excited crowd; Levisohn fearing for his immediate safety took refuge in the Commercial-Street Police-Station. The women later reported that they accused him because he looked like the Ripper, with his shiny black bag. Levisohn lived in St. Ann's-Road Tottenham. According to a story told by Dr Dutton, Levisohn was reported to have told Inspector Abberline that Klosowski was not Jack the Ripper and that he should investigate a Russian barber's assistant in Walworth Road about the Ripper murders.

LEVITSKI

Alleged accomplice with Miss Winberg of Dr Alexander Pedachenko. Levitski was supposed to have been the lookout, while Dr Pedachenko committed the murders. And according to William Le Queux Levitski also wrote the Jack the Ripper letters. It is then claimed that he was exiled with Winberg to Yakutsk, Russia.

JACOB LEVY

Jacob Levy was suggested as a Ripper suspect by Mark King in Ripperologist, 26 December 1999 and 27 February 2000. In The (2006) book: Crimes of Jack the Ripper, author Paul Roland suggests Jacob Levy as a "very likely" suspect in his mind.

Levy was born in Aldgate in 1856 to Joseph and Caroline Levy, his father, being a butcher at 111 Middlesex Street, Spitalfields, it was a trade his son would subsequently follow him into. In 1881 Jacob Levy was listed as living at 11 Fieldgate Street, Whitechapel, with his wife Sarah, and their two children. In 1886

302

he was committed to the Essex County Asylum, after complaining of hearing strange noises, and saying that he felt compelled to do acts that his conscience could not stand, he also felt that if he was not restrained, he will do acts of violence to someone. In 1888 Levy was listed as living at 36 Middlesex Street, with his wife and children. On 15 August 1890 he was taken to the City of London Lunatic Asylum, Stone in Kent, and admitted as an insane person, his occupation was noted as a butcher and the cause of his illness was listed as mania. He was described as in good health; his height was given as 5 ft 3 inches tall, and his weight as 9 stone 3 pounds. Levy died of general paralysis of the insane (tertiary syphilis) on 29 July 1891. Theorists have speculated that Levy may have been the City police suspect, Detective Constable Robert Sagar referred to when he said:

We had good reason to suspect a man who worked in Butcher's Row, Aldgate. We watched him carefully, there is no doubt that this man was insane, and after a time his friends thought it advisable to have him removed to a private asylum. After he was removed, there were no more Ripper atrocities.

Another theory is that the man seen by Joseph Hyam Levy with Catherine Eddowes outside Church Passage, shortly before she was murdered, which caused him to become alarmed, was Jacob Levy. Joseph Hyam Levy was a butcher who worked at 1 Hutchinson Street. Jacob Levy was a butcher at 111 Middlesex Street, only 60 yards away, so it is quite possible that Joseph Hyam Levy knew Jacob Levy and may have recognised him that night with Catherine Eddowes. Dr Robert Anderson, Assistant Commissioner, Metropolitan Police CID, in his memoirs, The Lighter Side of My Official Life (1910), stated:

That the only person who had ever had a good view of the murderer unhesitatingly identified the suspect the instant he was

303

*confronted with him, but when he learned that the suspect was a
fellow-Jew he declined to swear to him.*

Was Joseph Hyam Levy, Anderson's witness, who would not
testify against fellow Jew, Jacob Levy?

JULIUS LIPMAN

A report in the News of the World 21 October 1900 reported:

*The death has just occurred in the East End of London of Julius
Lipman, nicknamed Leather Apron, a jobbing cobbler, who in
1889, unfortunately, fell under suspicion of being Jack the Ripper.
He was easily able to satisfy the world of his innocence, the
stigma of the suspicion never was overcome, the little business
he had was gone. and he went to another neighbourhood, where
he took heavily to drink; he died in the hospital of neglect and
semi-starvation.*

Little is actually known about Lippman and researchers have
speculated he was possibly the Julius Lippman, listed in the 1881
census as born in Birmingham, Warwickshire in 1861. His
occupation is given as a slipper maker, his address as 3
Richmond Street, Newcastle Upon Tyne, and is marital status as
unmarried.

JOHN LOCK

The Morning Advertiser, Thursday 4 October 1888 reported the
following story:

*At 6: pm on Wednesday 3 October 1888, considerable
excitement was caused in the neighbourhood of Ratcliff Highway
by the report that a man was seen roaming about there in a
suspicious manner, with what appeared to be bloodstains on his
coat. The man was described as respectably dressed and had*

somewhat the appearance of an American. A crowd had gathered and followed the individual around, uttering threatening cries of "Leather Apron" and "Jack the Ripper." The man, fearing for his safety, took shelter in the Victory public-house, but the angry and restless crowd remained outside until a policeman arrived and advised the man to accompany him to the King David Place Police Station. Upon arriving at the police station the man was questioned and said his name was John Lock, his age was 32 and that he was a Naval Reserve sailor who had come to England with his wife from Australia on 28 April 1887. He said he had left a friend's house at 85 Balcombe Street, Dorset Square, that morning and was making his way to the docks at Wapping with the intention of finding a ship when a crowd noticed the stains on his coat and began to follow him. His light tweed suit was carefully examined and the stains were found not to be blood but paint and grease. After the crowd had eventually dispersed, he was subsequently allowed to leave the station without charge.

THE LODGER

In the bestselling (1911) fiction novel The Lodger, Marie Belloc Lowndes, tells the story of a retired couple, who not altogether successfully, rented out rooms in their home. Just when it seemed their venture would fail, they managed to rent an upstairs room at a higher rate than was usual, to a quiet, deeply religious gentleman, who spent his days reading the bible aloud and his nights on nocturnal wanderings. The man, it was noticed, left the house late at night and did not return until the early hours of the morning, whereupon he would conduct strange experiments on the gas ring in his room. The elderly couple, after reading through the newspaper accounts of a madman called the "Avenger" who was terrorising London, murdering, prostitutes, caused them to become suspicious of their new lodger when they noticed that his

305

late night wanderings coincided with the occurrence of the murders. They became convinced their Lodger was the Avenger.Mrs Belloc Lowndes apparently got the original idea for her story after she overheard a dinner guest discussing how his mother's butler and cook had once rented a room to Jack the Ripper. This story, though originally a work of fiction, introduced to the general public the scenario of the mythical lodger who turns out to be Jack the Ripper. Three films have been made to date based on this story. The first, The Lodger A Story of the London Fog, was directed in 1926 by 26 year old Alfred Hitchcock, and starred matinee idol, Ivor Novello. The second a 1944 film starred Laird Cregar as the lodger Mr Slade. The third movie starred Hollywood actor Jack Palance best known for playing villainous roles. Mrs Belloc Lowndes story of the nocturnal religious fanatic, it transpires, does have some basis in fact. Lyttleton Stewart Forbes Winslow, an early theorist and expert on matters of legal sanity, contacted the police with his suspicions about a Canadian, G. Wentworth Bell Smith. Smith had taken lodgings with Mr and Mrs E Callaghan in Finsbury Square and aroused their suspicions when he stayed out late at night, wore a different suit every day, talked and moaned to himself and claimed all prostitutes should be drowned. Mr Callaghan took these suspicions to Winslow, who in turn contacted the police. The police fully investigated Winslow's claims and found them to be without foundation. Winslow, however, for the rest of his life, convinced himself that he had not only identified Jack the Ripper but stopped his murderous ways by causing him to flee abroad. Another variation of The Lodger story was told by the painter and Ripper suspect Walter Sickert. Some years after the murders Sickert rented a room (believed to be 6 Mornington Crescent, Camden), and was told by the elderly couple who owned the property that the previous occupant of the room was Jack the Ripper. He was a veterinary student who would stay out all night, then rush out to buy the morning paper. He, also, on occasions, burnt the clothes he had been wearing the previous night. When his health began to fail his mother took him home to Bournemouth, where he died three months later. Sickert wrote down the man's name, believed to be Druitt, Drewett or Hewitt, in the margin of a book, said to be Casanova's memoirs. This book was given to Albert Rutherston, though, was lost during the blitz. A further variation on the story of the lodger, who transpires to be Jack the Ripper, is the mysterious occupant of 22 Batty Street, who aroused the suspicion of his middle-aged German landlady, Mrs Kuer, after he left behind a bloodstained shirt, along with instructions for her to wash it, claiming he would return for it shortly. On the advice of her neighbours, she contacted the police. The police took possession of the shirt and watched the house day and night, awaiting the man's return. This individual has been credited by theorists as Ripper suspect Francis Tumblety.

CHARLES LUDWIG

Charles Ludwig, also known as Charles Ludwig Wietzel, or Wetzel, according to various newspaper accounts, was a German hairdresser, born in 1848, he came to London from Hamburg in 1887-88 and found employment with Mr C.A. Partridge, a hairdresser in the Minories. He lived first in Church Street, with a German tailor named Johannes, from where he was asked to leave on account of his dirty habits, and later at a hotel in Finsbury. He was arrested by Police Constable Gallagher 221 H, after threatening 18-year old Alexander Freinberg with a long bladed knife, while drunk at a coffee stall in Whitechapel High Street, at 3 a.m. because he disliked the way Freinberg was looking at him. When the police later learnt from Ludwig's landlord that Ludwig had supposedly bloodstained hands and had earlier frightened a one-armed prostitute named Elizabeth Burns at Three Kings Court, Minories, in the early hours of Tuesday 18 September 1888, by brandishing a big knife, he immediately became a Jack the Ripper suspect. PC John Johnson, of the City of London Police, was walking his beat along Minories, when he heard a loud scream of "Murder!" The cry had emanated from a notorious trouble spot named Three King's Court. Hurrying in the direction of the scream, Johnson found a man and woman standing close to one of the railway arches. Johnson demanded to know what the man was doing. "Nothing," came the surly reply. The woman, who was evidently distressed, begged him "oh policeman do take me out of this," whereupon Johnson escorted them out of the alley onto Minories and ordered the man to be on his way. Once the stranger had gone, Johnson turned to the woman to see what other assistance he could render. "Dear me," she said, "he frightened me very much when he pulled that big knife out." We can only imagine Johnson's shock on hearing that he may well have had the Whitechapel Murderer in his clutches and had let him, quite literally, slip through his fingers! "Why didn't you tell me that at the time," he demanded of the woman. "I was too much frightened," she replied, coyly. Johnson carried out a quick search of the area in the direction the man had gone, but to no avail. Ludwig was described as 40-years old, 5 ft 6 inches tall, slightly built dark complexioned with a grizzled beard and moustache and who walked stiffly, as though something was wrong with one of his legs. Police received a "helpful" character reference of Ludwig from his landlord: "He is a most extraordinary man, is always in a bad temper, and grinds his teeth in rage at any little thing which puts him out. I believe he has some knowledge of anatomy, as he was for some time an assistant to some doctors in the German army, and helped to dissect bodies. He always carried some razors and a pair of scissors with him.

From what he has said to me, I know he was in the habit of associating with low women." While being taken to the police station Ludwig dropped a long-bladed knife, which was later recovered, the knife, it later transpired, was an ordinary clasp knife. When searched, a razor and a long bladed pair of scissors were found on his person; however, being a hairdresser this is hardly suspicious. He was still in custody on the night of the double murder, which confirmed that he was not Jack the Ripper.

SIR MELVILLE LESLIE MACNAGHTEN

Accused in 2007 by Sophie Howard, suggesting Macnaghten committed the crimes to embarrass Sir Charles Warren.

Born 16 June 1853, Woodford, London. Educated at Eton. Left school in 1872 to travel to India on behalf of his father to manage the tea business in Bengal. On 3 October 1878 he married Dora Emily Sanderson, with whom he had 4 children, two sons and two daughters. It was in India he befriended James Monro, who was the District Inspector General of the Police in Bengal. When Macnaghten returned to England, he was offered the post of Chief Constable (CID) by Monro, the Assistant Commissioner (Crime) at the time. Charles Warren the Commissioner of Police, opposed the appointment, it is speculated due to his dislike of Monro. On 9 November 1888, Warren resigned, and Monro became Commissioner. In June of 1889 Macnaghten was appointed Assistant Chief Constable, and then promoted to Chief Constable a position he held until 1903, when he was appointed Assistant Commissioner (CID) of the London Metropolitan Police. Knighted in 1907. He remained in office until 1913, when ill-health forced his retirement. Macnaghten Died 12 May, 1921

Macnaghten wasn't actually a member of the Metropolitan Police when the Jack the Ripper murders occurred in 1888. He would

309

later tell the *Daily Mail* that the greatest regret of his life was that he had joined the force six months after Jack the Ripper had committed suicide. Without publicly identifying the man he suspected of being the perpetrator of the murders, he told the newspaper:-

Of course he was a maniac, but I have a very clear idea who he was and how he committed suicide, but that, with other secrets, will never be revealed by me. I have destroyed all my documents and there is now no record of the secret information which came into my possession at one time or another.

He wrote his autobiography, Days of My Years, which was published in 1914. One of his most important statements on the Whitechapel murders was written in 1894, and is now known as the "Macnaghten Memoranda." The memoranda was written explicitly to refute claims being made in a newspaper that Thomas Cutbush, who at the time had been confined to Broadmoor Asylum, was Jack the Ripper.

In his memoranda – Macnaghten, wrote

Now the Whitechapel Murderer had 5 victims - & 5 victims only. Mary Nichols, Annie Chapman, Elizabeth Stride, Catherine Eddowes and Mary Kelly.

This established the idea of the "canonical five" victims of Jack the Ripper.

ALONZO MADURO

Mr Griffith S Salway, who worked for a City brokerage firm in Gresham House, Old Broad Street, London, came to know through his business dealings Mr Alonzo Maduro, who was a successful Argentinian businessman. Salway came across Maduro in Whitechapel and overheard him say that all prostitutes

310

should be killed. It is speculated Salway came across Maduro On the night Emma Elizabeth Smith was murdered Bank Holiday Monday, 2 April 1888, but Salway makes it clear he was referring to the murder of Martha Tabram, when he stated another murder was reported later that month, (Nichols) which would make it the month of August (not April). Maduro's behaviour became increasingly strange. When Salway met him for the last time in the Commercial Room of Anderton's Hotel in Fleet Street and discovered in the false bottom of Maduro's bag a bloodstained apron several instruments, and a large knife, it was at this point he became convinced Maduro was Jack the Ripper. Though kept his suspicions to himself until 1949, over 60 years after the event, when he told his tale to John Shuttleworth, editor of True Detective, magazine.

Maduro, was born in Buenos Aires, his mother died while he was in infancy. He was described by Salway as "perhaps a year or two under forty, with dark eyes and a swarthy complexion, clean shaven, stocky build, but quick and agile. Spoke with a barely discernible Spanish accent having spent a lot of time in the United States." The fact that he was allegedly in Whitechapel the night Emma Smith was murdered does not prove he was Jack the Ripper, because Emma Smith has largely been discounted as a Ripper victim. Before she died, Emma Smith claimed that she was assaulted and robbed by three men, one of them a youth of about nineteen years. She died the following day from peritonitis, as a result of a blunt object being thrust into her vagina. (Peritonitis is inflammation of the peritoneum due to a bacterial or fungal infection. The most common symptom of peritonitis is severe abdominal pain. The peritoneum is a thin membrane (covering), which lines the inside of the abdomen and surrounds and supports the abdominal organs, such as the stomach and liver).

In the (1999) book: Mammoth Book of Jack the Ripper authors Maxim Jakubowski and Nathan Braund's conclude that these two suspects Alois Szemeredy and Alonzo Maduro, we're one and the same

JAMES MALONE

James Malone appeared at St Helens Police Court, on 14 September 1891, charged as a lunatic wandering at large. After he was discovered by Constable Wilkes, wandering in a strange manner at 03:00, that morning. At the police station, when asked where he was going to, he said he did not know, but he knew that a lot of people were after him. He was a sailor, who had spent time in an asylum. His sister who lived in Tontine-street, said she was very much afraid of him, he was in the habit of throwing knives around, and calling himself "Jack the Ripper." He had previously been in an asylum, and had suffered from sunstroke while in India. He was sent to the workhouse for two weeks.

JACK MALTIMORE

The Stevens Point Daily Journal, Saturday, 9 December 1893 reported the following story:

A man who said he was Jack the Ripper applied to Sheriff Wheelock last Sunday evening for work. After talking with him Frank saw that the man was not in his right mind, and took him down to the jail and locked him up. He afterwards said his name was Jack Maltimore. He came here from Waushara county but says he has no relatives anywhere. He is strongly imbued with the doctrines of the anarchists and a great admirer of Gov. Altgeld of Illinois. When questioned by the Sheriff he said he had used dynamite; he also said he was handy with a knife. The former statement is probably the imagination of a disordered brain, but that he is a dangerous man to have at large there is no doubt. He says he is an Englishman and during the past summer worked on the World's fair grounds. On Wednesday he was examined by Dr C.F. Phillips and Dr Southwick, who pronounced him insane. He will be taken to the Northern Hospital near Oshkosh.

ROBERT MANN

Advanced as a suspect by M. J. Trow in the (2009) book: Jack the Ripper Quest for a Killer and the accompanying Discovery Channel documentary, Jack the Ripper Killer Revealed.

Trow used the 1988 FBI profile as the foundation for his theory. Special agent John Douglas, and Roy Hazelwood of the FBI were asked to use their acquired knowledge and collected data to prepare a criminal personality profile of the Ripper, made especially for the television documentary "The Secret Identity of Jack the Ripper". They concluded the following features of the profile:

• Was a white male, 28-36 years of age.

• Was of average intelligence, lucky not clever.

• Was single, never married, and had difficulty in interacting with people in general and women in particular.

• Was nocturnal and not accountable to anyone.• Blended in with his surroundings.

• Had poor personal hygiene, and appeared dishevelled.

• Was personally inadequate with a low self-image and diminished emotional responses.

• Was a quiet loner, withdrawn and asocial. • Was of lower social class.

• Lived or worked in Whitechapel, and committed the crimes close to home.

• Had a menial job with little or no interaction with the public.

• Was employed Monday to Friday, possibly as a butcher, mortician's helper, medical examiner's assistant, or hospital attendant (the proximity of London Hospital was noted in the profile).

• Was the product of a broken home, and lacked consistent care and stable adult role models as a child.

• Was raised by a dominant female figure who drank heavily, consorted with different men, and physically, possibly sexually, abused him.

• Set fires and abused animals as a child.

• Hated, feared, and was intimidated by women. • Internalized his anger.

• Was mentally disturbed and sexually inadequate, with much generalized rage directed against women.

• Desired power, control, and dominance.

• Behaved erratically. • Engaged in sexually motivated attacks to neuter his victims.

• Drank in local pubs prior to the murders.

• Hunted nightly, and was observed walking all over Whitechapel during the early morning hours.

• Did not have medical knowledge or surgical expertise. • Was probably interviewed by police at some point.

• Did not write any of the "Jack the Ripper" letters, and would not have publicly challenged the police; and

• Did not commit suicide after the murders stopped.

Robert Mann, born c. 1835, Mile End New Town. Pauper mortuary attendant in charge of the workhouse mortuary in Old Montague Street. An inmate of the Whitechapel Workhouse described as a labourer and dock labourer. Died in Whitechapel, in 1896, of phthisis, known at the time as consumption, we now know the disease as tuberculosis. Mann helped James Hatfield wash and lay out the body of Mary Ann Nichols in Old Montague Street Workhouse Infirmary. The police were criticised for allowing the body to be washed without adequate police supervision. Inspector Helsen insisted he had left strict instructions the body was not to be touched. These instructions were disregarded, and James Hatfield or Robert Mann instigated the washing of the body. At the inquest, the coroner Wynne Baxter instructed the jury to disregard Mann's evidence, as he was unreliable and had fits. Investigators noted strange behaviour in Mann, when the bodies of a few of the victims were present. For example, once he was specifically told not to touch a body, and he did so anyway. Mann was also present at the Annie Chapman inquest:

Robert Mansel [sic]: I have charge of the Whitechapel mortuary. On Saturday last I received the body of the deceased at the mortuary about seven o'clock. I was there most of the day. No one touched the body until the nurses came over and undressed it. I remained at the mortuary until the doctor arrived, and the door was locked. The police were in charge of it. No one touched the body except the nurses. I was not present when they laid the corpse out.

RICHARD MANSFIELD

Richard Mansfield was an American actor, though, was born in Helgoland, Germany, on 24 May 1857. The son of the operatic soprano, Erminia Rudersdoff, (1822–1882) and her second husband, English violin-playing wine merchant Maurice Mansfield. His father died in 1861 when Richard was 4-years old. Educated in Derby, England, he studied painting in London, though when this work failed to support him he turned to acting. He became a light comedy actor and singer with the D'Oyly Carte (Gilbert and Sullivan), provincial touring company. Married Beatrice Cameron an actress, in 1892. They had one child, Richard Gibbs Mansfield (1898-1918). At the time of the Ripper murders, he was starring in a production of Robert Lewis Stevenson's Dr Jekyll and Mr Hyde at Henry Irving's Lyceum Theatre. He came under attack and suspicion after many believed his convincing on stage transformation from a gentleman into a mad killer incited murder. His on stage transformation was achieved by the method of pre-painting the required face altering shadows in actors grease paint, this would be undetectable under normal stage light, then by the process of gradually introducing a coloured filter to the lighting, while simultaneously contorting his facial features, the monstrous visage of Hyde would eerily become apparent. In an attempt to stem criticism of him, Mansfield offered to present a special benefit performance for the Suffragan Bishop of London's home and refuge fund, who were trying to raise money to open a laundry for the employment of reformed prostitutes. The newspapers said Mansfield wisely selected Prince Karl a comedy in four acts for his benefit performance. Mansfield unfortunately, however, suffered financial loss due to falling audience attendances and cancelled the show. He died in New London, Connecticut, from liver cancer 30 August 1907 at the age of 50. At the time of his death, The New York

Times claimed, "He was the greatest actor of his hour, and one of the greatest of all times."

THEOPHIL MARY

A 29 year old male hairdresser named Theophil Mary, born in Alsace, Germany, was mentioned in the Scotland Yard files, 27 September 1888, and 19 October, having been arrested several times in Germany for assaulting women in Strasbourg and Bremen, stabbing them in the breasts and private parts with a sharp instrument. The attacks started in Strasbourg in 1880, and continued in Breman. 35 attacks were attributed to him. In 1881 he attempted to rape a 12-year old girl in his barber shop. The young girl was able to give a very good description of her assailant, and he was arrested the following day. Suspecting they had a possible Ripper suspect the British police contacted their German colleagues, only to find that Mary, had served a seven-year prison sentence, and had been rearrested immediately and was now serving a further twelve months at Oslebshausen prison for the Strasbourg assaults, and was not due to be released until August 1889; therefore was in prison when the Whitechapel murders occurred.

ARTHUR HENRY MASON

Mentioned in a Scotland Yard file which is now missing dated 18 December 1888. At 10:20 pm, 16 November 1888 John Hemmings of 11 Youngs Buildings, Kingston, and William Shulver of 201 Aspen Road, Starch Green, Middlesex, informed PC 548T, Robert Large, they were drinking in the White Hart public-house, Hampton Wick, Middlesex, and were talking about the "Whitechapel Murders," when another man Arthur Henry Mason who was in the public-house overheard their conversation and became excited. Mason's strange behaviour caused the men to become suspicious of him. They thought his description matched that of the Ripper in the newspapers, and duly informed PC Large. Mason lived at 12 Portland Road, Spring Grove, Kingston, London, and was employed as a compositor at Kelly and Co, Kingston. He was described as 32-years of age, 5 ft. 9 inches tall, fresh complexion with a thin face, whiskers and moustache. He was interviewed by the police and his statement was proved to be correct.

THOMAS MASON

On the 28 April 1895, the Chicago Sunday Times published a story in which it claimed the medium Robert Lees had received a psychic impression of the Whitechapel murderer. Seventeen murders later? The police asked for his assistance. Throughout the night Lees followed a psychic trail which ended at the house of an eminent Physician. The story goes on to say that the police questioned the doctor and his wife, eliciting the admission that the doctor suffered from occasional losses of memory, and had on one occasion regained it to find his shirt bloodstained. Proof of his guilt as Jack the Ripper was found in the house and he was committed to an asylum in Islington under the name Thomas Mason 124. Author Stephen Knight identifies Thomas Mason with Gull though miss-dates Mason's death as 1896. The real Thomas Mason was a 71-year old retired bookbinder whose address was given as Bookbinders' Alms Houses, Balls Pond, Islington. Mason, who was born in 1817, had no connection with Gull, or Jack the Ripper, and was never incarcerated in an asylum. He died in 1902 from bronchitis in Islington Infirmary.

OLIVER MATHEWS

Mathews aroused the suspicion of Richard Watson, of 21 Old Square, Lincoln's Inn who, while sitting next to him in the "Trevor"

318

Music Hall, Knightsbridge. Watson noticed that Mathews had in his possession a small black bag. Watson informed the police of his suspicions and Mathews was questioned and his bag searched. When his bag was opened it was found to contain clean linen. Mathews, who had resided at 14 Wharton Street, Kings Cross, for over a year, and whose appearance did not answer that of the Whitechapel murderer was able to satisfactorily prove his innocence.

ALFRED JOHN MATTHEWS

On 28 July 1889, Alfred John Matthews, of no fixed abode, was charged at Aston Police-court, with committing wilful damage to the house door of Mary Ann Riley, of Tamworth Road, Erdington. Matthews went to the house and kicked the door. When it was opened, he flourished a knife and said he was "Jack the Ripper." He was fined 1s and costs, or seven days imprisonment.

MAURICE

In 1884-85, a series of murders rocked Austin, Texas, the killer, known by the moniker, The Servant Girl Annihilator, was never apprehended. The newspapers speculated as early as 1888, that these crimes where connected to the Ripper murders. In November 1888, according to the Atchison Daily Globe, the Austin American-Statesman reported on a possible American connection to the Ripper: a Malay cook on an ocean vessel was suspected in the White Chapel killings. The article went on to report that a Malay cook had been working at a small Austin hotel called the Pearl House "near the foot of Congress Avenue." The Austin reporter learned a Malay cook named Maurice had worked there in 1885 before departing in January 1886. The last killings occurred just before Maurice left Austin. He told acquaintances that he was going to work aboard ships as a cook to earn his

319

passage to London for a fresh start. Stories of similar serial murders of women happening in port towns along major trade routes, like Nicaragua, Tunis, and Jamaica, were reported in the newspapers. The Pall Mall Gazette 18 February 1889, reported:

Some unknown criminal had perpetrated several murders of the well-known Whitechapel type upon the outcast women of Jamaica.

The New York Sun, 25 January, 1889, reported:

Six horrible Nicaraguan murders, in almost every detail the crimes and characteristics are identical with the Whitechapel Horrors. All the murders occurred in less than ten days.

The murders in Austin, Texas, began on 30 December, 1884, the Servant Girl Annihilator's, victims were initially all black servant girls. They were generally struck in the head with an axe, then raped. He killed eight times, seven of his victims were women, five black, two white. The last murder occurred on Christmas Eve 1885. The barefooted killer left bloody footprints at the scene of the crimes, the prints were distinctive: his right foot was missing a toe. Eyewitnesses accounts where conflicting: describing a white man, or a black man.

A 2014 episode of History Detectives identified another suspect. In 1885, Nathan Elgin was a 19-year-old black man living in Austin and working as a cook in a down town restaurant in close proximity to the crime scenes. One night in February 1886, a drunken, raging Elgin dragged a screaming girl out of an Austin saloon and into a nearby house. The police soon arrived and a cop named Bracken shot Elgin. The bullet lodged in his spine. Elgin was paralysed and died the following day. An autopsy revealed something startling: Elgin was missing his right toe. Sheriff Malcom Hornsby believed Elgin was the Servant Girl

320

Annihilator due to the distinctive footprints and the fact no murders were committed after his death.

Stephen Ryder, has shown conclusively that there was no series of murders in Jamaica, in fact, there was only one murder and that was solved. There was also no series of Nicaraguan Ripper, style murders.

FLORENCE MAYBRICK

In the (2017) book: "Jack n'est pas un homme." translated in English under the name "Jack is not a man". French author Pascale Leconte suggests Florence Maybrick as the Ripper. The book, is both fiction and non-fiction, part historical biography, part fantasy.

Born, Florence Elizabeth Chandler, in Mobile, Alabama, 3 September, 1862. Her father, William George Chandler, a banker and former mayor, died when she was a baby. Her mother the Baroness Von Roques, married twice more. While travelling to England, from New York, with her mother, she met cotton broker James Maybrick, on board ship. Maybrick was 24 years her senior. On 27 July 1881, they were married at St James's Church, Piccadilly, London. They lived in Battlecrease House, Aigburth, a suburb of Liverpool. They had two children, a son, James Chandler known as "Bobo" and a daughter Gladys Evelyn. After 5 years of marriage, Florence discovered that James had a long-term mistress. As soon as Florence found out about Maybrick's mistress, she stopped sleeping with him. Lonely and wanting a little romance, Florence began an affair with a businessman named Alfred Brierly but the affair was short-lived. In April, Florence had bought arsenic-laden fly paper around this time to lighten her complexion, she said — also a common practice at the time. James Maybrick's health deteriorated suddenly in April

321

of 1889, and he died fifteen days later on May 11. His brothers were immediately suspicious as to the cause of death and had his body examined. After an inquest, Florence was arrested for the murder of her husband. Florence was tried at St. George's Hall, Liverpool before Justice James Fitzjames Stephen, and convicted and sentenced to hang. Later commuted to 15 years imprisonment. The doctors could not agree on how James Maybrick died. One doctor thought it was arsenic poisoning, another thought it might have gastroenteritis. Maybrick didn't have enough arsenic in his system at the time of his death to kill him. A city chemist testified that he had supplied Maybrick with quantities of arsenic over a lengthy period of time. James was a hypochondriac and a drug addict. Florence Maybrick was finally released in 1904, after fourteen years in custody. She moved back to the United States. In later years she became a recluse, living in a squalid three-room cabin in Connecticut, with only her cats for company, she died penniless 23 October 1941, at the age of 79.

JAMES MAYBRICK

James Maybrick, was born 25 October 1838, in Liverpool. At the time of the Whitechapel murders he was a 50-year old Liverpool cotton broker. He was named as Jack the Ripper after a diary, purporting to have been written by him, came into the possession of Michael Barrett, an unemployed, invalid, former merchant seaman and scrap metal dealer from Liverpool. Barrett had been given the diary in a pub the Saddle Inn in Kirkdale, Liverpool by a casual friend Tony Devereux, a retired compositor at the Liverpool Echo. Devereux told Barrett to do something with it. Despite questioning from Barrett as to the diary's provenance, Devereux died shortly after from heart failure without ever revealing its true origins. After researching the hardbound 11 inch by 8½ inch 63-

page handwritten journal, Barrett discovered that the writer, who signed the diary Jack the Ripper, was James Maybrick. Publication rights to the diary were secured by Smith Gryphon Limited, who published the diary in 1994 amid worldwide interest and intense debate among Ripperologists as to the diary's authenticity, a debate that continues to this day. A series of scientific tests were carried out on the diary, which suggested it dated from the Victorian era. On 27 June 1994 Michael Barrett told the Liverpool Daily Post that he had in fact forged the diary, using a scrapbook bought from an auctioneer's and ink from the Bluecoat Art Shop, only to retract his confession, then confess to forging the diary once more, a claim he maintains to this day. In July 1994 Barrett's estranged wife Ann Graham, in a statement said she had had the diary in her possession since 1989, and that it was given to her by her father, Billy Graham now (deceased), who in turn had received it in 1950 along with a pile of other books from his stepmother. She had passed it to Tony Devereux to give to Barrett in the hope that he would write a story around it, as he seemed to have lost his purpose in life. She had not thought that he would attempt to publish it. Another story relating to the diary's provenance is that workmen found it under the floorboards that had been lifted for the first time in over a century at Battlecrease House, Maybrick's old home. The Dairy unfortunately is littered with errors. The writer of the diary claims to have placed Mary Kelly's breasts on the table. Left farthings at Annie Chapman's feet and attempted to remove Mary Ann Nichols, head, The writer of the diary also claims two further murders in Manchester, England, however no records of any such murders have to date been found. If the provenance of the diary was not enough to contend with, a ladies 18 carat gold half hunter watch, made by Henry Verity of Lancaster in 1846, supposedly owned by James Maybrick, was discovered shortly after the diary's appearance. Purchased as an investment for his granddaughter, by Mr Albert Johnson for £225 from Stewart's the Jewellers of Wallasey, Cheshire in July 1992 the watch Johnson noticed had the words, "I am Jack" J. Maybrick and the initials of his five victims scratched upon the inner case. Like the diary, the watches authenticity is hotly debated. Experts tested the watch and concluded that the scratches were decades old, and would be extremely difficult to fake and be made to appear old. Without the diary Maybrick would not be a Ripper suspect, he did not fit any of the eyewitness descriptions, his known handwriting does not match the writing in the diary, his health did not begin to fail until 1889, so there is no explanation as to why the murders suddenly ceased. Until the emergence of the diary, there is no evidence that James Maybrick was ever suspected or associated with the Ripper case. James Maybrick died in dubious circumstances on 11 May 1889, his wife Florence stood trial for murder and in a sensational trial was convicted of poisoning him with arsenic. At her trial, Edwin Heaton testified that Maybrick visited his chemist shop "up to five times a day to drink a preparation containing arsenic." Initially sentenced to death, her sentence was commuted to life imprisonment. She was released in 1904 and died 23 October 1941.

MICHAEL MAYBRICK

Named as Jack the Ripper in the (2009) book: The Diary of Jack the Ripper another Chapter by James Stettler, and more recently by the director of the classic British comedy Withnail and I. Bruce Robinson in the (2015) book: They All Love Jack, Busting the Ripper.

Stettler in his book makes the following claims, that the Ripper diary was not written by James Maybrick, but by Michael Maybrick. That Michael Maybrick was homosexual or at least bisexual. That Michael disliked women and hated his sister in law (Florence Maybrick) and was jealous and envious of his brother's relationship with a beautiful wife. It was this envy Stettler claims that drove Michael to commit murder. Bruce Robinson, who spent 12 years researching the case claims in his rambling, ranting, 800-page ode to insanity, that Maybrick, killed far than had previously been acknowledged, including the Ripper-like servant girl murders in Austin, Texas (1884-85) and his own brother James. Michael Maybrick was the younger brother of Ripper suspect James Maybrick. The fourth of seven sons of William Maybrick an engraver, and parish Clerk at St Peters Church, Liverpool, and his wife, Susannah who died 1 May 1880. William died in 1870 and is buried in Anfield Cemetery. Both his grandfather and father were minor composers.

Michael Maybrick, was Born 31 January 1841 at 8 Church Alley, Liverpool. A keen amateur cricketer yachtsman and cyclist, he was also a Freemason. From an early age, he had a talent for music. Known under his pseudonym "Stephen Adams" as the composer of "The Holy City." His songs were enormously popular, his early sea song "Nancy Lee" sold more than 100,000 copies in two years. On 9 March 1893, he married his 40-year old housekeeper, Laura Withers, and settled with her at Ryde on the Isle of Wight. Maybrick became chairman of the Isle of Wight Hospital, was a magistrate and was five times mayor of Ryde. His friends spoke of his charming personality, but others thought him arrogant and vain. He had been at Buxton for three weeks being treated for periodic gout when he died in his sleep of heart failure on 25 August 1913 at the age of 69. He was buried four days later at Ryde. He left an estate valued at £23.000.

SAMUEL McALLISTER

The Traralgon Record, Friday 7 February 1890 a weekly newspaper in Australia, reported the following story:

Samuel McAllister was charged on remand with insulting behaviour. Prisoner pleaded guilty. Senior-Constable Keon gave evidence that about 8am on the 31 the prisoner came to the police station and said he was "Jack the Ripper" and he had been chased by over two hundred men at the Tyers. The witness said that the accused was under the influence of drink, and he told him to go away and have a sleep. The prisoner replied that if he was not locked up he would do something serious. He was put in the lock-up, and soon after, had a very bad attack of delirium tremens. A doctor had to be called in, and the expense to the Government was over 2 pounds. A fine of 5s. or three days were inflicted.

JAMES McBETH

On 12 December, 1888, in Oldmeldrum, Aberdeenshire. James McBeth, a dishevelled looking, middle-aged pedlar, was charged with having conducted himself in a riotous and disorderly manner, while proclaiming he was "Jack the Ripper." He pleaded guilty, stating that he was in a deranged state with drink. He had five previous convictions against him, the last occurrence five years ago. He was sentenced to 14 days imprisonment.

GEORGE WILLIAM McCARTHY

On Monday 8 October 1888, Mr Kingsmill, the Relieving Officer, at the Elham Union Workhouse, Kent. Observed a man whose appearance aroused his suspicion, walking along the road towards the Union. He called the attention of the Master of the Union to the circumstances, should the man apply for admission.

326

The man, who complained of a weak heart asked to see a doctor and be allowed to enter the Hospital for a week or two, as he was feeling unwell. He gave the name of George Wilson, The man it is claimed, according to the attendants bore a striking resemblance to sketches of the Whitechapel murderer, which had appeared a short time ago in the Daily Telegraph newspaper. The man's manner was described as nervous and uneasy. He further aroused suspicion while being examined when it was noticed he had marks of blood on his shirt and trousers. He was detained, and the police called. The police, however, failed to detect any likeness of the man to the newspaper's description except about the "forehead." The police also felt the blood smears were indistinct. Superintendent Maxted questioned the man, who claimed his name was John Jeffrey, by which name he was known in the army. He had been discharged from the 16th Lancers at Dublin on the 8 August 1888. He produced his discharge papers which showed he was unfit for service. He arrived in London soon after his discharge, and tried unsuccessfully to obtain work. He admitted that he gave a false name when he entered the Workhouse, and he was very sorry he had done so. Superintendent Maxted asked the man to write his name, which he unhesitatingly wrote as "George William McCarthy," which he claimed was his real name. He stated that he slept at a lodging house in Red Cross Court for several nights, whilst attempting to find work. Then at Philip's lodging house, Dover. Before proceeding to the Union. The landlord bore out his statement, adding that the man was very quiet in his manner, and retired to bed very early. He was examined by Dr. Bishop, who found his heart quiet unaffected. He was described as 23 years of age, 5 ft 7 inches tall, medium build, dark brown hair, brown eyes a slight moustache, of superior appearance, dressed in a shabby genteel style, black cloth coat, check pattern waistcoat, and trousers (very torn), brown vest brown hard felt hat, and a pair of boots having several cuts across the uppers. On his person was found a pocket-handkerchief and a piece of sponge. He was the son of James McCarthy, a civil engineer, of Ivanhoe Road, Denmark Park, Camberwell.In newspaper and contemporary accounts he was known as, "The Elham Suspect."

JOHN McCARTHY

On the Morning of 9 November 1888 shortly before 10:30 am John McCarthy the landlord of 26 Dorset Street, this address is frequently referred to as 13 Millers Court, though is, in fact, one and the same. Sent his assistant to collect what rent he could from his tenant Mary Kelly. She had fallen behind with her rent to the tune of 29s. Kelly paid 4s 6d a week for the room. Bowyer knocked on the door of Kelly's room, but received no reply; he then tried the door, but found it was locked, he, then, reached inside the broken window pane and pulled back the dirty muslin curtain to be confronted with the mutilated body of Mary Kelly. A shocked Bowyer rushed back to McCarthy to report, 'Guv'nor,' "I knocked at the door and could not make anyone answer, I looked through the window and saw a lot of blood." McCarthy and Bowyer immediately rushed to Kelly's room and peered through the broken window. McCarthy would later recall.

"The sight we saw I cannot drive away from my mind, it looked more like the work of a devil than of a man. I had heard a great deal about the Whitechapel murders, but I declare to God, I had never expected to see such a sight as this, the whole scene is more than I can describe, I hope I may never see such a sight as this again."

McCarthy then sent Bowyer to Commercial Street Police Station, and after tending to his shop later followed him. Inspector

Abberline was informed by Inspector Beck that bloodhounds had been sent for, and Dr Phillips advised against forcing the door until the dogs had arrived. After a two hour wait, Inspector Arnold arrived at 1:30 am with the news that the dogs were not in fact on the way, and that the door was to be forced. McCarthy, armed with a pickaxe, then forced open the door on Superintendent Arnold's orders. It has been asked exactly why McCarthy had used a pick axe to open the door, when as landlord surely he possessed a spare set of keys? Also, why did he choose that particular morning to send his assistant round to collect the rent? McCarthy has come under suspicion from theorists, who suspect he was a regular client of Kelly's, and this could offer to explain why she had been allowed to accumulate rent arrears. It is also speculated that she may possibly have been blackmailing him. Another theory is that McCarthy may have been related to Kelly, and may have in fact been an uncle or a distant cousin.

John McCarthy was born c. 1849, in Dieppe, France; the eldest of six children to Daniel and Margaret McCarthy. He married Elizabeth Stephens in 1877, together they had six children. McCarthy ran a chandler's shop at 27 Dorset Street. He also owned several low-grade properties and let rooms known locally as "McCarthy's rents," and was reported to have lost a number of tenants following the murder. According to the East London Observer, McCarthy rejected a morbid offer from a theatrical man to buy or hire Mary Kelly's bed. It was also reported he turned down an offer of £25 from a woman who wished to stay at 13 Miller's Court. Possibly due to the attention in the press McCarthy's wife received a Jack the Ripper Postcard dated 11 November, postmarked Folkestone, in which the sender threatened, "Don't alarm yourself, I am going to do another, but this time it will be a mother and daughter." John McCarthy died 16

June 1934. He was buried at St Patrick's Roman Catholic Cemetery in Leytonstone.

JOHN AMOS McCULLY

At Portobello Police-court, John Amos McCully, described as a hatter, of no fixed abode. Was charged with entering the shop occupied by John Baillie, baker, 86 High Street, and annoying two shop girls, by declaring that he was "Jack the Ripper" and that he had murdered several women in Whitechapel. This declaration caused fear and alarm to the girls, one of whom has taken ill. He pleaded guilty and stated: "That he sometimes said he was Jack the Ripper for a piece of diversion, but he meant no harm by it." McCully was under the influence of alcohol when he committed the offence. A fine of 10s, with the option of five days imprisonment, was imposed.

JACK McCARDY

On 1 December 1888, the Minneapolis Chief of police received a letter signed William Hallen, alias Knife Stab, late of London, England. The letter stated that:

Unless all the select houses on First Street are closed up before 8 December, the Chief will have a reign of terror and blood equal to the Whitechapel of London.

The letter writer added that he was a pal of Jack McCardy, (pronounced McCurdy, in some newspaper accounts) alias Jack the Ripper, and that he had been in Minneapolis three days and wrote the letter in the West Hotel, before concluding that he was going to St Paul to make certain arrangements and would be returning on 8 December and that the dawning of the morning is not more sure than is the death of fifteen unfortunates by his hand. The newspapers reported that the police did not know

330

whether to set the man down as a crank, a practical joker or a desperado.

EDWARD McKENNA

McKenna was arrested on 14 September 1888 after acting suspiciously in Whitechapel throughout the day, and according to press reports, had threatened to stab people. When searched, his pockets contained, amongst other things an assortment of rags, handkerchiefs, women's purses, several metal and cardboard boxes, a small table-knife, rather the worse for wear, which he asserts he uses for the purpose of cutting his food, and a spring onion. Questioned by Inspector Abberline, at the Commercial Street Station, McKenna in his detailed statement said he peddled laces and other small articles for a living, and had just returned to London from Kent. He was confronted by several witnesses, who were not able to identify him as the man who had been chased in the neighbourhood by some boys, and who was alleged to have held a knife behind his back. Mrs. Lloyd and her daughter came from Heath-street. They were not able to identify him. Mr. Taylor, who on the same day had watched a man of suspicious appearance leave the Prince Albert public house and go into Bishopsgate-street, also could not say that M'Kenna was the same. A Mrs. Lyons was also called, and in her opinion M'Kenna was not the individual she had seen in Flower and Dean-street on the Sunday following the Hanbury-street tragedy. He was in consequence liberated. He was able to provide the police with the alibi that he was sleeping in a lodging house at 15 Brick Lane at the time Annie Chapman was murdered, Investigations confirmed his story. McKenna was described as five feet seven inches tall, slightly built with sandy colour hair, beard and moustache, he was shabbily dressed, with a careworn look he was wearing a cloth skull cap, which the newspapers said did little to improve his miserable appearance.

JOSEPH CAREY MERRICK

Joseph Merrick was mentioned as a possible Ripper suspect, with the following reasons given. That due to him residing at the London Hospital at the time of the Whitechapel murders, he had access to knives. That he had a grudge against women, being unable to have physical relations with them due to his disfigurement. And lastly, the reason he was never recognised was due to the fact that he wore a hood. These suggestions are, to say the least, not only ludicrous but also cruel. Purely because somebody suffers from a disfigurement or disability does not make them a monster. If those concerned had taken the time to research a little about John Merrick they would have discovered that throughout his short and unfortunate life he remained one of the kindest, gentlest and noblest of men.

Joseph Carey Merrick was born 5 August 1862 to Joseph Rockley Merrick, and Mary Jane (née Potterton) at 50 Lee Street, Leicester. He was the eldest of three children the other children were, William Arthur 1866-1870 who died of scarlet fever, and Marion Eliza 1867-1891. Marion it is claimed was born a cripple, she died of myelitis and "seizures." His father, was, variously in occupation as a Warehouseman, Cab Driver, Stoker, and Haberdasher. In the 1851 census he was described as an agricultural labourer. Mary Jane when younger worked as a domestic servant. The couple married in 1861. Joseph was born the following year, apparently healthy, but around the age of twenty-one months, tumours began appearing on his face and body, as his body grew so did the tumours, one "snout-like" lump of flesh extended several inches out of his upper-lip. These tumours later worsened to resemble cauliflower-like growths, the growths became so severe that he quickly became known by his unfortunate nickname. "The Elephant Man," To further add to his discomfort, at the age of 3 he fell, heavily damaging his left hip. Due to the family being poor, the untreated hip became diseased, which left him permanently lame. Joseph's mother died from bronchopneumonia, 19 May 1873 at the age of 36 when Joseph was 9-years old and though no photograph exists, according to eyewitness accounts she too was believed to have been physically disabled. At the age of 13, he found work rolling cigars in a factory, but after three years, his right hand deformity had worsened and he no longer had the dexterity required for the job. Following the death of his mother, his father married, Emma Warner, 3 December 1874. Ill-treatment by his stepmother, and a severe beating from his father forced Joseph to leave home, he was initially cared for by his uncle, until forced to enter the workhouse for a period of four years. In Joseph's own words:

I went to school like other children until I was about 11 or 12 years of age, when the greatest misfortune of my life occurred, namely the death of my mother, peace to her, she was a good mother to me; after she died my father broke up his home and went to lodgings; unfortunately for me he married his landlady; henceforth I never had one moment's comfort, she having children of her own, and I not being so handsome as they, together with my deformity, she was the means of making my life a perfect misery; lame and deformed as I was, I ran, or rather walked away from home two or three times, but suppose father had some spark of parental feeling left, so he induced me to return home again. The best friend I had in those days was my father's brother, Mr. Merrick, hair Dresser, Church Gate, Leicester.

In the 1881 census, his address is listed as the Leicester Union Workhouse, his age as 19 and his occupation as a hawker. In 1882, Merrick underwent surgery on his face. The protrusion from his mouth had grown to 8–9 inches and severely inhibited his speech and made it difficult to eat. He was operated on in the Workhouse Infirmary, by Dr. Marriott, and had a large part of the mass removed. For much of his life he was unemployed, and due to prejudice, unemployable. His attempts at hawking, door to door, where unsuccessful, his physical appearance frightening the public. As a last resort, he realised the only way to escape the poor law, lay in becoming a novelty in a freak show. He wrote to a local music hall owner Sam Torr, who agreed to promote him. His acquaintance Tom Norman agreed to take over Merrick's management. Norman observed Merrick asleep one morning and learnt that he always slept sitting up, with his legs drawn up and his head resting on his knees. His enlarged head was too heavy to allow him to sleep lying down and, as Merrick put it, he would risk "waking with a broken neck" When the show reached the capital it came to the attention of eminent Surgeon Frederick Treves, later to become Sir Frederick Treves, who came to hear of Merrick's condition and expressed scientific and medical interest in him, and presented him before the Pathological Society on 2 December 1884. Treves examined Merrick on two or three occasions, and on one of his visits handed Merrick his calling card. Treves later recalled in his 1923 *Reminiscences* his first encounter with Merrick:

He was the most disgusting specimen of humanity that I had ever seen... at no time had I met with such a degraded or perverted version of a human being as this lone figure displayed.

Merrick told Norman that he no longer wished to be examined at the hospital. According to Norman, he said he was "stripped naked and felt like an animal in a cattle market." Public enthusiasm for freak shows in England was dampening, shows were closed down by the magistrates and the police. Merrick's management took him to Europe, in the hope authorities would be more lenient, and he was no more successful than in England. He was deserted by his manager and had his £50 savings stolen. He slowly made his way back to England, by train and ship, exhausted, he arrived at Liverpool Street station, 24 June 1886, a policeman noticed a crowd of onlookers had gathered around Merrick, so helped into a waiting room, unable to make himself understood, he handed the police the card of Frederick Treves's Treves took him to the London Hospital, where he was washed, fed and put to bed. When Treves examined him, it was discovered that his physical condition had deteriorated considerably over the previous two years. With care his health improved, though Treves believed he had only a few years left to live due to a heart condition. A permanent home was found for Joseph at the London Hospital after the intervention of the British Royal Family. Here he became a society celebrity, receiving visits by the great and the good, his most distinguished guest was Princess Alexandra wife of the Prince of Wales. The princess, shook his hand, chatted and gave him a signed photograph of herself. She sent him a Christmas card each year. Merrick had spent his entire life, segregated from women first in the workhouse, then as an exhibit. Treves detecting signs of depression in Merrick, decided to introduce him to a woman friend of his, in the hope it would help him feel normal. Mrs Leila Maturin, "a young and pretty widow," visited Merrick. Though the meeting was brief due to Merrick becoming emotional, they kept in touch through letters. Treves believed that Merrick's hope was

335

to go to live in an institution for the blind, where he might meet a woman who could not see his deformities. Merrick's ability to speak was not as articulate as portrayed by the actor John Hurt in the 1980 film The Elephant Man, and Treves would often have to translate. This is possibly how the confusion regarding his Christian name came about, and why he was often referred to as John Merrick, and not Joseph Merrick. Merrick had clearly signed his name as "Joseph" in the few examples of his handwriting that remain. Joseph remained content with his life, grateful for everything that had been done for him. Treves said:

Merrick, I may say, was now one of the most contended creatures I have chanced to meet. More than once he said to me: "I am happy every hour of the day." Most men of Merrick's age would have expressed their joy and sense of contentment by singing or whistling when they were alone. Unfortunately Merrick's mouth was, so deformed that he could neither whistle nor sing. One thing that always struck me as sad about Merrick was the fact that he could not smile. Whatever his delight might be, his face remained expressionless. He could weep, but he could not smile.

Merrick filled his days with reading and constructing models of buildings out of card. In later years he spent time on holiday in the country, walking through the fields and sitting in the woods. He died 11 April 1890, at the age of 28, Merrick's death was ruled accidental and the certified cause of death was asphyxia, caused by the weight of his head as he lay down. Treves, who performed an autopsy on the body, said that Merrick had died of a dislocated neck. Knowing that Merrick had always slept sitting upright out of necessity, Treves came to the conclusion that Merrick must have "made the experiment," attempting to sleep lying down "like other people." His body was identified by his uncle Charles Merrick. He was denied the dignity of a burial, instead, his skeleton remains on permanent display at the London Hospital, where it is tirelessly examined by medical students. No real conclusion has ever been made, as to what condition Joseph actually suffered with. An exaggerated case of neurofibromatosis, a genetic disorder of the skin, was considered a strong possibility. In a 1986 article in the British Medical Journal, Michael Cohen and J.A.R. Tibbles put forward the theory that Merrick had suffered from a very rare congenital disorder called Proteus Syndrome, of which there have been less than 100 cases ever recorded.

On the 15 May 2004, a plaque was unveiled in his home town at 27 Wharf Street South, by the Lord Mayor of Leicester; it reads – "Joseph Carey Merrick 1862-1890, a true model of bravery and dignity for all peoples of all generations."

FRANK MILES

First suggested as a Ripper suspect in the 1970s, by Thomas Toughill, in correspondence with writer Colin Wilson. Toughill in his (2008) book: The Ripper Code, named Miles as the Ripper.

George Francis (Frank) Miles, was born 22 April 1852 in Bingham, Nottinghamshire, and was the grandson of Philip John Miles 1773-1854, an English merchant and politician for Bristol. His father, the Reverend Robert Henry William Miles, and his wife Mary (née Cleaver), had ten children, six sons; of whom Frank was the youngest, and four daughters. It was said his mother was a dominant woman who exercised a strong influence over him. Frank Miles was a partially colour-blind, well-known Painter, who specialised in flattering pencil drawings and portraits of society ladies. His work soon gained repute, and several pictures found their way into the Royal Academy, one of them, "A Flower Girl," being purchased by the Prince of Wales. In 1880 he won the Royal Academy's Turner Prize, and was an Oxford acquaintance

337

and friend of the playwright, Oscar Wilde, living in accommodation above Wilde in Salisbury Street from 1879-81. In 1881 the two lived together, possibly as lovers, at Keats House, Tite Street, Chelsea, one of his neighbours being Sir Melville Macnaghten. Miles close friendship with Wilde ended when Miles father wrote to him to express displeasure at his son's association with Wilde. Dependent upon his father's financial support, Miles faced with no alternative, severed their friendship. Wilde went to America, and Miles suffered a nervous breakdown. From this period Miles popularity faded, his drawings stopped selling and he became a recluse. Toughill claims "Oscar Wilde was hinting at his lover having been the killer when he killed off the painter in his novel, the Painting of Dorian Gray." Wilde's only novel is based on a gorgeous young man, Dorian, who wishes a painting of himself would grow old instead of him. His wish is fulfilled and he indulges in a hedonistic lifestyle, but the painting grows old and disfigured, serving as a reminder of how ugly Dorian has become inside. Dorian blames the artist, Basil Hallward for his fate and stabs him in a fit of rage. Thomas believes Oscar based the character of Basil on his lover Miles. In the book, the painter is killed on 9 November, 1888 the date of the last Ripper murder. In 1884 both his parents died. Miles was engaged to be married to Miss Gratiana Lucy Hughes (known as Lucy), daughter of Alfred Hughes (later Sir Alfred Hughes, 10th Baronet). But his incarceration to an asylum led to this falling through. Miles was afflicted by a cerebral malady, his mental health further deteriorated. On the 27 December 1887 he was confined to the Brislington Asylum near Bristol. An inaccurate report of his death was circulated soon after his confinement, the newspapers reported:

Frank Miles, the artist is dead, this announcement will bring sorrow to many hearts. Liked by many men, loved by many women. His powers never reached maturity, and his life ended in abysmal gloom.

Miles remained at Brislington until his death at the age of 39-years, on 15 July 1891. The cause of death was given as a combination of general paralysis of the insane, pneumonia and exhaustion. He is buried in the churchyard of St Mary's Parrish Church, Almondsbury near Bristol.

Even though it is rumoured Miles was homosexual, it is speculated he preferred exposing himself to young girls below the age of consent, for which the police once tried to arrest him. This story is rejected by Molly Whittington-Egan, who has traced the original source to a highly dubious account by Robert Shererd, Oscar Wilde's first biographer.

THOMAS MOLIN

In Montreal, an English gentleman of property, residing at Brighton, whose name was Ralph Boeheamil Husson, who went to Canada two years ago on account of declining health. While there he made the acquaintance of Miss Mulcahy, and they became engaged. His health growing worse, he wished Miss Mulcahy to marry him and accompany him to England. Her mother objected on account of her youth, and Mr Husson had to leave by himself. The engaged couple kept up a correspondence, and the marriage was arranged to take place. Accompanied by his father, a priest, and a friend of the family, the young gentleman set out for New York. This was, however, against the advice of the doctor, who said that an Atlantic voyage in the winter would most likely prove fatal. The party arrived in New York. And took a train for Bonaventure, a telegram being sent to

339

Miss Mulcahy to meet them at the station there. The young lady met them, and the party took sleighs to Mrs Mulcahy's house. On the way, however, young Mr Husson gasped for breath. He then motioned for the priest to read the marriage service. Miss Mulcahy, though greatly overcome, consented, and in St James's Street, in the sleigh, and in the open air the marriage took place. In two minutes afterwards the bridegroom fell back dead.

Soon after the ceremony the clergyman and father both checked on the new groom and said that he had already died.

They said they would take her to England but she bolted from the sled at Victoria Square.

Only later did she learn that the father, clergymen and all other involves were medical students who had conspired the whole event and the husband? It was a dissecting corpse taken from the medical school.

Mulcahy, in court said the driver of the sleigh, is an Englishman named Thomas Molin, who had been obliged to leave England because he was suspected of being the Whitechapel murderer.

Molin, remarked, "Yes, I have been known as Jack the Ripper, and have done considerable work of that kind in Paris." He was committed as a vagrant, and will be examined as to sanity. The detectives say he is a sane man, and was arrested in London, Ontario, some time ago as Jack the Ripper.

THE MONMOUTH RIPPER

On the 3 March 1888, a stranger, apparently a tramp, visited several houses in Monmouth, threatening the inhabitants. When he encountered only women present, he proclaimed himself as "Jack the Ripper". He entered the house of a florist, named Woodhouse, and she cried out for help, and a gentleman named

340

Pryce, hearing her cries came to her assistance. A few minutes afterwards he went to the house of Colonel Colls, and acted in a similar way to the servants in the kitchen. Mr Pryce followed him and was in time to see Col. Colls forcibly eject him from the house. The would-be "Ripper" took to the fields adjoining the river Wyre, followed closely by Mr Pryce and a baker named Clement. The man approached the river bank and jumped, and sank almost immediately. The Deputy-Coroner, in summing up, suggested that although the deceased deliberately jumped into the river, he might have done so intending to swim across the river and escape. Mr Pryce said the man was sober, of middle height, and about 40 years of age. The name of the mysterious individual is not known.

JAMES MONRO

James Monro was born in Edinburgh in 1838 and educated at Edinburgh High School and Edinburgh and Berlin Universities. His proudest boast was that he was born, bred and educated in Edinburgh. His father George Monro, was a solicitor. He was Assistant Magistrate, and Inspector General of police in Bombay, and resigned in 1884. He joined the Metropolitan police force in 1884 as Assistant commissioner in charge of C.I.D. And resigned in August 1888 because he was unable to gain complete control of the C.I.D from Metropolitan police commissioner Sir Charles Warren. He was head of the detective service-section D (an unofficial title), with responsibility for observing the activities of the Fenians. He later took over as commissioner, after Warren resigned on 9 November, and remained in the post until 1890, when he again resigned. He founded and ran the Ranaghat Christian medical mission in India 1890-1903. He contemplated retiring to Darjeeling, India, but instead returned to Scotland, and later Cheltenham where he died in 1920 at the age of 81. He was

341

said to be blessed with the instinct of a born detective. Tom Cullen regarded him as, "Possibly the only man at Scotland Yard who was capable of tracking down the killer." It was said of him:

"That he was loved by all the men who served under him, though, was said to have been a difficult character in other respects."

After his retirement, he said in the presence of his grandson James, "The Ripper was never caught, but he should have been." He left some papers with his eldest son Charles, in which he described his theory on the Ripper as, "A very hot potato." Unfortunately, the papers were said to have been burnt without his theory ever having been revealed. Monro did not publish any memoirs. Monro has been mentioned as a possible Ripper suspect by a theorist in Australia who claims Monro had a pathological hatred of Sir Charles Warren, though has offered no evidence to support this claim.

MORFORD

According to the Star newspaper 29 September 1888, the police had received a letter from a pawnbroker which suggested that a former surgeon named Morford, who had given way to drink, and disappeared from his lodgings in Great Ormond Street after the 10 September, and who had pawned some surgical knives at his shop, may be able to shed some light on the murders. Despite police efforts, Morford was never found. Apart from the newspaper article, there is no evidence to prove he ever existed. A search of the relevant medical directories has failed to reveal a doctor or surgeon named Morford. Neither does his name appear in any police files. Philip Sugden while researching did find a John Orford, a Senior Resident Medical Officer at the Royal Free Hospital in Gray's Inn Road (Medical Directory, 1888) which is close to Great Ormond Road.

GEORGE JAMES MORRIS

The 54-year old night watchman, and witness at Catherine Eddowes inquest. First suggested as an accomplice of Jack the Ripper 2 October 1888, then later in 2007 by Rob Hills. Born 8 February 1834 in Teddington, London, to John Morris and Elizabeth, his father's occupation in the 1841 census is recorded as a labourer. George served in the army for four and a half years. Joined the Metropolitan Police 22 December 1856, PC 211 T division (Hammersmith), resigned, 1863. Rejoined in 1864. Resigned again in 1882 due to ill health (stomach disease). Morris was night-watchman at the Kearley and Tonge warehouse in Mitre Square, going on duty at 7:00 am on September 1888. He occupied most of his shift by cleaning offices and looking around the warehouse. He had heard nothing out of the ordinary that night and claimed that "If there had been any cry of distress, I would have heard it." At 1:45 am 30 September, Morris was sweeping some steps inside as PC Edward Watkins knocked at the warehouse door, which was ajar (and had been for several minutes). Watkins said to Morris "For God's sake mate, come to my assistance." Morris got his lamp and went outside, asking "What's the matter?" to which PC Watkins replied, "There's another woman being cut to pieces." I said, "Where is she?" He said, "In the corner." I went over to the corner and shown my light on the body. Morris then blew upon his whistle and immediately left the Square to look for help via Mitre Street, heading toward Aldgate. Morris went to the corner of the square where Catherine Eddowes' lay and shone his lamp on the body. He immediately blew his own whistle and ran along Mitre Street into Aldgate, seeing nobody suspicious as he did so. In Aldgate, he was approached by two constables, PC James Harvey and PC Holland, who asked him what the matter was. He told them of the murder and they accompanied him to Mitre Square before he

343

went back to the warehouse. Morris claimed to have been in the warehouse constantly between 11:00 pm and 1:00 am the following morning

CHARLES MORSE

The Boston Daily Globe, Friday, 21 December 1888 reported the following story:

Bogus "Jack the Ripper." Charles Morse, a resident on North street, was arrested by officers of station 1 last evening on charges of drunkenness and disorderly conduct. It is alleged that Morse confronted two young women who were returning to their homes from their employment about 6:15, and asserted in a loud voice that he was "Jack the Ripper," and that he had come for them. They, badly frightened, appealed for protection to Patrol-man Phelan, who reassured them. Morse is said to have been much intoxicated.

EDWARD MORSON

In November 1888, Edward Morson, a 29 year old, labourer, was charged with being drunk and fighting, as well as using obscene language, in Lower Park-road, London. Morson was acting in a most disorderly and disgraceful manner, while declaring that he was "Jack the Ripper". Morson denied this, and said he was out and about to catch "Jack the Ripper". He was fined 7s, or seven days imprisonment.

WILLIAM M'PHERSON

On 12 November, 1888, William M'Pherson, an engineer, was charged at Dumbarton Police Court, with assault and breach of the peace. On Saturday night he went home and demanded his supper from his landlady. She said it was waiting for him. He was not satisfied, and made a further demand that a woman who was

344

in the home should be put out. He then seized a table knife and said "You have heard of "Jack the Ripper" I am he." M'Pherson, was sentenced to 30 days imprisonment.

JOHN MURPHY

On 13 November 1888 during a thorough police search of all the casual wards and other places of similar character, a man named Thomas Murphy came to the attention of the police when he was noticed behaving suspiciously at the Holborn casual ward. Constables were at once sent to the place and arrested a rough-looking fellow, who gave the name of Thomas Murphy. He was taken to the police station on Frederick Street, King's Cross Road, where a search of his person revealed a formidable looking knife with a blade about ten inches long. Murphy was detained on suspicion and questioned. The police proceeded to make inquiries at Woolwich and other places where it was said he had been a sailor. He was released without charge as he was able to prove he was elsewhere at the time of the Whitechapel murders. Murphy was born in 1864 and was said to be of no fixed abode, he was a Sailor from Massachusetts, and was described as 5 ft 8 inches tall, with a fair moustache and a fair complexion. He was wearing a blue jersey, a check coat and trousers, a "cheese cutter" cap and a duck pair of boots (a waterproof, shoe-like boot).

JOHN MURRAY

On 11 October 1888, in Wolverhampton, John Murray a seaman was charged with being drunk and disorderly, he was wandering around the town, acting strangely, and alarming people by proclaiming he was "Jack the Ripper." No attention was paid to his idle talk. He was taken into custody and fined 1s and costs or seven days imprisonment.

THOMAS MURRAY

Robert W. House, while conducting research at the London Metropolitan Archives in London, discovered an interesting individual named Thomas Murray. Murray had been admitted to an asylum, 8 June 1889. He was 30-years of age, single, with no occupation, though had previously been a bottler. His residence was given as 11 Burdett Street, Devons Road East, London. The cause of his insanity was given as sexual and alcoholic excesses, and he was described as dangerous to others. His sister, Ann Murray, stated that he was dangerous to live with, and repeatedly threw furniture around and threatened to kill her and their mother. He also threatened violence to children in the street, because he believed they were calling him "Jack the Ripper." He also believed his neighbours called him, "Jack the Ripper." It was said of him, "He remains very suspicious, and when alone says he hears voices."

JOHN MURRY

In October 1888, John Murry, 38 years old, a labourer, of 23 Charles-street, Soho-square, was charged at Enfield with riding in a third class carriage from Moorgate-street to Bowes Park, without having previously paid his fare (6d) with intent to defraud the Great Northern Railway Company. He was also charged with assaulting George Croxford, ticket collector, at Bowes Park, whilst in the execution of his duties. Murray, when asked for his ticket, used filthy language and claimed he was "Jack the Ripper". In his defence Murray, claimed he had a drop too much, to drink, and had fallen asleep on the train, which caused him to go past his stop. He was so bewildered, he did not know what he was doing. He was ordered to-pay 5s and costs for riding without a ticket, and 20s and costs for the assault on the collector or in default 14 days imprisonment.

346

EDWARD NELSON

In November, 1888, Edward Nelson, of Houghall, Durham, suddenly entered the grocer's shop of Mrs Pearson, Tudhoe Grange, in a drunken condition, and after declaring he was "Jack the Ripper" seized a piece of cheese, and in attempting to leave the shop in a hurry, banged his head against the door, smashing a panel, and cutting his head dreadfully. PC Johnson and Christison assisted Nelson to a doctor, who attended to his injuries. Nelson was fined 15s 7d, damages and costs.

JAMES NESBITT

On 23 July 1891, in Chicopee, Massachusetts, Samuel Alexander, a weaver, deliberately shot and killed James Nesbitt, at 5:30 this morning. Nesbitt, who was 29 years old, leaves a widow and one child. Alexander, is about 35 years old, and came from the north of Ireland, where he has a wife and several children. He was for seven years a soldier in the English army, serving the greater part of his time in India. He said that he shot Nesbitt because he thought he was "Jack the Ripper". On his person was found a knife, and a list of names, including some of the principal men of the city, whom he said he wanted to kill. He had a dream that his own wife was shut up in a dark room and would not be liberated until he had killed "Jack the Ripper."

JOHN NETLEY

John Charles Netley was born in May 1860, in Paddington, London, to John Netley an omnibus conductor and his wife Mary Ann (née Terry). His father was born in Pulborough, Sussex in 1831, died August 1912 at the age of 81. His mother was born in Paddington, Middlesex, in 1833, she died in November 1886 at the age of 53. His parents married 2 June 1857. He had five brothers, George Alfred, born 1858. William Henry, born 1860, died 1861. Albert James, born 1863, Francis Luke born 1865, Alfred Ernest born 1871, and three sisters, Mary Ann born 1868, died 1869. Margaret Lydia, born 1870, Agnes Louisa born 1874. He was employed as a Carman by Messrs Thompson McKay and Co and was described as a steady worker. According to Walter Sickert, Netley was broad shouldered, 5 ft 5 inches tall, with insecurity about his height. He was killed in an accident in 1903 when he was driving a van loaded with fish along Park-road when the wheel of his van clipped a high kerb, he was thrown from the vehicle and trampled by the horses, his head being crushed by the wheels of his own van. The inquest returned a verdict of accidental death, with a recommendation that the drivers of vans should be offered safety straps. An article from the Shepton Mallet Journal 25 September 1903, gave further details of the accident:

Van Driver Killed- A carman named John Netley, aged 43 years, of Amberley Road, Paddington, Regent's Park, on Saturday, when the wheel of the van came into collision with an obelisk near Clarence-gate. The driver was thrown from his seat into the roadway on his head, and the wheels of his van passed over him. Life was found to be extinct.

Joseph Gorman Sickert, the self-alleged son of the artist Walter Sickert, makes the unsubstantiated claim that Carman, John Netley, drove Sir William Gull and his co-conspirators around Whitechapel in his own carriage, while they committed the Jack the Ripper murders, and that the murders took place inside the vehicle. The bodies were then transported to the locations where they were subsequently found. The victims, it is claimed, were enticed inside by Gull then fed poisoned grapes. These claims, however, completely contradict the known available evidence. Blood splashes at the crime scenes clearly showed the victims had been murdered at the place where their bodies were discovered. Secondly, the contents of the victim's stomachs were carefully examined and failed to show any evidence they had been drugged or poisoned prior to their murder. The story of the grapes, originates from dubious witness Matthew Packer, a fruitier of 44 Berner Street, who claims to have sold grapes to a man, and a woman, he later identified Elizabeth Stride, at the mortuary as the woman he saw that night. Packer, originally told the police, he had no information to give. John Netley's actual involvement in the crimes varies according to which version of the Royal Conspiracy theory is being postulated at the time. Some theorists have speculated Netley was responsible for the murder of Elizabeth Stride and matched the description of her broad-shouldered assailant. Netley, it is also claimed, along with Frederico Albericci, murdered Emma Elizabeth Smith. Again, this claim contradicts the actual known events. Smith clearly stated before she died that she was attacked by three men, one a youth, about nineteen years of age.

JOHN NEWMAN'S RIPPER SUSPECT

John Newman, aged 34 a respectable looking man, described as a fitter, of 57 Lower Kensington Lane, London, was charged with being drunk and disorderly in Blackman Street. Police constable William Tilley was on duty when Newman came up to him holding a man by the collar. He told the constable he wished to give the man into custody, as he was "Jack the Ripper." The constable knew the gentleman who was being held to be a respectable man, who had lived for a long time in the neighbourhood. Newman was told to let the man go, and take himself off home. He did so, but told the constable he must take the consequences of letting the man go. Newman, returned a few moments later and refused to leave, whereupon he was taken into custody. The identity of the respectable gentleman accused of being Jack the Ripper is unknown.

JOHN NICOL

On the 16 February 1889, in Paisley, John Nicol, was charged with having, on the 6 February, pointed an unloaded revolver at a young woman in a confectioners shop in Smithhills Street, Paisley, and threatened her with being "Jack the Ripper," to the alarm and danger of the young woman. He pleaded guilty, and was fined £5, or 30 days imprisonment.

AUGUST NOCHILD

August Nochild, a 52-year old, portly German tailor of Christian Street, Whitechapel, was charged before Guildhall Magistrates with assaulting prostitute Sarah McFarly, by attempting to strangle her in Holborn Circus. McFarly, who stated she lived with a friend in Upper Rathbone Place, told the court that she had met the man in New Oxford Street, at about half past twelve, on the morning of 2 October 1888. The man asked her to go to his home in Whitechapel. When she refused his request, he seized her by the throat and said, "I will murder you if you don't. I have murdered the women in Whitechapel, and I would like to do another." Police Sergeant Perry 77 deposed that he was on duty in the area at the time, and observed Nochild speaking to the woman. He then saw the man suddenly, and without warning, seize the woman by the throat. Her cries of, "Police" and "Murder," ensured that he took Nochild swiftly into custody. The Sergeant, in his report, noticed both parties appeared to be under the influence of alcohol. Mr Alderman Stone did not think there was any foundation for the charge and dismissed the case.

WILLIAM ONION

William John Onion was accused of being Jack the Ripper by an unnamed member of the public, who wrote to the police on the 13 November 1888, and stated that the murderer is William Onion late of Colney Hatch, and Wakefield Asylums.Onion was born 24 December 1834, in Whitechapel. He was admitted to Colney Hatch Lunatic Asylum, 9 October 1868. He was admitted to the Stepney Workhouse 13 February 1873, with a bad hand. His address was 48 Flower and Dean Street. In 1874 he was charged with feloniously killing and slaying John Connor. Found guilty, he was recommended to mercy by the Jury and sentenced to one month's imprisonment. Reproduced here is the transcript from the Old-Bailey:

JAMES HOLMES. I am manager of the Old Rose public-house, St. George's Street—on the night of 12th June the prisoner and deceased were there drinking together with a third man—they were quarrelling—I told them to go outside, which they did—I stood at the door to keep them from coming in—I saw the deceased strike the prisoner two or three times and want to fight him; they were not violent blows—the prisoner said if he gave him one blow that would be enough for him, and he hit him one blow under the nose on the lip; he fell and caught his head against the side of the kerb—I went in and saw no more—they had been drinking, but were not drunk. Cross-examined by the Prisoner. The deceased had previously been quarrelling with another man—I did not hear you Bay "What is the use of two old pals quarrelling"—I did not hear you call for a pot of beer and say "You had better quarrel with that"—I would not serve you nor the other houses either—the deceased went on the top of the hill, and said "Come on, you are no man if you don't put up your dukes"—that was before you struck him—you were on the lower

351

part—there are stones there sticking out of the ground—he took every advantage of you. JOSEPH BRANSDEN. I am a cheesemonger, of 58, St. George's Street—on 12th June, about 8.15, I was in the Old Rose, and saw the prisoner and deceased there and another man who the deceased wanted to quarrel with, in fact they were all quarrelling together—I went away and returned again a little after 9 o'clock—the prisoner and deceased were then outside the house quarrelling again—the other man had gone away—the deceased struck the prisoner three or four times, and wanted him to go in the road and fight—the prisoner eventually went into the road; it is a steep hill—they put up their arms to spar, and the prisoner hit the first blow, hit the deceased under the nose, and knocked him down, his head struck against the kerb, and there he lay insensible. Cross-examined. The stones are very awkward there—it was not dark; there was plenty of light from the public-house—I don't suppose you wished to fight, but you did—you struck him, and he fell straight down with his head against the kerb, and there he lay as if he was dead. WILLIAM LYTHE (Policeman K 325). On the morning of 13th June, about 8.30, I saw the deceased Connor at his house—he was lying in an insensible state on the floor—I assisted to take him part of the way to the hospital, when I met the prisoner and took him into custody—I charged him with assaulting the man— he knelt down on his knees and kissed the deceased, and said "I shall be remanded for a week or two, but I shall get over it," and he made a similar remark at the station. Cross-examined. You did not say We shall get over it. HARRY THOMAS SHAPNEY. I am house-surgeon at the London Hospital—on 13th June the deceased was brought there about 9.30 in the morning—he was totally insensible—I examined him and found a bruise at the back of his head, and a cut through the upper-lip—the bruise might have been caused by a fall on a kerb-stone—he died about 1.30

the same day—I made a post-mortem examination—I found a small fracture of the skull, and he had extravasation of blood pressing on the brain—he died from the effect of it—the fracture tore across one of the small arteries—he was a well nourished man and all the organs were healthy. Cross-examined. I only saw two places, the bruise on the back of the head and the cut on the lip, the lip was entirely cut through—you were a patient at the hospital about four weeks before this with a fractured arm—it was the right arm. The Prisoner in his defence stated that he had only struck the blow in self-defence after being four or five times struck by the deceased, who had greatly provoked him. GUILTY —Recommended to mercy by the Jury — One Month's Imprisonment. He was admitted to the Stepney Workhouse again on 30 May 1875, this time of no fixed address. From 22 December 1882 to 2 March 1883, he was in Colney Hatch asylum. In 1885, he was acquitted of unlawful wounding. In November 1887 he was sentenced to 1 year's imprisonment for committing wilful damage.

The Following report is from the Star newspaper 20 November 1888:

The old man whom the Thames magistrate yesterday allowed to go free on a charge of drunkenness went to the Shadwell Police-Station last night and broke the window. He told the magistrate this morning that policemen followed him about to lock him up for being drunk, and that he smashed the window to save himself from being locked up. (Laughter) - Mr Saunders said: "The Court stinks with your name, and you stand in such bad odour that all policemen look after you, knowing you are a dangerous man." He would be sentenced to one month's hard labour.

He also served 14 days in Wakefield prison in September 1892, for drunkenness. He was described as age 61-years of age, 5 ft

353

6½ inches tall, with brown hair going grey. He served time in Wakefield prison again in 1898, at the age of 68, for being drunk and disorderly. Onion, notched up a total of more than 500 convictions in London alone for his drunken behaviour. And many more in other parts of the country. Upon his release from prison, he became a reformed character, and gave up drink, and became a poet. He died Monday 20 November 1916, of heart failure and chronic bronchitis.

MICHAEL OSTROG

Ostrog was named by Sir Melville Macnaghten in his memoranda as the third suspect, along with Druitt and Kosminski, as more likely to have been Jack the Ripper than Thomas Cutbush. Macnaghten described Ostrog as:

Michael Ostrog, a mad Russian doctor and a convict and unquestionably a homicidal maniac. This man was said to have been habitually cruel to women, and for a long time was known to have carried about with him surgical knives and other instruments; his antecedents were of the very worst and his whereabouts at the time of the Whitechapel murders could never be satisfactorily accounted for. He is still alive.

Ostrog, who used several aliases throughout his life, including Claude Clayton, Dr Grant, Count Sobieski, Dr Barker, Ashley Nabokoff, Max Sobiekski, and Bertrand Ashley, to name but a few, was a habitual petty criminal and confidence trickster, who was constantly in and out of prison or on the run from the authorities. His crimes were fraud and theft, usually items such as library books or silverware from colleges. His long criminal career started in 1863 when he was sentenced to ten months imprisonment for swindling hoteliers in Oxford. In January, 1874 he was sentenced to ten years imprisonment for larceny. In the

354

1881 census he is a prisoner at Portland Prison, his occupation is given as a surgeon, his birthplace as Poland. In July 1887 using the alias Dr Bonge, he was apprehended by the Cadets from Woolwich Barracks, after he was discovered attempting to steal a tankard. He told the court that he was on his way to play cricket when a fit of sunstroke gave him an irresistible impulse to run a race, which he thought he was doing when the Cadets chased him. It was in court that he began to show signs of mental instability and at one point picked up his coat as if to leave and declared he was off to France, if they did not mind, they did, and he was sentenced to six months hard labour. Certified insane while in Wandsworth Prison, he was sent to the Surrey Pauper Lunatic Asylum on 30 September 1887, where he was described as 50-years of age, Jewish, a surgeon, married and suffering from mania. He was released on 10 March 1888 as "cured" and continued his criminal career. He was admitted to Bansted Asylum 7 May 1891, where he remained until 29 May 1893. Where it was reported that he was suicidal but not dangerous to others. In 1898, he was charged in Woolwich for theft of books. He was arrested again in August 1900 for stealing a microscope and was sentenced to five years imprisonment, giving his address as 29 Brooke Street, Holborn. He was released from Parkhurst prison on 17 September 1904, and the last we hear of him was entering the St Giles Christian Mission in Brook Street, Holborn, there are no further records of him.

No records exist of his date of birth, but it has been estimated at about 1833, which would have made him at least 55-years of age at the time of the Whitechapel murders. Ostrog, born in Russia, was dark skinned with dark hair and moustache, without whiskers, hazel or grey eyes, long features, and was 5 ft 11 inches tall. Generally dressed in a semi-clerical suit. Ostrog, is said to speak seven different languages. Among his many dubious claims was that he had once been a surgeon in the Russian Navy. The census, asylum, and prison records state surgeon as an occupation, yet no records have been found to verify the claims by Macnaghten that Ostrog was a doctor, had medical training or carried surgical knives. Macnaghten's claim about Ostrog being habitually cruel to women also remains unsupported. There is simply no evidence to support the police claims that he was a dangerous man. There is also no evidence throughout his long criminal career that Ostrog used violence, particularly on women. After the double murder of Stride and Eddowes, the police, having made enquiries at the local lunatic asylums, would have noted that Ostrog had been certified insane, and had been released some six months previously, and after failing to report, some attention was then attached to him. Research by Philip Sugden, shows there is, some evidence that during the Whitechapel murders Ostog, was in prison in France. He was arrested on 26 July 1888 under the name Grand Guidon, an alias he had used in France before, and was held in custody until 18 November 1888 when he was sentenced to two years in prison. He was held in the lunatic wing of a French prison, until his release in November 1890.

DR. VLADIMIR PANTCHENKO

Author Rupert Furneaux, in the (1957) book: The Medical Murderer, tells the story of a St Petersburg doctor named Dr Dimitru Panchenko (his correct name according to the newspapers and court transcripts was Vladimir Pantchenko) who was a supplier of poisons and was suspected of being involved in several murders. In 1908 bankrupt Polish nobleman, Patrick O' Brien De Lacy married Ludmilla, the daughter of General Dimitry and Madame Buturlin, they were extremely wealthy, General Buturlin was worth 1,400,000 roubles, but had bequeathed their

356

fortune to their children, their son Captain Vassilli Buturlin, was to receive half, and the other half was to go to Ludmilla. In an attempt to get his hands on their entire fortune, Delacy decided to murder Captain Vassilli, with cholera and diphtheria germs, both diseases were at epidemic levels in St Petersburg at that time. He planned to obtain these from Dr. Pantchenko, for the sum of 620.000 Roubles. Pantchenko was a physician with a dubious reputation, he reportedly sold poison, faked death certificates, and produced pornography. Pantchenko killed Captain Buturlin, with the diphtheria toxin. General Buturlin immediately became suspicious about the death, and requested a post-mortem. Pantchenko, and DeLacy, were arrested. De Lacy was sentenced to life imprisonment. Panchenko, for his involvement in the plot, was sentenced to 15 years imprisonment. There is no evidence to connect him with the Whitechapel murders. It is possible Pantchenko may have been the basis for the Dr Alexander Pedachenko stories.

ALFRED PARENT

Parent, a Frenchman and a resident of Bacon's Hotel, Fitroy Square, St Pancras, London. Came under suspicion on 25 November 1888 after he offered prostitute Annie Cook a sovereign for sex and five sovereigns to spend the night with him. As the usual price for such services was about sixpence, Annie became suspicious of the man and reported him to the police. She told the police that she thought the reason he had offered more money than was usual for her services was so that he could get her indoors and murder her. Parent was able to satisfactorily prove to the police that he had nothing to do with the Whitechapel murders. He was born in 1834 and was 54-years of age at the time of the murders, and was described as 5 ft 6 inches tall, with white hair, whiskers and moustache.

ISAAC PASCO

In October 1888, Isacc Pasco who described himself as a "maker of flowers from vegetables," was charged with being drunk and riotous in Bridge-street. PC Lea, said the prisoner was quite drunk, and shouting that he was "Jack the Ripper." Pasco, claimed he was enquiring his way to some lodgings, when the officer met him and kicked him on the back. The constable denied this, and said the prisoner fell down. He was fined 5s and costs, or in default seven days hard labour.

GEORGE PAYNE

George Payne a labourer who spoke with a provincial dialect was an individual who certainly did his utmost in life to live up to his surname, he was charged on 5 October 1888, with being drunk in the street. Detective Sergeant Gurtner F Division, said he received information that at eleven o'clock on Thursday night a man in the Harrow-road had been heard to say he had committed half a dozen murders in the East End of London and had now come to the West End to commit half a dozen more. Gurtner swiftly apprehended Payne, who was taken into custody. Payne was described as one of those mischievous fellows who goes about terrifying people by boasting that he had done some horrible crime in the East-end. He was ordered to pay a fine of 10s or go to prison for seven days.Sergeant Gurtner, who arrested Payne, was John Gurtner, born 1853 in Shadwell, London. His address in the 1881, census is 104 Alberny Street. Police-station.

MARY PEARCEY

Mary Eleanor Wheeler was born in June 1866, in Kent, and little accurate information is known of her early life. One unsubstantiated story often told is that when Mary was around fourteen years of age her father, Thomas Wheeler was hanged on the 29 November 1880 at St Albans Prison, for the murder of a local farmer Edward Anstee. In his prison cell, Thomas had written a letter to the farmer's widow apologising for what he had done and asked for forgiveness and her prayers that his sins would not be visited upon his wife or daughter.

In fact her parents were James Wheeler a delivery foreman, from, Birmingham, and Charlotte A (née Kelly). Mary was said to have grown into a relatively attractive woman with "shapely hands" lovely russet hair a beautiful long neck and fine blue eyes. She was described as 5 ft 6 inches tall and weighed 9 stone. Her looks brought her to the attention of many men. In her late teens, she had a relationship with a carpenter named John Charles Pearcey and although they never married, she took his surname and continued to use it after they parted. Mary is thought to have suffered from frontal lobe epilepsy and was known to suffer from depression and also drank quite heavily, she never worked and spent much of her time in the company of wealthy men, one of these gentleman friends, Charles Creighton, a married man, rented rooms for her at 2 Priory Street, Kentish Town, North London. She then began an affair with Mr Frank Samuel Hogg, a furniture remover, who was married with a daughter named Phoebe. On the morning of 24 October 1890, Mary asked a young lad to run an errand for her and deliver a note to Frank Samuel's wife, who was also named Phoebe, inviting her round for tea. At 7:10 p.m. a woman's body was found lying on the pavement in Crossfield Road by a clerk named Somerlea Macdonald who was returning from work. The woman's head was wrapped in a cardigan, which a policeman removed to reveal the bloodstained face of Phoebe Hogg. At the morgue, it was discovered that she had suffered a fractured skull and a large wound to the throat, the wound was so severe that it had almost severed the head. An examination of the location where the body was found indicated that the murder had taken place elsewhere. Later that evening a heavily bloodstained black pram was discovered in Hamilton Terrace, about a mile from where the body had been discovered. The following morning in Finchley, the body of an infant was found, the child had died from suffocation. Frank Hogg and his sister Clara, on hearing of the discovery of a woman's body, went to the police station to report his wife missing. Frank then sent Clara to see Mary to inquire if she had seen Phoebe. Mary denied having seen Phoebe, but agreed to accompany Clara to the morgue to see if the woman's body was, in fact, Phoebe. Mary's behaviour at the morgue was strange, and she tried everything possible to stop Clara identifying the body. Clara, despite Mary's attempts to stop her, identified the body as that of Phoebe Hogg, and also identified the pram as hers. A neighbour told the police that she had seen Mary pushing the pram with a large object in it around the streets of north London on the evening of the murder. When Frank was informed that the body had been identified as that of his wife, he confessed to having an affair with Mary. The police, now suspicious of Mary, searched Priory Street and found bloodstains in the kitchen, along with a bloodstained poker and carving knife, two broken windows in the kitchen provided signs of a struggle. When questioned as to what use the bloodstained poker and knife had been Mary replied, "Killing mice." While her house was being searched, Mary sat at the piano playing popular tunes. Mary was arrested and charged with the murder of mother and child, and when searched, bloodstains were found on her clothing, she was found to be wearing Phoebe Hogg's wedding ring. Mary continually protested her innocence throughout the trial, found guilty, she was sentenced to hang. On her final evening she asked her solicitor to place a personal advert in the Madrid newspaper, the message read; "mecp last wish of mew, have not betrayed mew." Mary refused to elaborate on the meaning of the message, and was hanged on 23 December 1890, the hangman was James Berry. In his memoirs, he says of her:

"She was the most beautiful woman I ever hanged."

He described her in detail as having:

"big blue eyes with a languishing look in them, masses of wavy hair and lips like Cupid's bow."

Sir Melville Macnaghten said of her:

"I have never seen a woman of stronger physique.... her nerves were as iron cast as her body."

Madame Tussaud's subsequently commissioned a wax model of Mary Pearcey, and also purchased the pram belonging to Frank Hogg. William Stewart, in his (1939) book: Jack the Ripper a New Theory, suggested Pearcey as a possible Ripper suspect, when he noticed the similarities between the murder of Mrs Hogg and the Whitechapel murders. He noted the savage throat cutting, the killing in private and later dumping of the body in a public place, which he also believed was the Ripper's modus operandi, and would explain why no witnesses heard any of the Ripper's victims scream. Stewart's theory, however completely contradicts all the known medical evidence, which shows that all the victims were murdered where they were found.

ALFRED PEARSON

On the 8 October, 1888, Alfred Pearson, a moulder (a person who makes bricks), was charged at Brierley Hill Police Court with threatening Thomas Plant, and a lady friend, who were out walking, on Saturday night. Pearson suddenly appeared out of the darkness brandishing what appeared to be a butcher's knife, and cried out, "I am Jack the Ripper." The lady, fainted from fright. Pearson then threatened Plant, with the weapon. The lady was afterwards taken very ill with hysterics. Pearson, pleaded to the court that, he had no intention of hurting anyone. The bench commented on the folly of his conduct, and said he might have been committed. He was bound over to keep the peace, for six months; the weapon he was holding was in fact not a knife but a "trowel."

In the (2007) book, Jack the Ripper: The Satanic Team, Karen Trenouth, claims Alfred Pearson, the moulder, is actually Dr Alfred William Pearson, the surgeon.

DR. ALFRED WILLIAM PEARSON

In the (2007) book: Jack the Ripper: The Satanic Team, Karen Trenouth, claims Jack the Ripper was an Edinburgh-trained Surgeon, Dr. Alfred William Pearson who was assisted in the murders by five Aristocrats, Lord Arthur Somerset, Henry James Fitzroy, Herbrand Arthur Russel and William Humble Ward. Prince Albert Victor also assists by murdering Mary Kelly.

Alfred William Pearson, was born 22 May 1849, in Stourbridge. He studied medicine in Edinburgh. Married Elizabeth Ann Rogers, 1895. Second marriage to Wilhelmina Barclay Clark 1907, they had three children. Pearson died 21 April, 1920 in Wordsley.

In one of the chapters, in her book, Trenouth studied the photo of Mary Kelly's crime scene, and comes to the conclusion that several knives, scissors and other implements were left strewn around. Despite the photograph having been closely scrutinised over the years, no one else has come to the same conclusion as Trenouth. She also claims that Mary Kelly, worked for Charles Hammond when she arrived in London, and was aware of exactly

362

what was occurring at 19 Cleveland Street and informed Inspector Abberline, of her suspicions. When the aristocrats discovered, a woman called Mary had reported their secret goings on at Cleveland Street, they set out to murder prostitutes until they found Mary.

The author offers us a convoluted theory, with no evidence, for any of her claims.

ALEXANDER PEDACHENKO

According to which variation of the story is told, Dr. Alexander Pedachenko, alias Vassily Konovalov, alias Count Andrey Luiskovo, was sent by the Russian secret police or the Ochrana, to England to commit the Whitechapel murders, in an attempt to discredit the Metropolitan Police, whom they believed were being too soft on anarchists, socialists and dissidents. His accomplices in this were Levitski, who would be the lookout, and Miss Winberg, who would engage the prostitutes in conversation, before Pedachenko (Jack the Ripper) struck. With their mission accomplished, Levitski and Winberg were exiled to Yakutsk. Pedachenko was smuggled back to Russia, but could not stop killing, and attempted to murder a woman called Vogak in Petrograd before he was committed to an asylum where he died.He was born in Tver, Russia, in 1847 and worked in the local maternity hospital. He was said to be a barber-surgeon, who had previously lived in Glasgow, and who in 1888 was living with his sister in Westmoreland-road, Walworth, South London. He would take an omnibus across London Bridge, walk into Whitechapel and commit the terrible deed. He was described as having a curly waxed moustache and occasionally wore women's clothes. The original source of this story was William Le Quex, in the (1928) book: Things I Know about Kings, Celebrities and Crooks. Le Quex, claimed to have seen a copy of the January 1909 Ochrana

Gazette, the bulletin of the Czarist secret police, which advised all officers that Konovalov, alias Pedachenko, the murderer of a woman in Paris, in 1886, as well as the five Ripper victims of 1888, had now died in an asylum. There is no evidence that Pedachenko ever existed, or that Konovalov and Pedachenko were the same people. The murder he allegedly committed in Petrograd in 1888 is unlikely, as it was not named Petrograd until 1914, prior to that it was called St Petersburg.

JOHN BENJAMIN PERRYMAN

Perryman was charged before Lambeth magistrates with being drunk and disorderly. The incident happened on Wednesday night 14 November 1888 in the Old Kent-Road. Two detectives Leek and Reed, who were in the area at the time heard a disturbance and went to investigate; they found Perryman surrounded by an angry crowd. The man had caused considerable alarm by manhandling several females, flourishing his arms about, exhibiting a black leather bag and proclaiming he was "Jack the Ripper." With great difficulty the man was taken to the police station, the crowd followed closely behind. At the police station, a search of his person and his bag revealed a dagger and sheath, a life preserver and two pairs of scissors. When asked why he was carrying such items about with him, Perryman replied: "He was going to have them ground." His sister stated that she was aware he carried a dagger about his person, though for what purpose she did not know. She also said that had been intoxicated for a long time. Perryman, it is claimed, was known as the "Mad Barber of Peckham." (Not to be confused with the "Mad Pork Butcher"). At the Lambeth Police Court, Perryman, who seemed to regard the whole matter as a joke, was told that if he was not in his right mind, it would perhaps be necessary to send him to an asylum. Perryman, it is claimed looked astonished when his request to be allowed out on bail was refused. John Benjamin Perryman was 40-years of age at the time of his arrest.

Born in Rotherhithe, London, 16 January 1848. His parents were John Perryman a mariner and Eliza. He lived in Pennethorne-Road, Peckham and was in occupation as a hairdresser. In the 1861 census aged 13, he is an errand boy in the employ of Reuben Norman a hairdresser at 361 Rotherhithe Street, London. In 1872 he married Mary Ann Goodings, a dressmaker, born in Camberwell, London. In the 1881 census, he is aged 33, living at 4 Middle Street, Camberwell, London, still in occupation as a hairdresser. On the 22 November 1888, he was admitted by the police to Newington Workhouse. He died July 1889.

WILLIAM PETITT

On 2 January 1889, William Petitt, a 47 year old, bricklayer, living in Masboro Road, Hammersmith, was charged with being drunk and disorderly. Detective Cracknall was in North End Road when he saw Petitt, who was very drunk, chasing boys with a knife in his hand, saying "I am Jack the Ripper." Petitt, denied this saying it was nonsense. A boy named Daniel McIntosh, stated that the man came up to him and said, "I am Jack the Ripper." He saw the knife in the man's hand and ran away. Petitt, was fined 40s or 14 days imprisonment. Petitt, was born in 1842, in Cambridgeshire. He was married to Sarah, (née Cutts) born, 1851 in Suffolk.

GEORGE PIERILLI

The Morning Advertiser (London) 10 December 1888 reported the following story:

George Pierilli, 20, an Italian, of 8 Fleet Row, Holborn, was charged, before Mr Horace Smith, with being disorderly at Farringdon Road. Police constable Dunlop, 18 G, R said that late on Friday night he was on duty in Farringdon-Road when he saw a large crowd assembled and heard cries of "Murder" and "Police." Upon nearing the crowd, he saw the prisoner stripped to the waist, shouting "I'm Jack the Ripper; I will do for some of them." He ascertained that Pierilli had previously assaulted a woman, and had thrown her to the ground. Mr Horace Smith, in sentencing the accused to 14 days' imprisonment, described his conduct as most disgraceful.

Pierelli had, previously, been tried for rape, 12 September 1887.

GEORGE PIERELLI (18), Carnally knowing Florence Louisa Platt, aged between 13 and 16. MR. MEAD Prosecuted. Verdict NOT GUILTY.

Pierelli had also previously been sentenced to three months imprisonment for wounding, 3 April 1888.

WILLIAM PIGGOTT

Piggott came to the attention of the police after the landlady of the Pope's Head public house in Gravesend, Kent, heard him yelling his hatred and hostility toward women. PC John Vollensworth was summoned and found Piggott dazed and confused. When the Constable noticed an injury to the man's hand, which he was unable to satisfactorily account for, he was arrested. When questioned at the police station, Piggott made a rambling statement in which he explained that on Sunday morning the 9 September 1888 in Brick Lane, he came to the aid of a woman who had fallen while having a fit, and attempted to help her up, whereupon she bit him on the hand, causing the wound and the blood on his shirt. Superintendent Berry later recovered a paper parcel which Piggott had left in a fish and pie stall, it contained two bloodstained shirts, it was noticed that his shoes also looked like they had been wiped clean of blood. Inspector Abberline was summoned to Gravesend and returned to London with Piggott. Now looking a strong suspect, he was placed in an identity parade of seventeen men, before Mrs Fiddymont, Joseph Taylor and Mary Chappell, to see if they could recognise the bloodstained man seen in the Prince Albert public house shortly after the murder of Annie Chapman. Of the three witnesses, only Mary Chappell picked Piggott out as the man she had seen, before changing her mind and saying "she was no longer sure." The police eventually satisfied themselves that Piggott had nothing to do with the Whitechapel murders. He was treated for delirium tremens and discharged on 9 October 1888.Piggott was born in 1835 and was 53-years of age at the time of the Whitechapel murders. The son of a Gravesend insurance agent, Piggott was said to be a ship's cook, who at one time had owned his own pub in Hoxton, which he paid the sum of £8.000 for, but had since fallen on hard times. He was no stranger to the infirmary as he had previously been admitted there on 8 June from 19 Brick Lane, and discharged on 30 July again suffering from delirium tremens. In appearance, he was said to closely resemble John Pizer (Leather Apron). There is a suggestion that Piggott may have later been incarcerated in an asylum.

JOHN PIZER

John Pizer was born in 1850 in London and was the eldest son to Israel Pizer, and Abigail (née Moss). They were married in London in 1842. Israel was described as a "general dealer." John Pizer was a Polish Jewish boot finisher, of no fixed abode, who often resided at 22 Mulberry Street with his 70-year old stepmother, Augusta. John Pizer was better known as "Leather Apron." He came under suspicion after the murder of Mary Ann Nichols, when the newspapers reported that the police were looking for a man named Leather Apron, who had been ill-treating prostitutes in the area. According to a reporter from the Star newspaper, at least 50 women described the man who had been ill-treated them:

He is 5ft 4 inches tall and wears a dark close-fitting cap, he is thickset and has an unusually thick neck, his hair is black and closely clipped, he is aged between 38 to 40 and has a small black moustache. His expression is said to be sinister, his eyes small and glittering, his lips are usually parted in a grin, which is not only unreassuringly but is excessively repellent. He always carries a knife and gets his nickname from a leather apron he always wore. He was said to be a slipper maker by trade, though does not work. His name nobody knows, but they are all united in the belief that he is a Jew or of Jewish parentage.

Sergeant William Thick, who claimed he had known Pizer for eighteen years, knew that when people in the neighbourhood spoke of Leather Apron, they meant Pizer. Thick went to Mulberry Street shortly after 8 am on 10 September 1888 to fetch Pizer, who had been lying low on the advice of his brother. Pizer believed if he went outdoors he would be torn to pieces by angry mobs searching for Leather Apron. His brother and other relatives confirmed his alibi the night Annie Chapman was murdered. Pizer was taken to Leman Street Police Station, and when questioned he said he was unaware that he was known as Leather Apron until Thick told him so. While he accepted that he had worn a leather apron home from work, he had, in fact, not done so for some time, because he had recently been out of work. His neighbours, family and friends denied that he was known as Leather Apron.Pizer was soon cleared of any involvement in the Whitechapel murders. On the night Mary Ann Nichols was murdered, he had been staying at Crossman's lodging house in Holloway Road, and at 1:30 spoke to a policeman about a fire at

368

London Docks, which he then went to see. The fire had broken out at 8:30 that evening at one of the huge warehouses, and was extremely fierce and could be seen for miles around. Though brought under control by 11 o'clock, it was not fully extinguished until several hours later. He did not watch the fire long, before returning back to Crossman's, arriving there about 2:15 a.m. He paid his 4d for his bed, then sat in the kitchen and smoked a clay pipe, he slept until 11 am when he was awoken by the attendant. He later learnt of the murder from a placard he saw in the street. The police confirmed the account of his movements. It was reported that Pizer had received handsome compensation from the newspapers after slanderous stories were printed about him; the amount he received, however, was not as substantial as some writers have claimed, and may have been no more than £10. Worth about £200 in today's terms. The East London Observer gave this rather unflattering description of Pizer:

His face was not altogether pleasant to look upon by reason of the grizzly, black strips of hair, nearly an inch in length, short, smooth and dark, intermingled with grey, his head was slightly bald on top, his head was large and was fixed to the body by a thick, heavy-looking neck. He appeared splay footed and spoke with a thick guttural foreign accent.

Pizer said this description of him bore no more resemblance to him, as it did the man on the moon. Pizer was described by the Daily Telegraph, 11 September:

As a dark man, of slight build, with a small moustache and side-whiskers, his hair is turning grey. There is no foreign accent about his talk.

He died of gastroenteritis in the London Hospital, in July 1897, at the age of 47 years, after a lifetime of poor health.

ANTONI PRICHA

After witness George Hutchinson gave his detailed description of a Ripper suspect wearing an Astrakhan trimmed coat. seen with Mary Kelly, shortly before she was murdered, Edward Knight Larkin, a clerk in H.M. Customs 53 Pepys Road, New Cross saw Antoni Pricha, at 12 noon on 13 November, and told PC 61A Thomas Maybank that he thought he fitted the newspaper description of Hutchinson's suspect.Pricha was questioned, at King Street Station, but was soon able to satisfactorily prove his innocence and was released. He lived at 11 Back Hill, Hatton Garden EC, and was described as 30-years old, about 5 ft 6 inches tall, with long dark wavy hair and a long dark moustache. He was wearing a long dark brown Astrakhan trimmed coat. He stated he was Employed as an Artist Model at the Royal Academy.

THOMAS PRITCHARD

On 28 November 1888, at South Shields Police Court, Thomas Pritchard, a butcher, was charged with being drunk and disorderly. He had been going about with a knife, and people had been shouting "Jack the Ripper" after him. He was sentenced to 14 Days imprisonment.

OSWALD PUCKRIDGE

On 19 September 1888, Metropolitan Police Commissioner, Sir Charles Warren, wrote to the Home Secretary Henry Matthews and informed him of a suspect named Oswald Puckridge, who had been released from an asylum on 4 August 1888. Warren wrote:

He was educated as a surgeon, and had threatened to rip people up with a long knife, he is being looked for, but cannot be found yet.

Oswald Puckridge was born in Burpham near Arundel, Sussex, on 13 June 1838; he was the fourth of five children, born to John Puckridge a farmer, and his wife Philadelphia (née Holmes). On 3 October 1868, he married Ellen Buddle the daughter of a licensed victualler, John Puckridge, at St Paul's Parish Church, Deptford, and gave his occupation as a chemist. In 1870 they had a son Edward Buddle Puckridge. In the 1871 census, Oswald, is listed in occupation as a licensed victualler. In 1884, he was sentenced to six weeks hard labour, for causing the death of his dog. During election time, he painted the animal all over with the Liberal and Conservative colours and the dog was poisoned through licking the paint off. He appealed, his sentence and was granted bail, thereupon he escaped to the continent. While visiting friends in Sandwich, he was identified, and arrested. In November 1884, he was in court charged with assaulting a woman called Fanny Smith. When she failed to appear the charges against him were dropped. On the 11 November, he was arrested for being drunk and disorderly, the arresting officer P.C. Lyon, said he had never heard such filthy language. January 1885, he was back in court for assaulting Phillip Journeaux, in Springfield-road, by knocking off his hat. He was accompanied by a tame sheep. In November, he was in trouble for riding a horse into the Post Office, and attempting to send it by parcel post. He also frightened, a child so much it wasn't expected to live by wearing a sheepskin coat, (that explains the fate of the sheep). He was admitted to the Hoxton House Lunatic Asylum 50-52 Hoxton Street, Shoreditch, on 6 January 1888 and remained there until 4 August 1888. In 1888, he was described as Age 45, height 5ft.10, dark beard, whiskers & Moustache hair cut short & parted in Centre sallow complexion,

371

square shoulders, turns his toes out, walks quickly. Dressed black morning coat, dark vest & trousers & soft felt hat. He was admitted to Gloucester Lunatic Asylum, 11 July 1889, discharged 13 August 1889. He was admitted to the Devon County Lunatic Asylum, 6 August 1891, discharged 13 November 1891. On 9 August 1893 he was found wandering in Queen Victoria Street, London, and was admitted to Bow Infirmary, he was discharged on 18 August. He was admitted to the Holborn Workhouse in City Road, 18 September 1894, where he remained till 30 October 1894. He was re-admitted to the Bow Infirmary, on 5 February 1896, from Bridewell Police Station, he was discharged on the 14 February to the City of London Lunatic Asylum at Stone Buckinghamshire, being recorded as a danger to others. He was released on 9 July 1896, only to be readmitted on 19 August 1899. He was discharged once more on 18 October, before being admitted, on 28 May 1900 to the Holborn Workhouse in City Road, where his address was given as 34 St John's Lane, Clerkenwell, and his occupation as a general labourer. He died there on 1 June 1900 of bronchial pneumonia. In his will he left effects to the value of £300, to his son Edward Buddle Puckridge, grocer and provisions-dealer. The Thanet Advertiser 27 May 1899, reported that when Puckridge, was admitted to Romford Workhouse, he had on his person, over £555, a couple of purses containing £6 in gold, and half a £5 note. There is no evidence to substantiate the claim by Warren that Puckridge had ever trained as a surgeon; his marriage certificate stated his occupation as a pharmacological chemist. A little known fact about Oswald Puckridge, is in 1869, at the Wellington Lodge, he became a Freemason.

JAMES PURTON

James Purton, known as "Dragon Man" because of a dragon tattooed on his forearm, escaped from Chelmsford Prison in 1947 and 1948. He was at liberty for 8 days before being recaptured. On 1 October 1950, he was recaptured at Whippingham, East Cowes, on the Isle of Wight, after escaping from Parkhurst Prison. Purton was discovered hiding in an army camp under a bundle of army greatcoats and netting, during a search by a patrol of National Servicemen. The officer asked him "You are Joe Purton, aren't you?" Purton replied wearily "Of course I'm not I'm Jack the Ripper, didn't you know?"

EDWARD QUINN

Edward Quinn a 35-year-old labourer, appeared at the Woolwich Police Court on 17 September 1888, charged with being drunk. He had been drinking at a bar in Woolwich Arsenal, on 15 September when a tall, big man came in, engaged him in conversation, gave him beer and tobacco, then accused him of having committed the Whitechapel crimes, after Quinn's appearance caused suspicion. His hands and face were bruised, blood was also noticed on his hands and clothing. Quinn initially thought it was a joke, and laughed, but the man said he was serious and pointed to the blood. Quinn said: "Nonsense." The subject was then dropped. They both then left the pub together. The man walked him to the police station, and charged him with the Whitechapel murders. It later transpired that Quinn, had merely fallen over in the street whilst in a drunken state, banged his head against a wall, and badly cut and bruised his hands and face. He was not aware at the time how much the cut had bled, or how badly his clothes had become bloodstained due to his drunken condition. He was charged with being drunk and disorderly. At Woolwich Police-Court, Quinn, who denied being

373

drunk said: much to everyone's amusement, "I murder a woman, I could not murder a cat." He was later released.

THE RAILWAY POLICEMAN

Retired Metropolitan Police officer, theorist and police historian, Bernard Brown, in the true crime publication Murder Most Foul, made the suggestion that Jack the Ripper may have been a railway policeman, who used the underground to make good his getaway. The first tube station in Whitechapel was opened in 1876, and Shoreditch Station was less than five minutes' walk from Bucks Row, where Mary Ann Nichols was murdered. St Mary's Station was situated only a few yards from Berner Street, where Elizabeth Stride was murdered. Unfortunately, Brown does not name his police suspect. Brown believes the infamous "Dear Boss" letter received at the Central News Agency, On 27 September 1888, contained a vital clue as to the Ripper's identity. Though was misinterpreted for over a century, and a valuable clue lost forever.

Dear Boss I keep hearing the Police have caught me, but they won't fix me just yet. I have laughed when they look so clever and talk about being on the right track. The latter phase was a teasing reference to the railway. Yes, he was indeed on the right track-below ground!

Although it is true a policeman would inspire a degree of confidence in his victims, and allay any suspicions, the weakness of this theory is that no witnesses reported seeing a policeman with any of the victims shortly before they were murdered. Brown, during research, did discover the story of a well-known 40-year old prostitute named Emily Wood, a widow of 11 Hungerford Street, Commercial Road, East London, who in the early hours of Friday 7 January 1899 walked into Arbour Square Police Station and demanded to see the officer in charge. She appeared to be in a state of intoxication and was promptly arrested for drunkenness. When examined she was found to have been stabbed in a delicate area, causing a two-inch wound from which she was bleeding profusely. She was treated first at the London Hospital, and later at St George's Infirmary. Due to the loss of blood, Wood remained in a weak state, but eventually recovered from her ordeal. She then told the story that, while walking along Commercial Road, claimed that she was accosted and attacked by a tall, dark policeman with a black moustache, who stabbed her and left her for dead. Despite claiming to have known the officer for some time and could easily recognise him again, the policeman was never traced. Over several days 206 patrol-men and points men were paraded before her, but she was unable to identify her assailant. No evidence or records exist to confirm this story, interesting though it is.

FRANK RAPER

Frank Raper, was arrested at a public house, known as "Dirty Dick's," near Liverpool-street. While in the bar, and in a drunken state, he made a number of extravagant statements about the murder of Annie Chapman, and Polly Nicholls. A constable was sent for, when he arrived Raper, was openly boasting of being the murderer, and complimenting himself on the means he had adopted to destroy all traces of his identity. He was removed to the police-station, followed by a large and excited crowd. On being charged Raper said he had no settled address. After inquiries he was set free.

WILLIAM RAPSONG

In August 1889, a Frenchman, named William Rapsong, who said he was a sailor, caused a great commotion by running about in a mysterious manner, at Preston village, while declaring he was "Jack the Ripper." Police-constable Packman, spoke to the prisoner, who told him he was the only son of the Empress Eugenie, and that he was the brother to Baron Rothschild, who allowed him £36,000 a year to spend. The officer noticing the man was wearing workhouse clothing came to the conclusion that he was an escaped lunatic, and took him to the police-station. The doctor who examined him declared him sane, but said he might have been suffering from drink. The learned chairman, Mr. Serjeant Spinks, said the constable had acted prudently and wisely, but under the circumstances ordered the prisoner's release.

JOHN RICHARDSON

At 4:45 am on Saturday, 8 September 1888, 35 year old John Richardson, who lived at 2 John Street, Spitalfields, and worked as a porter at Spitalfields market, and who also helped his mother at her packing case business. Was on his way to work, when he called in at 29 Hanbury Street to check the locks on the yard where his mother ran her business from. A few months previously it had been broken into and a few items were stolen. Richardson, noticing everything was at it should be, paused to trim a piece of leather from his boot which was causing him discomfort when walking. Richardson, was described as tall, stout with dark brown hair, brown moustache, and a very pale face and who spoke with a rather husky voice, would later tell the inquest. "It was not quite light at the time, but there was enough light to see all over the place." He felt sure he would have seen a body if it had been lying there. One hour later, John Davis, while on his way to work, discovered the mutilated body of Annie Chapman, just yards from where Richardson had claimed to have trimmed his boot only one hour before.Dr George Bagster Phillips examined the body and declared that she had been dead for at least two hours, probably longer, putting the time of death at 4:30 am. At the inquest Inspector Joseph Chandler stated he had interviewed Richardson at about 6:45 on the morning of the murder, and was told by him that:

"He had been to the house that morning about a quarter to five. He said he came to the back door and looked down to the cellar, to see if all was right, and then went away to his work."

The Coroner: "Did he say anything about cutting his boot?

"Chandler "No."

On the 12 of September, Richardson's story had changed,

The Coroner: "Did you go into the yard?"

Richardson: "No, the yard door was shut. I opened it and sat on the doorstep, and cut a piece of leather off my boot with an old table knife, about five inches long. I kept the knife upstairs at John street. I had been feeding a rabbit with a carrot that I had cut up, and I put the knife in my pocket. I do not usually carry it there. After cutting the leather off my boot I tied my boot up, and went out of the house into the market. I did not close the back door. It closed itself. I shut the front door."

When the inquest learnt that Richardson carried a knife, and a leather apron belonging to him had been found under a tap in the yard, he briefly came under suspicion. Richardson, was requested to produce the knife he had used to trim his boot, accompanied by a constable. An examination of it showed it could not have been the murder weapon; it was an old, rusty blunt five-inch long table knife with half the blade broken off and no handle, he had generally used it to cut up carrots for his pet rabbit. If Richardson was, "Jack the Ripper," he would hardly have

377

produced the actual murder weapon for the police to examine. If the knife he used was an old, rusty blunt table knife, how was it able to cut a tough piece of boot leather? The leather apron, which the police took possession of when they searched the yard, was one he wore when he worked in the cellar, it had been washed by his mother Amelia Richardson, because "it was a bit mildewed," and had been left in the yard since Thursday and appeared to have not been moved. Albert Cadosch, a 23-year old carpenter, who lived next door at number 27, woke at about 5:15 am, then after a brief period went into his yard to use the privy, when he heard a woman's voice quite close to him say, "No." He believed it came from number 29. He went back into his house, and returned three or four minutes later, presumably to use the privy again, as he had recently had an operation at the hospital, when he heard the sound of something falling against the fence. The fence, was about 5ft 6 high. Cadosch at the inquest stated that he had heard no other sounds.

The Coroner: "Had you heard any noise while you were at the end of your yard?"

Cadosch: "No."

The Coroner: "Any rustling of clothes?"

Cadosch: "No."

When Cadosch left his house to go to work he passed Spitalfields Church and noticed the time was 5:32 am. Elizabeth Long, whose name was given as Durrell, or Darrell, in some newspaper accounts lived, at 32 Church Street. She was on her way to Spitalfields market where she worked as a cart minder, when she passed 29 Hanbury Street as the brewer's clock struck 5:30, and noticed a man and woman talking loudly. But not sufficiently so to arouse her suspicions. She overheard the man say, "Will you," and the woman replied, "Yes." By her own admission, she paid very little attention to the two. Yet four days later, on the 12 of September, at the mortuary, when viewing the body of Annie Chapman, was certain it was the same woman she had seen. Mrs Long was unable to give a good description of the man because she hardly saw his face, except to say that he was dark and wore a brown deerstalker hat, had a shabby genteel appearance and looked like a foreigner. She could not say what age he was, but looked to be over 40 and appeared to be a little taller than the woman, Chapman was 5 ft tall, so her companion was about 5 ft 2 to 4 inches. Mrs Long said she saw nothing to indicate that they were not sober and it was not an unusual to see men and women talking together at that hour, in that locality. If John Richardson's, Albert Cadosch's and Elizabeth Long's version of events are correct, then Chapman was killed around 5:15-5:30 and not earlier as Bagster Phillips had claimed. Dr Phillips later admitted that he may have miscalculated the time of death, due to the loss of blood from the body and the coldness of the morning. There is, however a discrepancy in the time, Cadosch, heard something falling against the fence, and the time Long saw the Couple.

John Richardson was born in January 1852, in Lambeth, London. He was the fourth eldest son of six children. To Thomas Richardson, a packing case maker, and his wife Amelia Manners (née Smily). The couple where married 3 May 1846, at St Leonards Church, Shoreditch. His father died in April 1884. His mother Amelia, died 30 October 1903, at the age of 79. He married Caroline Ann (née Chaffey) on Christmas Day, 25 December 1873, at St Thomas Church, Bethnal Green. They had three children, two sons, Thomas, and John, and a daughter, Amelia Janette. In the 1881 census he is living at 15 Caroline Street, in occupation as a militiaman. In the 1891 census he is living at 7 John Street, in occupation as a bricklayer. In the 1901 census he is living at 139 Vallance Street, in occupation as a market porter. In the 1911 census, he is living at 36 Ballance Road, Hackney. Still in occupation as a market porter. He died in Hackney 1935, at the age of 83. His wife Caroline died in 1924.

JOHN RIP

In October, 1888, a man named John Rip, was brought before the Mayor at the Town Hall, Ilkeston, Derbyshire, on a charge of being drunk, and with stealing a shilling from Priscilla Bennett, in Burn's street. She was on her way to her mother's house when, Rip, took hold of her arm, and asked her for some money. She told him she had none. He said that if she did not give him some he "Whitechapel, her." And that he was "Jack the Ripper." She began to scream, he put his hand over her mouth, and struck her in the face, which caused her nose to bleed. He then put his hand in her pocket and took out a shilling. PC Cosgrove, arrested the man for drunkenness. Bennett, identified him the next day as the man who had robbed her. He was sent to prison for three months. Rip, declared that he would buy a revolver and blow her brains out when he came out.

JOSE RIZAL

On 19 June 1861, Francisco Rizal Mercado and Teodora Alonzo y Quintos welcomed their seventh child into the world at Calamba, Laguna. They named the boy Jose Protasio Rizal Mercado y Alonso Realonda. He was the seventh child in a family of 11 children; 2 boys and 9 girls. Both his parents were educated and belonged to distinguished families. From an early age, Jose Rizal Mercado showed a precocious intellect. He learned the alphabet from his mother at 3-years old and could read and write at age 5. In May of 1882, Jose Rizal got on a ship to Spain without

380

informing his parents of his intentions. He enrolled at the Universidad Central de Madrid. In June of 1884, he received his medical degree at the age of 23. He travelled extensively in Europe, America and Asia, and mastered 22 languages. (Some reports claim 10) These include Arabic, Catalan, Chinese, English, French, German, Greek, Hebrew, Italian, Japanese, Latin, Malayan, Portuguese, Russian, Sanskrit, Spanish, Tagalog, and other native dialects. Rizal wrote Noli Me Tangere in Spanish; it was published in 1887 in Berlin. The novel is a scathing indictment of the Catholic Church and Spanish colonial rule in the Philippines. In the hope of securing political and social reforms for his country and at the same time educate his countrymen, Rizal, published, while in Europe, several works with highly nationalistic and revolutionary tendencies. Because of his fearless exposures of the injustices committed by the civil and clerical officials, Rizal provoked the animosity of those in power. Thus, he was imprisoned in Fort Santiago from 6 July 1892 to 15 July 1892 on a charge that anti-friar pamphlets were found in the luggage of his sister Lucia who arrived with him from Hong Kong. When the Philippine Revolution started on 26 August 1896, his enemies lost no time in pressing him down. Despite a lack of any evidence of his complicity in the Revolution, They were able to enlist witnesses that linked him with the revolt. Rizal was convicted on all counts and given the death sentence. On the morning of 3 December 1896, Rizal was shot at Bagumbayan Field. H e was buried in Paco Cemetery in Manila with no identification on his grave. He was 35 years old. Today, the people of the Philippines will honour him as their national hero. An article in the Philippine Daily Inquirer records Philippine urban legends that Jose Rizal was Jack the Ripper. In the attic of #37 Chalcot Crescent, the present day owners found a dusty old trunk which once belonged to Dr Jose Rizal. The following items were found inside a diary wherein Rizal confesses to the Whitechapel murders; and a glass jar with half a human kidney preserved in alcohol. The handwriting appears to match Rizal's and dates from about 1888. The following points are made against Rizal. In 1888, he was staying with the Beckett family at 37 Chalcot Crescent in Camden. He was a (ophthalmologist, eye doctor). He left London in January of 1889, and the Ripper killings stopped. He was working at the British Library at the time of the Whitechapel murders. After he died, his mother tried to procure his assets which consisted of some pretty nice jewellery including gold cuff links and other baubles of diamonds and amethysts (gold chain with a red stone seal?) The description of the chain and red stone seal; is significant because George Hutchinson described a suspect seen with the last victim Mary Kelly shortly before she was murdered wearing a chain with a red stone seal. At the time of the Ripper murders, Rizal was 27 years of age, was short, and had dark skin, dark hair and dark eyes.

PIERCE JOHN ROBINSON

Robinson came under suspicion on 14 January 1889 from his business partner, of 5 weeks, Richard Wingate, a baker, of 10 Church Street, Edgware Road. Wingate told the police that when they were discussing the Whitechapel murders, Robinson had suddenly gone very quiet. Robinson was keen to sell his share of the business and go to America. Further suspicion against Robinson was aroused when a letter he posted to Miss Peters, a woman he was living with at High Street, Portslade, was found. The writer of the letter expressed a fear that "He would be caught today." Inquiries by Superintendent Waghorn, Superintendent Arnold and Sergeant Thick revealed that Robinson had previously lived in Mile End, and was a religious fanatic, who was said to have had medical training and served a four-month prison sentence for bigamy.The proceedings of the Old Bailey:

27 February 1888 PEARCE JOHN ROBINSON (38) PLEADED GUILTY to marrying Adelina Sarah Bird, his wife being then alive. — Four Months' Hard Labour.

Robinson was soon cleared of any suspicion in regards to the Whitechapel murders, as he was with Miss Peters in Portslade on the night Mary Kelly was murdered 9 November. In 1888, he was described as 5 ft 4 inches tall, with a dark complexion, thick set, full short beard, and moustache. Wearing midshipman's hat anchor on the front, light jacket and vest, black trousers.John Pearce Robinson was born in 1849, in St Lukes, to Alfred Robinson a boot maker, and Frances (née Walters). He married Mary Ann Sorrell a tailoress, 13 October 1873 in Stepney. They had four children, three daughters and a son. In the 1881 census he is living at 18 Pollard Row, Bethnal Green, in occupation as a Baptist Missionary. His wife divorced him in 1891. He was admitted to Bexley Heath asylum 5 October 1899, where he died 16 May 1901. He left effect in his will to the value of £948 14s 8d.

STEPHEN ROURKE

In October 1888, Stephen Rourke, a warehouseman, living in Foster-street, Ardwick, Manchester. Was charged with using annoying and threatening language and behaviour toward Mrs Sarah Burgess, wife of a cab maker, living in Argyll-street, Hulme. According to Burgess, the man accosted her in Lower Moss Lane, Manchester, as she was making her way home at about twenty past twelve in the morning. Despite her refusal to have anything to do with him, Rourke persisted in annoying her, and followed her, as far as Clopton-street. There he asked her it she knew who he was. She replied that she did not, and be said he was "Jack the Ripper," He threatened her with violence unless she complied with his wishes. A passing young man came to her assistance and Rourke was taken into custody, by Police-constable John Moore. Rourke was described as young and respectably dressed. Burges, failed to appear in court, Inspector Robinson, told the magistrates that she was a woman of such dissipated habits that her husband refused to live with her. All the statement's she made the previous day as to her address and her husband's occupation were false. Rourke's employers gave him an excellent character reference, and said he had been in their service eight or nine years. With no evidence, he was discharged.

JOHN ROYALL

In July 1889 John Royall, described as a miserably-clad, 35-year old labourer, of Long Lane, was charged with violently assaulting and threatening to murder prostitute Nora Brown. On Saturday morning at about 1 a.m. Brown was standing near St Georges Church when Royall, approached her and inquired "how she was," to which she replied that "she was all right." He then invited her to have coffee with him, to which she agreed. While they were drinking the coffee Royall asked her if she would accompany him on a walk, to which she duly consented. They walked down a court in the borough, where Royall attempted to assault her. She resisted, to which he urged her to keep quiet, before adding, "If you don't, I'll rip you up," at the same time producing a knife from his pocket. She grabbed hold of his scarf, which was round his neck, and called out, "Police" and "murder." When Royall heard someone approaching, he struck her a violent blow in the face with his fist, cut the scarf with the knife and made off. Police Constable Albert Crancy 116M said, when he arrived on the scene the woman said to him, "Jack the Ripper has been trying it on me, he has run down there," pointing in the direction that

Royall had fled. The policeman quickly gave chase and apprehended Royall, who, when confronted with the allegation of assault, said, "It's a mistake." A large crowd quickly gathered, which made getting Royall to the station more difficult. When Royall was searched at the police station a large pocket knife was found on him. In reply to the charge against him, he stated that he was drunk. This claim was contradicted by the Constable who said that "Royall was quite sober at the time of the incident." He was remanded in custody for a week.

FRANCIS CHARLES HASTINGS RUSSELL

Francis Charles Hastings Russell was mentioned as a possible suspect by French author Philippe Jullian in the (1962) book: Edouard VII (published in the English language version 1967 as *Edward and the Edwardians*). Jullian fails to mention which Duke of Bedford was actually involved and also fails to offer us any evidence to substantiate these claims.

Born in Curzon Street, London, 16 October 1819. The son of Major-General Lord George William, and Lady William Russell. Grandson of John Russell, 6th Duke of Bedford. Russell was commissioned into the Scots Fusilier Guards in 1838. He was a Liberal Member of Parliament for Bedfordshire between the years 1847-72. When he succeeded to his dukedom and took his place in the House of Lords, upon the death of his cousin William Russell, 8th Duke of Bedford. He married Lady Elizabeth Sackville-West, daughter of George West, Fifth Earl de la Warr, on 18 January 1844. They had four children: George William Francis Sackville Russell, 10th Duke of Bedford (1852–1893); Lady Ella Monica Sackville Russell (1854–1936). Lady Ermyntrude Sackville Russell (1856–1927). Herbrand Arthur Russell, 11th Duke of Bedford (1858–1940). On 1 December 1880, he was made a Knight of the Garter. He died in 1891, aged

385

71 years at 81 Eaton Square, London, by shooting himself through the heart as a result of Insanity, while suffering from pneumonia. His ashes were buried at the Bedford Chapel of St. Michael's Church in Chenies, Buckinghamshire.

THOMAS JAMES SADLER

Thomas James Sadler was born c. 1838, in Stepney, London, to James Meal Sadler, a head clerk in a solicitors practice, in Lincoln's Inn Fields, and his wife Mary (née Hownett). James succumbed to consumption (tuberculosis) at the age of 27 when Thomas was 3-years-old. Educated at Primrose School, where he stayed until the age of 15. Upon leaving school, Thomas started working as an Under Clerk in London Docks. He was a sailor when he met Sarah Maria Chapman (b. 1851, Stoke, Rochester, Kent). They married in 1876 at St John's Church, Clapham. They had three children, Ruth, Daisy and Primrose. After their marriage, they went to live in Elephant & Castle, South London. Other addresses they lived at where Buck's Row, Tetley Street, Poplar, and later Colebrook Terrace, Bethnal Green. In the 1881 census, the family was living at 95 New Road, Whitechapel, where James was listed as a Dock Labourer. When on dry land, he was chiefly in occupation as a labourer in tea warehouses he also tried his hand as a, greengrocer, and a conductor. In 1888, after a quarrel the couple separated. Sarah left London to live with her mother in Chatham, Kent.

On Friday 13 February 1891 At 2:15 am 27-year old Constable Ernest Thompson 240 H was on his first tour of night duty between Chambers Street and Rosemary Lane and was just about to enter Swallow Gardens, when he heard footsteps, walking away from him, heading in the westerly direction of Rosemary Lane. When he turned under the railway arch into Swallow Gardens he saw the body of a woman lying on her back,

386

her throat had been cut from ear to ear and blood was still flowing from the wound. Upon drawing closer, the constable noticed she was still warm, and claimed that one of her eyes flickered open and that she was still alive, her new black crepe hat lay on the ground beside her. Thompson immediately blew his whistle to raise the alarm and the neighbouring beat officers, PC Hyde and PC Hinton, came running to the scene. They were soon joined by Police-constable Elliott, who was on plain clothes duty in adjacent Royal Mint-street. Elliot later stated that, shortly after 2 o'clock he had heard a whistle blown, and on going to Swallow-gardens saw a constable with his lamp turned on the body of a woman. He later stated that he was certain that he would have heard any cry from the woman, but everything was very quiet until he heard the whistle. Checking for signs of life, the officers found the body to be quite warm and they also felt a very faint pulse. PC Hyde was then sent to fetch the local medic, Dr Oxley, who arrived at the scene and pronounced life extinct. Soon, Dr George Bagster Philips, the Divisional Police Surgeon, had arrived at the scene and, on examining the body, he found two cuts to the woman's throat, which, he stated, were "sufficient to account for death." She died on the stretcher on the way to the hospital. Thompson had passed the spot 15 minutes before and was adamant that the body hadn't been there then. The woman was identified as Frances Coles, otherwise known as "Carrotty Nell," a 31-year old prostitute. Born on Crucifix Lane in Bermondsey on the 17 of September 1859, Frances was labelled as a particularly pretty woman throughout her time in Whitechapel. Dr Bagster Phillips examined the body and noted that the throat had been cut by a sawing motion, there were no mutilations or injuries to the body apart from the throat wound, and the victim's clothing had not been disturbed. Dr Phillips detected no surgical skill and did not think the knife used had been very sharp. As far as he was

387

concerned the perpetrator was not the same person who carried out the Whitechapel murders of 1888. A witness a Carman called William Friday, who was known to his friends as "Jumbo," came forward to say he had seen a man and a woman standing in a doorway about 1:45 am on the night of the murder, only half an hour before the body was discovered. He identified the victim's hat as the same one he had seen the woman in the doorway wearing. He went on to describe the man as stocky and looking like a ship's fireman. The police checked the docks and discovered that Coles had spent the last two days in the company of Thomas James Sadler, a 53-year old merchant seaman and fireman, on board the SS Fez, which was moored at London Dock. They spent most of February 12 1891 on a pub crawl around the area and by evening both of them were extremely intoxicated. Sadler was a former client of hers and, after a few drinks, they decided to spend the night together. At around 7.30pm that evening Frances turned up at a milliner's shop at 25 Nottingham Street, where she bought a black crepe hat, paying for it with 2s. 6d, that Sadler had given her some hours before. According to Peter Hawkes, the man who served her, Frances was "three sheets in the wind." Leaving the shop she had, according to Hawkes, gone off in the company of a man who had been looking in through the window whilst Coles was in the shop. Hawkes would later pick Sadler out of a line up at Leman Street Police Station as the man she had gone off with. Later that evening as the drunken couple passed through Thrawl Street, Sadler was suddenly and violently hit on the head by a woman in a red shawl. Upon falling to the ground, Sadler was kicked insensible by several men. When he regained consciences, he discovered that he had been robbed of his watch and money. Sadler believed he had been set up, and turned his anger on Coles, who had made no attempt to help him during the assault.

Eventually, he made his way to the London hospital, where his wounds were attended. The blood stains the police found on him were from his troubles that night. Upon inquiries, the police quickly learnt that Sadler had a violent temper and had returned to his lodging house covered in blood. When they also discovered that he had sold his knife to a man named Donald Campbell for a shilling and a piece of tobacco, they arrested him on Sunday 15 February 1891. Campbell a seaman, stated: "That he was staying at the Sailors' Home in Well-street, when a man came in and asked if he wished to buy his knife." Campbell took hold of the knife, opened the big blade, and said: "This is not an English Knife, the man replied: "No I bought it abroad, in America." Campbell felt the big blade, and a clammy feeling came over him. Campbell washed the knife, noticing as he did so that the water was slightly salmon-coloured." Sadler was interviewed by Inspector Swanson and charged with the murder of Frances Coles the following day. Sadler was described as 5 ft 6 inches tall, stoops a little, with a moustache and goatee beard. He was wearing a pilot cloth pea jacket, serge trousers and a black cap with a leather peak. The notion that he was also being suspected of the other Whitechapel Murders is borne out by the fact that he appeared in a lineup in which a witness to a previous case; possibly Joseph Lawende was used, although after confronting Sadler, the witness failed to identify him. All his discharge dates from ships dating back to March 1887 were checked and included in his statement. Enquiries were also made into Sadler's previous employment and addresses. Sadler received legal representation from the Seaman's Union who had collected some strong witnesses in his favour; as a result, charges against him were dropped on 2 March before the case could go to court. A young couple, Thomas Fowles and Kate McCarthy, came forward to say they were the ones seen in the doorway by William Jumbo Friday that night. The knife Sadler had sold turned out to be an old blunt knife, which, when examined showed it could not have been the one used to murder Frances Coles. He also had alibis for the previous murders, satisfying police that he was on board the S.S Winestead from the 17 August to the 1 October 1888. Evidently there were many who had been convinced of Sadler's innocence and, as Sadler left the court, he was greeted by a large crowd who proceeded to cheer as the cab drove him away. They ran after his carriage whereupon, according to *The Times*, "Sadler put his head out of the cab window and waved his hat." Despite being cleared of Coles murder, the police watched his movements and continued to show an interest in James Sadler for some time afterwards. In May 1891, Sadler and his wife reunited and were living together at 121 Danbrook Road, Streatham where they kept a chandler's shop. Sarah, wrote to the police, in March 1892, claiming her husband had assaulted her, and threatened her life. She did not press charges against her husband. The elderly lodger James Moffatt, also wrote to the police with his concerns, about, Sadler's aggressive behaviour towards his wife. Moffatt, described Sadler as "a treacherous and cowardly man" and feared him enough to ensure the door to his room was locked every night. He told the police, that he had been at sea for many years, but, had never heard such horrible language as that uttered by Sadler to his wife. After Sadler had threatened to cut his wife's throat, he was arrested. On 16 May 1892, he was bound over to keep the peace. The last we hear of Sadler is January 1893 when he told the police he was very wisely leaving the area.

Macnaghten in his 1894 memorandum, noted that::

Sadler was a man of ungovernable temper and entirely addicted to drink, and the company of lower prostitutes.

Macnaghten thought it unlikely that Sadler was in any way responsible for the earlier Ripper Murders.

JOHN SANDERSON

John Long a sea cook on the bark Annie Laurie, sailing from Shields, England to Iquique, Chile, told a reporter the tale of John Sanderson, a member of the crew, who early in the voyage, was taken ill, and became delirious and violent, and was subsequently put ashore in Iquique and sent to hospital. Shortly after Long also became ill, and was put in the bunk next to Sanderson, who was now delirious. Sanderson confessed to Long and a priest that he was Jack the Ripper. He said he was the son of a surgeon and knew how to handle a knife. He claimed he developed a taste for murder after one night meeting a woman in Whitechapel he killed and mutilated her in a dark alley. "I escaped, no officer seemed to get on my track, and the idea came to me that it would nice to kill a few others." He acquired an accomplice and the two wore butchers smocks to avoid suspicion of being seen bloodstained. "We were wild for blood. I was mad and nothing would satisfy me, but the sight of a bloody and mutilated body of a Whitechapel woman." He later told of how he worked on a farm in the country, before returning once more to the lore of the sea. Long says his story can be substantiated in every particular, and that if necessary he will do so. This story appears to be an amalgamation of the suspects John Anderson, Father of GWB, and the Malay sea cook Alaska.

COUNT SARDROUJI

Count Sardrouji, was mentioned as a possible Ripper in the (1935) book: Jack L' Eventreur by Jean Dorsenne. The book is a mix of fact and fiction.

Scotland Yard received numerous letters from a woman in Siberia calling herself the Countess Sardrouji or Sardrouk. In the letters, the Countess explained that her husband was Jack the Ripper and that he had committed suicide by throwing himself into the Thames, shortly after the murder of the last Ripper victim Mary Kelly. Some years later the Countess on a visit to London made Scotland Yard her first port of call. There she told detectives a tale of how her husband was a charming; though shy man, gay (in the old-fashioned sense of the word), and whimsical. In a series of letters to her, he confessed to having committed the London atrocities. By a stroke of "bad fortune," the countess lost the letters her husband had written when sailing along a river, swollen by floodwater in an unsuitable small, light boat, a wave swept away a valise she was holding which contained her husband's correspondence. Despite the loss of the letters the Countess claimed she could still prove her story. She led detectives to her husband's small house in the suburbs, which had remained closed up, and untouched since his death. The Countess told there was an item in the house which would prove his guilt. There amongst the dusty remains was a jar containing a human kidney, preserved in alcohol, along with several rusting surgical instruments.

REGINALD SAUNDERSON

Shortly before midnight on Sunday 25 November 1894 Augustus Louise Dawes, aged 28, was found murdered in a much-frequented thoroughfare, Holland Villas Road, Kensington. Her throat had been cut from ear to ear and a stick was found lying beside the body. A knife, believed to have been used in the murder, was later discovered in an unfinished building. Immediately the newspapers raised the inevitable cry of "Jack the Ripper." The newspaper reports are reproduced here:

392

KENSINGTON MURDER MYSTERY. WOMAN'S THROAT CUT IN THE STREET

A horrible discovery was made at Kensington in the early hours of Monday morning. A woman was found lying in Holland Park-road with her throat cut almost from ear to ear. A gentleman passing along Holland Park-road towards Melbury-road between 12 and one in the morning was the first to make the ghastly discovery. He saw a heap in the road near the residence of the President of the Royal Academy. On examination this 2heap" proved to be the body of a woman with a big wound in the throat, from which a great deal of blood had flowed. She was quite dead. Information was given to the police, and in a very short time a considerable body of constables arrived. The divisional surgeon was also sent for, and, having examined the body, he directed its removal to the mortuary. The police then, under Inspector O'Shea, began a search of the neighbourhood. The only thing, however, they came upon was an ash walking stick with a crook handle lying near where the body was found. The victim was a woman of the "unfortunate" class, and from the nature of the wounds in her throat, the police were at first inclined to regard the crime as of the "Jack the Ripper" class. In this belief it was reported to Scotland-yard. During Monday detectives from all parts of London, who had been engaged on the Whitechapel murders, and Dr. Bond, the Home Office expert, visited the Kensington mortuary and examined the body. It had been left unwashed so that an accurate judgement might be formed as to the nature of the murder. But, after examination, the detectives, as well as Dr. Bond, came to the conclusion that the crime had no resemblance to the Whitechapel murders. The spot where the body was found is a very lonely one at night, although it is fairly well lighted. On one side of the road are some old-fashioned cottages, and on the other numerous large mansions occupied by some of the leading

393

Academicians, including Sir Frederic Leighton and Mr. Val Prinsep. Sixpence in silver and two pieces of old newspapers were all that was found upon the body. The woman had been good-looking, with a broad forehead and aquiline nose, and a perfect set of natural teeth. She was dressed in a black skirt and jacket trimmed with astrachan, a red and black striped blouse, and a dark-brown straw hat done up with coloured ribbon, black stockings, and low shoes. Her underlinen was poor and dirty. Two rings of little value were upon the third finger of her left hand. Several women were taken to see the body during the day, but they had no personal knowledge of her. Early in the afternoon, however, a Miss Cremer and her mother, accompanied by a pretty, three-year-old girl, visited the mortuary and identified the body as that of Augusta Dudley, aged 30, and living at a common lodging-house (kept by Mrs. Cremer) in Clement's-road, Notting-dale. The little girl was the deceased woman's child. After leaving the mortuary Miss Cremer stated that the dead woman was of Scotch nationality, and, she believed, was very well connected. She, however, seldom spoke of her relations. Once she told them that some years ago she was a governess, but took to drink and went wrong. She was a great drunkard, and took very little food. On Sunday night the dead woman left her lodgings about five o'clock, saying that if ' all went well' she would return about 12 o'clock. The police, were rewarded after a diligent search by the discovery of a knife, with which the deed is supposed to have been committed, in a builder's yard at the back of Warwick studios, Warwick-gardens, about one hundred yards from the scene of the murder. It is a shoemaker's knife with a very keen edge, and when found was covered with coagulated blood. Miss Cremer states that the deceased went to live in St. Clement's-road, Notting-dale, about three weeks ago. She was greatly attached to her child and came home to see her every night. On

Saturday night last she stated that she had met two gentlemen, whose names she did not know, and with whom she went to a coffee-stall. She described one of her companions as tall and dark, and as carrying a walking stick which he "swung round," and the other was shorter and of fair complexion. The former asked deceased to meet him on the following (Sunday) night, and she overheard him make an appointment with his companion to play a game of billiards in the afternoon. The tall, dark man ultimately drove off in a cab, having agreed, after some discussion, to give the driver 10s., as the distance would be considerable. It has been ascertained that the dead woman and her daughter have been twice admitted to the Kensington infirmary. The first time was in April last, when her stay extended over some four weeks. She returned, still accompanied by her little girl, on Oct. 5, and remained until Nov. 10. In the course of a conversation with one of the infirmary officials she stated that she was born in the year 1867. Four years ago she left Bristol, where she was employed as a barmaid at the Prince's hotel, Totterdown, and came to London. At the time of her leaving Bristol she had a brother living in Colston-street. During her stay in the metropolis she had resided at Hammersmith, the addresses including Queen-street, Yeldham-road, and Porten-road.

Dawes was described as a comely woman. A young man, 21-year old Reginald Saunderson, immediately came under suspicion for the crime. Saunderson, whose state of mind, it was said, had caused his family in December 1888 to send him to an institution at Hampton Wick, near Kingston upon Thames. He left the institution on 25 November 1894 claiming he was going to attend divine service at a local church and was not heard again for some time. Police checks at the institution led them to identify the stick which was found at the murder scene as one

395

Saunderson had taken from another pupil. They also discovered he had taken a knife from the carpenter's shop with him when he had left. He was traced to a relatives house in Belfast and promptly arrested. The police received a letter in his handwriting signed Jack the Ripper, claiming how he had committed the murder in Kensington. Reginald Traherne Bassett Saunderson came from a well-connected family; his father was Colonel Edward J. Saunderson, the Orange leader, and Member of Parliament for North Armagh. He was a descendant of Mary Tudor, and one of his aunts was Lady Maria Henrietta Fitzclarence, whose husband was the grandson of William IV. At the time of the Whitechapel murders, he would have been 15-years old. He was described as tall and handsome, an expert at football, rowing and swimming. He was adjudged insane, and committed to Broadmoor Asylum, where he died in 1943.

SAMUEL SCAR

In August 1890, a labourer, named Samuel Scar, was charged with being drunk and disorderly. Scar while very drunk, was creating a disturbance, he threatened to stab a woman in Whitehall. Mrs. Yates, was walking along Whitehall, when Scar, came up to her with an open knife in his hand and said, "I'm Jack the Ripper, and will rip you up." She ran to two gentlemen who were passing for protection. They told her not to be frightened, as the man was only drunk, and probably meant no harm. Mr. Henry Haydon, a gentleman living in Peckham, corroborated her story, and said that he had knocked the knife out of the man's hand. Scar declared it was "a got-up story," and said he was not drunk. The magistrate, said it was clear the witnesses had spoken the truth, as they were entire strangers to the prisoner. It was also quite clear the prisoner was too drunk to know what he was doing. He was on his way to work. He was sentenced to 14 days imprisonment for being drunk and disorderly.

DR. JOHN WILLIAM SANDERS

Mentioned as a possible suspect by researcher Jon Ogan. His name is often incorrectly stated, and confused with fellow Ripper suspect John William Smith Sanders. He is also not connected to the three insane medical students who had attended the London Hospital, whom the police were attempting to find.

Dr Sanders was born in London in 1859. First Prizeman in Medicine, Surgery, (1879), and Prizeman in Anatomy, (1877). A Fellow of the British Gynaecological Society and a Member of the British Medical Association. Educated at Guys Hospital, where he was a House Surgeon and Gynaecologist. He was for a time Medical Officer of the Croydon Fever Hospital. He then became the resident Medical Officer of the Bethnal Green Infirmary. At the time of his death, he was the Medical Superintendent of the St George-in-the East Infirmary, Princes Street, E, as well as Surgeon to the St John Ambulance Brigade. He died from heart failure, while under anaesthetic, 7 January 1889 at the age of 30. Apart from having the requisite medical skills, there is no reason to suspect him, other than his death occurring shortly after the murder of Mary Kelly, which fitted some theorist's explanation for the sudden cessation of the murders. In his will he left effects to the value of £416 1s 6d.

JOHN WILLIAM SMITH SANDERS

Inspector Donald Swanson, in a report to the Home Office dated 19 October 1888, mentions three insane medical students who had attended the London Hospital. Two had been traced and eliminated from their inquiries, but the third was believed to have gone abroad. Enquiries were made of the suspect's last known address 20 Aberdeen Place, St Johns Wood, London, where it was believed a woman named Sanders had lived with her son. Sanders, mother Laura née Tucker in fact, lived at 20 Abercorn Place. The police made a mistake in identifying the correct address. Sanders had not gone abroad, but had been placed in an asylum and was incarcerated at the time of the Whitechapel murders. John William Smith Sanders was born 6 October 1860 in Milton, Gravesend, Kent, and was the son of Henry Shearly Sanders, an Indian army surgeon, who committed suicide, 5 February 1867, at Mount Aboo, Bombay, by shooting himself while temporarily insane. Smith Sanders entered the London Hospital as a student on 22 April 1879. In 1881 he was placed in an asylum after subjecting his family and friends to outbursts of physical violence, despite it being claimed he had previously been of a gentle and passive nature. In February 1887 he was moved to Holloway Asylum in Virginia Water, after suffering fits of violence. He was later transferred to West Malling, and finally in 1899 to the Heavitree Asylum in Exeter, where he remained until his death at the age of 39, on 31 March 1901.

SCHULSE

The Following report appeared in The Newark Daily Advocate 30 October 1891:

Reported in Berlin, the alleged Jack the Ripper, Schulse, is much broken down by his imprisonment, and it is believed he may confess his criminal career. The London police have made a request for the official documents, including the testimony at the inquest, to be forwarded in the original, or in copies to London, on the grounds that the crime of Schulse closely resembles the East End horrors.

THE UNKNOWN SECRETARY

According to William Booth, the founder of the Salvation Army, a secretary, he once employed, but refused to name, made a sinister prediction concerning an alleged future victim of Jack the Ripper. Booth related that on 10 February 1891 his secretary became twitchy and agitated on hearing people discuss the Whitechapel murders, and suddenly exclaimed! "Carrotty Nell will be the next to go." Booth and his friends agreed, this was a strange and morbid thing for the usually timid man to say. Three days later, 25-year old prostitute Frances Coles (nicknamed Carrotty Nell), was murdered. Thomas Sadler was arrested for the murder, but later released through lack of evidence. Booth's secretary, who had predicted Carrotty Nell's fate, vanished into obscurity before the police could question him about his sinister foreknowledge. This story appears to have confused Salvation Army General William Booth, who did not favour any suspect, with Salvation Army Commissioner David Cricton Lamb, (1866-1951) who suspected a visiting sign writer, he had employed who had visions of blood, he mentioned Carrotty Nell would be the next victim.

JACK SHAW

The following articles appeared. In the Atlanta Constitution newspaper 4 December 1910: and the Iowa City Citizen 5 Dec 1910:

JACK THE RIPPER' HELD IN CALIFORNIA

AMan Thought To Be the London Fiend Is Under Arrest Having admitted during lucid moments to the police that he fled from England fifteen years ago in fear of being arrested as "jack the Ripper," who committed the notorious Whitechapel crimes of the late eighties, Jack Shaw is being detained in the insane ward of the county hospital. Shaw was arrested through the efforts of the Legal Aid Society, the complaint being that he attempted to murder Edith Tyson, his half-sister, last Wednesday. The man's mental condition was found to be such that he was locked up in the insane ward. His past life will be investigated, and the local authorities will notify the London police of their suspicions. Shaw has not admitted he is the notorious "Jack the Ripper" but his constant references to the subject indicate that it is deeply impressed on his mind. He is 50 years of age

THINK PRISONER 'JACK THE RIPPER

Officers Arrest Man Who Tells of Having Been Suspected of Whitechapel Crimes PROWLS AT SISTER'S HOME John Shaw to Be Held on Insanity Charge Pending an Investigation In the opinion of Deputy Sheriffs Wood and Crowley, John Shaw, arrested yesterday, charged with being an insane person, may be "Jack, the Ripper," whose atrocious crimes kept the Whitechapel district in London in a panic during 1888 and 1889, and who escaped, although scores of detectives tried to run him down. The deputies Intended to arrest' Shaw on a charge of attempting to kill his half-sister, Edith Tyson. When they located him he was in such a state of mind as to suggest that he is Insane. He told them that the face of his dead brother, Fred Shaw, haunted him. Fred Shaw was killed several months ago, a coroner's jury concluding that he met death by a fall down an elevator shaft in the Central National Bank building. At the time of the young man's death, Shaw was closely questioned by the police but allowed his liberty. He was later arrested at the instigation of his sister, on a felony charge. The case was dismissed In Justice Summerfield' court when the offence charged was proven to have been committed outside of the county

REFERS TO WHITECHAPEL CRIME

400

Shaw, In his rational moments, but still fearful of the return of the vision of the face of his brother, told the deputy sheriffs that he fled from England 15 years ago to escape arrest on suspicion of being the notorious Whitechapel criminal. Other statements he has} made cause the officers to believe they have effected the capture of the long-sought fugitive. He will be held on a charge of Insanity until a rigid investigation has been made into his past life and the English authorities are informed. Shaw is 45-50 years old. He walks with a half crouch and a slight limp. His right arm is crippled from a bullet fired by his brother in San Francisco when the two, the sister alleges, were quarrelling over her. Edith Tyson has been looked after by the Legal Aid Society, which Is in reality back of the prosecution of Shaw on a charge of attempting to kill her Wednesday night at the home of a family on the east side where she was living. Numerous complaints have reached the sheriff's office of Shaw's actions in prowling around the home of his half-sister. Several nights ago, he was alleged to have seized a young woman in the backyard of the house evidently mistaking her for his- half-sister. She screamed for help and he released his grasp. Deputy Sheriff Wood is convinced that Shaw Is the man - tor whom the English police have been looking for many years. "Statements he made during his rational moments,'" the officer said yesterday, "lead me to believe that we have effected a capture that Is not only important to us in connection with young Fred Tyson's death, but developments may show, as I think more than likely, that he Is the man who has committed the Whitechapel crimes. Shaw is in the ward for the Insane in the county hospital.

Shaw whose Christian name was variously given as Henry, Jack or John would have been 23 years of age at the time of the Whitechapel murders.

JAMES SHAW

Scotland Yard had information that wife murderer James Pennock, a labourer, employed on the North-Eastern Railway, of Pickering, North Riding, Yorkshire was travelling under the name "James Shaw" on board the steamer SS Wyoming. Pennock, a railway platelayer, had murdered his wife Hannah, on 7 November 1888, with an axe. He was described as 47-years old, 5 ft 8 inches tall, stout build, with ginger hair and whiskers, and a protuberance the size of a walnut on his head. Shaw was arrested, on 23 November 1888, when the ship docked in New York. Shaw, a farm labourer, admitted his real name, was Heddington, but declined to say why he was travelling incognito. He claimed to live in Leeds, and that he had kissed his wife, and children goodbye on 9 November 1888, saying, he was going west, seeking a better life. Shaw came under suspicion because he apparently fitted the description of Jack the Ripper. In his pocket was found an illustrated account of the Whitechapel murders. Shaw could neither read nor write, and was confused in his accounting for the presence in his pocket of the newspaper containing the Whitechapel story. (*Presumably* as it was illustrated *he carried it to look at the pictures*) Deputy Marshal Fred Bernardt interviewed Shaw and satisfied himself that he was not the Whitechapel Murderer. Neither was he James Pennock, as he was two inches shorter than the Yorkshireman, and had no walnut on his head or scar where it might have been.

WILLIAM SHEALS

On 17 October 1889, William Sheals accosted four females, and told them he was "Jack the Ripper." The incident happened in the Thames Police Court district. When Police-constable 613 K remonstrated with him, he deliberately kicked him, and when he was arrested exhibited renewed violence. He was sentenced to one month hard labour.

WALTER SICKERT

Walter Richard Sickert was born on 31 May 1860 in Munich, Germany, and was the eldest of six children. His father Oswald Adalbert Sickert, was Danish and employed as an artist for a comic journal. His French-educated mother, Eleanor Louisa Moravia, was, due to money received from one of her relatives, the financial mainstay of the family. They moved to England in 1868 and Walter attended University College School, Bayswater College School and Kings College School, Wimbledon, where he graduated in 1877. His first love was the stage, and for a while, he worked as an actor under the name "Mr Nemo" with Henry Irving's company at the Lyceum, where he was said to be proficient in the art of make-up. His period on the stage would be ultimately unsuccessful due to financial restraints. Having shown some early artistic talent he studied painting under Alphonse Legros at the Slade School of Art, London, and in 1879 met the American artist James McNeill Whistler, and for a while became his assistant. All Sickert's early work was signed, a pupil of Whistler. In 1883 while in Paris, he met the artist Edgar Degas, who influenced him to produce striking studies of music halls, it was the start of a friendship which lasted until Degas death in 1917. In 1885 Sickert married Ellen Melicent Ashburner Cobden, twelve years his senior and the daughter of Liberal politician Richard Cobden. The marriage was childless and said to be unhappy, due to, it is claimed, Sicker's infidelity. They moved into 54 Broadhurst Gardens, South Hampstead, where he used the top floor as his studio. The couple separated in 1896 and divorced in 1899. Sickert moved to Dieppe, where he stayed for the next seven years. He moved back to London in 1905 and took studios at 8 Fitzroy Street, and 76 Charlotte Street, and rooms at 6 Mornington Crescent, Camden Town. His work from this period now consisted almost entirely of music hall scenes and the grim faded life of Camden Town. Camden he asserted had been, "So watered with his tears that something important must sooner or later spring from its soil." It was in Camden in September 1907 that a part-time prostitute named Emily Dimmock was found murdered in her bed, at 29 St Paul's Road. Her throat had been cut, but the body had not been mutilated. She had last been seen in the company of a man named Robert Wood, who was arrested and charged with her murder but was later acquitted. The murder became known as "The Camden Town Murder." Sickert would make reference to this murder, and the Whitechapel murders, in several of his drawings and paintings. One such painting entitled, "Jack the Ripper's bedroom," which he painted in 1908 was inspired after being told a tale by his landlady at Mornington Crescent that the previous tenant, a young veterinary student, was Jack the Ripper. A prolific and influential art critic, with a talent for stimulating heated debate, he criticised the technique of Whistler, his former teacher, though, would not tolerate any criticism of Degas, whom he called, "The lighthouse of his existence." Between 1908 and 1910 he taught at Westminster institute, and later, at various other schools. In 1911 Sickert married Christine Drummond Angus, his student, eighteen years his junior. Her death in 1920 caused Sickert to suffer a nervous breakdown. His behaviour became erratic and he became more eccentric as time passed. The death of his mother in 1926 did little to lift his depression. He married his third wife, the painter Therese Lessore in June 1926, and they lived together in Islington. He took a studio at 10 Cecil Square, Margate, and also had a house in Margate. In his later years he began to paint scenes based entirely on newspaper photographs or Victorian

404

magazine illustrations, and in 1938 moved to Bathampton, Bath. In 1941 Sickert was honoured with a one-man exhibition at the National Gallery in London. He died at the age of 81, on 23 January 1942, in Bathampton. At the time of the Ripper murders, Sickert was 28-years old, almost 6 ft tall, with light brown hair a fair moustache and a fair complexion.

Walter Sickert was first mentioned in connection with Jack the Ripper by Stephen Knight in the (1976) book: Jack the Ripper the Final Solution. And later by Jean Overton Fuller in the (1990) book: Sickert and the Ripper Crimes, and more recently by bestselling crime author Patricia Cornwell first in her (2002) book: Portrait of A Killer, and subsequently in the (2014) book: Chasing the Ripper, and the (2017) book: Ripper: The Secret Life of Walter Sickert. And by Paul Christian in the (2018) book: The Inevitable Jack the Ripper.Fuller's hypothesis that Sickert was the Ripper is based on the claims made by Florence Pash, a friend of Sickert's, who told Fuller's mother Violet Overton Fuller, who in turn told her daughter, that Sickert knew the identity of the murderer and painted clues into some of his pictures. Also that the murders were connected to an illegitimate child of an unnamed member of the royal family. Cornwell, in her book, makes the claim that Sickert became a serial killer after Whistler, whom he idolised, went on honeymoon with his new bride, and the thought of Whistler been in love and enjoying sexual relations with a woman, was the catalyst that finally sent him over the edge. Cornwell also believed he never stopped killing and may have claimed as many as 15 (down from her previous estimate of 40) victims, including children. She also claims to have found mitochondria DNA evidence, shared by only 1% of the population, linking Sickert to at least one Ripper letter. If Sickert wrote any of the Ripper letters, it does not prove that he was the Ripper, for there is no evidence that any of the Jack the Ripper letters were actually sent by the murderer. Cornwell errors in assuming that an operation in Sickert's childhood left him with a malfunctioning penis. It is believed it was rectal, and not penile surgery that he underwent, and his sex life, by all accounts, remained unimpeded. Cornwell's book, though sensationalist and highly speculative, unfortunately, suffers from the same oversights as Fuller's book, and employs selective facts and poor scholarship to support her case, and provides us with no real proof that Sickert was Jack the Ripper. Cornwell, it is said has spent nearly $7 million of her own money in an attempt to prove Sickert was the Ripper. Paul Christian in his book, claims a recently-uncovered painting contains hidden clues that suggest the artist Walter Sickert, was "Jack the Ripper." The painting shows a scene on the streets of London featuring three figures, one is believed to be the Ripper and two are thought to be his victims, Mary Kelly and Martha Tabram.There is some evidence that Sickert may not even have been in England at the time of the Whitechapel murders, as during the whole of September he may have been on holiday in France, a letter written by Ellen, Sickert's wife, to her brother-in-law Dick Fisher dated 21 September, suggests that Walter had been in France for some weeks.

SICKERT'S VETERINARY STUDENT

Some years after the Whitechapel murders the artist Walter Sickert took a room in a London suburb, believed to be 6 Mornington Crescent, Camden. The owners of the house, an elderly couple, told him that the previous occupant of the room was Jack the Ripper, who was a delicate-looking veterinary student whom would stay out all night, then come home in the early hours, before rushing out to buy the morning newspaper. He also occasionally burnt the clothes he had been wearing the night before. When his health began to fail, his widowed mother took

406

him home to Bournemouth, where he died three months later. Sickert wrote the man's name in the margin of a book (said to be Casanova's Memoirs) which he gave to Albert Rutherstone. The book, it is claimed, was lost in the blitz. Donald McCormick, the writer and author, claims to have been told this story and remembers the student's name as Druitt, Drewett or Hewitt. If the room mentioned in the story was Sickert's studio at 6 Mornington Crescent, then the last occupant was an Egyptian medical student named Waller.

JOSEPH SILVER

Proposed as a Ripper suspect by South African historian Charles Van Onselen in the (2007) book: The Fox and the Flies. Born Joseph Lis, (which means "Fox" in Polish), in 1868 in Kielce, Poland, one of nine children to tailor and petty criminal Ansel Lis. He was more commonly known by the alias Joseph Silver, but also used the names Joe Liss, Joe Eligmann, James Smith, Joseph Schmidt, Charlie Silver, Charles Greenbaum, Abraham Ramer and Ludwig. He was known in Johannesburg as the "King of Pimps." Lis started his criminal career in London, committing further crimes in New York, South Africa, and South America. He served time in Sing Sing, Pentonville, and Wormwood Scrubs. In the early 1890s, he was described as 5 ft 8 ½ inches tall, 140 pounds in weight, with grey eyes, brown hair and a sallow complexion. His face was full of pimples and pitted with small scars. Silver was a cruel and sadistic pimp, racketeer, white slaver, burglar, rapist, and police informant. Van Onselen makes the following points. Silver was in Whitechapel at the time of the Ripper murders for the birth of his daughter. As a pimp and brothel keeper, he would have been familiar with the prostitutes working in the local area. Jack the Ripper was known to write brazen letters to the papers. Silver was litigious, wrote bold letters

407

to newspapers. He also had bitter and violent relationships with women all his life. Van Onselen believed Lis's attempt to conceal his presence in England in the latter half of 1888, made him a plausible suspect. While there is good documentary evidence Silver was in London in the late 1890s Van Onselen, offers us no real evidence Lis was actually in Whitechapel, London in 1888, it is purely speculation. Joseph Lis would have been 20-years old at the time of the Whitechapel murders. He had been found guilty of theft and espionage and was probably executed in mid-1918 in Poland.

CLARENCE SIMM

In 1992 an article appeared in the publication Weekly World News in which widow 103-year old Betty Simm, described as in failing health, but mentally alert and vibrant, claimed that her late husband Clarence, had made a death-bed confession to her in 1951 that he had as a teenager killed 14 prostitutes, to free them from a life of sin. Betty then aged 16 had met her husband Clarence a 36-year old widower and prosperous accountant in London in 1905. Within 2 years they had married and moved to Yorkshire, they had a son, Walter born in 1909, died 1992. It is claimed Clarence stopped killing when he met and fell in love with his first wife. He confessed his crimes because he did not want to die with his horrible deeds still weighing on his conscience. Betty, who lived in seclusion in Southern Spain, said of her husband that he was "Always a very quiet man, extremely private who treated me like a queen." Betty took a lie detector test to substantiate her story and was told there was less than half of one percent chance she was lying. The lie detector test, however, only proves Betty was telling the truth, it does not prove her husband was telling the truth. Neither do we know which murders he referred to. If he committed any murders at all, it is unlikely to have been the Whitechapel murders. To arrive at his figure of fourteen victims you would have to include not only the Torso Murders but the murder of Emma Elizabeth Smith, who before she died clearly stated that she was attacked by at least three men. And also that of Rose Mylett, whom the police believed was not even murdered, but in fact had choked to death on her own stiff collar while drunk.

GEORGE ROBERT SIMS

George Robert Sims, was born 2 September 1847 in Kennington, London, the oldest of six children to George Sims a prosperous merchant, and Louisa Amelia Ann (née Stevenson) president of the women's provident league. Educated in Eastbourne, then Hanwell Military College, and Bonn University. Three times married twice widowed; none of his marriages produced children. He married Sarah Elizabeth Collis, in 1876, Annie Maria Harriss, in 1888, and Elizabeth Florence Wykes in 1901. He took up journalism in 1874 and enjoyed wide popularity as a novelist, playwright and poet. He is perhaps best remembered as the author of the much-parodied ballad, It Is Christmas Day in the Workhouse. He used his excellent police contacts to write about the Ripper murders for the publication The Referee, under the pseudonym Dragonet. He also contributed numerous articles from 1879-1883 about the bad condition of the poor in London's slums in various newspapers. A self-alleged Ripper suspect Sims claimed that in 1888 a coffee stall holder in Whitechapel saw a portrait of Sims advertising his latest book, and believed he was the likeness of a suspicious man with bloodstained cuffs who had come to his stall shortly after the double murder, and announced to the stall holder that he would hear of two more murders the following day. Sims would make frequent references to this story and appeared to believe the Ripper looked exactly like himself.

In the 1911 census, he is 63-years of age, married to Elizabeth Florence (née Wykes) his occupation is listed as dramatic author and journalist. His address is 12 Clarence Terrace, St Marylebone. A successful playwright, his most notable success was the melodramatic play The Light o' London, first produced in 1881. His autobiography, My Life Sixty Years Recollections of Bohemian London, was published in 1917. Sims later came to believe the rumours that the Ripper was Montague John Druitt. In 1913 to counter these rumours Inspector John Littlechild wrote to Sims naming Dr Tumblety as a more likely suspect, this became known as the Littlechild letter. Sims died at his home in Regent's Park of liver cancer at the age of 75 years on the 4 September 1922.

HENRY SKINNERTON

On 21 October 1888 Henry Skinnerton, described as 50 years of age and a labourer, of High Street, Chingford, was charged with assaulting Henry Corney, and with wilfully breaking 25 panes of glass, the property of John Cricks, of High Road, Woodford. The damage caused was estimated at £1. The assault happened at about 10:40 pm on Sunday evening. Corney was returning home, accompanied by a friend, when Skinnerton, for no apparent reason, seized Corney by the throat and exclaimed, "I am Jack the Ripper, I killed the women in Whitechapel, and one in Hatton gardens." Skinnerton then ran away but was chased by Corney and his friend. After a long chase, Skinnerton got as far as the rear of Mr Crick's house, it was here that the panes of glass were broken. Skinnerton had jumped upon a lean-to and smashed a quantity of glass in the fanlight. After a struggle, he was removed to the police station. Skinnerton, it was said, had previously been of good character. The magistrate ordered him to pay a fine of 2s 6d and also the costs of the proceedings, 20s, in all amounting to a total of 1.12s, or in default go to prison for 14 days with hard labour.

THE SLAUGHTERMAN

In the (1965) book: Jack the Ripper In Fact and Fiction, Robin Odell makes the suggestion that Jack the Ripper was a Jewish shochet or a ritual slaughterman, who, after the Miller's Court murder was discovered by his own people, and dealt with in accordance with their own brand of justice. The man's identity was never made public. The police at the time considered the possibility that the Ripper may have been a Jewish slaughterman and made visits to Jewish abattoirs. The khalef, a shochet's ceremonial knife, was examined by police surgeon Dr Gordon Brown to see if it was capable, in his judgement, of inflicting the injuries on Catherine Eddowes body. Dr Brown said in his opinion, such a knife, single-edged and lacking a point, could not have been used. Dr Bagster Philips thought the murder weapon must have been a very sharp knife with a thin narrow blade, at least six inches to eight inches long. Questioned by the coroner, Philips thought that the knives normally used by slaughterman, which were well ground down, might have been used. Major Smith claimed to have checked on the movements of all the local butchers and slaughterers in the area. Chief Inspector Swanson reported that seventy-six butchers and slaughterers had been visited, and the character of the men employed had been enquired into. The butchers came in for a good deal of attention, and it was considered a significant fact that there always existed a slaughterhouse in close proximity to the scene of the murders. According to Forbes Winslow, in his book recollections of forty years detectives disguised as slaughtermen obtained work in several of these houses in order to keep a sharp eye on what was going on. It was stated that the murderer might be a woman in disguise of a slaughterman.

G WENTWORTH BELL SMITH

Smith, a Canadian, had come to London in 1888 to work for the Toronto Trust Society, which had offices in Goldman Street, St Paul's. Smith took lodgings in April with Mr and Mrs Callaghan, at 27 Sun Street, Finsbury Square, and came under the suspicion of Mr Callaghan, who noticed that he kept three loaded revolvers hidden in a chest of drawers in his room. He also stayed out late at night, changed his suit every day and talked and moaned to himself. Smith, also according to Mr Callaghan, was a religious fanatic, who appeared obsessed with prostitutes, saying that they should all be drowned. He was also noted as coming home at 4:00 am on the 7 August, the night Martha Tabram was murdered. The next morning, when the maid went to make his bed, she found a large bloodstain on the linen and a shirt hanging with the cuffs having recently been washed. Convinced that Smith was a lunatic, and therefore Jack the Ripper, Callaghan took his suspicions to Dr Forbes Winslow, a Ripper theorist and expert on matters of sanity, having founded the British hospital for mental disorders. Winslow was convinced that Smith was the Ripper, and claimed that given the help of six Constables could catch him. The police investigated the claim and came to the conclusion that there was nothing in it, and that Smith was not Jack the Ripper. On the statement Callaghan gave to Winslow to show to the police, the date in which Smith had returned to his lodgings late had been altered from the 9 August to the 7 August, to make it appear that it was the night Martha Tabram was murdered, and make Smith a more plausible suspect. Smith was described as 5 ft 10 inches tall, with dark hair a full beard and moustache, a dark complexion, foreign in appearance, multilingual. It was also claimed that he was knock need and walked with his feet wide apart and probably wore false teeth.

NEWLAND FRANCIS FORESTER SMITH

Newland Francis Forester Smith was born 15 October 1863 in Cinderford, Gloucestershire. The son of clergyman Henry William Smith and Sarah Adeline (née Croome). Educated at London University 1881-87, and Lincoln's Inn 1887-90. In the 1881 census, he is an undergraduate London University. Living at 16, Macaulay Road, Clapham, Wandsworth. On 17 November 1883 in Jubbulpore, Bengal, India he married 22-year old Sophie Dawes Swinhoe. They had three children, William born 1884. Francis, born 1885. Reginald born 1887. Called to the bar in June 1890. Certified insane October 1890, and sent to Holloway Asylum and Sanatorium, Virginia Water, Surrey. Discharged October 1891 but re-admitted immediately, on an urgent order, his case notes recording that he believed himself, "Accused of being Jack the Ripper." According to legend his room in Virginia Waters was known as "Jack the Ripper's room." In 1891 his address was 61 Trouville Road, Clapham Park. On 9 February 1894, he was transferred to the Cane Hill Asylum, Coulsden, Croydon where he died from organic brain disease and full degeneration of the heart on 23 July 1898, at the age of 35 years.

JOHN SMITH

In 1889, at the Frome Police-court, John Smith, a rough looking tramp, was charged with begging and making use of threats. The prisoner called at the home of a Mrs Sheppard, 32 Fromefield, and wanted to sell the servant a book. She refused to but the book or help him in anyway. He put his foot against the door, and insisted on seeing the master or mistress. Then said "I am Jack the Ripper, and I will kill you." She slammed the door in his face and watched him through the window. He leaned against a wall oppisite the house, swore very badly, and said he would kill the girl if he had to wait a year. He took a knife from his waist and drew it across his throat, to show her what he intended to do. He was sent to prison for 21 days with hard labour.

WILLIAM SMITH

The Maitland Mercury & Hunter River General Advertiser, Tuesday 23 July 1889 reported the following story:

A man, giving the name of Wm. Smith, of the "sundowner" type, called at Warranook station on Wednesday evening, asking for work. He was given food and a bed for the night. Yesterday afternoon he had an altercation with one of the employees. He then went to the men's hut, seized a meat chopper, and, while the men were at tea, attacked a Chinaman, giving him a fearful blow on the back of the head and across the cheek, causing very deep wounds. T. Cook, a man with only one leg, interfered, and Smith dealt him terrible blows on the head and shoulders while on the ground, striking him repeatedly across the neck with the back of the weapon. He then dropped the weapon and made for the homestead. Seizing another chopper from the kitchen, he rushed through the hall of the house, where he was confronted by Mr Ayrey, who presented a revolver and ordered him to throw up his arms. The man cried, "Don't shoot me." He was then secured. A messenger was despatched for the Rupanyup police, and Smith was handed over, remarking to the constable that he was "Jack the Ripper" and that they had got him at last. The two injured men are in a very precarious condition.

WILLIAM SMITH

In January 1904, a rough-looking man, named William Smith, was sentenced to six weeks imprisonment at Marlborough-street

Police Court, for being drunk and disorderly, and assaulting a constable, while proclaiming he was "Jack the Ripper." He had previously severed a prison term for a similar offence.

SOLOMON

After the murder of Mary Kelly, it seemed anyone who had committed the crime of murder was considered as a possible Ripper suspect. Solomon was mentioned in the Home Office files, after a letter was received from the officers at Woking prison, dated the 15 November 1888, which suggested that Solomon, the murderer, may be Jack the Ripper. The Home Office file continued to say that his was an ordinary criminal case.

HENRY ARTHUR GEORGE SOMERSET

Named as a co-conspirator in the books The Ripper and the Royals, and Epiphany of the Whitechapel murders. Somerset was born 17 November 1851, the son of the Eighth Duke of Beaufort, and his wife the former Lady Georgiana Curzon. Nicknamed "Podge" by his brothers. Head of the stables of the future King Edward VII then (Prince of Wales). Major in the Royal Horse Guards. Linked with the Cleveland Street scandal, where he was identified and named by several young men as a customer of their services. Interviewed by the police 7 August 1889, and again on 22 August, Somerset obtained leave from his regiment and permission to go abroad. He returned to England briefly, though fled to France when tipped off charges against him were imminent. He settled in France and never returned to England. He died there on 26 May 1926 at the age of 74.

JOHANN STAMMER

A man named Jonas, contacted Sir Augustus Paget, the British ambassador in Vienna, claiming he knew the identity of Jack the

Ripper. He requested £165 to enable him to travel to London to find the man. Paget advanced the money out of his pocket. When he demanded another £100 it was refused. The Home Office considered the man a fraud and the matter a hoax, and recommended reimbursing Paget from the Metropolitan Police funds. Jonas said the murderer was a former San Francisco butcher, Johann Stammer, who had killed his mistress and child in New York. He used the name John Kelly when in London, and was now a ship's cook. Described as aged 35-38, medium height with broad shoulders, strongly marked features, brilliant large white teeth, and a scar due to a stab under his left eye. He walked like a sailor and was believed to be in Liverpool.

CHARLES STANDEN

On 3 October, 1888, at the Derby Police Court, Charles Standen, was charged with drunkenness and disorderly conduct on St. Thomas's road. When apprehended by Police-constable Allbutt, Standen threatened the officer, and said he was the Whitechapel murderer. When approaching the lock-up he began to cry. He was fined 10s and costs, or 14 days' imprisonment in default.

DR STANLEY

Dr Stanley was the fictitious name given to the Ripper by Leonard Matters first in The People in 1926 and later in his (1929) book: The Mystery of Jack the Ripper. Stanley was a cancer specialist at an unnamed London hospital, who also had a private practice at his house in Portman Square. Matters described Stanley as a refined, courteous elegant, man of about fifty years, full of wisdom and good. It is said Dr Stanley took revenge on the prostitute, who on boat race night 1886, gave his beloved son Bertie, (some reports claim the son was called Herbert), who was a brilliant medical student, with a bright future ahead of him, a particularly virulent form of syphilis that killed him within two years. The prostitute's name was Mary Kelly. After killing her, along with her friends, Dr Stanley fled to Buenos Aires in Argentina, where he died in 1918 from cancer. Stanley told a deathbed confession to the physician in charge of the hospital, Dr Jose Riche a former student of his. Riche, in turn, told the story to an English journalist Leonard Matters. Unfortunately, no records exist in any London hospital for Dr Stanley, or at his residence in Portman Square. Neither are there any records of him in any Buenos Aires hospital. It should also be noted that syphilis takes far longer to kill than two years. The first signs of syphilis occur approximately one month after infection, the symptoms, then recede and the disease stays dormant for a period of up to ten or twenty years, before the third stage manifest itself. Death generally occurs within a further three or four years. Matters makes the assumption that the victims were known to each other, though there is no evidence to support this claim. There is also no evidence to substantiate the claim that Mary Kelly had syphilis.

ROBERT LOUIS STEVENSON

A member of the public, wrote to the police, asking who wrote Jekyll and Hyde and if he was a likely Ripper suspect.

Robert Lewis (later "Louis") Balfour Stevenson, was born in Edinburgh, on 13 November 1850. And was the only child of respectable middle-class parents. His father Thomas was an engineer. His mother, was Margaret Isabella Balfour. Throughout his childhood, he suffered chronic health problems that confined him to bed. At the age of seventeen he enrolled at Edinburgh University initially to study engineering, he later studied law. Stevenson developed a desire to write early in life, his first published volume, was An Inland Voyage (1878). He met his wife Fanny Osbourne, in September 1876, she was a 36 year old

417

American, married (although separated) with two children. She divorced her husband in 1878, and the two married in 1880, they remained together until Stevenson's death in 1894. Stevenson's health always fragile declined, he suffered from haemorrhaging lungs, and was confined to his bed. While bedridden, he wrote some of his most popular fiction, most notably *Treasure Island* (1883), *Kidnapped* (1886), *Strange Case of Dr. Jekyll and Mr. Hyde* (1886), and *The Black Arrow* (1888). The Strange Case of Dr. Jekyll and Mr. Hyde opened in London in early August 1888, at the Lyceum Theatre, with American actor Richard Mansfield performing the dual role of Jekyll and Hyde. The *Pall Mall Gazette* referred to the perpetrator of the Ripper crimes as:

Mr. Hyde at large in Whitechapel.

Mansfield's nightly transformations were absolutely terrifying his audiences, this led to speculation that Mr Hyde's persona might not be all down to acting, and some were even wondering if Mansfield himself might be responsible for the Ripper murders. The play so shocked its audience that parallels began to be drawn between Mansfield's Hyde and the homicidal maniac who was ripping open prostitutes in Whitechapel at the time. On 29 September 1888 the final performance of Jekyll and Hyde was announced. Stevenson's final years were spent in Apia, in the Samoan islands, where he decided to build a house and settle. Apia was a perfect location because the climate was tropical, he would never again endure the harsh winters of his native Scotland or England. Robert Louis Stevenson died of a stroke on December 3, 1894, at his home in Vailima, Samoa. He was 44 years of age. He was buried at the top of Mount Vaea, overlooking the sea.

LEWIS STEMLER

In May 1915 a 31-year old Austrian, out of work waiter, named Lewis Stemler, was suspected of being Jack the Ripper after he was accused of frightening a group of five and six-year boys, by chasing them along First Avenue. When he was arrested, he was found hiding in the hallway of a house in Seventeenth-Street, New York. He had been chased there by the father of one of the boys he had frightened. Feelings in the area were already running high before Stemler frightened the children. A young boy, Charlie Murray, who lived on First Avenue, had recently been brutally murdered; the murdered boy's mother had received a letter stating that as soon as the present excitement had died down he would kill another child. Stemler at the time of the Whitechapel murders would have been 4-years old.

JAMES KENNETH STEPHEN

Michael Harrison, in the (1972) book: Clarence Was He Jack the Ripper? Made the suggestion that Stephen and the Duke of Clarence were lovers at Cambridge, and when the affair ended, Stephen became unhinged and decided to kill prostitutes on dates which had some significance to Clarence, such as birthdays and religious festivals. Harrison's theory that the Ripper killed ten women, which included Annie Farmer, who was not even murdered, is important because Harrison believes Stephen was acting out one of his own poem's Air Kaphoozelum, in which the song's villain kills ten harlots. Harrison also claimed that Stephen's poetry displayed signs of sadism and misogyny, thus proving his hatred of women. In one of his poems, A Thought, Stephen wrote:

> If all the harm that women have done,
> were put in a bottle and rolled into one,

419

earth would not hold it,
the sky could not enfold it,
It could not be lighted nor warmed by the sun,
such masses of evil would puzzle the devil,
and keep him in fuel while time's wheels run.

But if all the harm that's been done by men,
were doubled and doubled and doubled again,
and melted and fused into vapour,
and then were squared and raised to the power of ten.
There wouldn't be nearly enough, not near,
to keep a small girl for the tenth of a year.

James Kenneth Stephen was born on 25 February 1859 and was the second son of Judge Sir James Fitzjames Stephen, the judge at the Maybrick trial. He was educated at Eaton and Kings College, Cambridge, and was elected President of the Cambridge Union, a public political speaking forum. In 1883-85 he became tutor to Prince Albert, and was awarded the Whewell scholarship in international law, and called to the bar 1884. In the winter of 1886, while on holiday in Felixstowe, Stephen, while out riding, was struck by a sail from a windmill. In a variation of this story, it was said that he had been struck by a projection from a moving train. Though the injury was considered minor at first, and he made, what appeared to be a complete recovery, it was said his brain had been permanently damaged and he slowly went insane. Up until the accident, there was no evidence Stephen had displayed any signs of mental illness, and he continued his political public speaking. Upon recovering from his accident after treatment from family physician Sir William Gull, Stephen took up writing and contributed articles to The Pall Mall Gazette and the Saturday Review. In 1888 he founded his own weekly newspaper The Reflector. It was to last only 17 issues before folding, due to

420

lack of support. The last issue was published on 21 April. He returned to Cambridge to lecture and teach and in 1891 published two volumes of poetry, Lapsus Calami and Quo Musa Tendis. On 21 November 1891 Stephen was admitted to St Andrews Hospital, Northampton, which was a mental health asylum, after being found naked and ranting in his room under the misapprehension that there was a warrant out for his arrest. He remained there until his death at 4:21 pm on 3 February 1892. The official cause of death was given as mania, refusal of food and exhaustion.

At the time of the Ripper murders, he was 29 years of age almost 6 ft tall, dark haired and clean shaven. Stephen had no known base in the East End. Also, the suggestion that the dates of the murders had some significance to Clarence is without foundation. There are no known dates of importance to Clarence on the night of the double murder, nor the murder of Annie Chapman. There was a history of mental illness in Stephen's family, his father, who was at one time felt by his family and friends to be destined for high public office, later went insane and spent his final days in an asylum. Also, Stephen's cousin, the novelist Virginia Woolf, (author of Mrs Dalloway and To the Lighthouse) attempted suicide several times, before filling her overcoat pocket with stones and drowning herself in the River Ouse near her home in 1941.

ROBERT DONSTON STEPHENSON

Robert Donston Stephenson was born on 20 April 1841 at 35 Charles Street, Sculcoats, Hull, the son of a seed oil mill owner Richard Stephenson, and his wife Isabella (née Dawber). He was by his own account, well travelled and educated and studied medicine in Paris and chemistry in Munich, under Dr James Allen. In 1859 while in Paris, he met Lord Edward Bulwer-Lytton and was initiated into the Hermetic Lodge of Alexandria. Stephenson himself claims he served as a field surgeon from 1860 to 1863 in Garibaldi's army of Red Shirts, in their fight for Italian unification, and claimed to have performed appendectomies without anaesthetic. Stephenson throughout his life was fascinated by the occult and claims he travelled to Africa in the 1860s to study black magic and witchcraft. One of many unsubstantiated tales told by Stephenson of his early life was that while in Africa he claimed to have murdered a female witch doctor, and killed the seducer of his favourite cousin, dipping the girl's handkerchief in the man's blood. Also, that he was party to the murder of a Chinaman during the second Californian gold rush. Stephenson travelled widely to India and America, acquiring further knowledge of black magic practices. In 1863 family pressure would force him to take up a mundane position with the customs office in Hull, it is alleged he was fired in 1868 for consorting with prostitutes. He also believed he was superior to the position. In 1869 he moved to London and worked as a freelance journalist for the Pall Mall Gazette. It is not clear from this period how he supported himself financially, as the freelance work was infrequent. There is a possibility he was receiving an allowance from his parents. In 1871 he is listed in the census as living at 2 Acorn Court, Strand, London, lodging with a compositor John Murray and his wife Martha. On 14 February 1876 using the name Roslyn D'Onston Stephenson, he married Ann Deary, in St James's Church, Holloway. In 1881 they are listed as living at 10 Hollingsworth Street, North. What happened to Ann Deary after 1886 is unknown. There are no records of her death, yet from this period Stephenson referred to himself as unmarried. On 11 May 1887, a woman's dismembered body was found floating in the Thames at Rainham, Essex. Some theorists have claimed this was the body of Ann Deary, and that this was Stephenson's first experiment in ritual murder. Until more is known about Ann Deary, this claim remains highly speculative.

On 26 July 1888 Stephenson checked himself into the London hospital complaining of tension and sleeplessness; he was treated for neurasthenia, or nervous exhaustion, and was discharged on 7 December. Therefore was a resident during the duration of the Whitechapel murders. He was thus only a few brisk minutes' walk from the site where Nicholl's Chapman, Stride and Eddowes met their deaths. Some theorists have suggested Stephenson faked his illness, and that in fact he only required bed rest, so would not have been a security priority and could easily have sneaked out during the night to commit the murders, and return without arousing suspicion. It was during his stay at the London hospital that Stephenson met Dr Morgan Davis, who was a surgeon there. Davis, while visiting one of his patients, Dr Evans, who shared a semi-private ward with Stephenson, gave a graphic account of how the Ripper victims had been murdered and sodomised. Stephenson, upon hearing the news from W T Stead, editor of the Pall Mall Gazette, that Mary Kelly had been sodomised, became convinced that Davis was Jack the Ripper. Upon leaving the London hospital, Stephenson confided his suspicions about Dr Davis, to George Marsh, an impressionable unemployed ironmongery assistant and amateur detective, of 24 Pratt Street, Camden Town. They met two or three times a week over a drink at the Prince Albert public house to discuss the murders. They also drew up an agreement to share the reward money on the conviction of Davis as the Ripper. Stephenson signed the agreement under the name, Sudden Death. After a falling out between the two men, Marsh went to Scotland Yard on 24 December 1888 and made a statement in which he claimed that Stephenson was, in fact, Jack the Ripper. Two days later Stephenson went to Scotland Yard and explained his Dr Davis theory. He also wrote to the police and the newspapers with his theories about the murders. After the double murder of Elizabeth

Stride and Catherine Eddowes, he wrote to the police suggesting that the Goulston Street graffiti spelling of the word Juwes, was actually "Juives" which was French for Jews, thus indicating that the killer was of French nationality. Some authors have suggested Stephenson deliberately drew attention to himself so that he would be dismissed as a crank and nuisance, masking the fact that he actually was Jack the Ripper. Inspector Roots, who took Stephenson's statement and who had known him for twenty years, indicated no suspicion in his report and did not believe Stephenson was the Ripper. He described him as, "One who has led a bohemian life, drinks very heavily, perpetually fuddled and who always carries drugs to sober him and stave off delirium tremors". While there is no evidence that Dr Davis was ever questioned or suspected by the police, Stephenson was questioned on at least two occasions, though his suspect file has since been lost. In 1890 Stephenson was living in Southsea with his lover, the novelist Mabel Collins, and it was here that he met Collins friend and rumoured lover Baroness Vittoria Cremers. Stephenson and the Baroness went into business together and formed the Pompadour Cosmetic Company in Baker Street, on the site where Baker Street tube station now stands. The venture, however, did not last long, and the company folded in 1891. It is said that Cremers doesn't appear to have thought too highly of Stephenson. After first finding him inoffensive, she would later become uncomfortable in his company. On one occasion Cremers saw Stephenson drawing an upside down triangle on his door, he told her he had done so to keep out an evil presence. Initially, Mabel Collins was happy to care for Stephenson, who was now clearly in financial dire straits and provided him with money and a home. One day, Mabel went into the Baker Street office and told Vittoria that Stephenson had shown her something that convinced her he was Jack the Ripper. She refused to say why she had come to this conclusion, only that she wanted to be free of him. In the late 1920s-30's. Cremers told journalist Bernard O Donnell that she once went into Stephenson's room, without him ever knowing, to look for and steal some compromising letters that Collins had written to Stephenson. Under the bed, she found in a tin case seven neckties that were stained with what appeared to be blood. Stephenson had once told Cremers he knew who the Ripper was and went on to tell his, Dr Davis story, complete with a description of how the killer hid the organs he removed from his victims behind his necktie's. Cremers, upon having a conversation with Stephenson, when he stated there would be no more Ripper murders, and finding the bloodied neckties in Stephenson's room, became convinced, along with Mabel Collins, that he was Jack the Ripper. In the 1920's the ties were supposedly in Aleister Crowley's possession, Crowley boasting that they had belonged to the Ripper, who was a black magician and surgeon known to him. He went on to name the man as Stephenson, whom he believed had died in 1912. Stephenson in later life appeared to lose interest in black magic and converted to Christianity. He wrote the book: The Patristic Gospels, which was published in 1904. There is no documented record of Stephenson's death, and no evidence to confirm Crowley's claim that he died in 1912. Researcher and author the late Christopher Scott discovered documentary evidence relating to the death of Dr Roslyn D'Onston on 9 October 1916, of oesophageal cancer his address was listed as 129 St John's Road, Islington. Cremers described Stephenson at the time of their first meeting as:

Unassuming in appearance, a man one would not look at twice, 5 ft 11 inches tall, fair and moustachioed, his hair was thinning at the sides, his teeth were discoloured, his eyes were dead, his clothes were old and worn yet spotlessly clean, had a military bearing and was the most soundless man she had ever heard. One who could stand behind you without you ever have heard him approach.

D' Onston wrote articles under the name, Tautriadelta. One such article he wrote for W.T. Stead's spiritualist magazine The Borderland, 1 December 1888 convinced Stead that the writer, he had known for many years was Jack the Ripper. The article stated there were six murders, and not five, and the murder sites formed the pattern of a sacrilegious cross. In his favour as a Ripper suspect: Stephenson, by booking himself into the London hospital, was in the location where and when the murders occurred. He had the medical knowledge and skill to commit the murders, and remove the body parts, and was suspected by at least four people, Marsh, Collins, Cremers and Stead. He was familiar with the area, and his inoffensive and cultured manner would have won the trust of his victims. He may also have contracted a venereal disease from a prostitute and may have harboured a grudge against them. Against him being the Ripper: He lived almost thirty years after the last generally accepted Ripper murder. He does not match in age or height any of the eyewitness sightings of the Ripper. How was it possible for him to leave and re-enter the hospital on at least four separate occasions to commit the murders without arousing suspicion. His attempts to insert himself into the Ripper story as an authority on the subject may have been nothing more than an effort to gain more freelance work. Many of his stories about his life and exploits appear to be just that, stories. Unfortunately, to view Stephenson as a serious and credible suspect we have to rely heavily on both the testimonies of Stephenson himself and Vittoria Cremers, whose links to Aleister Crowley leaves one sceptical of the validity of the claims.

JOHN STEWART

In November 1888, at the Glasgow Central Police Court, a middle aged man named John Stewart, an engine fitter, admitted at the Central Police Court, that on Saturday afternoon, in Graeme-street, he brandished a knife and threatened to stab a woman, named Annie Macdonald, who resides at 10 M'Pherson-street. He threatened to "Jack the Ripper" her. When escorted to the Police-station, he shouting out in a very loud voice that he was "Jack the Ripper." Stewart was sentenced to 30 days imprisonment

MR STEWART

On 31 November, 1888, a man was arrested at the Crystal Tavern, Mile End Road, London, on suspicion of being the Whitechapel murderer. He met a woman there whom he urged to accompany him, but she refused. He also met a photographer who was soliciting for orders. He asked the man if he could take some photographs, using expressions which included suspicion. He gave the name Mr Stewart, and his address 305 Mile End Road. He was taken into custody, at the police station, he gave the name of Ever, and he appeared to be a Polish Jew.

STREET GANG

After the murder of Mary Ann Nichols, the police briefly suspected that she, like the previous killings of Emma Elizabeth Smith and Martha Tabram, had perhaps been perpetrated by one of the local street gangs operating in the area at that time. They noted that the murders had all occurred within three hundred yards of each other. Inspector Abberline quickly ruled out the theory of any connection between the deaths of Smith, Tabram and Nichols, and perceptively concluded that the Nichols murder was the work of a lone killer. A woman named Margaret Hayes, who, like Smith, lodged at 18 George Street, also stated that she was assaulted on the same night as Emma Smith was murdered. Hayes was struck in the mouth by two men, who then ran away. Hayes claimed there had been some rough work that night. Emma Elizabeth Smith before she died claimed that she was assaulted and robbed by three men, one of them a youth of about nineteen.

On 7 September 1888 The Weekly Herald reported:

The officers engaged in the case are pushing their inquiries in the neighbourhood as to the doings of certain gangs known to frequent the locality, and an opinion is gaining ground amongst them that the murderers are the same who committed the two previous murders near the same spot. It is believed that these gangs, who make their appearance during the early hours of the morning, are in the habit of blackmailing these unfortunate women, and when their demands are refused violence follows, and in order to avoid their deeds being brought to light they put away their victims. They have been under the observation of the police for some time past, and it is believed that, with the prospect of a reward and a free pardon, some of them might be persuaded to turn Queen's evidence, when some startling revelations might be expected.

Several authors have named gangs which were allegedly known to the police and believed to be operating in the area at that time, robbing and blackmailing honest tradesmen, fleecing drunken sailors and threatening prostitutes. The Blind Beggar Mob, a title derived from a public house in the Mile End Road where they used to meet, usually confined their criminal activities to the West End. The Hoxton Mob, or Hoxton High Rips, who were suspected of committing the Ripper murders. The Green Gate Gang and the immigrant gangs, the Bessarabians and the Odessians, as well as the gang, which was suspected of killing Emma Smith, the Old Nichol Gang, who operated around Old Nichol Street, at the top

428

of Brick Lane, close to where Smith was murdered.In the (1934) book: Lost London. The Memoirs of an East End, Detective, Ex-Det. Sergeant Benjamin. Leeson points out how much we owe to the quiet and unceasing efforts of the Metropolitan police. He tells us about

The Blind Beggars Gang, the Bessarabians, the Odessians and other formidable organizations of which the very names have been forgotten. The gangs worked at public sales rooms, race meetings, railway stations and football grounds. During the rush at turnstiles they selected their victims at will, removing watches and chains, money, tie pins. A protest from a victim was a signal for a ferocious melee which actually gave them further opportunities for their nefarious work. A Daily News journalist reported in early September that the general consensus, particularly among the women of the area, was that it was a gang that had "done this.

While the possibility remains that a gang may have been responsible for the murder of Emma Elizabeth Smith, there is no evidence to suggest they committed the Whitechapel murders. There has been some speculation that the Ripper may have originally been a member of one of these street gangs. Unfortunately, little accurate information is available to confirm how many of these street gangs actually existed.

GEORGE SULLIVAN

George Sullivan, 48 years old was charged with being a lunatic wandering at large. Sullivan was seen in the Whitechapel-road by Police-constable 269, surrounded by a crowd. He had a bible in his hand, and was shouting that he was "Jesus Christ" and had come down from heaven to save the people. He was arrested and taken to the police-station. He said he had been in the Bow

Cemetery, where people came out of their graves on their way to heaven and shook hands with him. A Dr. examined him and found the insanity was no doubt owing to drink. It was stated that the man had been in various asylums, and on one occasion was charged, on his confession, with being "Jack the Ripper". He was discharged, and taken to the workhouse.

GEORGE SWEENEY

Sweeney, a 27-year old labourer of 20 Chiswell-street, Camberwell, was charged at the Southwick Police Court with being drunk and disorderly in the borough High Street. Police constable Robert Walsh stated that he found Sweeney in the borough shouting that he was "Jack the Ripper." A crowd had gathered around him and was beginning to become excited. Sweeney blamed his behaviour on a toothache. He was told by the court, that his behaviour was disgraceful. He was fined 20s, or fourteen days hard labour.He was born in Camberwell, London in 1860. In the 1881 and 1891 census he is a prisoner in Wandsworth. Sweeney was also admitted to the workhouse on several occasions. He died in 1897.

ALGERNON CHARLES SWINBURNE

It is said, "A more unlikely candidate for Jack the Ripper would be harder to find than poet and critic Algernon Charles Swinburne."

Algernon Charles Swinburne was born 5 April 1837 at 7 Chester Street, Grosvenor Place, London, the son of Admiral, Charles Henry, and Lady Jane Henrietta, he spent most of his childhood on the Isle of Wight, where his parents and grandparents had homes. As a child, Swinburne was nervous and frail. Educated at Eaton 1849-53 and later Balliol College, Oxford 1856-60, he left without a degree and lived off an allowance from his father. He contributed to periodicals in the Spectator and Fortnightly Review.

The first poem he had published under his name was in 1865 Atalanta in Calydon, a poetic drama modelled on a Greek tragedy; it was received with critical acclaim. His lifestyle was said to be as energetic and extravagant as his poetry. Throughout the 1860's and 70's, his life was a cycle of alcoholic collapse, drying out at home in the country, then returning to London, where he would begin all over again. A decadent poet, he is perhaps best remembered for The First Book of Poems and Ballads 1866. The poem's emphasis on masochism and flagellation was met with outrage and admiration, in equal proportions. He took a sardonic delight in what the critic and biographer Cecil Lang call "Algernonic exaggeration." When people began to talk about his homosexuality and other sexual proclivities, he circulated a story that he had engaged in pederasty and bestiality with a monkey- and then ate it. Oscar Wilde called him:

A braggart in matters of vice, who had done everything he could to convince his fellow citizens of his homosexuality and bestiality, without being in the slightest degree a homosexual or a bestialiser.

His self-indulgent masochistic tendency excesses resulted in him suffering a breakdown in 1879. Weakened by epilepsy and alcoholism, destitute, and homeless, he was rescued from near death by his friend and legal advisor, Walter Theodore Watt Dunton 1832-1914, an English poet, novelist and critic, who took him into his home in The Pines, Putney, and persuaded him to moderate his habits, which he did, becoming a more respectable figure. It was said of Watts that he saved the man and killed the poet. He spent the remaining 30 years of his life in a manner as subdued as his youth had been wild. His health slowly and completely restored. He saw less and less of his old friends, his growing deafness, he was afflicted from about 1875 onwards, may have accounted for some of his decreased sociability. He produced 23 volumes of poetry in those last 30 years, which his critics agreed where more focused and mature, though apart from the long poem *Tristram of Lyonesse* (1882) and the verse tragedy *Marino Faliero* (1885), they lacked much of the verbal ingenuity that had made his youthful poems so enduringly popular. He died in Putney, London, of influenza 10 April 1909, at the age of 72. He was nominated for the Nobel Prize in Literature every year from 1903 to 1907 and again in 1909. He was described as abnormally short a little over 5 ft tall, with narrow, sloping shoulders, slight build and tiny hands and feet. His eyes were green, and his disproportionately large head was topped by a great aureole of bright red hair. His habit of fluttering his hands and hopping about provoked Henry Adams, to compare him to a "crimson macaw."

ALOIS SZEMERDY

Rumours that Szemerdy may have been Jack the Ripper was first reported in the Daily Graphic in 1892, and later by author Carl Muusmann in the (1908) book: Hvem Var Jack The Ripper, (Who was Jack The Ripper).On 26 July 1876 in Buenos Aires, a young prostitute, Caroline Metz, was murdered. Baptiste Castagnet, who lived with her and was also her pimp, was waiting in the room next door while Karoline was with a client when he heard screams. He rushed in to find Caroline on the floor, blood pouring from a wound to her throat. On the bed lay a sheath knife covered in blood, a man's black felt hat, an umbrella with a handle made of steel and a grey cloak and vest with a gold watch and chain inside. Castagnet became a suspect, and was arrested, and held in custody for 17 days before being released. Word soon began to spread that Alios Szemerdy was, in fact, the murderer after items left in the victim's room had been identified as belonging to him. He fled to Rio de Janeiro in Brazil but was arrested during a

432

street festival. After his defence had skilfully managed to convince the court of his innocence, on 12 September 1881 Szemerdy was acquitted of the murder of Caroline Metz. In 1885 charges of robbery and murder were brought against him and he was placed in a lunatic asylum in Buenos Aires, Argentina. In August 1889 he arrived in Vienna, and registered his address. He was next living in Budapest with a widow, Julianne Karlovicz, for whom he worked in her pork butcher's shop. In 1892 he was in back in Vienna, where he was arrested again on suspicion of robbery and murder. A series of robberies against pawnbrokers and watchmakers had occurred, and one victim had died after being struck over the head with a blunt object. A goldsmith in Prezburg remembered a man called Szemerdy had robbed him of a watch, two years earlier, and informed the police. Szemerdy was arrested, but before he could stand trial committed suicide by hanging himself in September 1892. The pawnbrokers, who survived the attacks, were shown the body of Szemerdy, and at once identified him. One witness said, "If you have seen that beard once, you will never forget it." Szemerdy, who described himself as a surgeon, though in other reports was said to have been a sausage maker, was believed to have deserted the Austrian army, 7 July 1863, and spent some time in a mental institution. Szemerdy was born in 1844 and was 44-years old at the time of the Whitechapel murders. He was described in newspaper reports as tall and thin, with a bronzed complexion, brown smooth hair, a thick bushy moustache and beard, sensual unsteady small eyes, and large muscular hands. He had a habit of wearing his coat buttoned up to his chin in military fashion.

ROBERT TANNER

On the 14 November 1888, at the Penarth police-court, Robert Tanner, 15 years of age, was charged with hacking the ornamental trees growing in Beach-road. He was seen by Henry Adams, with a small hatchet, wilfully hacking at the trees. Adams remonstrated with him, but only received impudence for his pains. A lady also, noticing the damage he was doing to the young trees, spoke to him. His only reply was "Now you see "Jack the Ripper." The damage was estimated at 5s. The magistrates ordered him to pay a fine of £2 and costs or one month's imprisonment.

CHARLES TAYLOR

On Tuesday, 20 November 1888, Charles Taylor, a schoolboy, of New Queen-street, rushed up to another boy Oswald Gould Smith, in North Marine Road, Scarborough, said he was "Jack the Ripper," and stabbed him in the throat, with a knife he carried about his person. The wound a severe one was dressed by Dr. Cross and Mr J. W. Teale, surgeon.

MR TAYLOR

In John Blunt's Monthly 16 December 1929, a recently discharged Broadmoor patient, (name unknown) gave an interview in which he claimed that a former inmate had been known to both warders and patients as "Jack the Ripper." The article called him by the pseudonym, "Mr Taylor." The patient who was regarded as a doctor, was detained for thirty years. Described as a quite mild-mannered, studious man, of great knowledge and culture, famous for his love of scientific books, and his fondness for diagnosing the ailments of people he came into daily contact with. He was caught after one of the murders, but was never charged with the crimes as he was immediately pronounced insane, and incarcerated. While working in the garden, he made an unsuccessful escape attempt, while climbing a wall, when a chisel fell out of his pocket onto a glass frame, the noise alerted the staff, and he was captured in the nick of time.

434

He died shortly after. At Broadmoor he was always known as Jack the Ripper.

OLGA TCHKERSOFF

Olga Tchkersoff was named as Jack the Ripper by author and former policeman Edwin Thomas Woodhall, in the (1937) book: When London Walked in Terror.

Olga, a 24-year old immigrant from Russia, described as dark, olive-skinned and handsome, came to England on 22 February 1887 with her parents and younger sister, blond, blue-eyed, fresh complexioned 19-year old Vera. Olga, a skilled needlewoman, soon found work from the local Jewish traders and the family bought a large run down house in Spitalfields, with Olga wishing to use the many rooms in the house for tailoring and dressmaking. Her father, Ivan, however, had other ideas, he decided to let every room and all available floor space to as many people and for as much rent as possible. Madame Tchkersoff, herself was apparently not too particular who stayed there. Vera soon fell under the influence of some of the more undesirable women in the house, and much to the consternation of her elder sister became a prostitute. Her parents spent the rent money on alcohol, and both died in 1888 as a result of drink. Her father, Ivan from pneumonia caused by excessive drinking, and her mother from a fall while in a drunken state. The death of her parents and the fact that her beloved sister had fallen into prostitution, convinced Olga that this class of creatures who had brought Vera to her ruin were to blame. She was overheard saying that if she had her way, she'd hack them all to pieces. Her sister Vera died on 28 July 1888 from septic poisoning after an illegal abortion Olga quickly cleared the house of all the tenants, except for an Old Russian couple, whom she allowed to stay on as caretakers. One day the old housekeeper, who looked after the property, saw Olga dressed in men's clothing. On commenting about this, he was told that she was trying out a new style of clothing for men. Knowing Olga to be a forward-looking tailoress, he thought no more of it. A short while later, while she had been away from the property for some time, he entered her room and began to look around, opening a chest of drawers he discovered wrapped in a towel a large bloodstained clasp knife, and noticed still smouldering in the fire, the partly charred remains of a man's jacket and trousers. Putting all the clues together, the old man realised that Olga was, in fact, "Jack the Ripper." Feeling some empathy toward her, with them both being Russian, plus the fact that he was very fond of her and knew the traumas she had suffered since she came to England, he decided to cover up her crimes, and destroyed all evidence implicating her in the Whitechapel murders. Two days later he set sail for America, he dropped the knife overboard. No evidence has been found to prove that Tchkersoff ever existed.

TEENAGE JACK THE RIPPER

In 1962 while researching his (1965) book: Jack the Ripper In Fact and Fiction, author Robin Odell, received a number of letters from a gentleman in Blackpool, Lancashire. The man made the claim that his father, who was born in Dundee in 1873, was Jack the Ripper. His father would have been 15 years of age, when the murders commenced. He stated that the man worked as an apprentice to an engineer's wood pattern maker, and was described by his son as an honest, kind and gentle fellow. His motive for the crimes was revenge against prostitutes, because his master, a journeyman tradesman in his early thirties, had died at the London hospital in 1889 after contracting a venereal disease. The murder weapon he used was a Swedish lock knife.

436

WILLIAM THICK

Sergeant William Thick was accused of being Jack the Ripper by a member of the public, Mr H.T Haslewood, a law clerk, who wrote to the police on the 10 September 1889 saying: "That he had very good grounds to believe that, the person who committed the Whitechapel murders was a member of the police force, and whose name he would forward." Haslewood admitted that his suspicion was based on very slight evidence, "but with the help of the police records could ascertain where this person was on the respective days of the murders." Haslewood wrote to the police again a few days later, this time naming his suspect as Sergeant T. Thicke, misspelling Thick's name. He stated that: "Thicke should be watched, and his whereabouts ascertained upon other dates where certain woman have met their end." Written in the margin of the letter was the official police response to the accusation, "I think it is plainly rubbish, perhaps prompted by spite."

William Thick was born in Salisbury, Wiltshire, on 20 November 1845. His parents, Charles Thick and Mary (née Shepperd) had married in 1841. The family home for the first 10 years of young William's life was Bowerchalke Dorset, a far cry from the streets of Whitechapel. At the age of 14, he gained employment as a Carter at West Chase Farm. He left for London at the age of 23 and joined the police force in 1868 (warrant no. 49889) and was appointed to H-division, Whitechapel. According to Walter Dew, he earned the nickname "Johnny Upright," due to his uprightness, both in his walk and his methods. He was described as 5 ft 8 inches tall, stout-built, with dark hair and a heavy drooping yellowish moustache. The press at the time commented on his striking checked suits and went on to describe him as a smart officer. F. P Wensley, ex-Chief Constable CID, described Thick as,

"One of the finest policemen he had ever known." On 4 November 1872, he married Hannah Ellison. In the 1881 census, he is living at 19 Nottingham Place, Mile End Old Town. In the 1891 census, he is living at 81 Demsey Street. Thick retired from the police force in 1893. His most prominent action during the Ripper investigation was the arrest of John Pizer (Leather Apron). In the 1901 census, he is still living at 81, Dempsey Street, Mile End Old Town, employed as a Railway Police Inspector. In 1902 he showed Jack London around the East End when the writer was researching his (1903) book: The People of the Abyss. He died 7 December 1930 at the age of 85.

CHARLES THOMAS

On 12 November 1888, Charles Thomas a 51-year old labourer was charged at Clerkenwell Police-court with being drunk and disorderly. The incident happened in Crowndale-Road, St. Pancras early on Sunday morning. Police constable 550 Y said the prisoner was surrounded by a crowd of onlookers and kept shouting out, "I'm Jack the Ripper." In his defence Thomas simply said he was "sorry", he was sentenced to 14 days hard labour and was told that any man brought before the court for shouting in the street that they were the Whitechapel murderer would go to prison without the option of a fine.

DR. WILLIAM EVAN THOMAS

Dr. William Evan Thomas was born in Llanfairpwllgwyngyll, on the Isle of Anglesey in North Wales in 1855, and was baptised on the 7 December 1855. The son of local pharmacist and postmaster, in Aberffraw, Anglesey, Wales. Henry Parry Thomas, (1831-1914) and his wife Ann (née Evans). His parents married 1 September 1855. He had one brother, John Henry, born 1864. And a sister Ellin Eliza, born 1858. Thomas had a surgery at 190 Green

Street, Victoria Park, a distance of three-quarters of a mile from Whitechapel. According to local oral tradition in Anglesey, Thomas, suffered a nervous breakdown, and returned home on 11 June, 1889, He slept that night with his father, who thought it advisable to watch him. While his father was distracted in the shop talking, his son was seen going behind the counter with his pipe in his hand. After taking something from a drawer, he left. His father followed him in a few minutes, and failing to find his son downstairs, he went into his bedroom, he found him lying on the bed dead. He had taken an ounce bottle of prussic acid from the shop, and had swallowed about half its contents. At the inquest, a verdict of suicide during temporary insanity was recorded. His suicide occurred (7 months after the last Ripper murder), he was 33 years of age. He left in his will effects to the value of £228. Thomas fits the criteria for those theorists seeking a suspect with the requisite medical knowledge and whose suicide, coincided with the cessation of the murders.

FRANCIS THOMPSON

An English poet, and ascetic (An ascetic person has a way of life that is characterised by rigorous self-denial or self-discipline; usually because of their religious beliefs). Thompson was first suggested as the Ripper by Richard Patterson in the (1998) book: Paradox, and more recently in works by the same author, Francis Thompson & the Ripper Paradox, (2014), and Jack the Ripper The Works of Francis Thompson, (2017).

Thompson was born at 7 Winckley Street, in Preston, Lancashire, on 16 December 1859 to a respectable Catholic family. His father, Dr Charles Thompson was a homeopathic doctor. His Mother Mary was a governess, who had previously failed in her attempt to become a nun, she died at the age of 58 on 19 December 1880 from a liver complaint. Francis Thompson was named after

St Francis of Assisi. The family moved to Manchester in 1864, shortly after the death of his sister, Helen, at the age of 15 months of consumption. Thompson, as a young man, was described as "shy, untidy, unpunctual and unobservant." He entered the Catholic school of St Cuthbert's, Ushaw College in Durham, where he excelled in Latin, English and Greek. Taking an interest in poetry from an early age, his writing ability was described by the English master as the best production from a lad of his age. In 1877 he failed his studies for the priesthood. His teacher, Father Tate, wrote to Thompson's father telling him:

With regard to Frank, I have been most reluctantly compelled to concur in the opinion of his director and others that it is not the holy will of God that he should go on to the priesthood.

On the advice of his father, he spent the next six years studying to be a surgeon at Owen's medical college, but he was to fail the medical examinations three times. In 1878 he entered his name on the register of the Manchester Royal Infirmary, where he studied anatomy. He continued writing poetry, and in April 1888 had one of his poems The Passion of Mary published in Merry England, a minor Catholic literary magazine. The editor Wilfred Meynell, had been trying to trace the unknown author who had submitted the work a year earlier. Recognising Thompson's brilliance, Meynell and his wife offered him a home. It was around this time, 1879 that he became addicted to opium, after being treated with laudanum for a serious lung infection. Laudanum was prescribed as a painkiller and sedative, it was also a popular method of suicide. From 1885-88 Thompson spent the majority of his time as a homeless vagrant in the Dockland area of London, and claimed to have fallen in love with a prostitute, who took him in and cared for him. She encouraged him to continue writing. Much of his later work recognises his gratitude for her kindness.

Her name is unknown. He died at the age of 47 on 13 November 1907, of tuberculosis when his reputation as a poet was at its height. His most famous poem, "The Hound of Heaven" which described the pursuit of a human soul by God, was to sell over 50,000 copies. When he died, he weighed only 70 pounds (5 stone). He was buried in Kensal Green cemetery. He was described as of medium height with a slight build, which made him appear taller, sunken cheeks, dark brown hair, which appeared almost black, with a small grey beard, wearing frayed clothing and a great Ulster coat and necktie. There is no record Thompson was suspected at the time of the Ripper murders.

DR. LEONARD BOOKER THORNTON

Michael Thornton, after watching a channel 5 documentary on Jack the Ripper, became convinced his grandfather, Leonard Booker Thornton was Jack the Ripper. He told the story to the Daily Mail 26 December 2006.

Leonard Booker Thornton (Len to his friends) was born on 24 September 1859, at 24 London Terrace, Bethnal Green. London. The son of Mary and Tomas Thornton a well-to-do master linen draper, who owned several shops. When he learnt his son did not want to follow him into the family business, but plan to study medicine instead, he told him he must earn the money to pay for his own tuition. At 18 years of age, Len went to work for a local blacksmith, transporting sick, elderly and lame horses, to the slaughterhouses in Whitechapel, where he learned how to dismember the carcases. He studied anatomy at the London Hospital in Whitechapel Road, where he performed amputations and other surgical procedures. Qualified chemist and druggist. On 26 July 1885, he married Hannah O'Sullivan, an Irish Catholic. The marriage was not without tension, with Hannah being Catholic and Leonard atheist. Their first child Mabel was born in

1886, but was to remain sickly throughout her life; she died at the age of 23, unmarried. It was during the pregnancy of their second child, Reginald Leonard Thornton, Michael's father, that Len began coming home in the middle of the night with bloodstained clothing, which he explained away as a consequence of his hospital work. Len was 29 years of age at the time of the Whitechapel murders, 5 ft. 7 inches tall, with a small carroty moustache. Doreen Gillham, Michael's half-sister, told him that Len was a man who had secrets. "A dark side to his life." She told how, after the murder of Mary Jane Kelly, he was briefly arrested, and questioned, then followed by plain clothes officers. In the 1881 census, he is in occupation as a manufacturing druggist, living at 401 Cold Harbour Lane, Lambeth. In the 1901 census, he is 41 years of age, in occupation as a chemist & sub-postmaster. Living in Landor Road, Stockwell. In the 1911 census, he is 52 years of age in occupation as a chemist and druggist pharmacist. Living at 113-15 London Road Stockwell. His wife Hannah died 21 March 1932 at the age of 72. When Len developed cancer and was nursed by Michael's half-sister, he said to her, "Thank you for looking after me, but if you knew what I have done in my life; you would not even come near me." There is no evidence to the claim, he was arrested and questioned, about the Ripper murders. He died on 23 September 1935 at the age of 75. He left effects in his will to the value of £3997. 3s.8d.

DR. NIGEL TORME

In an article in the publication Weekly World News 1 August 2000, workers tearing down an old bakery in London have discovered the mummified remains of Jack the Ripper. The body which was found in a secret chamber beneath the bakery has been identified as that of Dr Nigel Torme. Found alongside the body was bloody surgical knives, a small phial of poison, and two unidentified women, who had been stabbed and dissected. The building was once the home of Dr Nigel Torme, who had lived there in the late 1800s. The doctor withdrew from society and disappeared in 1900. French criminologist and Ripper expert, Dr Jeanne Benot, stated "The women in the cellar were killed in exactly the same vicious way as the Ripper victims in 1888." Benot also claimed the overcoat he was wearing matched perfectly a piece of material found at the murder scene. The wearing of the coat in the bakery heat Benot believes was his way of confessing to his crimes, knowing the coat would be matched by the authorities to the cloth fragment. A relevant search of the records has revealed no person named Dr Nigel Torme. This suspect appears to be a variation of the 1 April 1985 Daily Express skeleton found in the pub cellar story.

TOM TOTSON

A letter was sent from 1 Wood View terrace in Bradford, York, to the City Police in London claiming that a game of "Spirit tapping" had revealed the Ripper was about to strike and the police should concentrate on 20 Wurt Street WC (Whitechapel).The letter, and signature were illegible in part.

This evening some of my children were experimenting with the table, to see if it would rap a sound people affirm it does under certain conditions-- It rapped out "more more murders tonight in London"-- and in reply to our questions it said that another woman wd__be Killed by the same man, whose name it is said is Tom Totson, 30, Wurt-St. W.C. and that we must send you a Telegram as at foot kind must write you as above. Whether there be such a street or such a person I do not know; but partly from a motive of curiosity and partly to relieve myself of what might for anything I know to the contrary, be a heavy responsibility, I have done as I was told. If there is no such street please drop me a

443

line, but unless the above information is of value in tracing the offender, do not. In [crossed out] allow anything of this to be known past yourself. I could have passed it over as a thing of no account but for thinking that there may be [underlined] "From things in heaven and earth than are dreamt of in our philosophy"

Tom Totson was unable to be traced, the address 20 Wurt Street, does not exist, in London. The letter writer B Baraclough, is credited as living in York. However, there is no Wood View terrace in York. Wood View terrace is in Bradford, his correct address therefore is 1 Wood View Terrace, Bradford, Yorkshire.

EMIL TOTTERMAN

In December 1903 Emil Totterman, a Finnish sailor, was arrested at the Sailors Union boarding house at 37 South Street and charged with the murder of prostitute Sarah Martin. The murder occurred on 20 December 1903, at Kelly's Hotel in Walker Street, New York, a stone's throw from where an elderly prostitute and tenuously linked possible Ripper victim named Carrie Brown had been murdered thirteen years earlier. Sarah Martin's body had been mutilated, the injuries comprising of two deep wounds to her throat, a gash three inches deep, extending from armpit to armpit, a large vertical wound in her abdomen and minor mutilations targeting the genitalia. This led to the inevitable newspaper speculation that Totterman, who also used the alias "Carl Nielsen" was Jack the Ripper. The headline of the New York Times 22 December 1903, proclaimed: "Police Say They Have Ripper Murderer." Despite the newspapers proclaiming his execution, Totterman was spared the death sentence, on account of his heroic efforts during the Spanish-American War, where he received three medals for bravery and was considered a war hero. Sentenced instead to life imprisonment, he escaped from Sing Sing prison 20 August 1916 and remained on the run for eight months. Recaptured 24 April 1917 he was released 24 December 1929 and returned to Finland the following year. Totterman at the time of his arrest stated he was 41 years of age, though, was believed to have been 35-years old when he was arrested in 1903. The official court and police records state his age as 29 years in 1904. Totterman was born in 1875 in Finland, which would make him 13 years of age at the time of the Ripper murders and 16 years of age at the time of the Carrie Brown murder.

FRANCIS TUMBLETY

Tumblety was named as the Ripper by Stewart Evans and Paul Gainey in the (1995) book: The Lodger the Arrest and Escape of Jack the Ripper, after the discovery of the Littlechild Letter in February 1993 by Stewart Evans. The letter was dated 23 September 1913 and was written by Inspector John George Littlechild to the journalist George Sims. Littlechild was the head of Special Branch from 1883-93. In his letter Littlechild recounts his suspicion of a doctor; the relevant extract of the letter is as follows:

I never heard of a Dr D in connection with the Whitechapel murders, but amongst the suspects, and to my mind, a very likely one was a Dr T which sounds much like a "D." He was an American quack named Tumblety and was at one time a frequent visitor to London, and on those occasions constantly brought under the notice of the police, there being a large dossier on him at Scotland Yard. Although a sycopathia sexualis subject, he was not known as a sadist, which the murderer unquestionably was, but his feelings towards women were remarkable and bitter in the extreme, a fact on record. Tumblety was arrested at the time of the murders in connection with unnatural offences and charged at Marlborough Street, remanded on bail, and got away to

Boulogne. He shortly left Boulogne and was never heard of afterwards. It was believed he committed suicide, but certain it is, from that time the Ripper murders came to an end.

Francis Tumblety was born in Canada in 1833, though, was of Irish descent, to James and Margaret Tumblety, the youngest of eleven children, his family moved to Rochester, New York, when he was a child. As a teenager, he sold books; one former Rochester neighbour claims pornographic books, to the canal boat owners between Rochester and Buffalo. He left Rochester at the age of 17 and returned 10 years later claiming to be a great physician. He became rich, setting himself up as a quack doctor selling potions such as "Tumblety's Pimple Destroyer" and became known as the "Prince of Quacks." He is known to have attempted at least one crude abortion on a prostitute, Philomene Dumas. Tumblety was arrested on 23 September 1857, but after some legal haggling, was released on 1 October. No trial was ever undertaken. He was practising medicine in Toronto in 1860, claiming to cure all diseases. The death of James Portmore, a man he was treating for kidney disease, soon caused him to flee. In 1865, using the name J.H. Blackburn, he was accused of being involved in the assassination of President Abraham Lincoln and was imprisoned for three weeks, but it appeared to be simply a case of mistaken identity, and he was soon cleared. He wrote a short pamphlet about his ordeal The Kidnapping of Dr Tumblety. He next moved to Washington, D.C., and it is claimed once gave an all-male dinner party, where he lectured his guests on the evils of women, and proudly displayed his extensive collection of anatomical specimens, including the wombs of every class of women which he kept preserved in glass jars, the contents, filling every shelf. Tumblety was a flamboyant figure, and shameless self-publicist, who had by this time taken to riding around on a white horse, accompanied by a pair of greyhounds, wearing elaborate uniforms, complete with rows of medals. In 1874 Tumblety was in Liverpool, England, and began a stormy homosexual relationship with the writer, 21-year old Henry Hall Caine which continued till 1876. His landlady in New Orleans said that Tumblety, "Received a great many visits from young men between the ages of 16-20 years, with whom he appeared very intimate, some of them remained with him all night." In 1888 just prior to the start of the Ripper murders, he allegedly took lodgings at 22 Batty Street, these lodgings were said to have been watched by officers from Scotland Yard because Tumblety was suspected to have had strong Fenian sympathies. His landlady gave the police a blood-soaked shirt, which she had found in his room, and Tumblety became a prime Ripper suspect, though the police felt they did not have enough evidence to arrest him. On the 7 November 1888 two days before the murder of Mary Kelly, he was arrested and charged with four counts of gross indecency and indecent assault with force against four men, Albert Fisher on the 27 July 1888, Arthur Brice on 31 August, James Crowley on 14 October and John Doughty on 2 November. Due to appear at the Old Bailey on 20 November, Tumblety hearing that his trial was postponed to 10 December, jumped bail, on 24 November 1888 and using the alias Frank Townsend, fled, first to Boulogne, France, then to New York, arriving on 3 December on the steamship La Bretagne hotly pursued by Inspector Andrews. Upon arrival in America, Tumblety who was living at the home of a Mrs McNamara 79 East Tenth Street, was kept under surveillance by the New York City police department, probably on account of the newspapers mentioning that Tumblety was wanted in connection with the Whitechapel murders. Tumblety gave Andrews and the New York Police the slip. Tumblety briefly appeared again in 1890 in Washington, D.C., when he was arrested on a charge of being a suspicious character for loitering in the shadows. When searched he was found to have several thousand dollars' worth of valuables on him. Tumblety lived for the last ten years of his life with his sister in Rochester, New York. He died in St John's hospital St Louis, Missouri, on 28 May 1903 at the age of 73 under the assumed name of Dr Townsend. He left an estate worth in excess of $150,000.Tumblety in 1888, was 55 years of age, over 6 ft tall, with broad shoulders, black hair tinged with grey, and a large dyed black moustache, waxed at the ends. Tumblety was almost certainly homosexual, and there is no evidence, as some authors have claimed, that he was bisexual, his companions throughout his life were young males. There is also no reference to him ever consorting with female prostitutes, nor any evidence of him showing violence toward women. There is an unsubstantiated story that as a young man Tumblety met and fell in love with a woman some years his senior, they quickly married, but the marriage ended when he learnt his wife had been in the habit of going with other men, and in fact was a prostitute. It was said at this point Tumblety gave up on all womankind. Littlechild, in his letter at no point, stated for a fact that Tumblety was Jack the Ripper, only that he was a likely suspect. He was also incorrect when he stated that Tumblety was never heard of again after he left Boulogne. We know he was followed to New York and was watched by the New York police department.

JOHN TYSON

On 7 December 1888, John Tyson, a champion boxer, was charged, with stealing a pair of boots from the shop of Rosa Gertrude Hammond, a Bootmaker, of High-street, Tooting. Tyson was seen walking away with the boots under his arm. A constable followed and arrested him. He was very violent, and said he was "Jack the Ripper," and threatened to kill the constable when he

448

came out of prison. When asked by the magistrate, what employment, he followed, he said he was a hard-working man. He added that he was the champion fighter of the world for some years. He was told that he would find that stealing was not so lucrative, and was sentenced to seven days imprisonment with hard labour.

UNIDENTIFIED SKELETON

The Daily Express 1 April 1985 ran an article under the headline:

PUB SKELETON COULD BE JACK THE RIPPER

It was reported that, in the bricked up cellar of the Old Bull and Bush public house in North End road, Hampstead, a skeleton has been found by a builder renovating the cellar. Remnants of clothing still attached to the remains suggest that the individual had been a toff.

The article went on to say:

Rusting surgical knives, found alongside the skeleton, suggest at his likely profession. It was believed that the man was hiding in the cellar when he was overcome by the lack of ventilation and was entombed when building work commenced to seal off the cellar. The skeleton was examined and was said to have belonged to a right-handed man, about 30-35 years of age and 5 ft 10 inches tall.

Any actual credibility to this story ends with the date of the newspaper article, 1 April (April fool's Day).

UNKNOWN

Despite hundreds of suspects since 1888, having the finger of suspicion pointed towards them, there remains every possibility that 130 years later, the person who came to be known as Jack

449

the Ripper has still not been brought to our attention and is completely unknown to us. A man whose name may now, in fact, never be known.

NICHOLAS VAN BURST

Van Burst, a Dutchman, was a resident of Bacon's Hotel in Fitzroy Square. He was arrested after accosting several women at Kings Cross railway station on the night of 25 November 1888. He briefly came under suspicion of being the Ripper, but was satisfactorily able to account for his movements on the nights in question, and was subsequently released. Van Burst was described as 50-years old, 5 ft 11 inches tall, with dark hair and a moustache. He was said to have been respectable in appearance.

VINCENT VAN GOGH

The artist's painting "Irises" supposedly contains concealed images of the face and body of Ripper victim Mary Jane Kelly, Dale Larner argued in the possibly forthcoming, non-forthcoming, (2018) book: "Vincent Alias Jack." He also alleges Van Gogh's handwriting matched a Ripper letter from 19 July, 1889. And the lull in the sending of the Ripper letters, 23 December 1888, to 7 January 1889, can be explained by Van Gogh been in the hospital having cut his own ear off. The author also claims Van Gogh was in London when the Ripper murders occurred. The book failed to reach its crowdfunded target of $8.000, with only $544 pledged, and appears to have been cancelled.

Considered the greatest Dutch painter after Rembrandt, Van Gogh was born 30 March, 1853, in Groot-Zundert, Netherlands. His father, Reverend Theodorus van Gogh, was a Protestant pastor. His mother was Anna Cornelia Carbentus. At age 16 Vincent started to work for the art dealer Goupil & Co, in The

Hague. Taking little interest in his work, he was dismissed from his job at the beginning of 1876. Following in his father's footsteps, he became a Protestant minister. In 1879 he took up a post as a missionary at Petit-Wasmes, in Borinage in Belgium. He was dismissed for "undermining the dignity of the priesthood" when he showed support for his impoverished congregation by sleeping in a small hut on straw. His brother Theo, a hugely influential figure in his life convinced van Gogh that if he wanted to make an impression on the world he should become an artist. He received lifelong financial, and emotional support from his brother. This friendship is amply documented in a vast amount of letters they sent each other. He studied in Brussels and Paris, and was influenced by the new impressionist painters: Monet, and Renoir. He adopted brighter, more vibrant colours and began experimenting with his technique. His artistic career was extremely short, lasting only from 1880 to 1890. During the first four years of this period, while acquiring technical proficiency, he confined himself almost entirely to drawings and watercolours. In 1888, he rented and decorated a house in Arles, with the intention of persuading Gauguin, Toulouse-Lautrec, and others whom he believed had similar aims, to join him. Gauguin arrived in October 1888, their relations rapidly deteriorated, because they had opposing ideas and were temperamentally incompatible. On Christmas Eve, 1888, van Gogh exhausted, and showing signs of mental instability, snapped. He argued with Gauguin and, reportedly, chased him with a razor and cut off the lower half of his own left ear, which it is rumoured, he then offered it to a prostitute as a gift. It is speculated that it was actually Gauguin who mutilated van Gogh's ear and that he did so with a sword. A story in circulation suggests that Van Gogh, took a blade to his ear after reading reports in Le Figaro about Jack the Ripper slicing off one of Catherine Eddowes' ears. Gogh, however, took responsibility for the event and was hospitalized. Van Gogh returned home two weeks later, and resumed painting, shortly after he once again was showing symptoms of mental disturbance and was sent back to the hospital. At the end of April 1889, fearing for his sanity, he asked to be temporarily shut up in the asylum at Saint-Rémy-de-Provence. Van Gogh stayed there for 12 months. It was in the asylum that he painted "Starry Night" which became his most popular work. The last two years of his life where his most prolific as a painter. Creating nearly one painting per day. Despite his creative achievements, the artist thought of his life as terribly wasted. He wrote to his brother:

I feel-a failure. That's it as far as I'm concerned-I feel that this is the destiny that I accept, that will never change.

In despair of ever being able to overcome his loneliness or be cured, he killed himself by shooting himself in the stomach, He did not die immediately. When found wounded in his bed, he allegedly said, "I shot myself. I only hope I haven't botched it." That evening, when interrogated by the police, van Gogh refused to answer questions, saying, "What I have done is nobody else's business. I am free to do what I like with my own body." He died two days later, 29 July, 1890, at the age of 37. His brother Theo unable to come to terms with his brother's death died 6 months later and was buried next to him. The name of Van Gogh was virtually unknown when he killed himself. Of the more than 800 oil paintings and 700 drawings that constitute his life's work, he sold only one in his lifetime. They include landscapes, still-life, portraits and self-portraits. Van Gogh has been mythologized in the popular imagination as the quintessential tortured artist. His art became popular after his death, in the late 20th century, his work sold for record-breaking sums at auctions around the world

The Van Gogh Museum in Amsterdam is dedicated to Van Gogh's work and that of his contemporaries.

HENRY VANN

In November 1888, in Neath, Port Talbot, Wales, a man described as of exceedingly rough exterior, appeared at the Falcon Inn, Old Market-street, and claimed to be "Jack the Ripper". It is stated he was brandishing a glittering weapon, and threatened to cut up a woman know as "Nancy Bull". A struggle ensured when a man named William Perrin attempted to seize the man. PC Vincent, arrived and took the man into custody. A large and excited crowd followed, many of whom expressed a desire to lynch the suspect. At the police-station the man gave his name as Henry Vann, of no fixed place of abode. When searched no weapon was found in his possession.

VANZETTI'S SUSPECT

On the evening of 18 October 1887 Mr P. Jose Vanzetti, an Italian, was standing with his wife and children on the harbour at Genoa, awaiting the arrival of the ship the Savoye, which was to take them to Brazil. While his wife and children wandered around the quay, Vanzetti idly passing time began to listen to two men that he could overhear talking, one spoke, Vanzetti believed possibly with an English accent, and the second, with a bad Italian accent. They said:

I have accompanied you this far. I have been to India and have done all that you wished, and have had more than enough of it already. I do not wish now to run my head against the English police, for believing me; London is not like India, as you know even better than I do. When you have ripped up two or three women, there will be the devil of a row and who knows how it will end.

453

Vanzetti said he was suddenly gripped by a strong curiosity to see what the men looked like. He went on to describe their appearance as, "When seen once, would remain impressed for a lifetime." He said the man, who spoke Italian, was short of stature, thin, very pale with a low forehead, small black eyes with black hair and moustache. He wore a long dark frock coat and a black glazed hat. The second man, who spoke with an English accent, was rather tall, large boned and stout with a high forehead, bushy eyebrows, prominent cheekbones and a large nose. He had no moustache, but whiskers of a light brown colour and two eyes, which, when half closed, seemed to "flash fire." He wore a long dark grey overcoat and a hard hat. Vanzetti claimed his first thought was to go to the nearest police station, but this action would result in trouble, and delay his sailing. He continued on his journey and went to Brazil, and forgot the matter completely, and was only reminded of it when he read of the Whitechapel murders in the newspapers. Vanzetti waited almost two years before contacting the authorities with his story. Vanzetti was described as a person who could be relied upon and gave lessons in Italian and gymnastics in the neighbourhood of Sao Paulo. It is not known what action, if any, was taken, though Inspector Donald Swanson appeared to think the story was too vague and too much time, over 2 years had elapsed since the mysterious strangers were seen on the quay in Genoa.

NICOLAI VASSILI

Born in Tiraspol in the province of Cherson, Ukraine in 1847, Nicolai Vassili, Wassili or Nicolai Vasilyeff, as the British press referred to him at the time, was educated in Tiraspol and at Odessa University. He inherited sufficient income for him to support himself without the need to work. As a young man, he joined one of the many fanatical sects which lay outside the

Russian Orthodox Church, the Skoptsy, referred to as "The Shorn" in English language newspapers. The Shorn condemned all sexual relations, even within marriage, as impure. The Russian church's attempts to suppress the sect resulted in Wassili going into exile in Paris, where he took lodgings in the Rue Moufetarde. In the daytime, he would toil away amongst piles of religious books, and at night would wander the streets calling on prostitutes to repent and join the Skoptsy. It was in 1872 that he met and fell in love with a young prostitute called Madeline, whom he had tried to reform. When he called on her, he was told she had fled, but left him a note which read:

I thank you a thousand times for all your kindness. I respect but cannot love you. I am grateful, but why should I sacrifice all my life to my gratitude? That which brought us together separates us. You have saved me, but you ought not to ask me as a reward. I cannot reconcile your roles of gutter preacher and lover. Forgive me and forget me!

It was her rejection of him, which contributed to his mental breakdown, and the start of a killing spree which left Madeline and four prostitutes dead within two weeks. All were stabbed in the back and mutilated. He was arrested after a streetwalker he had attempted to kill shrieked out his name to the police. He was committed to an asylum in Bayonne and was released as cured on 1 January 1888, whereupon he declared his intention to go to London. The press, noticing the similarities with the Whitechapel murders, quickly theorised that Wassili may have been Jack the Ripper. There is, however, no evidence Wassili ever existed. There are no records of his arrest or committal to an asylum. There is also no evidence to confirm that a series of murders actually occurred in Paris. The only crimes which bore any similarity to the Whitechapel murders happened in 1875 in the district of Rochechouart, when five or six women were assaulted, though none were murdered. The reports of his supposed murders in Paris are from European newspapers that often garbled their account of events, and very often resorted to copying each other without accurately checking their facts. Wassili in accounts was described as tall, lean, with broad shoulders strong, with a brawny form, burning black eyes and a pale waxy complexion.

WILLIAM WADDELL

On the morning of Sunday 23 September 1888 in Birtley Fell, a small Northern mining village in County Durham. John Fish, a fitter at Ouston Colliery, was on his way to work at Eighton Banks, at around 7:20 a.m. when, at a point known as Sandy Cut, he discovered the body of a young woman near a railway line. Her clothing was ruffled and there was blood on her underclothing and right cheek. Fish, who claimed he knew instantly the woman was dead, ran to fetch local constable John Dodds. The constable after a brief examination of the body and a quick inspection of the area for clues recognised the victim as a local woman, Jane Beardmore, more commonly known in the district as Jane Savage, (her stepfather's surname). She was popular, 27 years of age, 5 ft tall, quite stout, and in poor health due to a heart condition. She lived at the White House Cottage with her mother, stepfather and half-brother. She had been visiting the Gateshead Dispensary, where she had received medicine from time to time. When the body was examined it was discovered she had sustained horrific injuries, they were deep wounds on each cheek, her throat had been cut and she had received wounds to her breasts and abdomen, her intestines were protruding. Money found in her pockets clearly showed robbery was not the motive for the crime. Due to the mutilations, the press immediately speculated that the murder was committed by Jack the Ripper, whom it was feared had ventured north. Inspector Thomas Roots and Dr George Bagster Phillips (who had performed the post-mortem on the second Ripper victim Annie Chapman), travelled to the North of England to investigate. The police quickly satisfied themselves that the murder was not linked to the murders in Whitechapel, and was, in fact, "a local affair." Dr Phillips gave his opinion that it had been a "clumsy piece of butchery" and the abdominal mutilation was carried out more as an afterthought, to make the killing resemble the work of Jack the Ripper. A young local man William Waddell, a Gateshead factory worker and labourer quickly came under suspicion, as he had recently been Jane's lover until she had ended the relationship. Waddell matched the description of a man described as about 5 ft 9 inches tall, seen by the miner, James Gilmore, arguing with a short, stout woman at around 9:00 pm on the night of the murder. Waddell caused further suspicion to fall upon him when he fled the district. Two days after the murder, he traded in his clothes, which appeared to be bloodstained, at a clothing broker in exchange for clothes of a lesser value. It was nearly a week before Waddell now christened the "Birtley Ripper" was apprehended. Found guilty and hanged at Durham prison on Wednesday, 19 December 1888 by hangman James Berry. This is an extract from the letter Waddell wrote to his brother:

Dear Brother, you must not trouble yourself too much about me, as it may be for the best. The Lord knows what is best for us, so I will leave it all in His hands, for I am happy to tell you that I have made my peace with God, and if I die I know I am going to a better place, where no sorrow ever comes, and I hope to meet you all there by-and-by, for I can trust all to the Lord now, and He will hold me up. Dear Brother, I must tell you that I am very happy now since that I gave my heart to God, and found in Him a

Saviour, for the Lord is my Shepherd, I shall not want. I shall not be afraid to die and leave this unhappy world, as it is nothing but a world of sin and sorrow, and there is nothing good in it.

Waddell had received the last visit in his cell from his brother and sister and had put his affairs in order. The following day when the Dean asked him if he would like to confess, he replied in the affirmative. In answer to the Dean, Waddell, with an affecting display of emotion, said: "Yes, sir, I did it." After a pause, the Dean remarked, "Whatever could have possessed you to commit such a crime?" Waddle in reply attributed the crime to his having been so drunk as to having entirely lost his mind. He also stated "That he had been reading the accounts of the Whitechapel murders in London, and his mind must have been deranged."Waddell was described by the newspapers As a sullen, morose individual, 22 years of age, 5 ft 9 or 10 inches tall, with brown hair, small and sunken blue eyes, a very bad walker, has tender feet, walks with his toes out and leans well forward. It was said that he was far stronger than he appeared.

Jane Beardmore was born in Walker, Northumberland, in 1861, to Thomas Beardmore, and Isabella (née Jobling). Her surname was variously described as Beetmore, Beadmore, Boatmoor and Beedmore in contemporary newspaper accounts.

WALTER

In the (2010) book: Jack the Ripper's Secret Confession, David Monaghan, and Nigel Cawthorne, suggest a new suspect for Jack the Ripper, "Walter" the writer of the book: My Secret Life. They claim the following points to Walter as Jack the Ripper

• Walter details his tactics of giving bonnets as sexual inducements. Mary Ann Nichols was found with an unexplained bonnet.

458

• Walter's privately printed sex memoir, My Secret Life is dated 1888, the year of the Ripper killings.

• Walter uses "low whores" in East London during bouts of poverty. He hates himself for doing so.

• Walter is a violent sexual sadist.

• Walter knows Whitechapel. He had based himself at the Gunmaker's Proof House in Commercial Road, Aldgate for stalking women and voyeurism. This is within a four-minute escape radius of all Whitechapel murder sites.

• Walter uses knives for sex purposes, carrying blades to make peep-holes.

The book was published between 1888 and 1894 and consisted of eleven volumes, and over 4,000 pages. The highly disorganised text is the memoir of a gentleman's erotic sexual experience. Billed as a classic of Victorian pornography, the book was never meant for general distribution. Publication of the book was repeatedly banned over the years. The author of the book identifies himself only as Walter. The true identity of whom Walter actually was is unknown, several names have been suggested, and the most popular candidate is the writer, book collector and authority on erotic literature, Henry Spencer Ashbee.

Ashbee was born 21 April 1834 in Southwark, London, to Robert and Frances Elizabeth (née Spencer). Prosperous and respectable he was fluent in Greek, Latin, Spanish and several other modern languages. He travelled extensively throughout his life. In 1862 he married Elizabeth Jenny Lavi daughter of a wealthy Hamburg merchant in Hamburg Germany. Ashbee was part of a loose collective of writers and intellectuals who discussed and wrote about sexual matters frankly. This fraternity included Richard Francis Burton, Richard Monckton Milnes, Algernon Charles Swinburne, and others. He bequeathed to the British Museum antiquities, prints and drawings, and his entire library, running to thousands of volumes, including the world's largest collection of *Don Quixote* manuscripts and the largest collection of Cervantes literature outside of Spain. It was bequeathed on one condition, they also accept his extensive collection of private, erotic literature. They accepted. It is speculated the trustees exploited a loophole to destroy some of the more offensive matter, which is of "no value or interest" including cheaply produced Victorian erotica. He separated from Elizabeth in 1893. He died 29 July 1900, at the age of 67, in Hawkhurst Kent.

WILLIAM HUMBLE WARD

Proposed as a co-conspirator, in the (2006) book Epiphany of The Whitechapel Murders, by Karen Trenouth

Born in London 25 May 1867, Son of William Ward, First Earl of Dudley, and Georgina Elizabeth, (née Moncreiffe), daughter of Sir Thomas Moncreiff, seventh Baronet. His mother was described "As one of the great beauties of her generation." Educated at Eton; he inherited great wealth and the Earldom upon the death of his father in 1885. Described as tall and handsome, though slightly lame from a childhood accident. In 1891 he married Rachel Anne Gurney, born 1867, daughter of Charles Henry Gurney and Alice Prinsep. Intelligent and forceful, though with a reserved even absent manner, she was described as "Beautiful as a marble statue." They had seven children, four sons, William Humble Eric, Roderick John, and twins George Reginald and Edward Frederick, and three daughters. Lady Dudley drowned 26 June 1920, at the age of 51, while sea-bathing in Ireland. Lord Dudley married the musical comedy actress Gertie Millar, 30 April

1924. Mayor of Dudley (1895-96). Conservative politician. Secretary to the Board of Trade (1895-1902). And an extravagant and controversial Lord Lieutenant of Ireland (1902-05). Governor-General of Australia (1908-11). With the Liberals still in power, he held no further public office. During World War 1 Dudley commanded a Yeomanry unit in Egypt and Gallipoli. He died of cancer in London on 29 June 1932 at the age of 65. He was succeeded by his eldest son William. The former Australian Prime Minister Alfred Deakin wrote about him:

His ambition was high, but his interests were short lived... He did nothing really important, nothing thoroughly, nothing consistently … He remained … a very ineffective and not very popular figurehead.

JOHN PETER WATSON

In December 1888, in Cupar, Fife, Scotland. John Peter Watson, a boy of 13 or 14 years, was charged with writing a number of threatening letters to farmer David Edie. In the letters he threatened to murder him and his family. It is also alleged, he sent similar letters to the Reverend. Douglas Arbroath. Edie was so alarmed, he had a policeman watch his home for a considerable time. The letters were signed "Jack the Ripper" and "Catch Me if you can."

JAMES WATT

On 3 December, 1888, a farm labourer, employed at Ormiston Farm, Colinton, named James Watt, pleaded not guilty to a charge at Edinburgh City Police Court, of behaving in a disorderly manner, by brandishing a pocket-knife and using threats of violence towards several little girls. He followed and frightened them. He threatened one girl by flourishing a knife, and declaring he was "Jack the Ripper." A man named Russell arrested Watt and handed him over to the police. Watt, said he did not remember anything about the incident because he was drunk. It was stated in evidence he was quite sober. He was fined £2, with the option of 20 days imprisonment. The authorities thanked Mr Russell for his prompt action.

DR WILLIAM WYNN WESTCOTT

Westcott has been mentioned as a Ripper suspect in newspaper articles by theorists who believe the murders were occult sacrifices. The Ripper victims were alleged to have been ritually killed in a churchyard, and then the bodies dumped where they were later discovered. This theory, however, completely contradicts the known medical and police evidence which shows the victims had been killed where they had been found. There is no evidence Westcott was suspected at the time of the murders.

Westcott was born in Leamington, Warwickshire, on 17 December 1848, both his parents died before he was ten-years-old, his father Peter Westcott, was a doctor, who died in 1852. His mother, Elizabeth Mary (née Hill) died in 1857. He was adopted by his uncle, Richard Westcott Martyn, who was a surgeon by profession. Educated at the Queen Elizabeth Grammar School at Kingston-Upon-Thames, London, he studied medicine at University College in London, and qualified as a physician in 1871 and became a partner in his uncle's medical practice in Somerset, in the West Country. Described as "docile, scholarly, industrious, addicted to regalia and histrionics." Westcott became a Freemason, on 24 October 1871, when he joined the Parrett and Axe Lodge # 814 in Crewkerne, and in 1887-88 along with G Samuel Liddle Mathers and Dr. William Robert Woodman, founded a hermetic society, the order of the Golden Dawn, an occult society whose membership would include W.B. Yeats, Aleister Crowley, and briefly, the writer and poet Oscar Wilde.

462

Westcott published an enormous number of works, besides his medical treatises. Many of his writings were in the form of brief handbooks, dealing with such subjects as Alchemy, Astrology, Death, Divination, Numerology, Serpent Myths, Talismans, and Theosophy. In the field of medicine, he published materials on such subjects as alcoholism and suicide. On 18 February 1873 he married Elizabeth Burnett, the couple would have five children, two boys and three girls. He moved to Camden, and in 1881 became coroner for central London, a position he would hold until 1910. He was said to have conducted more than ten thousand inquests during his period as coroner. He was awarded the freedom of the City of London in 1884. In 1896 Westcott was requested by the political authorities to cease his occult activities with the Golden Dawn. The order was said to be achieving notoriety with the press, and it was not seen fit for a coroner of the crown to be made a shame of in such a way. He immediately severed all outward ties with the Order. Tragedy struck in 1906, and 1907, when both of his sons died. In 1918 his second daughter committed suicide. After the death of his daughter, he retired and went to live in Durban, South Africa with his family. His wife died in August 1921, and his daughter died in February 1924. Westcott, died on 30 June 1925, of Bright's disease. In his will he left effects to the value of £10779 18s 3d.

FREDERICK WHITE

Frederick White, aged 42, who described himself as a commission agent, was charged with using threatening language to a young woman named Mary Ann Galling. The woman was entering Moorgate Street railway station on Wednesday evening, when the prisoner, whom she did not know and had never seen before, attempted to strike up a conversation with her. She pointedly declined to have any conversation with him, whereupon he struck at her saying, "I will rip you up, I am Jack the Ripper, if I don't do it now I shall know you again." The woman ran away, whereupon the man proceeded to follow her making an attempt to trip her up. Galling quickly, and rather, fortunately, ran into police Constable Stringer, who apprehended White and took him into custody. In court, White made a rambling statement in answer to the charge and was fined 10s.

MARY ELIZABETH ANN WILLIAMS

In the (2012) book: Jack the Ripper The Hand of a Woman by ex-solicitor John Morris, Dr John Williams, Wife, Mary Elizabeth Ann Hughes, known as "Lizzie" is revealed as Jack the Ripper.

Lizzie was Born 7 February 1850, the daughter of Richard Hughes, a wealthy stockholder of a successful tin company in Swansea, and Anne (née Thomas). Described as a very kind, refined religious person. She was 22 years of age, when she married her husband in 1872 he was 32 years of age. Morris, in his book, believes the case against her is very strong and makes the following claims. That she killed her victims because she could not have children, and ripped out their wombs while in an unhinged state, as her revenge on those who could. That the personal items of Annie Chapman, were laid out at her feet in a feminine manner. That her husband was having an affair with the last Ripper victim, Mary Kelly. That remnants of a cape, skirt, and hat were found in the ashes of Mary Kelly's fireplace, though Kelly had never been seen wearing them. That Lizzie would have easy access to surgical knives, with her husband being a surgeon. That she confessed her crimes to her husband, which caused his early retirement. A letter found among his personal correspondence read: "Thank you for the forgiveness and for keeping my secret." The letter also included the line "you are the centre of my world." The identity of its author has never been

464

proven but has been suggested it was written by Lizzie to her husband. Mrs Williams was never questioned in connection with the murders. Morris claims she suffered a nervous breakdown immediately after carrying out the murders. Two years afterwards she was shown to be living back in Wales with her father while her husband remained in London. She died of cancer in 1915, at the age of 65.

DR JOHN WILLIAMS

In the (2005) book: Uncle Jack, Tony Williams, and co-author Humphrey Price, presented to us an entirely new Ripper suspect in the form of the eminent Victorian doctor Sir John Williams. Tony Williams, a descendant (his nephew) of Sir John, became suspicious of his illustrious ancestor when he chanced upon a handwritten letter held at the National Library of Wales, along with Sir John's personal possessions. A letter by Dr Williams to a person called Morgan, recently credited as Dr Morgan Davis, an alleged Ripper suspect himself. In the letter, the Dr makes his apologies for not been able to meet as arranged, as he would be attending a clinic in Whitechapel. The letter was dated 8 September 1888, the date the second Ripper victim Annie Chapman was murdered in Hanbury Street. Also found among the doctor's possessions where a surgical knife, about six inches in length, so well used that the point had been snapped off, three slides containing! "Animal matter" a diary belonging to Sir John from 1888, with many pages missing, and a notebook from 1885 which listed an abortion, he had performed on a woman called Mary Anne Nichols, (the name of the first Ripper victim was Mary Ann Nichols, without an extra e). An examination of a facsimile of the original notebook showed that it differed from the one published in Uncle Jack, and had clearly been tampered with, a claim vehemently denied by Tony Williams. In presenting his theory against Dr Williams the author also makes the following claims. That the Ripper victims, at one time or another, may have attended the Whitechapel Workhouse Infirmary while Dr Williams may have worked there. That he may have known Mary Kelly while residing in Wales, and that they were both possibly lovers. That he resembled in likeness the description of the man seen by eyewitness George Hutchinson with Mary Kelly shortly before she was murdered. That the motives for his murderous rampage were due to his wife's inability to have children. That Dr Williams, desperate to have children, and intent on looking for an answer to his wife's infertility, used the women of the East End as guinea pigs on which to practice his surgical skills, in the hope of finding a cure for infertility. When this failed to provide the answers, he took this a stage further. He removed the organs from his victims, to complete his research, and as the authors claim, perhaps may even have gone so far as to attempt to transplant these organs into his infertile wife. And finally, the reason for the cessation of the murders was that after murdering his former lover Mary Kelly, on 9 November 1888, he suffered a breakdown, which resulted in his and Jack the Ripper's early retirement.

John Williams was born on the 6 November 1840 in Blaenllynant, Gwynfe, Carmarthenshire, Wales. Third son of David Williams a farmer and Congregationalist minister, who died in 1842 from typhoid fever when John was two-years-old. His mother Elinor, was described as a strongly religious character, with high standards and expectations. She would stay and farm Blaenllynant after the death of her husband. Instead of following a career in the ministry like his mother wished, John Williams chose a career in medicine. He attended the Normal school in Swansea, and in 1857 studied mathematics at Glasgow University. He returned to Wales in July 1859 where he was apprenticed to surgeons and apothecaries in Swansea. In 1861 he studied medicine at University College Hospital, Gower Street, London, and gained his MRCS, MB, MD, and was a prize winning student. After qualifying, he returned to Wales and began working as a GP in Swansea. It was while in Swansea that he would join the Freemasons. It was at this time he met his wife to be, Mary Elizabeth Ann Hughes, known as Lizzie. She was described as a "refined, religious girl." She was the daughter of a Welsh industrialist Richard Hughes. The couple was married in 1872, he was 32 years of age she 22. The couple moved to London, where he quickly gained a reputation as a leading Obstetrician. He would later become President of the Society of Obstetricians and Gynaecologists. Created a baronet by Queen Victoria in 1894. He retired from his London practice in 1903 and moved to Aberystwyth Wales. His wife Lizzie died in 1915, whereupon Sir John threw all his energies into establishing the National Library of Wales and donated 25,000 rare books and manuscripts from his personal collection. He also bequeathed to the Library a very large sum of money. Considered by his peers as a vain, difficult and aggressive man, he was knighted in 1902 and died on 24 May 1926 at the age of 86.

JOHN WILLIAMS

On 15 October 1888 a man named John Williams was brought before Chorley magistrates under the following suspicious circumstances. On Saturday night he went into a public-house, and drew from a sheath a long, sharp knife, at the same time boasting that he was "Jack the Ripper," and had already polished off four victims and that he meant to do another. A paper was found on him which showed that he had recently travelled in the neighbourhood of London.

JAMES WILSON

On Tuesday 27 November 1888, shortly after 12 o'clock midday, a man was pursued by an angry crowd (according to the newspapers the numbers exceeded 200) through the streets of Belfast. The crowd, swelling in numbers, called out, "Jack the Ripper," and chased the man up Little Donegall Street, and down Birch Street. The man turned the corner of Carrick Hill and took refuge in the cellar of the first house that he came to; where it is claimed he frightened some children. Police Constables Britten and M'Guirk, who had joined the crowd in pursuit of the individual, searched the property and duly arrested him. The crowd following closely behind kept up their cries of, "Jack the Ripper" while the man was escorted to the police station. At the police station, and while the man was being questioned, the crowd, who were obliged to remain outside, believing the Whitechapel Murderer had finally been apprehended gave vent to their feelings with frequent outbursts of cheering. The man, who was described as about 43 years of age, gave his name as James Wilson, and his occupation as a comedian, which was interpreted by the Sergeant in charge as meaning a ballad singer. It was discovered that the defendant was wearing two hats-a soft hat being inside a felt one-and carried two walking sticks. He claimed that he had been on tour through the provincial towns, and had called at Lisburn, and several places in County Antrim. The charge entered against him was that of indecent behaviour, but it appeared he was arrested more for his own safety than for any breach of the peace that he may have committed.

WINBERG

An alleged accomplice, along with Levitski, of Ripper suspect Dr Pedachenko. Winberg, who was described as a young tailoress, would apparently engage the victims in conversation, lulling them into a false sense of security, before the Ripper, Pedachenko, struck, while Levitski would keep watch. It is then claimed she was exiled along with Levitski to Yakutsk, Russia.

DR LYTTLETON FORBES WINSLOW

Dr Lyttleton Forbes Winslow was born 31 January 1844 in Guildford Street, Marylebone, London, the son of psychiatrist Forbes Benignus Winslow, and Susan (née Holt). Educated at Rugby and Downing College, Cambridge. He grew up in the private asylums owned by his father. He would later join his father in practice, and upon his death in 1874, took over the running of the two Hammersmith asylums. After a family feud, this responsibility was removed from him. In 1878 his reputation and career took a blow from which they never fully recovered when he attempted to have Mrs Georgina Weldon, a popular aspiring opera singer, falsely committed to a lunatic asylum at the request of her estranged husband. Mrs Weldon sued Winslow along with her husband. The court case was widely publicised and caused public outrage. Winslow was viewed as an embarrassment by the medical establishment. With his career in tatters He thereafter turned his attention to the solving of crime by Sherlock Holmesian methods, and with a little manipulation of the evidence, came to believe he knew the identity of Jack the Ripper and believed if given a team of six Constables could apprehend the murderer. Winslow wrote:

I determined to throw myself heart and soul into the matter, and wrote a letter to the press in which I set forth my theory that a dangerous homicidal lunatic was prowling about London. Arrests were made by the score, principally of people of a low class who inhabited the locality where the murders were committed. I, however, refused to believe that the murders were committed by one of the lower classes. I gave it as my opinion that the

469

murderer was in all probability a man of good position and perhaps living in the West End of London. When the paroxysm which prompted him to his fearful deeds had passed off, he most likely returned to the bosom of his family. After the fifth and sixth murders, however, I changed my views. The exact similarity in the method of murder and the horrible evisceration of the body showed too much of a methodical nature ever to belong to a man who committed the deeds in a fit of epileptic furor. Considerable anatomical knowledge was displayed by the murderer, which would seem to indicate that his occupation was that of a butcher or a surgeon. Taking all these things into consideration, I concluded that the perpetrator was a homicidal lunatic goaded on to his dreadful work by a sense of duty. Religious monomania was evidently closely allied with his homicidal instincts, because his efforts were solely directed against fallen women, whose extermination he probably considered his mission. Many homicidal lunatics consider murder to be their duty. Jack the Ripper possibly imagined that he received his commands from God. I communicated my ideas to the authorities at Scotland Yard, and expressed my opinion that I would run down the murderer with the co-operation of the police. I explained that lunatics can frequently be caught in their own trap by humouring their ideas. If opposed, however, they bring a devilish cunning to bear which effectually frustrates all efforts to thwart their designs. I proposed to insert an advertisement in a prominent position in all the papers, reading something like this: "A gentleman who is strongly opposed to the presence of fallen women in the streets of London would like to co-operate with someone with a view to their suppression." I proposed to have half a dozen detectives at the place of appointment, and seize and rigidly examine everyone who replied to the advertisement. Scotland Yard, however, refused to entertain the idea; and as it was quite impossible for me, as a private citizen, to seize and detain possibly innocent persons, the idea was abandoned.

Winslow gave a lecture in New York, where he claimed the Ripper was:

A young man, of slight build, with light hair and blue eyes who was a medical student from a good family who studied very hard and attended service every morning at eight o'clock at St Paul's Cathedral.

His principle suspect was G. Wentworth Bell Smith, a Canadian, who had come to London to work for the Toronto Trust Society, and who lodged with a Mr and Mrs Callaghan at 27 Sun Street, Finsbury Square, Islington. Callaghan said:

That in April 1888 a gentlemanly-looking man called in answer to an advertisement. He engaged a large bed-sitting-room in his house, and said that he was over on business, and might stay a few months or perhaps a year. Before he came there he told them that he had occupied rooms in the neighbourhood of St Paul's Cathedral. The proprietor and his wife noticed that whenever he went out of doors he wore a different suit of clothes from that which he wore the day before, and would often change them three or four times a day. He had eight or nine suits of clothes and the same number of hats. He kept very late hours, and whenever he returned home his entry was quite noiseless. In his room were three pairs of rubbers coming high over the ankles, one pair of which he always used when going out at night. Mr Callaghan, also noticed that he kept three loaded revolvers hidden in a chest of drawers, and talked and moaned to himself. And according to Mr Callaghan, was a religious fanatic, who appeared obsessed with prostitutes, saying that they should all be drowned. On the date of the second murder, the lodging-

house keeper was sitting up late with his sister, waiting for his wife to return from the country. She was expected home about 4 a.m., and the two sat up till then. A little before four o'clock the lodger came in, looking as though he had been having rather a rough time. When questioned he said that his watch had been stolen in Bishopsgate, and gave the name of a police station where he had lodged a complaint. On investigation this proved to be false, as no complaint had been lodged with the police. The next morning, when the maid went to do his room, she called the attention of the proprietress to a large bloodstain on the bed. His shirt was found hanging up in his room with the cuffs recently washed, he having washed them himself. A few days later he left, saying that he was going to Canada, but he evidently did not go, because he was seen getting into a horse car in London in September 1888.

Convinced that Smith was a lunatic, and therefore Jack the Ripper, Mr. Callaghan took his suspicions to Dr Forbes Winslow to investigate. Winslow said:

The rubber shoes, which I took possession of, were covered with dried human blood. They had been left behind by the murderer in his rapid departure from the lodging-house. In addition to the rubbers there were three pairs of woman's shoes and a quantity of bows, feathers, and flowers, such as are usually worn by women of the lower class. Some of the latter were stained with blood, and were in my possession.

Winslow contacted the police. His story was fully investigated and shown to be without foundation. This did not stop Winslow, from trumpeting his theory at every given opportunity, and for a great many years afterwards, claimed credit that his efforts had forced the Ripper into abandoning murder and fleeing the country.

472

Winslow himself tells us how he spent, day after day, night after night, in the Whitechapel slums:

The detectives knew me, the lodging house keepers knew me, and at last the poor creatures of the streets came to know me. In terror, they rushed to me with every scrap of information which might, to my mind, be of value to me. The frightened women looked for hope in my presence. They felt reassured and welcomed me to their dens and obeyed my commands eagerly, and I found the bits of information I wanted.

According to authors Donald McCormick, and Tom Cullen, Winslow, through his persistence and his constant projection of himself into the Ripper story, caused the police to briefly suspect him, and to check on his movements at the time of the Ripper murders. A letter dated 3 October 1888, from C. J. Denny, a medical officer, to the City Police accused Winslow, because his letters to the Globe newspaper, showed signs of incipient insanity. When Winslows´ claims about knowing the identity of the Ripper were reported in the English press Scotland Yard sent Chief Inspector Donald Swanson to interview him. Winslow immediately retracted his story. He said the story printed in the newspaper was not accurate and misrepresented the entire conversation between himself and the reporter. Winslow, an expert on matters of legal sanity, wrote the Handbook for Attendants on the Insane, in 1877 and in 1890 founded the British hospital for mental disorders in London. The clinic provided free treatment for poor patients suffering from mental disorders and nervous disease in a "modest building" in Euston Square. It was called the British Hospital for Mental Disorders. In his memoirs: Recollections of Forty Years (1910), he states, "I have breathed the atmosphere of lunacy for a period extending over sixty years." Winslow made a statement to the effect that "Spiritualism was driving people

473

insane in America and filling the asylums of that country with its victims." In later years he publicly stated that while at the time that he made this assertion he honestly believed it to be true, he had since learnt that he was mistaken and would not make any such statement now. He died at the age of 69 on 27 May 1913 of a heart attack.

WIRTOFSKY

Mr George Strachey contacted the police in Dresden, Germany to inform them that a young American-German medical student of his named Julius I Lowenheim, had mentioned to him his suspicion about a Polish Jew, whom he used to meet at a Christian home in Finsbury Square, called Julius Wirtofsky. Wirtofsky had consulted Lowenheim on a special pathological condition which was troubling him, and told Lowenheim that he wished to kill the person concerned, and all the rest of her class. Lowenheim, who stated that he could identify Wirtofsky without fail, had previously contacted the police in London about the matter but failed to receive a reply. Apart from his alleged grudge against prostitutes, nothing else is known about Julius Wirtofsky.Julius

Lowenheim was born 16 August 1870 in Berlin. In 1890 he is listed as a passenger on board the Belgenland, destination Philadelphia. In the 1901 census, he is a merchant's clerk, aged 34 years a prisoner in Holloway. He died 7 September 1933 in St Louis, Missouri.

STARR WOOD

British caricaturist, joke cartoonist journalist and illustrator, born 1 February 1870, in London. Eldest son of of a customs officer, great-grandson of Captain Starr wood. Educated at the Stoke Newington Collegiate School. Starr Wood, who also used the pseudonym, "The Snark" was a self taught artist who first worked at first as a Chartered Accountant in a debt-collecting business in the City. On one of his calls he was mistaken for Jack the Ripper, and pursued by a mob. He escaped by hiding in a railway cloakroom. An autobiography written in 1907 about Starr Wood, gives further details.

On one occasion, I remember, my work nearly led to being torn in pieces by an infuriated populace. No, I had not been tearing the mattress from beneath the dying widow. I was in Whitechapel on some dunning errand when luck would have it, I was almost an eye-witness of one of the terrible Jack the Ripper outrages. At all events, I came upon the scene of one of them just after it had been discovered by a policeman. He was actually stooping over the body when I arrived. I was carrying a black bag, and this, coupled no doubt with my well-known ferocity of appearance, induced some idiot in the crowd, which quickly collected, to denounce me as the murderer. I was little more than a smooth faced boy at the time, but, none the less, so unstrung were the nerves of the people, so damning was the evidence of my black bag, that the cry was taken up in deadly earnest, and I had literally to run for my life, eventually shaking off my pursuers in the purlieus of Shoreditch, an unpleasant experience which kept me awake for many nights.

After his first drawing was published in 1892, he turned freelance cartoonist, contributing to many publications including *Chums, Fun, Judy, Chips, Parade, John Bull, Bystander, Humorist, Passing Show, Tatler, Strand* and *Punch* from 1898 until 1935. He died at the age of 74 in 1944.

JOHN JOSEPH WOODS

Following the murder of the second Ripper victim Annie Chapman, on 8 September 1888, a suggestion was made that every streetwalker on the street after midnight should be either arrested or provided with a police whistle. A young prostitute named Eleanor Candy (spelt Candey in some newspaper accounts) and described as a single woman took the latter advice. She picked up drunken 18-year old Joseph Woods, the son of a licensed victualler, near the Waterworks office in Commercial Street, shortly after midnight, on Tuesday 25 September 1888, and during a conversation with him confided that she never ventured out after dark without her police whistle. Woods in reply said: "And I never go out without my trusty little knife if you want to know who I am, I am the Whitechapel murderer." Woods took hold of her in a disgraceful manner and produced a knife. Candy blew her police whistle and Woods was immediately arrested by Police–sergeant Brading for indecent assault. At Portsmouth Police-court, Candy said the prisoner, Woods, and another unnamed, man approached her and accosted her in a very rough and threatening manner, and seized her by the waist and then her throat, breaking her necklace in the process. He then threw her to the ground and assaulted her. She remonstrated with him, and he thereupon produced a clasp knife, exclaiming, "Look at this, I'll put it right through you." She said: "Are you one of the Whitechapel men," to which he replied: "Yes, I am." Woods was described as drunk, but Candy as quite sober. In court, Candy said: "Ever since the Ripper murders, she had carried a whistle for protection, but had never used it before this." The clerk asked her "If she carried it about with her during the day," she replied: "No, only at night." The clerk then asked her: "You have no reason to suppose that he is the Whitechapel murderer?" She replied: "No, sir." much to the merriment of the court. The magistrate sided with Woods and dismissed the charge of assault against him, and regarded the matter as a stupid freak. He was, however, bound over to keep the peace in the sum of £10 and was duly ordered to find a surety for a like amount. His accomplice was never identified.

John Joseph Woods was born in 1869, in Portsea Island, Hampshire. The son of George Woods, ex-Seaman, RN now a publican, and his wife Catherine Julia (née Cottrell). In the 1871 census, he is living at 2 Telegraph Street Magnet Beer House, Portsea Island, Hampshire. He married 22 year old Priscilla Washington Sargent, in December 1895, they had four children. She died in June 1907 at the age of 34. In June 1910 he married Florence Mary, (née Howell) and they had three children. In the 1911 census, he is in occupation as an engine fitter, living at 43 Froddington Street, Southsea. John Joseph Woods died at the age of 61, in 1930 in Portsmouth. His wife died in June 1971, at the age of 84.

MANUEL CRUZ XAVIER

37 year old Portuguese cattleman Manuel Cruz Xavier. Suspected along with three other men. Jose Laurenco aged 26, Joao de Souza Machado aged 41, and Joachim da Rocha aged 23. By Edward Knight Larkins. For further information see the suspect Jose Laurenco.

INSPECTOR Y

In the (1935) book: Jack l'Eventreur by, French novelist Jean Dorsenne, Inspector Y was allegedly a police officer involved in the hunt for Jack the Ripper. He was described as "delicate, sensitive, over emotional, feminine in nature, though loyal, energetic and intelligent." He made a great many enemies among his colleagues at Scotland Yard and there were questions about both his methods and his morals. There was even a formal complaint by a young woman who claimed to have been attacked and knocked to the ground by him in the course of an inquiry which he was making at her home. On two occasions he came close to being dismissed. Inspector Y surprised many of his work colleagues one day when he announced he was shortly to be married, though the real shock to his colleagues was in meeting his soon to be bride, described as dominant, some twenty-years-older than him, short, dumpy red-faced, with a double-chin and the beginnings of a moustache and beard. Many years later the wife now older, larger and sporting a full moustache and beard, went to pay a visit to one of her husband's old work colleagues, there she told a tale of how she had killed her husband by cutting him open with a knife as he slept. It was an act she had been mulling over for years since her husband had confessed to her he was "Jack the Ripper." Her husband told her their marriage two days after the death of the last Ripper victim Mary Kelly, had been a means to suppress his insatiable lust to kill which had simmered inside him. Her motive for her crime, she explained, was to save her own life, after he had threatened to finish her off, like his previous victims. She committed suicide, that very evening by hanging herself in her cell, using strips torn from her dress.

C. J. Morley is the author of the following Jack the Ripper books. Jack the Ripper Eliminating the Suspects. (2004). Jack the Ripper 150 Suspects. (2005). Jack the Ripper a Suspect Guide. E-book (2006). Jack the Ripper the Suspects. E-book (2011). Jack the Ripper the Suspects. (2011).

INDEX OF SUSPECTS IN THIS BOOK

35. CHARLES BOND
36. JOSEPH BONNY
37. WILLIE BOULT
38. JOHN BRENNAN
39. JOHN BRINCKLEY
40. WILLIAM WALLACE BRODIE
41. JOSHUA BROOK
42. GENERAL BROWN
43. THOMAS BROWN
44. CHARLES BRUYN
45. EDWARD BUCHAN
46. WILLIAM BULL
47. HANS BURE
48. EDWIN BURROWS
49. WILLIAM HENRY BURY
50. CALOR
51. JAMES CARNAC
52. FRANK CASTELLANO
53. FREDERICK RICHARD CHAPMAN
54. WILLIAM LEONARD CHAPMAN
55. CHARLIE THE RIPPER
56. FREDERICK NICHOLAS CHARRINGTON
57. ALMEDA CHATELLE
58. RANDOLPH HENRY SPENCER CHURCHILL
59. GEORGE CLARK
60. JOHN CLEARY
61. DAVID COHEN
62. DR. COHN
63. JOSEPH COMPTON
64. CLAUDE REIGNEIR CONDER
65. JAMES CONNELL
66. GEORGE COOPER
67. BOSTON CORBETT
68. MARIA CORONER
69. NATHANIEL COUSINS
70. DOUGLAS COW
71. FRANCIS SPURZHEIM CRAIG

72. THOMAS NEILL CREAM
73. CHARLES CROSS
74. GEORGE CULLEN
75. GEORGE CURTEIS
76. THOMAS HAYNE CUTBUSH
77. THE DARTMOOR SUSPECT
78. JOHN DAVIDSON
79. JOHN DAVIDSON
80. JOHN DAVIES
81. JOHN DAVIS
82. DR. MORGAN DAVIS
83. DR. HAROLD DEARDEN'S BROTHER OFFICER
84. FREDERICK BAILEY DEEMING
85. HENDRIK DE JONG
86. HARRY DENKER
87. JOSEPH DENNY
88. LOUIS DIEMSCHUTZ
89. MICHAEL DEVINE
90. CHARLES LUTWIDGE DODGSON
91. PETER DONALD
92. TIMOTHY DONOVAN
93. ERNEST DOWSON
94. BETTY DOYLE
95. SIR ARTHUR IGNATIUS CONAN DOYLE
96. MONTAGUE JOHN DRUITT
97. WILLIAM HARVEY DRUITT
98. DR THOMAS DUTTON
99. W H EATON
100. FRANK EDWARDS
101. BLACK ELK
102. JOHN MOSES EPPSTEIN
103. JAMES FARLEY
104. FATHER OF GWB
105. COLLINGWOOD HILTON FENWICK
106. CARL FERDINAND FEIGENBAUM
107. WILLIAM ALFRED FIELD
108. JOHN FITZGERALD

109. JOHN ALEXANDER FITZMAURICE
110. JOSEPH FLEMING
111. FOGELMA
112. WILLIAM JOHN FOSTER
113. JOHN FOY
114. ROBERT FULLERTON
115. PATRICK GALLAGHER
116. GAVIN
117. ANDREW JOHN GIBSON
118. WILLIAM GILBERT
119. GEORGE ROBERT GISSING
120. WILLIAM EWART GLADSTONE
121. JAMES GLEN
122. BENJAMIN GRAHAM
123. WILLIAM GRANT
124. ALFRED GRAY
125. JAMES GREEN
126. WILLIAM GRIFFITHS
127. PETER GULAURA
128. DR WILLIAM WITHEY GULL
129. ELIZABETH HALLIDAY
130. FRANK HALL
131. EDWARD HAMBLER
132. THEOPHIL HANHART
133. ROBERT HANSOM
134. JAMES HARDIMAN
135. WILLIAM HARDIMAN
136. PETER J HARPICK
137. JOHN HARRIS
138. JOHN HARVEY
139. THE HAVENT RIPPER
140. GEORGE HAWKES
141. WILLIAM HAYDAY
142. DAN HAYES
143. JAMES HEAP
144. WILLIAM HAYNES
145. JAMES HEAP

146. THOMAS HEFFERON
147. GEORGE RICHARD HENDERSON
148. STEPHEN HENDERSON
149. WILLIAM HENLEY
150. HENNELL
151. THOMAS HENRY
152. CHARLES Y HERMANN
153. JOHN HEWITT
154. THOMAS HEYWOOD
155. JOHN HILL
156. WALTER HILL
157. BENSON HILTON
158. ALFRED HINDE
159. HANS HOCHKISS
160. H H HOLMES
161. WILLIAM HOLT
162. MIRIAM HOWELLS
163. HENRY HUMPHREY
164. GEORGE HUTCHINSON (AMERICAN)
165. GEORGE HUTCHINSON
166. HYAM HYAMS
167. JACK IRWIN
168. BENJAMIN ISAACS
169. JOSEPH ISAACS
170. JACOB ISENSCHMID
171. JACK THE FLASHER
172. JACK THE RIPPERS
173. JACOBS
174. HENRY JAMES
175. WILLIAM JAMES
176. JILL THE RIPPER
177. JILL THE SAILOR
178. JAMES JOHNSON
179. JOHN JOHNSON
180. JOHN SOLOMON JONES
181. NATHAN KAMINSKY
182. JAMES KELLY

183. JOHN KELLY
184. THE KENNINGTON SUSPECT
185. CONSTANCE KENT
186. MICHAEL KIDNEY
187. SEVERIN KLOSOWSKI
188. KARL KNAPPE
189. BERTRAM KNUTSON
190. VASSILY KONOVALOV
191. AARON KOSMINSKI
192. MARTIN KOSMINSKI
193. H C KROMSCHROEDER
194. ARBIE LA BRUCKMAN
195. JAMES DAVID LAMPARD
196. JOHN LANGAN
197. JOHN LANGHORN
198. EDWARD LARMONTH
199. JOSE LAURENCO
200. HENRI DE TOULOUSE LAUTREC
201. JAMES LEADBEATER
202. JOHN LEARY
203. HENRY EDWARD LEEKE
204. CHARLES LE GRAND
205. KING LEOPOLD II
206. ARTHUR LEVENDON
207. WOLF LEVISOHN
208. LEVITSKI
209. JACOB LEVY
210. JULIUS LIPMAN
211. JOHN LOCK
212. THE LODGER
213. CHARLES LUDWIG
214. SIR MELVILLE LESLIE MACNAGHTEN
215. ALONZO MADURO
216. JAMES MALONE
217. JACK MALTIMORE
218. ROBERT MANN
219. RICHARD MANSFIELD

220. THEOPHIL MARY
221. ARTHUR HENRY MASON
222. THOMAS MASON
223. OLIVER MATHEWS
224. ALFRED JOHN MATTHEWS
225. MAURICE
226. FLORENCE MAYBRICK
227. JAMES MAYBRICK
228. MICHAEL MAYBRICK
229. SAMUEL McALLISTER
230. JAMES McBETH
231. GEORGE WILLIAM McCARTHY
232. JOHN McCARTHY
233. JOHN AMOS McCULLY
234. JACK McCARDY
235. EDWARD McKENNA
236. JOSEPH CAREY MERRICK
237. FRANK MILES
238. THOMAS MOLIN
239. THE MONMOUTH RIPPER
240. JAMES MONRO
241. MORFORD
242. GEORGE JAMES MORRIS
243. CHARLES MORSE
244. EDWARD MORSON
245. WILLIAM M'PHERSON
246. JOHN MURPHY
247. JOHN MURRAY
248. THOMAS MURRAY
249. JOHN MURRY
250. EDWARD NELSON
251. JAMES NESBITT
252. JOHN NETLEY
253. JOHN NEWMAN'S RIPPER SUSPECT
254. JOHN NICOL
255. AUGUST NOCHILD
256. WILLIAM ONION

257. MICHAEL OSTROG
258. DR. VLADIMIR PANTCHENKO
259. ALFRED PARENT
260. ISAAC PASCO
261. GEORGE PAYNE
262. MARY PEARCEY
263. ALFRED PEARSON
264. DR. ALFRED WILLIAM PEARSON
265. ALEXANDER PEDACHENKO
266. JOHN BENJAMIN PERRYMAN
267. WILLIAM PETITT
268. GEORGE PIERILLI
269. WILLIAM PIGGOTT
270. JOHN PIZER
271. ANTONI PRICHA
272. THOMAS PRITCHARD
273. OSWALD PUCKRIDGE
274. JAMES PURTON
275. EDWARD QUINN
276. THE RAILWAY POLICEMAN
277. FRANK RAPER
278. WILLIAM RAPSONG
279. JOHN RICHARDSON
280. JOHN RIP
281. JOSE RIZAL
282. PIERCE JOHN ROBINSON
283. STEPHEN ROURKE
284. JOHN ROYALL
285. FRANCIS CHARLES HASTINGS RUSSELL
286. THOMAS JAMES SADLER
287. JOHN SANDERSON
288. COUNT SARDROUJI
289. REGINALD SAUNDERSON
290. SAMUEL SCAR
291. DR. JOHN WILLIAM SANDERS
292. JOHN WILLIAM SMITH SANDERS
293. SCHULSE

487

294. THE UNKNOWN SECRETARY
295. JACK SHAW
296. JAMES SHAW
297. WILLIAM SHEALS
298. WALTER SICKERT
299. SICKERT'S VETERINARY STUDENT
300. JOSEPH SILVER
301. CLARENCE SIMM
302. GEORGE ROBERT SIMS
303. HENRY SKINNERTON
304. THE SLAUGHTERMAN
305. G WENTWORTH BELL SMITH
306. NEWLAND FRANCIS FORESTER SMITH
307. JOHN SMITH
308. WILLIAM SMITH
309. WILLIAM SMITH
310. SOLOMON
311. HENRY ARTHUR GEORGE SOMERSET
312. JOHANN STAMMER
313. CHARLES STANDEN
314. DR STANLEY
315. ROBERT LOUIS STEVENSON
316. LEWIS STEMLER
317. JAMES KENNETH STEPHEN
318. ROBERT DONSTON STEPHENSON
319. JOHN STEWART
320. MR STEWART
321. STREET GANG
322. GEORGE SULLIVAN
323. GEORGE SWEENEY
324. ALGERNON CHARLES SWINBURNE
325. ALOIS SZEMERDY
326. ROBERT TANNER
327. CHARLES TAYLOR
328. MR TAYLOR
329. OLGA TCHKERSOFF
330. TEENAGE JACK THE RIPPER

331. WILLIAM THICK
332. CHARLES THOMAS
333. DR. WILLIAM EVAN THOMAS
334. FRANCIS THOMPSON
335. DR. LEONARD BOOKER THORNTON
336. DR. NIGEL TORME
337. TOM TOTSON
338. EMIL TOTTERMAN
339. FRANCIS TUMBLETY
340. JOHN TYSON
341. UNIDENTIFIED SKELETON
342. UNKNOWN
343. NICHOLAS VAN BURST
344. VINCENT VAN GOGH
345. HENRY VANN
346. VANZETTI'S SUSPECT
347. NICOLAI VASSILI
348. WILLIAM WADDELL
349. WALTER
350. WILLIAM HUMBLE WARD
351. JOHN PETER WATSON
352. JAMES WATT
353. DR WILLIAM WYNN WESTCOTT
354. FREDERICK WHITE
355. MARY ELIZABETH ANN WILLIAMS
356. DR JOHN WILLIAMS
357. JOHN WILLIAMS
358. JAMES WILSON
359. WINBERG
360. DR LYTTLETON FORBES WINSLOW
361. WIRTOFSKY
362. STARR WOOD
363. JOHN JOSEPH WOODS
364. MANUEL CRUZ XAVIER
365. INSPECTOR Y

Printed in Great Britain
by Amazon